Outrunning Death

The Amazing True Story of how Jenene Lehman Conquered the Incurable…and You Can Too

A Book by Adam James

*Julie ~
Anything can be healed.
Peace & Harmony
Jenene*

Copyright © 2016 by Adam James

All rights reserved, including the reproduction in whole or in part in any form.

Names have been changed to protect the privacy and anonymity of those involved.

To all those who were told they couldn't, but did.

Namaste

I want to tell you about a woman who by all appearances is just another person going about living her life, much like everyone else. Like many women, she wears several hats. She's a wife. She's a mother. A worker. A daughter. An altruist. An aunt. She's also a healer. How she came by that descriptor is the story I am going to tell.

I want the whole world to know. Why? So all who read this may be as astounded, inspired, and touched as I have been from the time I achieved understanding. How have I been a part of this story for so long? I am this woman's only child, the very reason she has done so much to hold fast to her life despite enough health obstacles to complicate—or end—a dozen lives.

In so many ways my mom is the exception to the rule. Are you overwhelmed by stress? You can get through that. Have you been abused? You can get through that. Have you experienced great loss? You can get through that. Have you been told you're dying of an incurable disease, condemned by a diagnosis? You can get through that too.

How do I know?

My mom has survived all that and so much more. She would tell you herself if she wasn't of so humble a grain. In a time when everyone wants his or her own reality show, she would rather have a personal conversation and it would only for sake of greater understanding arise organically if any element of her remarkable life were to emerge in the form of an anecdote.

Self-aggrandizement tends to make others see a show-off. Heroes of the battlefield are made by the convictions of their buddies. Champions are only respected by history if their bouts earn beaming reviews. Legends are made first by whispers and then by shouts. Since my mom won't tell you herself, it leaves it up to me to start the whispers, to lead the shouts. Because in a way, my mom is legendary, and doubt if you might—in any case there are so few living legends—all I ask is you give me a chance to convince you.

My mom's name is Jenene Lehman and this is her story. Though this all may seem incredible, even logic defying, I assure you every word is the absolute truth. Great healing is possible.

Chapter 1
Health Horror

If wishes were horses all would have a full stable, wishes for happiness, for love, for understanding, for the wellbeing of loved ones, for money, for all those things just out of reach.

To wish for good health would in no way change the fact that in one way or another Jenene Lehman had been sick for a long time. Worse yet, she was getting sicker. Jenene had gained enough horse sense in her three decades to know wishing loses value when what you desire is the end of a lifelong dilemma. By the fall of 1990 she was wise enough to know mere wishes would never save her life.

That was forever ago now. When a dozen aspects of life impeded on one another and the worst one of all was a brooding thunderhead darkening the horizon. Not one to shrink from adversity, after an abusive marriage, painful losses, and enough poor health to beleaguer anyone, Jenene had proven her will to endure and fight, to persevere. What she lacked was the simple commodity of time.

In a life of too much illness, Jenene recognized the signs. Even still she had tried to ignore the symptoms. Mother to a son with chronic bronchial asthma, wife to a second husband offering her another chance at love if only she could prosper it, and overwhelmed caregiver to two elderly relatives in their eighties, time to be sick simply did not exist.

As it stood she never scratched off every item on her daily to-do lists. Not when the running joke was, "We got to bed early last night…early in the morning." Juggling responsibilities was wearing her out and being sick—with something she was beginning to recognize as insidious—would maybe prove no one is shatterproof even if she had rebounded continually in her short life.

What made that Monday remarkable was that Jenene and hubby Russ were enjoying the extravagance of eating lunch out. This odd occurrence was made possible by the rare coincidence of sharing a day off and a gift certificate proffered by a support group for families caring for geriatric relatives.

Downtime was more often than not an unaffordable commodity.

A state-provided aid was back at the farm watching after Lal and Herb yet Jenene was uneasy. The service offered much needed respites when constant care became necessary, this being before the "I've fallen and can't get up" ad campaign turned the world on to medical alert services. Yet as adequate as their care, Jenene always worried. It had been a tough period.

The siblings were still recovering from the death of their younger brother, eighty-one-year-old Bill the previous year. The car accident that took Bill diminished both, Herb having been in the accident, Lal having broken mentally by the unexpected loss. Herb was sharp as ever; Lal had lost her acuity to the Alzheimer's thrown into overdrive by her forceful grief.

Bill was the one not too proud to ask Jenene and family to move to the farm. He saved all three from nursing homes. Now he was gone and the family had yet to emerge from the sorrow. Bill's sudden death drove home many realities, not the least of which how life can turn on a dime. Anything could happen; a slip, a broken hip…a hastened death. From something that happened even before we moved in Jenene was clued in to how fragile The Seniors were becoming.

Decades of labor can equal swollen varicose veins and Lal's toil left her legs besieged. The tiny unnoticed scratch through her nylons of one engorged vein meant a small amount of bleeding followed by scabbing. Cut to bedtime, when she pulled down those nylons unaware she was uncapping a gusher when the scab matted in the material was torn off. Blood geysered all over the wall like a scene from a murder.

Had Jenene and her son not been staying at the farm following the implosion of her first marriage there's no telling what might have happened.

As the crow flies it was less than ten miles from the state capital building yet the place was so deep in the boonies the paramedics wound up lost. They weren't as lost as they thought, though. Jenene saw the ambulance prowling around the end of the long drive as the emergency operator explained the problem. "They are literally at the end of the driveway right now," she had informed the operator calmly but tersely, terrified her aunt was bleeding to death while precious seconds were lost.

I would guess more by luck than know-how the paramedics chose to come up what they probably mistook for a field road, and Lal was saved. It wouldn't be the last 9-1-1 call placed from the farm.

Coming through something like that might bolster some. Jenene was only made aware of how delicate The Seniors were by then. And that horrific event was more than a few years ago. Age catches up and when it does is a terrible bully, one medication and care can only stave off so long.

To think the reason they were out was the perceived quality of their care. Not that Jenene felt they did a bad job. It was only that their competence could only be measured by the day-to-day ups and downs. Not by coordinated actions from some rulebook they were playing by because no such book existed.

Due to the time they had invested in caring for her three elderly relatives, Jenene and Russ knew more than even the leader of the support group and their wisdom had earned appreciation. Being the one with the most answers when you have questions was not ideal. Joining the group because they felt they needed help and finding little more than moral support was disheartening.

I really thought they would have more advice, she thought as they awaited their order in a deli-style restaurant in New Port, Minnesota. *All they have are pats on the back I don't think I deserve because I'm only going on instinct and I don't ever really know if what I'm doing is right.* She felt buried by all she didn't know. Crushed almost to powder. And it was this train of thought that preceded the familiar pain—she could have no idea her insecurity, her fear of falling below expectations, was spurring her body to self-attack.

No, no, not again. Where's the nearest restroom?

The irksome rumbling within her digestive tract made her stand straighter. *Do I look sick? Can the people around me tell how uncomfortable I am?*

Throughout her life she stomached a lot, maybe too much.

All the good smells that should have enticed only shed light on her distress. No matter how pleasantly aromatic, instead of the savory scents entering her nose and rousing up growls of hunger they stirred only inner turmoil.

Food had become her nemesis. It could run through her like a cat burglar or revolt and come straight back up like a smash and grab looter. She could never be too far from a bathroom. The vomiting, cramps, and diarrhea were sapping her of life, draining her of vitality and energy. Yet it was easier to ignore than to face what she was beginning to think would be a hard truth.

If she stopped to think about it, to really consider how sick she was getting, it would have been too overwhelming and terrifying.

Just too much to do....

She had reason to be leery of her illness and of doctors. Throughout her life she had been burdened with poor health—had what her father termed a "used" body. She was the veteran of several surgical procedures, one of which may have been the cause of her distress.

Talcum powder contamination from latex gloves used during a surgery to remove her gallbladder may have caused the intrapertoneal adhesions predicted to kill her by thirty. She was told the uncontrollable scar tissue growth would bind her organs and ultimately crush them like fruit in a press. Surgery to remove the scar tissue would be a catch-22—it would only spur more growth, worse adhesions.

She refused to believe she would die, and defied the expiration date her doctors tried to impose.

But maybe the doctors had been right after all. Maybe adhesions *were* killing her. The pain was worsening as she waited; sweat had sprung up on her brow and it felt as if her insides were alternately in a vice and being stabbed with red-hot knives. She wouldn't be able to make it home before the terrible fireworks.

"I'll be back," Jenene said to her husband and adjourned to the ladies' room. She had grown accustomed to using public restrooms. Necessary but never fun, she was content if they were relatively clean. If you used them often you learned quickly there could be a huge sanitation disparity between public restrooms.

A lot were maintained. Many weren't.

Some stank. Revoltingly.

To her benefit this restroom reeked of cleanser rather than urine. Even in moments of duress you have to find the little upsides.

Not able to put it off she settled onto the cold toilet seat. The knowledge she was about to expunge razor blades in no way prepared her for what felt like clawing and squeezing hands wringing her insides.

She slammed a palm against the wall as she was wracked by agonizing spasms.

Her eyes misted.

She tried to breathe through the corkscrewing pain. In through the nose, out through the mouth, slowly, to assert control, and the breathing helped. Somewhat.

Like when in labor.

The pain was comparable. Only she wasn't birthing life…she was birthing a hideous warning of impending death.

A final gush and the event had concluded. With luck there would be no encore. Left out of breath, exhausted, a moment of reflection was wasted gathering her wits in the thoughtless way we do when recovering from something that has just put our body to task.

With wariness she rose from the toilet. When her hazel blue eyes took in the horror her heart dropped like a rock. Terror can be galvanizing and in that instant she could only stare.

The white bowl was muddied with thick red blood!

How can there be so much blood? Oh my! Breathe. Breathe. Is this a symptom of the adhesions? I don't think it is. What's wrong with me?

Closing the lid against the ghastliness, she had to face facts. Flushed. Wanted to cry but held her composure. Swish, swish, chug-glug-glug she heard the whoosh of her life sucking away.

Jenene was thirteen years old the last time she had an experience like this. That time the prognosis was a devastating anal fissure that nearly killed her. This was different than that whole humiliating experience. The color of the blood—darker—seemed to indicate it was coming from deeper inside.

I don't have a choice anymore. It's not just pain. I can handle pain. I need a doctor to tell me what's wrong. I have to know….

But what will it cost me?

When she had gotten sick during her first marriage it had been a game changer. The adhesions had meant there was little chance of getting pregnant and a real threat that if she were to, carrying a pregnancy to term would be impossible. There was also the fact, as her doctor keenly pointed out: it was extremely unlikely she could live through an offspring's childhood even if her womb could support life.

If you can't even give me a baby, what are you good for?

Resentment destroys marriages even if it proves pointless. And if being sick put too much focus on her she feared contemptuousness would ensue; a life of emotional deprivation left Russ needy and requiring validation she may not be in a position to give. There was also the fact that in their short marriage she learned her new husband had been taught a lot about quitting.

For now he was hanging in.

With their life so full of dilemma she could only guess for how long….

Had she been sure then there was no reason for concern a lot less worry would have followed her around like a hex on legs.

With the help of slow breathing the pain dispelled the way a snail crosses a sidewalk, in wiggly increments, one miniscule twitch at a time.

With their earnings and other sources of income already stretched to transparency, she couldn't afford to be sick. Making herself secondary even when it came to her health was a bad habit but one of those necessary evils that complicate a life. Her obstinacy was not entirely in consideration of others; the gall of some doctors had prospered an aversion.

There was also how people would be toward her. From past experience she knew being sick inspired a lot of emotion in others and too often meant she was an object of pity. Sympathy was one thing but she took exception to being pitied for one simple reason: pity should be reserved for those who are doomed and she would never concede to doom as a possibility.

Such steadfast devotion to hopefulness was contradictory because her personal assessment of her strengths belied the notion she could take on more without breaking. Yet unbowed and unbent she would have to remain. Whether she was weak or strong much needed doing. Whatever internal mechanism makes her unbreakable has sustained her through a life of continual ups and downs.

Despite her reservations this was the day Jenene decided to put her life in the hands of doctors. The huge amount of blood had swayed her. Only she would prove a hot potato. After being handed around she would find diagnosis without real help.

The blow of what she was experiencing being labeled Crohn's disease—mysteriously the life-ending adhesions had retreated—would only be the beginning. One quote from a well-intentioned but helpless doctor stands out: "You are full of hundreds of bleeding ulcers. And beyond drug treatment"—such drugs had too high a psychological price and only dealt with symptoms—"there's nothing we can do. If even one of them perforates…you probably won't survive it. I'm sorry, but you're going to die from this. It's only a matter of time."

Chapter 2
An Imperfect Life

Being uprooted and moved to Wisconsin at the age of twelve was far from the worst thing that happened to Jenene in her young life but at the time it registered as a grand scale calamity to her 'tween mind….

On the edge of Highway 12 like a spur on a bone, about ten miles outside Woodville sits an old county plow depot converted into a restaurant. For the better part of half a century it has served the bucolic and picturesque area as a stopover where the beer is ice cold, the coffee piping hot, and the steaks prepared to taste.

An area hallmark, everyone knows the Wilson Nite Club. Neon beer lights in the windows make it a beacon in the night, a cool place to stop in the summer and a toasty holdover in the winter.

Its namesake, the flyspeck town across the highway and a railroad track, is a rural backwater of subtle consequence, a place where in that day you could watch grass grow or the residents sneak around. Back then it could have competed for the most bars per capita, there being no less than four at any given time for a population of about eighty people. Other than a feed mill, hope in a bottle had been the only business there for some time, since there was little money in fooling around.

In 1972 Bob and Lois Davis bought the Wilson Nite Club after much debate. There had been many considerations that included the possibility of purchasing one of those newfangled burger joints that in modern times can be found about everywhere.

Had they gotten in on a fast food franchise the whole family would now be loaded but neither foresaw the future boom. Instead they made the safe choice. The Nite Club had many regulars as well as a steady flow of travelers who preferred the leisurely scenic route to the decade-old Interstate 94.

Was there another mitigating circumstance behind the decision to acquire the Nite Club? After all it meant abandoning a nice neighborhood, displacing their family—Jenene and four-year-old Jeff—and relocating from Cottage Grove, Minnesota, to Wilson. Only an hour away but it might as well have been a thousand miles. Was there reason for the distance?

Jenene thought so. Upon the announcement they were moving, she was stunned, heartbroken, and inconsolable. *Why did I complain to Lal? I should have kept my mouth shut!*

The situation was worsened when her dad took her on a road trip to see their new home. The excursion with her dad was welcome if slightly strained since she had dared speak of him to Lal. He wanted her to be happy. He also wanted her to be understanding and accepting. He expected nothing less.

"It's going to be fantastic," he said. "A fresh start for all of us"—she didn't feel in need of a "fresh start"—"and you'll see, you'll make new friends and before long it'll be like it was before—"

Before? Before she blabbed? She looked at him sidewise. Bob's cherubic face held a hint of a grin bordering on roguish or maybe was only an expression of knowing. Wisdom showed in the wrinkles around his squinty eyes, each a brand earned with some lesson or other. Still. Was he crazy? This was crummy! Even worse, she was sure she caused it all!

Tallish, bearish, ever so slightly mawkish when it came to his passions, and hawkish when it came to his goals, he wore thick-rimmed eyeglasses, rocked a militaristic flattop haircut, and was partial to drab slacks and dressier polo shirts.

For a man so large rotundity was no limitation. He was exceptionally light on his feet. So much so, when he crossed a floor it was almost as if he levitated. He carried himself with an air of immovable confidence to match his stout girth, and was a natural born charmer on the order of all the famous smooth talkers. He could be downright silky. And he was convinced he could sell her on the move.

"—And I bet you'll be really happy. We'll have our own business and it'll make it so I'm around a lot because I'll be running the Nite Club fulltime and its right next door to where we'll be living. You'll be able to come visit, maybe even help out. There's a jukebox and a pool table and a big jar of pickled eggs—"

"I don't like pickled eggs."

"I don't know if anyone who isn't drunk likes them."

"So you brought them up to let me know you're going to let me get drunk?"

"I don't know about that, maybe an occasional drink. I would rather you didn't but if you were to, I would rather you do it in front of my face instead of behind my back."

A daughter usually impartial to her dad's charms, she listened to his blandishments and wanted to believe this all wasn't one of the worst things she could imagine. Maybe the move would entail new privileges as appeasements. Even then would it be worth it?

They arrived early and the current owner had yet to appear with keys. Seeing the Nite Club for the first time persuaded her to try at least to be upbeat.

Maybe it'll be really great. It's such a big building. And my parents own it, so I'll probably have run of the place.

Under the purview of most children, compartmentalization allowed her to have completely contradictory feelings about the impending change. This meant she was not entirely predisposed to being obdurate in the matter of moving. On the one hand it could be murder; on the other the whole thing could be an amazing adventure.

Or so she desperately wanted to believe.

Bob said, "I'll show you around," and they went on the grand tour of Wilson.

Since the tour lasted all of three minutes after crossing the railroad tracks and ended when they arrived at the weedy lot of a gas station that looked like a refugee of the 1930's, perhaps calling it a "grand tour" was an overstatement. When Bob said, "I'll show you again," and she realized that was really the whole town, Jenene began to cry.

Not much to explore here. Oh but there was: bars, dens of ill repute with lax standards regarding carding. That would come about soon enough.

Sob she didn't; no grand theatrics from her. She cried the silent tears of those who internalize.

Not so much that she was judgmental out of hand; had she grown up in this place she would likely be just as unhappy about moving to Cottage Grove. The problem was contrast. Cottage Grove was a booming city with large residential neighborhoods.

Not to mention other kids living nearby.

There would be no neighborhood of friends here. No close friends at all. No friends like her best friend, Mary, who she had known since they were three. "You can write letters," her parents said, "maybe visit each other in the summer." What were letters and occasional visits compared to seeing each other almost every day?

Disappointment continued once inside the Nite Club. Maybe her dad talked it up too much; he was a born salesman who knew how to sell the sizzle even if the meat was a piece of chuck. The stale stink of grease and cigarettes infiltrated her nose the instant they stepped inside. Jenene was reminded of a place she remembered as not only unpleasant but crummy.

The tavern associated with the resort on Bone Lake where she and her family stayed a week every summer was a rustic sort of place that seemed dingy and unwelcoming to a little girl who had never before been in such a place. Perhaps it was because it was old and not the sort of establishment where an emphasis was put on downplaying the accrued dinginess. When it burned to the ground later to be rebuilt, it seemed a far cheerier and open place, due in part to the freshness lost to the previous building.

Standing there in the dim bar, the dining room to the left, the Nite Club was too reminiscent of the pre-burned tavern. It seemed like the sort of dreary place she would rather not be. Any hope that it was somehow better than the grungy tavern dissipated. Had she known that day this place would become the epicenter of her life for the next several years she may have sobbed openly after all.

The whole scenario reminded her of when Lois announced she was pregnant with Jeff. They promised her a little sister—really got her jazzed on a little sis, in fact, so much so she was simply delighted by the notion—only to deliver a brother.

Perhaps it was fitting Jeff was born in 1968, the year ads everywhere implored "Pray for Rosemary's Baby." An angry little eight-year-old Jenene would have had no problem labeling him the antichrist.

"Send him back," she said after evaluating the pink-cheeked cherub for a minute and concluding they had lied to her knowing full well this result was possible. Had they not lit the fire and fanned the flames of excitement over a little sister it was likely the sense of being betrayed wouldn't have been inflicted and she wouldn't have felt burned.

As it stood she learned a lesson about deception. How even what could seem like a harmless lie to coddle a child could cause great hurt and cynicism.

So far as her parents knew after the move Jenene was her usual sullen self. Had they ever questioned why her disposition would be so dour even before the life-shaking move and not assumed it was normal childhood moodiness, maybe they would have asked questions and gotten to the root of why she was miserable.

They had no idea Jenene had a secret. One she had wanted to tell…but because no one ever thought to ask—she would think they didn't *care* to ask—her subconscious decided to bury it deep, where it would remain hidden, and like an undiscovered abscess causes illnesses attributable to other causes, would cause her many problems easy to blame on other circumstances.

Like ostriches with their heads in the sand, her parents' ignorance, at least when it came to her feelings, was unshakeable. If they had no idea how truly devastated she felt after being forced to put such distance between her and the places and people with whom she was familiar, how would they ever isolate and identify a much bigger problem?

At the time of the move it was easier to identify the unhappy surface as the reason she felt so mucky. The secret had been submerged into the darkness…where it would remain—until she was faced with degenerative disc disease and the need to know where the injury began would bring it to light.

For Jenene it was easy to blame her discontent on all the change, and all she missed. As much as she cared about Mary and liked her old home, it didn't take long to figure out she missed the farm worst of all. The farm was the greatest place ever because it was where The Seniors lived.

I shouldn't have complained to Lal....

Lal, Bill, and Herb were in some ways a truer family than her parents. They were her elderly great aunt and great uncles, the unmarried siblings of her grandmother. Someday to take care of them she would turn her whole life upside down. But at that time she was only a kid with a great affection for these people who let her be herself.

It pained her she would miss unrecoverable time. Their advanced age made her acutely aware of their mortality.

Jenene could remember the very instance in which she learned about death. When the finality and the eventuality were hastily explained to her, as it was probably explained to many children that day. The cataclysmic event of November 22, 1963 was the sort of game changer that led to a lot of hasty explanations.

A pleasant enough wait on a fall day, she and her sitter were parked on the toll bridge in St. Paul Park as a barge chugged by on the mighty Mississippi. Breaking news on the radio shattered the peacefulness. President Kennedy was assassinated. She didn't understand who the president was, only that he was a big deal. But she did understand that he had been killed, which meant he was dead, which meant he was a goner, which meant there was no coming back.

The Seniors were old and going to die and she had to move away.

They were such an important part of her life….

The distance left her feeling hollow and infinitely alone. They were so instrumental in her happiness she doubted she would be capable of any joyful feelings so long as they lived so far away. They were her sugar. Giving them up was like swearing off candy and renouncing all forms of play.

Even more importantly, they were the ones who took care of her when she was sick, the ones always willing to listen, and the ones who actually let her be a kid. Well, Lal and Bill. Herb was a little scary, what some call a curmudgeon, and was no stranger to making a little girl cry with his gruff nature…or shooting trespassers in the butt with rock salt. Still, the old boy had his charm.

The prospect of visits in no way reduced her sour feelings. With the farm on the outskirt of Cottage Grove and only a few miles away as the crow flies from their old house, visiting them had been part of the routine of her life; what was an occasional stay on the farm compared to that?

Pain and anger and disenchantment were boiling up inside her yet she internalized rather than express how badly she felt. Even if she wanted to scream and wail and carry on about the blatant unfairness of it all, there was no forum for her outburst, no audience for her tantrum. In her mind, they just didn't care when it came to her true feelings. Her mother was always one to remark, "Whoever said life is fair? Fair is just a word in the dictionary."

Quiet, introspective, and guarded, Jenene had learned to conceal her feelings at home and to instead put up a barricade. This had gotten her labeled by her mother as gloomy, which was better than the label expressing herself would have incurred—spoiled brat. Her mother had grown up so poor she wore holey shoes to school and she felt any child who did not have to worry about such things had no reason to complain.

The move meant she would rarely get a break from the confines that led to her gloominess.

There was no room for outbursts of any kind. No room for a child with a voice. "I never should have been a mother," Lois would tell her, not to be mean or cruel, but more as an admission that she really had no idea how to live up to the role.

Everything about Lois implied dedicated career woman. Housewifely she was not. She was slim, carried herself with regality earned not inborn, and dressed in conservative attire to ensure the very sight of her implied respectability. To that end she wore her blonde hair in an old lady hairdo akin to a beehive way before her time so no one would mistake her youthfulness for softness because she was hard as granite. In nearly every photo of her from the past she holds firmly a strict no nonsense expression: all serious, all business.

Lois had to fight against the stigma of being a "career girl" in an era when women were expected to stay in the home. When her stridently self-assured manner prompted the question "Are you a feminist?" in the days when women were burning their bras and bucking traditional roles, she would reply, "Nope. I'm for Lois."

Ice maiden Lois was the perfect claims adjustor. She had no sympathy. When a little boy involved in an accident needed only a Band-aid, the payout she authorized exactly covered the price of one Band-aid. Bob said to her, "Jeez, Lois, you could've at least given him enough for an ice cream cone." No dice. Impersonal. Unaffected. Ice maiden Lois would break bread with her best friend's enemy and wouldn't shed a tear at her husband's funeral.

Lois' strictness, her severity, her seeming indifference, her inability to relate, and her lack of understanding weren't personal but instead reflected her austere childhood, which unfortunately for them both left her unprepared to raise a daughter with an emotional temperament.

She would swear to you and anyone who would listen that no daddy issues contributed to her marrying a man eleven years her senior, and maybe it's true, but her decadent wayward father was definitely absent enough it would be unkind to judge her for seeking an older, wiser mate to compensate for what she missed out on. All she had been denied, perhaps emotional support was not a quantifiable expectation. So she never developed a need for it or an ability to offer it to those in her life.

There is an old photograph of Jenene as a little girl sitting on the front step of The Senior's farmhouse, clutching a bouquet of wildflowers, crying. The flowers were presented to Lois only to be icily rebuffed. "Get those weeds out of the house," she had bellowed.

A harbinger of the Crohn's and lupus, it is no wonder Jenene suffered ulcers in her throat as a child, a persistent and painful nuisance that plagued her early years. There was so much she had to repress and hold back that her anger and frustration had to manifest somehow. Since she internalized it all, she was a subdued child whose tantrums showed in poor health rather than in displays of open theatrics.

Chapter 3
In the Wake of Major Changes

So the doozy of a move happened and overnight Jenene's whole life changed irreversibly.

The sudden awareness of the impermanence of life was stark and sobering; nothing cherished would last forever and the gossamer daydream of believing otherwise was dissolved.

They left a nice abode in Cottage Grove to move into the small one-bedroom house adjacent to the Nite Club. No longer did she have her own bedroom; she was forced to bunk with her obnoxious little brother (later so Jenene had her own room their parents slept on the living room hide-a-bed but that was a few years away). What was worse, as she had suspected Wilson had few kids her age. If it would happen at all it would take her time to prosper any friendships like the ones she left behind.

The whole situation was infuriating!

Denied an opinion, shorn of an identity, Jenene resolved to find escape by filling her time constructively. To her dismay this oftentimes entailed babysitting the constantly bratty Jeff. The kid was as attention-starved as her. But instead of being aloof like her, he displayed his unhappiness with all sorts of naughty shenanigans. He was developing a habit of shifting blame to her, too. She had yet to decide if it was funny or sad.

Even if he was a handful, babysitting was better than nothing. In an environment that was about as stimulating as a padded room in an asylum, to maintain her sanity it was worth doing about anything to evade the tedium, boredom, and total lack of stimulus.

As for Jeff, he made due in their new environs by trying to pass off a constant stream of fibs. Whatever he was caught doing he would invariably blame on Jenene. The habit became so ingrained it would continue years after she moved out. He also found clever ways of circumventing rules. He was always seeking loopholes that would keep him out of trouble.

Jeff was the spitting image of Dennis the Menace, a little boy always on the wrong side of trouble with squinty eyes and a puckish grin. He was tiny until a bowel-obstruction was found—a diet of only peanut butter and grilled cheese sandwiches has consequences—and dealt with; then he was a weed on the edge of a compost site, one that would grow into a stout and sturdy plant.

One example of his ingenuity was how after being expressly forbidden to go over the highway—vehicles whizzed by at 55mph—Jeff managed to cross Highway 12 to the facile body of Wilson, where there was at least a small playground. Able to explore on his side, he ambled his way on down the highway and discovered…a culvert. A quick shimmy through and bingo, he was on the other side without technically breaking the rules by going under rather than over the road and avoiding traffic completely.

Jenene could be defiant too. She developed into a voracious reader, which sounds like a good thing. But what was her literature of choice? Whatever would make a banned books list. The film version of *The Exorcist* was released and of course her mother forbid her to read the original book, so naturally she sought a copy and devoured the crazy tale of a possessed little girl in a modern city and found it a little scary but mostly strange.

Peyton's Place, for all its luridness, did not interest her as an entertainment because it did not take her long to pick up on the tomfoolery going on around her. When such a storyline too closely mirrors your surroundings it does not seem titillating…just sad.

The Valley of the Dolls and *The Happy Hooker* were enlightening tales, one of drugs and one of sex; one fictional, one purportedly real, both were filled with the sort of vulgarly enticing mental junk food supplied through reality programming today. How strange it was, to be so bored her biggest defiance was reading books her mom found questionable.

Other less wholesome forms of defiance would follow.

Waitressing was a natural extension of a desire to keep busy.

The sometimes hurried, sometimes nasty, sometimes wacky job bore many responsibilities. Yet it seemed like a decent way to fill time since Jenene would bank more money than the quarter an hour she made babysitting.

At the outset unaware touchy-grabby hands were the real downside of the job, in the beginning it was performance anxiety causing her angst. It was always important for her to do a good job. Her whole life she had watched her parents work, watched them sacrifice and put their work ahead of all else, and she had gotten the idea the only chance she had of getting the attention for which she yearned was to do a good job no matter what task was at hand.

Looking out from the edge of the dining room, she was more than anxious. She knew she had to perform. Nepotism wouldn't keep her in a job. If she failed to attain and maintain a reasonable standard, she would be replaced. Then it would be back to babysitting the true brat of the household.

Cut off from the bar by a wall, the dining room was one of two separate worlds, well lit, tables coordinated to maximize space, each with a cloth and the appropriate number of placemats.

It was beginning to fill with families, older couples, some retired, and men stepping out with their girlfriends. Beside it, the bar was darkened for ambience and filled with men and women on the make.

Later. The night in full swing. It was a carnival to the nose. Fried food. Beer. Sizzling meat. Wafting cigarette smoke. Intermingling. With the scents of industry, sweat and dust and cow manure. Perhaps a diaper or two was adding to the aroma, too. There were a lot of big farm families.

The jukebox played country tune after country tune, an endless cycle of testaments to the hard side of love, the good side of drinking, and the importance of having a fine dog.

Glasses clanged on the bar.

Country repartee was exchanged with drunken bravado.

Once in awhile a fist would fly, most often between brothers, and the fracas would be directed to the parking lot, where if a cop happened by he would stop and be a spectator because in that day it was no crime for two men to fight it out so long as no weapons were involved.

Figuring out quickly there was no magic formula to the job, only hard work, Jenene found her groove. Smile. Be pleasant. Take their orders, keep their drinks filled, prevent their kids from wandering off, listen to their complaints or praise, and help the busboy clean up after they vacated. Not too difficult. Even if a lot of the tips were disappointing.

Busying herself stacking dirty plates and drawing together silverware, she was totally unprepared for a bee sting to her right butt cheek. But a bee hadn't gotten into the dining room.

The man's pinch surprised her so much she jumped. She wanted to cry out ouch! But repressed it, pasting on a facsimile of a smile.

Not only was it a shock, but it hurt too. In the aftermath it felt like a crab had gotten her with its pinchers. At least a bee sting can be relieved with baking soda.

Turning on a dime, she saw the culprit. He was married, in his thirties. He had a mouthful of bad teeth and the swagger of a fellow who knew his way around the world. Or thought he did. He was smiling enticingly. Shamelessly. What could a grown man want with her? She was a child. His oldest was not much younger than her. Could he really want to do sex with her? The idea repulsed her. His wife had taken their children to the bathroom. She would be back any minute and he was propositioning a child.

Jenene wanted to slap his hand. Snap at him that he was a scumbag. Tell him how disgusting he was, how rude.

Yet all she could do was smile. Take it. It had been explained to her. It was part of the job, catering to the customers, placating them…and putting up with their advances apparently.

It was so outside her realm of understanding. Only a few months ago, her days entailed playing Barbie with her girlfriends and spending time with The Seniors. No men treated her as anything other than a child, not a sex object certainly.

Since his advance had failed to elicit much response, negating his air of chumminess, the flagrant cheater belched, "Can I get another beer?"

"Right away," she replied, breathing a sigh of relief because she had an excuse to rush away. She was none too anxious to return, to get within reach of the handsy customer, but it was the job.

The initial pincher proved to be the first of many such men. Yet Jenene kept waitressing. Even if the tips were paltry and the grabby hands a nuisance, what else was there to do? Stay in and baby-sit the bratty little squirt?

Of course the tips were only paltry until the seasoned waitresses, who made good tips, told her that she'd need to take the pats and pinches with good humor if she wanted more than nickels and pennies. When you looked stunned and put-off, it ensured the fellow who motivated such a response wouldn't be too keen to leave a decent tip.

In time, she would have a following of older men intent on tricking her out of her innocence. She was initially so ignorant she had no idea what these men expected from her, what they were seeking to gain, why they were so interested in her except to blame it on whatever mysterious notions of sex were in her mind. It was confusing and flustering and in many ways a nuisance because it was not acceptable subject matter to discuss.

She was getting an incomplete education full of innuendo, hints, and schoolyard misinformation.

One memory that exemplifies the transition from ignorance to awareness revolves around a comment made by a young bartender Bob had hired.

"Hey, come here," the sly man called her.

"You have an order up?"

"No. I need to tell you something."

"What?"

"My brother has the hots for you," he said as if that should have some special significance to her.

His brother was at least five years older. Having never heard the expression, she had no idea what he meant so implored him to clarify.

"You know, he likes you. A lot. He thinks you're cute."

His words fell short of the implication behind them yet the inference was unmistakable. What the heck else would a much older guy want to do with her? Talk about dolls? Talk about what it's like to be too young to have a driver's license? Or, more likely, he saw her as someone he wanted to fool around with, whatever that meant. *That's a little gross...maybe a lot gross. He doesn't know me at all. He's way older. And he thinks it's good he wants to...to.... Ew!*

"Tell him no thanks," she said indignantly.

Instead of being flattered by all this male attention, she was disgusted. She resolved to never marry a man from anywhere around Wilson or even a man from the state of Wisconsin. The attention was not only uncomfortable; it was offensive. Being objectified began undermining her confidence (Would she ever be seen as more than a piece of meat? Would she ever be listened to? Would she ever be taken seriously?) and made her seek escape.

Drinking began with experimentation and grew into habit. More than what she was allowed before her parents' eyes. She became a slush, a boozer, a real drunk; but she was secretive enough it was an attribute known to no one but her.

Chapter 4
Wrinkles

Family is a funny thing. Subject to all manner of weirdness and misperception. Dysfunction too.

Misunderstandings, especially ones given weight by lack of clarification, can tincture the better part of a life.

Born on February 9, 1960, the year Coca-Cola began canning its soda and Alfred Hitchcock's landmark *Psycho* was released, Jenene's early years were a matter of dispute, for a time even labeled taboo, until illumination much later in life shed a revealing light on the past.

The dispute arose from a suspicious memory ignited when Jenene noticed some inconspicuous evidence. Speculation began with an observation: in the photo album, her parents were in Jeff's baby pictures, but not hers.

This reminded Jenene she lived on the farm when she was little. She remembered Lal being her world, Lal being her provider and protector. Her parents only arrived later…to snatch her away.

In her teens she built up the courage to ask her dad about the photo discrepancy and her memories. His response was to tell her never to ask her mother about that time because it was sure to "make her cry" and ended the conversation there.

The inference Jenene took was that she was perhaps the product of an affair since Bob had previously been married to a fashion model with whom he had a son. He would say no more other than to confirm she had spent a time living on the farm. The subject seemed to pain him.

So she dropped it.

And for most of her life she received no explanation. She recognized her parents were an unlikely couple and her dad had probably feared old emotions stirred up would create a heady brew of resentments or regrets. Sometimes it boggled her that her parents ever ended up together. A chance meeting at a car dealership where Bob was a salesman set them on a path that would lead to kids, marriage, and the whole shebang.

With their age difference, it was improbable Bob and Lois would meet let alone marry; yet there were commonalities that brought them together. Lois may have been Bob's physical junior but on the playing field of maturity her difficult upbringing and dogged spirit made her his equal. There was also the fact they shared similar impoverished backgrounds that tempered them into consummate go-getters.

Lois's early childhood was spent on Grey Cloud Island, near the farm. Much like she would later do to her own children, she was moved unhappily to Dixon, Illinois. In 1953 she graduated from high school and three months before her eighteenth birthday returned to Minnesota, intent on a better life.

From our perspective brave but from her own just another thing she had to do to accomplish her goal Lois took an apartment in Minneapolis and set about finding a career. In the city she was relatively close to The Seniors and better able to find her forte.

From the humblest beginnings in the mailroom of the Hartford Insurance Company, the never-say-die worker Lois rose through the ranks at a surprising clip.

This was pre-feminism and women were expected to keep house. Lois refused to be denied. She would never consign herself to being a frumpy dumpy housewife with a mind only for housework and child rearing. Family life was of little interest; she had too much of it growing up, forced to watch after her two younger brothers while her mother worked and her estranged father gallivanted.

A career was for her and that was what she earned, ultimately rising to the level of claims adjustor, her favorite position, and beyond, to levels of management someone without a college degree could not achieve today.

Bob grew up in Carthage, Missouri, and struck out even younger, at fourteen, due to a less-than-stellar home life marred by half-siblings who hated him for being the only offspring his parents shared.

In what may have actually been an attempt to kill him (it's not for this writer to speculate on the intentions of children—only to divulge the facts), they fed him the corrosive liquid lye, used to make soap and explosives.

The resulting esophageal stricture, an acute narrowing of the esophagus, led to a year of eating only bananas, creating an aversion for the fruit that haunted him the rest of his life (after a heart attack in later life he was advised to eat half a banana a day for the potassium; he followed the advisement to a tee, eating a perfectly parceled banana half and not a smidgen more).

Another time his evidently dastardly half-sibs pushed him down a mineshaft and only came clean a day later, meaning as a small child he spent several claustrophobic hours trapped and terrified in a pitch black hole.

Perhaps tempered by those experiences into someone less afraid of death, shortly after striking out on his own he used his half-brother's identification to join the war effort. World War II was in full swing and he felt it was his duty. He joined the Navy in an attempt to find the sense of family he never had at home.

Stationed on an aircraft carrier, Bob became the unlucky recipient of a Purple Heart when a mortar blew him to smithereens. If any luck were involved it was that he wasn't paralyzed, disfigured, or killed. Beyond a deep pocket of scar on his back that sort of worked like a bass mouth and could eat fingers or loose change, the war left him with fewer lasting impacts than too many with whom he served.

Twenty-two months in traction meant little entertainment other than fantasizing about the future. He came home from the war intent on capturing the American dream. For him that meant business ownership, a goal easier to daydream than actually achieve. And Indy car racing: more a hobby but a way to prove his worth to himself that was a whole lot of fun.

To improve his salesmanship, he worked car lots, which was his vocation when Lois strutted into his life near the end of a disastrous first marriage. Even if he was so good at making sales they said he could "sell freezers to Eskimos," a disconnection between him and his fashion model wife fractured his personal life. She persisted on blaming Bob for cursing her with what was in the 1950's a career-ending pregnancy. Their son, Bobby, was the personification of all his mother's problems.

This meant her resentment carried down to their son. She refused to even remotely care for little Bobby. This forced Bob to come home periodically throughout the workday to tend to the baby's needs. At the child custody hearings it was no surprise she went so far as to outright refuse custody.

By the time of the divorce his foray into racecar driving had led to a wall of trophies. In court they were awarded to his ex wife; she destroyed the whole lot out of immature spite. Bob didn't give a damn. The sort of braggart who cared about a bunch of trophies was a person who misunderstood what Bob saw as the point. What mattered to him were the actual achievements, placing in the prestigious Daytona 500 being the biggest.

Bob and Lois were married after the divorce was finalized and she put a stop to what she viewed as racing nonsense.

Where the dispute laid was in the timeframe of when their marriage occurred, before or after Jenene's birth. Aware it was well after she was born, a full two years, Jenene never questioned her mom as to the sequence of events or why she had lived on the farm. She never dared broach this taboo subject even after her dad died.

Jenene assumed her mom didn't want her and for that reason abandoned her into Lal's care. All while her dad pushed to create a family. This belief for decades tainted her view of her mother. Then one day Lois brought it up as if the subject was in no way forbidden and her explanations changed Jenene's entire view of the past.

While Bob dealt with his divorce he insisted Lois and Jenene maintain distance. They lived with a family in North Minneapolis. The woman of the house was Jenene's sitter while Lois worked. One day Lois came home to find Jenene "screaming [her] head off and soaked from head to toe" while the woman talked on the phone oblivious to the situation. For this reason Lois entrusted Lal with Jenene's care.

Jenene was sent to the farm for her protection…not because she wasn't wanted. The revelation restructured her view of her mother, her father, and the past. All those years believing her mom wanted to abandon her created a wedge from as early as she could remember.

Had she known the truth, perhaps the gulf she felt could have been shortened, even eliminated. Learning her mom had tried to do the right thing while her dad wanted to keep them a secret made her reassess all her feelings.

Most of her childhood her dad was the parent she was close to, the one she saw as more than a parent, as a friend. Not that there was a lack of awkwardness when he first came into her young life.

When the dust from his divorce had cleared, Bob was there, sixteen-year-old son in tow, to collect Lois and Jenene. They moved into a house in Cottage Grove, where they lived until the eventual move to Wilson. For a little child the transition was jarring and confusing. But Bob worked his magic on Jenene.

Despite so shaky a beginning, she recalls many fond memories. He had a way of making her feel special. He was managing an out of town upscale restaurant to advance his proficiency. When Jenene visited he made sure to lavish her with attention. This included extravagant dinners. Never one to prize food, she nevertheless loved the lobster she was allowed to order.

Three petite tails prepared to perfection and slavered in butter, the lavish meals were daddy's love served up on a fancy plate.

Now she had to contend with the notion that he repressed the story not to spare her mom but to shed a better light on himself.

Although her love for her dad couldn't be diminished, her respect for him took a hit. He had prospered the wedge…and by doing so had created misunderstandings that undermined her relationship with her mother during those important years when a teenage girl can use a mom.

Perhaps had she known, had she understood the truth, their relationship would have prospered instead of decayed.

Maybe they were destined to have a strained rapport. One of Jenene's earliest memories of her mother came from the time shortly after the four of them moved in together.

Not that Lois ever made her feel guilty about the accident.

For a woman who could be stern, even callous, her toddler inadvertently allowing a spring-action gate to swing shut and demolish her nose might seem like a perfect reason to become unhinged. Not to Lois. That was the thing about her mom. Even as she extolled that fairness didn't exist, she had her own sense of fair play. To her an accident was an accident and not call for punishment.

Maybe seeing blood splashing all over the sidewalk, knowing she was the cause, made her take on more blame. The event traumatized her in that minor but poignant way all but the luckiest of people experience at some point. Because her mom was new to her, practically a stranger, and seemingly not easy to impress, she never felt like she could live down the inadvertent accident she caused.

The accident and all the blood was the first upsetting part of that day. The second was Bobby driving them to the hospital. She had yet to develop any confidence in Bobby, or would she; he was a mystery to her and would remain enigmatic until he came clean decades later.

The then sixteen-year-old was a powder keg of anger. No doubt to spare him from knowing his dad sired a child before the divorce was final, he was told Jenene's father was killed in Viet Nam. Not a complete idiot, he never believed it for a second. The deception only fueled his fury.

Jenene was too young to understand why he seethed with anger yet sensed there was something frightening about the large young man. Feeling Bobby's aversion, perhaps an emotion as advanced as loathing, made for one scary car ride. Their lives were in his care and she didn't trust him one bit.

Had Jenene been older it would have been apparent to her he was not keen on the situation in general, Lois in particular. The defiant Bobby often butted heads with his father's young wife. Jealousy was as much to blame as resentment. Who were this haughty woman and her quiet child to take his dad? Who was his mother to shove him away? Who was his dad to let it all happen?

Even if he got them safely to the hospital that day she had good reason to distrust....

If the years following that incident proved anything, it was that a lack of early bonding does not make for a good mother-daughter relationship. The communication breakdown was only furthered by the relocation to Wisconsin. Had things gone differently perhaps when she suffered the anal fissure that nearly took her life she would have been comfortable telling her mom as soon as she saw the blood in the toilet—instead of procrastinating for days.

By the time she was bleeding out, the mutual disconnect made revealing private matters to her mother almost out of the question.

Chapter 5
Humiliating Crisis

Picture a teenage girl, self-conscious of her body, awkward with her whole identity, rising from the toilet to a bowl full of bright red blood not of the menstrual variety. What would she feel? Revulsion? Aloneness? Terror?

Jenene experienced all three. By the time she saw the blood, she had no one she felt comfortable divulging such a problem to, no one it wouldn't mortify her to tell. She was close to her dad but not so intimately she felt comfortable speaking of those things that concern women. Never once did they discuss her menstrual cycle or sex. There was also the matter of his teasing....

If she had Lal, maybe she could have told her. But Lal was a state away...too far away. Was it purposeful creating that distance?

Misperceiving a clueless father's teasing as mean barbs—the things he said never failed to make her deeply uncomfortable—

can cause a young girl to run to help. To some kids it all would have been water off a duck's back. To a sensitive girl unsure of why her parents seemed so strange and remote it was too much.

Lal reacted by making it clear his behavior was uncalled for and said it would stop…or else.

No parent takes a threat to take away his or her child lightly; not even if the threat is levied by a loving, softhearted aunt who's only intention was to soothe a hurt niece.

Was it because she ran to Lal and Lal had stood up for her that they had to move far away?

So she chose not to say anything about the blood spilling out of her every time she sat on the toilet. All she could do was isolate herself, struggling with her misery alone, and be blindly hopeful the bleeding would stop yet terrified the flow would continue unabated.

The headache became her constant companion on the first day. A dull thump at the start: a dull banging in her temples, bam, bam, bam, that evolved to a strident booming throughout her whole skull, bang, bang, bang!

Day by day, as she continued to bleed, the pain worsened as the tapping became drumming, intense pressure pushing its way out like a root that cracks then fractures the pot that holds it, pulsing, undulating, and causing her constant nausea, lightheadedness, and malaise.

Blind hope was fading.

Terror was metastasizing.

It was the September of 1973. Eighth grade started like a landmine going off and all the shrapnel that hit was the line up of teachers she quickly concluded would make for an agonizing quarter. The rigors of school lent to more stimulating environs than the banality of her home life but when her teachers were fusspots and prigs, the sort of people who made the learning experience without fun, she dreaded going to school and it was shaping up to be a dread-filled quarter.

A little over a year in Wisconsin had jaded and hardened her. Made her realize for whatever problems she used to face in her old school or her old neighborhood, they were nothing compared to the unhappiness she felt living in Wilson and going to school in Spring Valley. The about-face her parents had so hoped for had yet to manifest and even if they were deluded enough to have faith it still might, she had no such delusions.

Spring Valley, a pleasant little hamlet that as its name implies is nestled in a valley, is fifteen miles from Wilson, which meant a long boring bus ride on hilly, windy roads. She missed walking to and from school with her friends. There was also something to be said for only being five minutes from home.

Puzzlingly, her popularity soared in her new school. She was an oddity…a kid from the Cities who really didn't seem to give a care about much of anything.

There was another new girl from Minnesota but she had less cachet because her parents weren't business owners and she had an attractive older sister. That Jenene's parents owned a restaurant where many of her classmates often ate with their families was an even greater differentiation; she would stand coolly behind the bar and nod when they said hello or look right through them if they said nothing.

To her peers, her detachment seemed to come off as the height of sophistication. No one really cared to know her but they all wanted her to come to their birthday parties and sleepovers.

There were friends in and out of her life, but not like her peeps in Cottage Grove, who liked her for her and not because she transferred from a place they had all sorts of funny ideas about, as if she came from a foreign land and not from a distance of less than a hundred miles.

So far as she knew, the biggest difference didn't reflect well on the area. Never in Minnesota had a grown man touched her inappropriately and it was a constant irritant when she waitressed. To be fair she had no experience waitressing in Minnesota. So it was possible it could have been the same. But in her experience it seemed men in Minnesota still viewed her as, well, a child.

Having been indoctrinated from birth in the ways of the area, her peers could not relate to her or her complaints. If she harped about the blatant pinchers, she was met with envy and not the mutual disgust she expected. The consideration she was getting was the sort for which many young ladies yearned. The notice of older men meant the world to them, and all she did by shedding light on it was cause them to dismiss her as ungrateful or as a liar because who wouldn't want a grown man giving her the appreciation of a good pinch?

All of it was an atomic pain in her butt and apparently that bomb had gone off.

Sans friends good enough to confide her problem and no confidants nearby, she harbored her secret in miserable silence.

Had it been three days or four? A little dizzy, a lot groggy, she couldn't remember. Life had become an unreality, a cartoon, and she was a character composed of animation cells, only layers were missing and she was incomplete, only an outline instead of a fleshed out being. Could she hide that lethargy virtually had her in a stupor? Conceal that she felt so removed, so unreal? Through scarceness she thought it possible but was her thinking clear enough to make such an assessment?

Jenene's lassitude even drew the interest of Lois, the woman who only seemed to take note of her when she was doing something wrong.

Lois looked her up and down quizzically. "What's wrong with you?"

You know that stressful instant you're put on the spot and have to come up with an answer? In that instant, even in her diminished state, Jenene evaluated her entire relationship with her mother and weighed her options.

Their relationship was strained from all those underlying antipathies—a child abandoned, a mother challenged—and external strife caused by the transformative changes in their lives. It didn't help that the only way to get her mother's attention was to address her by her first name because the label "mom" never took.

What crass thing might Lois say about this? Would it lead to a clash? Jenene didn't have the energy to absorb criticism. She remembered how shortly after the move when she flubbed a fruit and marshmallow salad her mother made her feel stupid, really excoriated her in front of everyone.

Sure, what she did wasn't the brightest thing. But was it worth kicking her when she was already down?

Jenene was sent to the Nite Club for a tub of sour cream intended for the salad. The Seniors were coming for a visit and she wanted to lend a hand. Not yet kitchen and cooler savvy, what she brought back and mixed into the salad was sour cream spiced with onion and garlic. This went over like spoiled salami with her mother while everyone else reacted as if it were a humorous bungle.

The problem with their relationship ultimately came down to a mutual misunderstanding neither was big enough to overcome. What they shared was an inability to relate to each other. Their priorities and opinions differed so significantly compromise was a never-ending negotiation and neither was willing to concede. As the parent, Lois would win because she would put her foot down and stop listening.

The differential in authority helped nothing; only intensified Jenene's feeling of unfairness. If she dared mention this, she got the same response: "Fair is just a word in the dictionary."

With buttocks tightly cinched, instead of revealing her true problem, she would only say, "I have a really bad headache. It's making me feel sick." No lie in that.

"I'm taking you to the doctor," Lois declared.

One thing about her mother, she was quick to solicit medical consultation.

Illness not so much worried Lois as repulsed her. Those with queasy stomachs can't afford to experience certain sights or smells. One time Jenene vomited on her bedroom floor. Sparking Lois to vomit alongside her. Too queasy to spend another instant in the presence of the mess, she closed the door. And waited for Bob to come home, thus he with the strong constitution was tasked with clean up.

As Lois hustled her out the door Jenene was more than reluctant to go. It had nothing to do with being afraid of doctors. Twice in Cottage Grove a doctor was summoned to their house to tend to her, once for mumps, once for chicken pox. These events and the removal of her tonsils all came before the age of ten. So she knew the benefits of treatment.

The mortification was what it all came down to ….

Every mile that brought them closer to the doctor's office in Menomonie also brought Jenene closer to an inevitable revelation. The embarrassment of it was enough to make her choose death over disclosure.

If the doctor figured out her real problem, he would probably want to poke around down there and that she wasn't comfortable with; whether or not he was a physician made no difference to her. Maybe if there had been someone whose hand she could hold, whose words would have assured and consoled her, she wouldn't have been so resistant. Feeling utterly alone, she wanted nothing more than to retreat from her problem and solidify her seclusion.

The idea that maybe her mother would go along with her when it came to concealing her true ailment grew out of the flawed logic of desperation.

Not thinking clearly, brain really in the fog, it was the only thing she could think to do. She didn't really believe she cared all that much for her, would be fine going along with the hush-up. So the decision to confide in her mother was made…if she promised not to tell.

"I won't say anything I promise," she replied impatiently. "What is it?"

"The thing is…."

Explaining was as horrible and embarrassing as she expected, as painful as crawling through broken glass on hands and knees, as baring as stripping and running through the Nite Club's dining room on a Friday night naked. She was in no way accustomed to making such personal divulgences. It wasn't like her letters to Mary and Lal were filled with the personal disclosures they might have shared were they in a room together.

Even at that young age she had the tendency to be a hermit; the barricade that made her life gloomy also made her a loner because when nothing is ventured, nothing is gained, the reason she had trouble making any close friends in her current surroundings. It was easier not to put expectation on others because then nothing was expected of her. Today she may have been diagnosed as depressed; at that time she was just a mopey teenager and that may have been worst of all, that she felt there was no one who could commiserate with her, no understanding to be found.

Telling brought no relief. Her mother listened, her mien giving no indication of how she felt about it, and Jenene could only hope she would keep her promise.

Jenene was alone in the examination room. She felt weak, on the brink of collapse, in fact.

The pain in her head was a constant drone. Feeling so faint the real difficulty lay in keeping her eyes open at all; they were teary, constantly blinking, getting blearier by the instant. She had no idea how near death she was, how much of her life had been allowed to run out of her body. Blood is life, which is why blood donations are so important.

The cheery Filipino doctor entered in a flourish, a small jaunty man, tossed down a file, thoroughly washed his hands, sat on his wheeled doctor's chair, and positioned himself in front of her. "Your mother tells me you have another problem," he said. "How about you tell me what's going on."

Frowning, Jenene knew the jig was up. A tsunami of fear and horror swept her away. Was it the feeling of doom? At that moment it sure felt that way.

Within an hour, she was in emergency surgery, undergoing a fissurectomy to repair the anal fissure out of which her life was draining. It wasn't even her first surgery; the first had been more routine, tonsil and adenoid removal, which was almost a bonus since she was allowed a lot of ice cream afterwards. It hadn't been so scary that time and not at all as degrading.

Later in life she would have the sentimentality of a nudist but that would be after she learned to be comfortable with her body. At the age of puberty, she still felt the weight of shyness, the conspicuity of being seen by others, and wished she could be anywhere else in the world.

The lead up, stripping and donning a gown, having a needle poked into her vein for an IV, being put on a gurney that would convey her to the operating room, all of it made her feel like a bug pinned on a board for display. The actual details were all a blur in the end but the experience would be so oft repeated in the coming years elements of it would blend into the amalgamated memory of many surgeries.

One thing would stand out to her from that particular surgery.

On the verge of being put under, the operating lights like UFOs hovering overhead, the medical staff shuffling around, what was on her mind was her mother's duplicity. Even if it saved her life, a trust was broken.

If her mother was going to tell, she should have told her she was going to tell. Going behind her back the way she had, promising not to tell only to take the first opportunity to notify the doctor, revealed a missing facet to her character: trustworthiness.

If she had only said, "I have no choice but to tell the doctor," trust wouldn't have been as much of an issue, even if she had initially promised. If she had taken it upon herself to sell the idea of telling, perhaps she could have convinced Jenene of the importance of being honest instead of revealing her personal willingness to be dishonest.

Embarrassment only described it to a degree. Humiliation only described it to a degree. It was so mortifying to drop her pants and have her private zone scrutinized over she would have rather died. In time she would learn not to be shy. Calluses develop through exposure and she would be exposed many times to come, as the ebb and flow of her health required her to endure ever more invasive procedures. But during that first major health scare she was still a neophyte, an innocent.

In the end, it wasn't the local Lotharios that took Jenene's innocence…it was the health scares that exposed her to the medical establishment. She would face so many health problems in the years ahead her dad would first make the comment, "It's like you got a used body."

Chapter 6
Oasis

When mothering was absolutely necessary, such as in the wake of the fissurectomy, Jenene was shipped off to the farm.

Lois had no interest in mothering and it worked to Jenene's benefit because it got her exactly what she wanted, to be with Lal, Bill, and Herb.

The farm had factored in more so than she feared when they first relocated. Perchance between Bob restricting his teasing, therefore limiting her reason to protest, and the distance already in place, worries were mollified. However it was whenever Jenene was sick or recuperating that she was sent to the farm to convalesce under the gentle, loving touch of Lal, the sympathetic ear of Bill, and the grumbly but mostly silent protective eye of Herb.

The farm had remained her refuge and without those respites she might have lost her mind.

"Come on in, Honey-child," Lal invited and embraced her in consoling arms. "We'll make sure you get better."

The warm atmospherics of the farm made for a perfect recovery zone. Put up in the room that once belonged to her great-grandparents, during the fall and winter months its placement above the woodburning furnace made it comfortably toasty.

Nothing was more soothing than being wrapped in a hand-sewn quilt bright with the colors of past fashions minced and assembled into a new artful iteration. Lal was a natural seamstress not to mention a skilled embroiderer. Embroidery of the Lord's Prayer was one of her masterpieces. She made enough doilies to supply Buckingham Palace.

Lal would keep her fed with delicious foods that because she ate so many restaurant meals seemed like delicacies. True home cooking can unwind the cockles of even the most entwined heart. Lal's canned peaches were unmatched.

A man whose heart was so light it could float, Bill would keep her company with his humor and whimsy and fill her heart with helium so it could float too.

Yet he could imbue his words with such weightiness serious lessons could be imparted and absorbed. There was one in particular Bill would reiterate with regularity: almost whenever she spent time with him, in fact. It was simple, played into the golden rule of treat others as one wants to be treated, and was the motto, "What goes around comes around. Be it good be it bad."

When she was very young, she would ask what he meant.

"If you're a bad person," he explained. "If you sell spoiled grain to your neighbor. If you tell lies that lead to others' pain. It will all come back on you. It goes both ways. You bring your neighbor some cookies, why they might just bring you a pie. You spread kindness it will be kindness that comes back to you."

Ever after he would remind her as though it were never far from his mind. Maybe it was why he conducted his life so admirably. So few people have no enemies. Bill had to be one of them. To Bill the effort to make a friend, no matter how great, paid off more than pursuing the callousness of building enmity. Between Bill and her dad she became a whiz at turning her shoulder.

Herb's contribution to her visit was to ignore her, which was better than getting the backside of his tongue.

It was only when she got home that she felt homesick—for the farm.

Chapter 7
Nightmare

Jenene experienced what proved to be a precognizant dream for the first time later that fall, capping off what thus far had been the most tumultuous year of her life. This vision would so terrify her she would misconstrue the event and believe for some time a warning was somehow an instigator because knowing…stopped nothing.

Her grandma Lucille, Lois' mother, and Lal were preparing to go on a three-week-long road trip and beforehand Lucille was staying with them overnight in Wilson. Sort of the old dame of the family even though by today's standards she wasn't really all that old at fifty-eight, she was a welcome guest even if she would never quite inspire the affinity Jenene felt for Lal. Quite a contrast separated them; Lal was warmer, kinder, and more grandmotherly, Lucille was loyal but spiteful, selectively affectionate, and deluded from a start in life that left her unprepared for what came later.

A change of life baby, Lucille Violet, born on November 30, 1915, was the pampered princess of the family. While Lal scrubbed floors, peeled potatoes, and mended the family's clothes, labor that in old age would leave her with a deep hunch in her back, "Babe," as the family nicknamed her, enjoyed the simple task of reading out loud to their mother.

As a young adult, she secretly married the good-for-nothing, hell-on-wheels local horse trainer. The man was a conniver, womanizer, and pretender; a maker of broken promises; no less than a scourge. Relationship eventually unearthed and rightly forbidden, Lucille smugly produced the marriage license. Too late for an annulment, she was pregnant.

In a time of hardship, her life was one of relative ease. As hardworking farm folk who knew the land, the family were spared the extreme meagerness so many suffered during the Great Depression yet it was no less a time of tight belt-cinching and careful penny-pinching. But Babe would know none of the privation her siblings struggled to avoid until the consequences of her decisions walloped her with a dose of stiff reality.

It's not so much that she chose to live in a way the family disapproved (this writer has been accused of living outside the norm and thus respects those who live on their own terms), but that she remained in the home and took all the benefits of the family, while bald-faced lying to the people supporting her, makes her a rather dastardly character in any estimate.

Subsequently she uprooted her family to raise her children, Lois, and her brothers, Uncles Bob and Dick, with her husband, Chester in Illinois.

When her husband exited stage right to gad about with a succession of girlfriends, she concocted a lie to save face. Perhaps brought up with too much leniency and indulgence to ever admit her bad decisions had led her astray, she had no problem attempting to mislead her children, peers, and family. Since he was a fireman, she told her brood and anyone else who would listen that he was forbidden from leaving the firehouse, and it was why he didn't live at home nor was often able to visit.

Even after her children were adults and no longer so ignorant as to believe her deception, she continued to live the fraud that her marriage wasn't snapped and for all intents and purposes as dead as a snake with a broken spine. Meanwhile, a philanderer of the first order, her ne'er-do-well husband used the excuse of having a wife to conveniently waylay his girlfriends' marriage plans.

When the rebellious man dropped dead with a grin on his maw and a twinkle in his eye, several of the women who inspired his final expression emerged from the woodwork to mourn him. Smirk plastered on a face otherwise severe, Lucille told Jenene, clutching her hand so hard it ground her metacarpals and made her wince as much as the vindictiveness in her grandma's chillingly spoken words, "He's my husband and I'll have the last laugh. Mark my words. The last laugh will be mine."

Jenene had no idea what she meant and only replied, "Yes, Grandma. Can you please loosen your grip?"

The man's death was enough to inspire tears not understood by her mother, who asked her dad, "Why is Jenene crying?"

Sure he had promised her a pony and never delivered, but he was her grandpa.

Years after those events Lucille traveled from Illinois to spend the night with the Davis family before proceeding the next morning to collect Lal. Geographically far removed, Jenene only saw her grandma once or twice a year and her visit was anxiously awaited.

Her grandma could be a kindly, saccharine, and jovial woman or she could be unapproachable, discourteous, and even scornful.

What permutation of her grandma would arrive?

Lucille proved to be in a euphoric mood. Such vibrancy imbued her it was infectious. She brimmed with delight and anxiousness to embark on her long desired and hard-earned vacation.

Lucille bunked with Jenene in Jeff's bed, which meant they slept side by side like girlfriends at a sleepover. There would be no late night gabfest. Lucille's vacation was starting in the morning so she was as anxious to go to bed as a kid on Christmas Eve.

Jenene settled in and soon drifted off to sleep…

Into dreamland…

Or perchance some other place….

Like a scene projected on the big screen, Lucille was a damsel in distress stranded on the side of a dusty road. She had a flat tire. Typical of herself, she surveyed the damage standing in the road rather than on the side of it, wringing her hands in the fashion she used to attract attention. No! There was a car coming. A flash of chrome and the car struck her. She flew through the air like a bounced ball and hit the ground like a brick. The heels knocked off her feet she was instantaneously struck dead.

And she lay where she landed, expired on the side of the road.

My grandma's dead….

The realization made the scene suddenly pull her away in a protracted zoom until she could see only blackness in the instant before her eyes snapped open.

Propelled out of sleep, upon jolting awake Jenene sat up, rolled on her side, and breathlessly stared at her slumbering grandma. The woman slept serenely, breathing deeply and evenly, at total peace.

Quite the opposite, a sense of urgency welled and pulsed inside Jenene. Emotion rose in her, forcing her to swallow back a gasp. She was certain her grandma was going to die very soon. She would be hit by a car and killed in the near future…probably on her vacation. When else? She would be far from home.

It was the strangest feeling; an eeriness that stemmed from a spike in her very soul. She just knew in a way no less ethereal than any inexplicable instinct. Logically, there was no reason she should feel that way.

The sense of knowing would be exacting. The toll of the genuineness of the feeling would be one of the albatrosses she would carry around her neck. What was different about this dream? Why did it resonate so deeply? When was it decided she would become the purveyor of clairvoyant warnings? Exactly why did she believe so strongly that was what she had experienced?

She just did.

After a life of coddling before her marriage was revealed, the universe seemed to punish Lucille for her duplicity with a shiftless malingerer for a husband who left her in the lurch with three kids.

Desperately poor, Lucille was barely able to scrape by and keep her children fed. She went to work at the "State School," the lovely euphemism in those days for the mental institution. She worked in the laundry. A hot, tiring, laborious job, for years she faithfully punched the timecard and put her nose to the grindstone because she had backed herself into a corner and the only way out was to admit she had been wrong.

She had spurned the family only to get burned but she was far too imperious to ever seek the sort of amends that would have brought her fully back into the fold. She never admitted her marriage was over, would sign every card from "Lucille and Chester" or "Grandma and Grandpa" until the day her husband died, twenty-eight years after their split up.

As inconclusive as she tried to make the situation, the whole family knew the disreputable Chester was no more part of her life than any of their lives. He'd blow in for a birthday like the peepshow that came with the carnivals in the old days, make boastful and empty pledges like the girls in such tents, and abscond shortly thereafter, leaving a metaphorical vacant patch in his wake, one left unfilled by promises broken before they were even made. His death marked an end to the lying but the lies flourished.

So it was after much leanness that Lucille was finally able to afford an escape. By that point in her life she was living a meager existence in a hotel room lined with books and magazines stacked in every conceivable open space; she worked and had little else going.

The vacation was the first not in five years, even ten or twenty, but ever. Contrastingly, Lal, who never married, though also part of the labor force, enjoyed a far freer and more pleasant life than Lucille in the years after their parents passed away; she had crisscrossed the nation and seen all the sights, accruing a massive collection of keepsakes.

It was finally Lucille's turn to get out and strut her stuff and it would quickly become apparent she was in no mood to entertain that any kooky foreboding dream was a reasonable forewarning to forestall or cancel or in any way interfere with her trip.

"You can't go, Grandma, you can't," Jenene gave her final plea. "Please don't. Please...."

Lucille was preparing to head out that morning in her yellow Monte Carlo. She would take I-94 into Minnesota and follow a series of secondary roads to the farm. Lal would be waiting there with her luggage lined up on the porch. They would probably have a light lunch of soup and sandwiches so Lucille could visit with Bill and be grumbled at by Herb. Then they would climb into the Monte Carlo and be off...to face whatever fate would travel beside them on the road.

Jenene had to broach the uncomfortable—chilling—topic and she had decided it was like entering a cold swimming pool—sometimes it's better to hop right in. It might have been better to test the waters with a toe, but that was one dive she had to make spontaneously or she would have been the kid bravely climbing up the ladder to the top of the high dive only to lose heart when surveying the drop spurring a tail-between-the-legs dismount.

She began her impassioned plea as Lucille prepared and loaded her bags. She explained the dream, cried, generally carried on, and at the conclusion of her explication, Lucille patted her on the cheek and said thinly, "Please don't take away my only vacation, Honey-child."

Making the usage significant, the endearment "Honey-child" was bestowed and used by Lal not Lucille. It was so different her using that pet name. That was somehow confirmation to Jenene she wasn't coming back. Even if she didn't want to believe it was true. Or why she was so certain.

Jenene buckled and abandoned her argument because she recognized the futility of saying more. She lost. Simple. No amount of intellectualization could grant an acceptable enough explanation to force belief.

This vacation was to be dispensation for many years of heartache, toil, and unmet dreams. Lucille's refusal to be deterred was understandable in retrospect—why would she think a child's nightmare was in any way a warning? Extrasensory perception wasn't mainstream subject matter and even had it been, why would she think her granddaughter possessed some sort of psychic power to foretell her death? It was the stuff of dime store novels.

Her grandma hugged her and she couldn't help but stiffen; a dead woman embraced her, condemned by her inability to accept an important message…if what she felt so strongly were true.

Tears obscuring her vision, Jenene watched her grandma drive away.

As she feared, their goodbyes in the Nite Club's parking lot proved to be their last words. Her dream would prove either an ineffaceable prognostication or incredible coincidence.

Either way within two weeks her grandma was dead.

Ten days later.

October 13, 1973. Teacher conferences meant that Thursday was the start of a four-day weekend, so Jenene was home when the call she had been waiting for came.

In the interim since Lucille departed she had told herself she was mistaken, being stupid, acting paranoid, and in the end she would be proven wrong. Yet every time the phone rang she would cringe, suffused with fear the nightmare would come true.

She was home alone so it was up to her to answer when the phone rang. An operator, calling from Enid, Oklahoma, invaded her ear. The woman asked hurriedly for Jenene's parents. It displeased her to be informed they were unable to take the phone.

"Can I take the call?" Jenene asked tentatively, her heart sinking, already knowing exactly what the call meant. *Oh my god*, she thought. *I dreamed grandma was going to get killed and sure enough this is the confirmation. Did I predict it or did I somehow…make it happen?*

"How old are you?" enquired the operator.

Had she not been impaired by an inability to lie, she may have been connected to the call. Instead she effectively stymied herself by replying truthfully, "I'm thirteen," at which point the operator gave her a phone number to hand off to her parents.

Anxious to learn if her fear had fermented into a stiff belt of truth, she practically threw the number at her dad when he arrived and informed him, "Grandma's dead."

Kicked into action, he dialed the number immediately and the operator connected him to Lal. Jenene watched her dad as he spoke. When Lal said, "Babe is dead," he parroted, "Babe is dead," and she got the verification she expected.

A beer truck pulled up behind the Nite Club, located right beside their house, and Bob signaled to Jenene to go sign for the delivery. When she returned, he was pale and had only one question. "How did you know your grandma was dead?"

Ready to tear the operator a new one, Bob had learned she had told Jenene nothing—in fact, she hadn't even told her who was calling. It could have been anyone Bob and Lois knew.

Jenene's emotions passengers on a plane that crashed the instant she heard the operator in her ear, shot down by the substantiation she so feared, she didn't want to explore the wreckage and study the information on the black box. Not now. Not so soon. Not when the debris was still glowing.

But Bob was a born talker and, besides for his hardheadedness in some regards, was empathetic enough to appeal to her with simple understanding.

So Jenene bared her soul and told her dad every detail of the dream, few though there were. She then put particular emphasis on the intensely felt assurance upon waking from the dream that it foretold an event that would happen in some capacity even if the details would prove different.

Surprise would be the first sensation that would begin to restore her emotional balance. Instead of being met by skepticism what her father presented was openness not always part of his character—as close as they were, there were subjects that made huge divisions in their relationship. Disbelief never crossed his face. He listened with earnestness that evolved into intent interest and finally emerged as total captivation. He wore an almost mesmerized expression.

Perhaps it was partly because he believed she wouldn't lie to him—couldn't, maybe. Knowing his daughter to be exceedingly honest would make it easier to grant veracity to her story. But perhaps it was because he was a touch superstitious, too. He never suggested it was merely a coincidence or twist of fate. He saw it as a warning—one that should have been heeded.

"Promise me, if you ever have a dream like that again," he said, "you'll tell me…right away. And if it's about me, I want to know even faster."

They shared a special rapport insomuch as she felt she could trust he wouldn't judge and label her but she didn't exactly expect to be believed.

"I will," she promised, failing to add that she hoped she would never have a dream like that again.

She failed to persuade Lucille but convincing Bob granted her some consolation. She avoided asking him if he thought it was feasible her fear was true, that somehow she willed or conjured or in some other way caused the accident. She was afraid he would confirm the possibility. Since he didn't bring up any such concept neither did she.

Even the possibility of fault plagued her with guilt. Guilt would be an emotion that would cause Jenene intense vexation throughout her life because she always found it easy to blame herself.

Saddled not only with her grandma's death but also the horror of her supposition that by dreaming a car hit Lucille it, well…caused a car to hit her, Jenene, as illogical as it might seem, absorbed a mix bag of feelings that went into a stewpot where it all stagnated into a heady brew. In time it coagulated into a brick that would sit heavily upon her mind for several years.

Selfless Lal, the gallant big sister, would in the days after the accident repeat over and over, "It should've been me."

A flash flood in Enid precipitated the accident.

Seeking higher ground, Lucille and Lal were crossing a street as hurriedly as they could manage with floodwaters slowing them down. Lal was in front, clutching her baby sister's hand, and felt the jolt when the speeding car struck her.

The driver stopped and jumped out. He was a young man. In that moment he had saucers for eyes. He exclaimed, "Oh my god," leapt back in his car, and sped off as if pursued by a drove of banshees…never to be identified to this day.

The instant she was struck the cause was lost. Lucille's entire left side was pulverized. While they waited on an ambulance Lal cradled her head and kept it out of the water. Soothed her in her final moments as only Lal could. Held her as her life slipped away as if carried on the current spilling across that flooded street in Enid, Oklahoma.

Did she perhaps give a thought to her granddaughter in her final moments? Recall her warning? Her adamancy? Wonder if perhaps she should have heeded? Or was she stuck in the immediacy of her moment of dying and never gave it a second thought? In a life so much can be left unsolved, so many questions unanswered.

In a life…

Mysteries abound.

The crime remains unsolved to this day. The young man, if he remains alive, is now a man older than the woman he killed. Have the banshees of a guilty conscience pursued him ever since? Or did the banshees get him long ago?

At her funeral, Jenene saw what Lucille meant when she said she would have the last laugh: she was laid to rest…right beside her husband. Every time the ladies' man's past loves visited his grave, they would be reminded that after all, she was his wife, the one and only; let their sinful tears sear the hallowed ground upon which they fell. Ha, ha.

Chapter 8
Paternal Lessons

"Jenene, always keep in mind, it isn't what you know, but who you know that's important," Bob declared. "The right association can make all the difference."

To Bob business wasn't about out-gimmicking the competition or cornering a market; it was about making irresistible merchandise through quality; but he knew nothing went as far as the right word of mouth.

"I know, dad, and always take a fool for what he says, not what he means."

"And don't waste your time listening to someone who only chatters to hear their brains rattle."

It amused Jenene her dad seemed to have a maxim for all situations.

While Lois commuted to the Cities for her beloved Hartford, Bob ran the Nite Club. As much as her mom was away and as little as they connected when she was home, Jenene found it unproblematic to bond with her dad. They had innumerable conversations.

Bob was the parent she believed truly cared about her. Probably because he would give her a hug and tell her he loved her. Bob was the one quick to defend her and give her an ear or an earful that was worthwhile and not uselessly critical. When they butted heads it could be as fierce as a pair of quarrelling rams but they could mostly come to an agreement without too much skull crashing.

Besides the taboo subject of the past, there was really only one disagreement they shared. Otherwise in most ways they were best pals. Only vaguely authoritative, he treated her like an equal in most regards, although he took great exception to any young man attempting to court her. She admired him for his work ethic, his people skills, and the way he handled Lois, such as when it came to Jenene sleeping in the Nite Club on especially hot nights.

This bone of contention came about the first summer. It was a heat wave and as it was a less common amenity they had yet to install air conditioning in their home. There had been a robbery and Lois thought it a bad idea since it was possible the unknown assailant might return. Bob overruled her. "She can't sleep," he justified.

Every time she declared she was sleeping over there, Lois would arch an eyebrow at Bob but she never said a word because he had closed the matter. That was the way her parents were, rather than argue they traded off who won the battles so that each prevailed about equally.

Jenene's relationship with her dad was also contradictory; his teasing, a form of jocularity that was an adjunct of his salesman manner, to him nothing more than poking fun, could make her sick with discomfort, even caused so much embarrassment she dreaded bringing friends into his presence, and yet she loved him enormously.

And there was the way she made Bob uncomfortable. Immeasurably. It was from there that the father and daughter's one true disagreement derived. Perhaps the discomfort she caused was deeper, in some way more weighty; whereas his teasing was ultimately triviality espoused as drollery, Jenene's ideas challenged his core beliefs.

Bob was raised in a backward environment in which racism thrived and he had learned to tow the line. A hook imbedded so deeply he embraced rather than rejected what much of the north had accepted as nonsense attached the line to him. Even though he quit his home to escape the nastier side of racism, in his opinion the races were different and shouldn't mix.

Miscegenation was what galled him; if anything fogged his eyes with red it was a black man canoodling with a white woman. Whites were at the top of the food chain. Other races were not welcome to interbreed with those fair of skin. It seems doubtful his prejudice went so far that he viewed other races in an entirely negative way; he was simply opposed to mixing.

They would be sitting on the sofa in Cottage Grove watching "Bonanza" on TV—Ben, Adam, Hoss, and Little Joe in color. They were the first family in the neighborhood with a color television; children would line up at the screen door in wonder. And Jenene would bust out with, "I think the cowboys should marry the Indians. That way no one has to fight. I think if all the people of different colors married each other and had kids, everyone would be colorful and no one would have to be against anyone else just 'cause they look different."

From the minds of babes comes audaciousness….

Bob would be flabbergasted. "That's not right," he would attempt to "correct" her, "white people should have babies with white people and only white people because they're white. Just like black people should only have babies with black people." The Muhammad Ali birds of a feather flock together argument.

"I don't think so," Jenene argued. "White people and black people make really cute babies."

The accent he could hide mostly save for when he overheard the dialect of his youth was like the bias ingrained in him from birth, absent except when churned up. Serving an interracial couple irked him but failed to churn him up. Yet Jenene had the power to shake his every conviction from the time she was little by expressing her notion of people of all colors mixing to the point of unity.

Whether or not the March on Washington was fresh on minds and equality was winning out over intolerance, where he had come from the things she was saying could still get even a white person lynched. Bob never condoned taking life or committing violence due to skin color. In his perfect world segregation would have been embraced across the board without violence and no intermixing would have gone on, but if achieving that perfect world could only happen through what can be deemed war, he was against what some of his contemporaries called the movement.

His daughter had to be such a grand conundrum to him, full of ideas so outside his beliefs they had to be taught…but by whom? Lal, Bill, and Herb had no bent toward racism but nor did they go out of their way except through actions to express a belief one way or the other in such regards. Not Lois. With so little conversation between them, she hadn't filled the girl's head with talk of expanded race relations. So who?

Is racism taught? Can prejudice be inherent? Jenene was naturally nonjudgmental in terms of race and later sexual orientation. If she held any bias it was against those who were cruel, who inflicted pain to others and animals, or who mocked people they perceived as weak.

Even toward them she was tolerant, though, since for them she was sympathetic enough to feel for them. Hate was never a component in her makeup, nor senseless criticalness of a fellow human being based on skin pigment or ethnic background. Quite the opposite, she was born totally open to all people—as are all people until they are taught otherwise.

Bob would remain stymied. No matter what he said it went in one ear, circled only long enough to meet rejection, and zipped on out the other. When he dared to declare he would disown her if she ever married or even dated outside her race, Lois stood in opposition…and that was a dispute she won.

The argument was made as much on Jenene's behalf as on the behalf of her own unbiased nature. For a woman imbued with coldness and limned with ice, Lois was warm to people of all shapes and colors. To her people were people, to be judged on their merits or lack thereof.

Perhaps it was by default that Bob became the preferred parent since such a conflict of beliefs existed between them. Bob's duality confused Jenene; he was a southern gentleman and a redneck cad, loyal open friend to everyone and ignoble covert hater of non-whites.

Bob was certainly every bit the conundrum to Jenene that she was to him: his racism was so mislaid, so pointless, so limiting, so dehumanizing, so outside the rest of his character. Why couldn't he grow? Evolve? Develop into a better man for no longer being hampered by the weight of his extreme disapproval bordering on hatred.

However, did Bob's bigotry make him a bad person?

Even though he held views this writer feels are repulsive, he beliefs were not violent. He escaped the south because he did not believe in the violent brand of racism that was fomenting. So far as Jenene knows he never used a racial slur. He had no truck with name-calling. In matters of business he was the opposite of discriminatory. He never turned away a customer. To him a whites-only policy would be ridiculous since everyone's money was green. He would never dare express his views in even the remotest way when interacting with black people.

This was demonstrated one afternoon when a black fellow drifted in with his arm snug around a voluptuous white woman sporting a thick mane of red hair. They spent hours drinking at the bar. By all accounts, Bob was the same welcoming soul, bright and full of palaver, as with any other customers. Even if the sight of them put a spike in his gut, the experience showed him people really aren't all that different from one another.

Reconciling his feelings as opposed to hers would be a trial, but in finding acceptance for her dad's mulish grip on prejudice Jenene found a deeper acceptance for all people. If she knew her dad as basically a good man, did that not mean the capacity was in even the worst people to exude decency, kindness, even goodness? There are many strata to each of us, layering that makes us complex individuals capable of all manner of duality, hypocrisy, and paradox.

Any instilled prejudices he might have harbored did not stop him from loving Sammy Davis Jr. or getting on the O.J. Simpson bandwagon in 1978 when he was the most popular man in America (oh the irony). It is possible had Bob lived long enough, he would have outgrown the past. With me as his pushy grandson, I am certain.

So on the issue of racism they agreed to disagree agreeably.

In all other matters she invariably got her way; he supplied her the lock pick of negotiation and she time and again used it to spring his safe.

We can too often be touched by events very removed from our personal lives but no less poignant for the fact they happened to a stranger.

On the morning of September 21, 1973, a Friday, on the bus ride to school the radio announcer dropped terrible news. American singer-songwriter Jim Croce was killed in a plane crash the previous day. His songs had thunderstruck the country and several of his hits were on the radio and on the Nite Club's jukebox, among them "Time in a Bottle" and "Don't Mess Around with Jim." He was the only musician she and her dad both liked and his sudden death was a sucker punch.

Sure, musician deaths were ridiculously common; small planes should be recognized as anathema to the whole profession based on number of untimely deaths. But this was a performer that actually bridged generations in a way like few others. He had a little boy, a young pretty wife, and hit records.

The specter of death was very present her thirteenth year. By the end of her anguish-loaded twelve months, Jenene was ready to turn her attention to as many distractions as she could find.

Even then she suspected her physical ailments were the result of her mental state. With regularity she continued to drink to make life more interesting. School was easy enough. The time she missed during her convalescence was no fuss to make up. Even with all the distractions she could find, she was still bored out of her mind.

What she needed was something to devote herself to, something to care about in the wake of one of the most shaking events of her life. She had no idea such a thing was going to fall into her lap, sort of anyway. But first she would have to convince her dad she was ready for way more responsibility.

Chapter 9
Head Cook

The Nite Club's cook went into the service and Bob found he was in a pickle when no desirable applicants emerged.

Unable to find a dependable replacement he was forced to kibosh the kitchen until further notice. The bar just about made enough profit it wasn't absolutely necessary to serve food, so he figured it better not to toy with the customers who would be loyal if they could get consistent reliable service.

"I could cook," Jenene suggested.

She had befriended the Nite Club's young cook, Mike, and they argued so much people prophesized they would get married. He dared to call Bob "Dad." Always fighting for whatever little attention she could get, she did not take kindly to him being so familiar.

Mike offered to show her around the kitchen. She declined not because he was such an annoyance but because she had her doubts she could match his pace. He kept up when they were busiest and nary got a complaint.

With the kitchen closed, Jenene began to plot. Her only income came from babysitting and that wasn't keeping her in her vices. Her vision included reshaping the menu to fit her ability and reopening the kitchen. If all went to plan it would get her out of the dining room at the same time.

Convincing him to let her begin cooking part-time was no easy task. "It'll just be simple," she reiterated continually. "Cheeseburgers, chili, fries. For the bar customers: you know they're always asking for more than chips and pretzels. Nothing that would be too much for me to handle."

"Don't put the cart in front of the horse," her dad replied. "It's a lot of responsibility. You have school. I just don't think it would be so hot an idea."

Because she was expected to work, wanted desperately not to continue waitressing should the kitchen reopen (off the front line in the war with touchy-grabby customers, she had no intention of going back), and was endlessly bored even if Jeff made things interesting, Jenene was relentless. It was just that the more she considered cooking, the more she wanted to run the kitchen. If it was only open for part of the week, she felt it would be a challenge she could succeed at if only she were given the chance.

Jenene knew she could wear her dad down with persistence. It worked. That the customers still wanted to be fed helped. Consummate businessman, Bob wanted to meet demand. He did his best to pull double duty and run a limited kitchen but he was always being pulled in two directions. Jenene seized the opportunity to be his assistant. He taught her the basics. Before long she was doing most of the cooking.

Using the leverage of the customers' desire for a greater menu, Jenene was able to pique his interest in hiring her as the Nite Club's official cook.

"Keep up your grades," he advised, "but remember, too, never turn your back on the food. Burned is burned."

Jenene got her way and it felt good being trusted with the responsibility.

Of course what she had bit off soon proved to be a huge mouthful but she was intent on chewing it up.

Not only was she tasked with cooking but keeping the kitchen clean. Bob was a stickler about cleanliness; they were running a respectable, even classy place, not some greasy spoon. She had to agree. As bad as her first impression of the Nite Club, with her dad acting as its heart and soul the place had taken on beaming life not evident during that initial visit.

So she proudly kept the kitchen meticulously clean. Got up close and personal with bleach and cleansers as well as scour pads and sponges. The vent hood regularly needed attention. Every surface. Deep-frying oil leaves trace on everything in the kitchen and if not wiped off habitually with degreaser develops into a thick yellow goop only removable with a scraper, and with great effort. A bit of that had met her when she started out and she vanquished it never to allow a vainglorious return.

Without a mother who cooked and a father whose culinary skill didn't exceed chili, burgers, and southern fried chicken, beyond the nuts and bolts Jenene had to learn food preparation on her own. She went by the recipes inherited with the place. Her menu grew as she learned and her skills developed, from beer-battered fish and specially spiced grilled steak to homemade au gratin potatoes and bleu cheese dressing.

Encouraged by the positive results, she began to consider a career in cooking.

Soon after taking over the kitchen, others heard Bob address Jenene by the nickname Cookie. The moniker stuck.

It was probably assumed the designation was due to her being the cook. In truth it came about when she was a little girl. Bob would take her around with him to friend's houses and car dealerships. Since she was a tiny thirty-five pounds, everywhere they went she asked for a cookie. One friend, a swinging bachelor, always had the best cookies. She was sure to ask him.

Her penchant so amused him he christened the pet name.

The Nite Club turned out to be so much more than a business. It had a soul and life's blood.

Jenene established a solid routine. Expediently. It was always her way. Shifts could be long but she maintained. The steady cascade of compliments inspired her to do an even better job.

What she liked most was being treated like an adult. She showed maturity and it was rewarded. Bob forgave her splashes of defiance. He believed in her because he thought she had a good head on her shoulders. He trusted her because if confronted she was honest.

After closing in the early days she and her parents often went to the Indianhead truck stop for a late night dinner. Right off I-94, the 24-hour diner was only a few miles away. A bunch of the Nite Club's bar patrons would join in for a sobering meal before dragging their pickled carcasses home.

It never struck her as strange until later that they ate at home rarely, or that on so many of these nights they ate with their extended family of regulars. The assemblage lent vibrancy otherwise absent. Stories were told, jokes cracked, and a real sense of camaraderie matriculated. These after parties were some of the best memories of those years.

Meanwhile Jeff was oblivious in his bed. That was until he happened to wake one ill-fated night. For a six-year-old it can be scary finding no one else in a dark house. For Jeff it was terrifying when he discovered even the Nite Club was dark.

They came home to a house as empty as Jeff found. The mystery was solved quickly. Infuriated at the betrayal, he made his way to the neighbor's at the top of a tall hill. They had to convince him to come home. He was hurt and angry and thereon Jenene or Lois had to remain home for his sake.

There's a photograph of Jenene standing in a bar holding a drink. Who was the photographer? To this day no one knows. Taken when Jenene was fourteen, an anonymous informant sent the photo to her dad.

She had tested limits and had gotten away with it for some time.

Everyone thought they should have their nose in her business so any of a number of folks could have been the culprit. The world was full of voluntary stool pigeons.

Jenene was frequenting the bars across 12 for a while before the unknown tattler struck. None of them carded her. By then no longer the tiny waif of a child she had been, she had blossomed—she experienced her first period in fifth grade—and had enough bosom and curves to not invite suspicion she was underage.

The drinking age was only eighteen at the time and driving while intoxicated had yet to become too much of a crime, so her ability to get away with underage drinking in public for so long can probably be blamed on a generally more permissive prevailing attitude. It was also a time when parents could send their child to the store with a note to pick up a pack of cigarettes and no one batted an eye.

Had any of the bartenders bothered to ask her, she would have confessed immediately and taken her chances. It was possible pouring on a little charm and flirt would be enough for the bartender to ignore her bad-girl lawbreaking. Men were easy that way. A hint of promise made all the difference.

Lying was not within her skill set; she put herself above deceptiveness as a matter of integrity and irreproachability. She would rather stand her ground stubbornly when caught in an act of wrongdoing than attempt a lie. Maybe that was part of the uprightness her dad had instilled; he always would tell her, "If you don't lie you never have to worry about your story." It went hand in hand with, "I swear you'd cut off your nose to spite your face," when her stubborn resolve put them at odds.

When Bob lifted up the photo for her to examine, he said, "You want to tell me about this?"

"Not really," she replied.

Whoever had taken the photo covertly and sent it anonymously to Bob must have known he would not be swayed by hearsay.

Bob took her to each bar and made introductions. "This is my fourteen-year-old daughter, Jenene. She's fourteen. Fourteen everybody. Fourteen…."

Her barhopping days were over for the time being. Cripes. At least the true extent of her drinking hadn't been revealed.

Maybe for her sake it would have been better had she been exposed.

Chapter 10
Perceptions

The fall following Lucille's death, Jenene had another uncanny dream.

This one was not so much a premonition for the unfortunate she saw dead as an early warning for her of the world's dangers. Even the young for all their feelings of indestructibility are not indemnified from devastation. The specter of death breathes down all our necks from the instant of birth.

Sleep could be such a marvelous respite from the waking world. To Jenene it was never the realm of living death as viewed by Edger Allan Poe until she began having the dreams in which she walked side by side with Death.

This night Jenene was seemingly on foot. She appeared mid-stride on a lonely black road. It looked like so many of the backcountry roads after dark, a bumpy strip of asphalt juxtaposed against darkest night. Familiarity offered no comfort in what might be the middle of nowhere.

A starless sky bore down on her with inky blackness so deep there was a sense of infinity.

Her focus went immediately to the horrendous sight before her as she was propelled toward a terrible accident. A dismantled car was deeply ensconced in a ravine, a warped, contorted mess of metal and broken glass. What her eyes captured next made her want to turn around and run in the opposite direction.

I don't want to see this!
But she had no choice other than to look.
I don't like horror movies!
It was out of her control.
I don't want to be in one!

The mangled human body was a sight she wanted to close her eyes against—only the set of eyes she could close were already lidded and in violent throes of REM sleep.

What skin on the body was visible implied the victim was a young woman. Unable to tell at first glance who she was because there was too much blood, Jenene knew instinctually it was a school chum who lay twisted on the ground. Her name was Michelle.

Thunderstruck again, it was that same sense of eerie knowing that preceded her grandma's death. Inexplicable knowledge, one of those strange extra senses that unwittingly aid us and go by the titles intuition or instinct or gut feeling, would one day be as common to her as eating or sleeping but was then still more frightening to her than anything else she had ever faced. Even scarier than the things she dared not recall….

Once close enough details came into focus. Even through the streaky mask of blood she could see she was right. Michelle was the one who lay broken on the asphalt.

The realization snapped her wide-awake. Breathing labored, heart jumping hurtles, she fought to snatch back her breath and rediscover her composure.

Why would she dream Michelle was dead? Was she going to die too? If so, when would it happen?

In her grandma's case, the hit and run accident occurred ten days after the dream.

Was there time to warn Michelle?

If so, could she be convinced?

Michelle was someone she saw only in the educational environment, yet she was someone Jenene was fond of and always happy to see. She was a pretty girl with olive skin and fine features who didn't know how nice-looking she was and because of it had that sweet insecurity of many a young woman prettier than she believes. She was also as bright as a sunny day. She was just one of those really nice people who cheers up your day.

Were they close enough that Michelle would believe her and take precautions?

Or would it be like before?

Jenene's worry kept her up the rest of the night.

Next morning she was on edge yet enervated.

Maybe she could have lived up to her promise and spoken to her dad. But he didn't know Michelle. Not that he was insensitive. It was just that he might wonder why she was dreaming about a girl so insignificant in her life he had never before heard her name.

There was only one person to whom she wanted to unburden and it was at school where she hoped to find her.

After the slowest bus ride of her life, she searched frantically for Michelle, asking around like an investigator canvassing after a murder, seeking clues concerning the girl she saw dead in her dream, information that would reveal Michelle was alive and well. Coming up disappointingly with a giant goose egg made her head hurt. Word was the same all around. No one had seen Michelle.

Was it a bad sign?

It seemed so. Michelle was not known to miss.

So upset it bordered on distraught, Jenene had to release some of her worry lest she lose her mind. Mr. Cribbage would maybe think she was crazy but she felt it would be better to speak to him. A peer might spread around what she said and make gossip of her. He was her favorite teacher because she had concluded he was the only adult in the school she could trust. He happened to teach her least favorite subject, algebra.

Benevolent and fair, Mr. Cribbage was a spirited fellow with a positive attitude toward teaching and his students. He was permissive of Jenene's quirks and they got along splendidly. He was a far cry from the line up of teachers that had so distressed her; it was evident teaching was more than a job to him, more than an ego trip.

Mr. Cribbage listened patiently. If he passed judgment he didn't let it show on his face. When she had finished explaining the dream of the night before and the one of the year previous and her forceful worry, he said, "That seems like an incredible coincidence but I can't discount the possibility. But listen, Michelle's probably fine."

"You think so?"

He smiled reassuringly. "I would wager on it."

"When she shows up, will you help me convince her…to be careful for awhile?"

"Sure thing—it's probably good advice for all your classmates," he mused. "Although it is strange that not only is Michelle absent, her brother is too."

Whether or not he was humoring her made no difference. Jenene was at least in some small way conciliated. There was still the challenge of persuading Michelle to believe if she was too careless it was possible her death was imminent. Who would want to believe such a premonition?

Jenene went to lunch and forced food down her throat, still feeling all kinds of wrong even if she had Mr. Cribbage on her side. She felt detached; too distracted to inhabit the same plain of existence as those bustling all around where she sat like an almost unseen ghost that faintly glowed just enough so no one ran into her or plopped down in her lap. Getting the gruesome image of Michelle's damaged body out of mind was proving complicated.

So dang real....

In her next class an odd event occurred. The message over the loudspeaker advising Jenene to go to Mr. Cribbage's classroom was so anomalous it seemed like the sort of signal the call from the operator had been.

Hesitation in no way slowed her gait.

Sure enough when she arrived Mr. Cribbage advised her to take a seat. Her spirits sank into the doldrums because the heavy feeling of awareness was again resting on her mind.

"Michelle's brother just came in to tell us," he said. "Michelle was killed in a car accident early this morning. From what he said, it sounds like it happened very similarly to how you described it from your dream." He looked at her differently. His eyes were wet with emotion yet also quizzical.

Jenene was processing. Here again. Unbelievable. The realization made her heart beat jarringly in her chest. She would never embrace the dreams. Not then, not ever. They were too difficult to face. Nor would she become desensitized to them.

"I thought there might be time," she said warily. "I thought I would have a chance to convince her."

Mr. Cribbage was open to her experience and his willingness to discuss it eased some of her discomfort. "Maybe these dreams aren't warnings about events that can be changed," he speculated.

"What are they then?"

"I don't know. Extrasensory powers, so far as I know, don't necessarily follow rules. Maybe there's some other significance. Maybe a message for you."

"Thank you. Believing me helps. The dream really freaked me out. Then figuring out Michelle wasn't here really had me scared. I still can't believe she's gone."

"This kind of thing makes you think about how fragile life really is."

"I wish I could have stopped it from happening."

"You've really blown my mind today," he said with genuine awe. "Even if it wasn't a warning for you to pass along, I can't help but believe you knew. You really knew." Then added,

"You have to promise me if you ever have a dream about me, you'll get in touch."

"You'd want to know?"

"If it's possible I can avoid dying, you better believe it. I like to think sometimes, such as in my case, it would be a warning with plenty of time to set me on the straight and narrow."

An odd bit of synchronicity, in 1997 Jenene would contact Mr. Cribbage because he was coincidentally listed as a reference on a potential employee's application. Unsure if he would even remember her, she said, "I was a student of yours; when I was in your class my name was Jenene Davis—"

"Did you have a dream about me?" he cut her off. A score of years ago and his memory was crystal clear.

"No, no dream. You're a reference. I need to ask you about…."

"Oh thank goodness," he gushed. "You had me thinking I better make sure the life insurance is paid up!"

In Michelle's case the timeframe indicated her death and Jenene's dream coincided. It was puzzling. Was she supposed to be a soothsayer dispensing warnings or was she only a seer, cursed to bear witness while being rendered inert, impotent?

When she studied astral projection years later she realized it was probable that was how she saw the aftermath of the accident—she had projected herself there. Even if in that instance the dream was less a premonition than an event witnessed, it was no less uncanny, no less eerie.

But why—and what—was she supposed to observe?

Seeing such things felt like more of a curse than a gift. There would be more dreams. In some cases she would be able to affect the outcome. In others she would suffer the frustration of coming up short when a life hung in the balance.

In light of future events, the dream or spiritual journey to see a dead girl even before law enforcement was aware of the accident, was likely meant to be a warning aimed directly at Jenene.

Chapter 11
Duality

By 1975 Jenene "Cookie" Davis was the triumphant head cook with a personal staff…and a practicing alcoholic.

Getting caught going to the bars had done little to deter what was evolving into chronic alcoholism.

Despite her drinking, she ran a tight ship and built up a respectable business with a large and varied menu. She never let the drinking get in the way of her work even if she let it get in the way of her schooling. The fact that she maintained a B average when she would drink during the school day is either a scathing indictment of the Wisconsin school system or a testament to her ability to pull off whatever she needed to in the pursuit of what she wanted; if her grade slipped, she would have lost her kitchen.

And whatever she was doing in there she was doing right. She could rely on her regulars, who she saw week-in, week-out, some for years. Folks would wait up to an hour for a table. The job was so important to Jenene later she would without a second thought skip her senior prom to work; a rather odd distinction when you consider how important an event the prom is to most teenage girls.

The accolades poured in. Her food was praised along with her promptness; she could manage twenty tickets and get piping hot food out speedily without compromising quality.

Word of Jenene's success and youthfulness drew the interest of local newspaper reporter Betty Brandt, who wrote an article about the fifteen-year-old cooking wunderkind. The distinction made her something of an exhibit piece beyond her usual cachet. Never the purpose for cooking, she in no way intended to earn any local celebrity and though she enjoyed the prestige, she wasn't quick to get a big head just because her picture was in the paper.

It wasn't about impressing anyone other than herself...and her dad, too.

Jenene's entrepreneurial spirit was a birthright passed to her by both parents but refined by her dad.

Business ownership meant the world to Bob; it showed in his devotion. He ran the Nite Club as if on a mission and it was paying off with a huge clientele of happy regulars. Even though so much was sacrificed to prosper his dream, Jenene respected his honest effort to ensure success. Through rolling up his sleeves continually, working up endless sweats, and being nothing short of tireless when it came to prospering solid connections to folks, what is today known as networking and then was known as being personable, Bob kept the Nite Club hopping.

"It's not what you know, it's who you know," was an adage Bob expressed almost as often as he said, "Keep your friends close and your enemies closer." He could haggle, finagle, cajole, dicker, and convince about anyone it was their idea to give him his way. Most often people so took to him it didn't even take all that much effort.

Bob's meetings with Margaret "Ma" Klund were as much about networking as mutual respect and understanding. Ma owned Ma's Roost, a beer joint in eyesight of the Nite Club. The porcine woman, garbed in a loose-fitting dress, would with the discomfort of hard work waddle her way in regularly, take a stool at the bar, and chitchat with Bob over several cups of coffee.

Vice versa, he would as often mosey on down to her establishment for the gabfest. Bob admired her for being a flourishing business owner in a man's world while juggling the hardships of being a widow and single mom. She admired his savvy.

If you looked out the west-facing window in the kitchen you could see Ma's diminutive honkytonk. The lady's abode was the Quonset beside her business, an even smaller structure most would mistake for a tool shed. Being as she was such a large woman it was the shell to her clam.

Rather than view each other as competition, Bob and Ma worked together to draw more patronage to their area. They knew there would be runoff. Both would be benefited no matter who presented the promotion they concocted. Ma only had a license to serve beer, so the Nite Club stood in a more favorable position anyway.

Ma had to sidestep the law to offer food but no one begrudged her serving up an occasional special. All-the-better if the special was a local favorite Jenene had no interest in serving, such as Lutefisk. Ma supplied the area's connoisseurs of the Norwegian delicacy. Jenene was happy not to step on her toes or stink up the Nite Club's kitchen.

The days Ma's kitchen was open they had to batten down the hatches in the Nite Club. As many fans as there were of the carefully prepared lye-soaked cod, the olfactory barometer of as many deemed it an eye-watering stench. One of those acquired tastes, if prepared correctly the consistency is gelatinous yet flaky.

In this author's estimate it tastes almost like shellfish if drenched in melted butter.

Jenene never saw the appeal.

Bob would grin and say, "To think she sells out every time."

Watching Bob work the bar, cultivating business and customer relationships tirelessly, taught Jenene a variety of communication skills. A rare trait, he inspired loyalty in nearly everyone he met. Even when rowdy patrons had to be hustled out for fighting or getting fresh, he often received a shame-faced apology soon after.

There was no denying that besides Jenene's cooking, Bob's spirit and force of will made the Nite Club a popular destination. He was the archetype of a raconteur, engaging, charming, droll, fascinating, and infinitely likeable. He was a combination storyteller, comic, jester, boss, and sympathetic ear. Folks passing through would stop in and become so mesmerized by his showmanship they would from that point forward trek from a distance of an hour or more away as often as monthly just to enjoy his antics.

Hand's on all the way, there was no pawning work off on others if he could do the job himself.

During the summer of 1974 Highway 12 was repaved. Bob finagled it so the gravel in their parking lot got a cozy blanket of black tar too, in hopes a tendency toward unruly parking would be stemmed. Much like a plant needs to be pruned to grow properly, they learned paving meant little without direction since patrons still managed to park kookily.

Of course Bob personally dealt with the problem. With a narrow roller he painted lines and made designated spaces. "Don't bother me while I'm out there, Cookie," he advised before heading out. "It'll be hard enough getting the lines straight without being distracted." A large man, meaning it was a strain, it took hours but he accomplished his goal and ended the parking confusion.

Bob wore many hats during those years and handyman was one that won him accolades from the regulars for his handicraft prowess. He would self-effacingly respond, "Yep, I'm a jack of all trades but a master of none."

Of the two, as previously stated he by and large wore the parenting hat because he was the one who was there. Even if the freeway were being closed in her wake, Lois went to work in the worst blizzards, never one to capitulate to Mother Nature…or family obligation. That was when Bob's parenting was most needed. When he and the kids were waiting for Lois to get home from work so they could go to dinner only to have her stroll in an hour or more late, without a call, she would explain that she had needed to stay late and deny any knowledge of solid plans.

Maybe he was disapproving of her nonchalance and was resultantly cynical because Bob would say, "Know your place, children—Hartford comes first, then family," to which Lois would retort, "Oh, Bob," as if it weren't a sad truth but a joke.

The Nite Club was Bob's adopted baby but when it came to his flesh and blood it would always come second. After matriculating in a family so cracked he ran away to war and the disgrace of divorce ruptured his first attempt at constructing a family, he was determined to make this family work like a fine-tuned mechanism. The four of them would never quite run with the efficiency and elegance of a Swiss clock; even if they were only the equivalent of a cheapo wristwatch that told the right time, he was happy.

Lois something of an enemy combatant, it was only natural Jenene took her dad's side and often deferred to him. Since he was an ally of sorts as parents go, she knew she could trust him and would only come to trust her mother years later. She recognized his savvy and wanted to emulate his better attributes while learning from his worst. Being at odds with her mom kept her by his side.

She even joined him at Tavern League meetings and would for a time serve as Secretary/Treasurer; since she was a minor, technically it was Bob's position but she did the work, taking the minutes at meetings and writing the monthly newsletter. She set herself up a little office in the Nite Club and took the duty seriously.

Being treated like an adult always appealed to her. Adulthood just wouldn't come fast enough.

When she wasn't working, reading, or doing homework, since there were few other thrills, Jenene perfected her pool game. When the Nite Club was closed, she would practice, sometimes for hours, learning angles, improving her game.

In turn, she became a bit of a shark, hustling the guys who would hang around to flirt with her. Putting on the charm she picked up from her dad through osmosis, even as they were losing their pants without the pleasure of actually losing their pants, they were amused enough to keep playing as they continued to wheedle and flirt ineffectively.

Playing men didn't interest her, nor did their attention; the thrill was in pitting her skill against theirs because they always figured they were better than a girl. It was also good practice dealing with people. They would flirt and she would parry. Not too many boys interested her but for the few who did she wanted to be prepared.

It was so easy to get their attention and it was kind of mystifying to her, their attraction.

Five-foot-two and 115 lbs., Jenene was petite but felt fat. She looked upon her curviness as a detriment. Tight clothes were the fashion of the day; the real diehards needed pliers to pull up their zippers. Stuffing her body into the absolute smallest jeans she could fit into did nothing for her body image.

Some thought she was good-looking but what did they know? In her teens she had yet to realize the subjectivity of attractiveness. That even if she had a problem with her reflection others might find her beautiful. There was a nearby influence that was beginning to show her there was something to presentation and attitude.

The town's strumpet—there was always a big rig sans a trailer parked near her house—really wasn't beautiful but many seemed to think so. Ms. Round Heels became a curiosity. She would show Jenene how to get the sexy sort of nails that tapered like the movie stars'. She wore her makeup garishly and smoked unfiltered cigarettes so there were always bits of tobacco stuck to her glossy teeth and rouged mouth. Not one to emulate, Jenene nevertheless found her fascinating. Men flocked to her for one reason and one reason only.

The strumpet's best features were her pampered hands. Jenene's own fingers ended with blockish nubs instead of thinning femininely the way she would have liked. The strumpet taught her to reshape her fingers with pressure and the results are evident today: her narrow fingers taper and support nails that are a manicurist's dream and nightmare.

Bob would ultimately put an end to her chumming around with the strumpet when the woman's son seemed too interested.

Since her dad refused to allow her a romantic life, any she had required absolute secrecy. More on that later....

Chapter 12
Coming of Age

With a promise the perks would outweigh the snags, Jenene's parents sequestered the last part of the summer of 1975 for a family trip.

The meticulously planned three-week expedition was a humdinger, a round-the-country road trip in a topper-equipped pickup pulling a tent camper that culminated with a stop at Disney Land for Jeff and heat stroke crossing Death Valley for Jenene. This after a run in with an "undertow" in the ocean she narrowly survived. Only Jenene would almost die twice on vacation. Such bad luck dogged her too often.

To me the trip represents the epitome of the bygone road excursion; back when a gallon of gas cost 43¢ and enough of the locals were also vacationing they could close their restaurant without hurting business. Jenene welcomed the break from work. Welcomed time away. What wasn't so welcome was catering to a bratty brother, which was a task that fell invariably to her.

They kicked off the trip by crossing Minnesota and North Dakota, glorious scenery giving way to flat monotony. Once the surroundings turned boring Jenene read. Since they would be visiting the ocean she thought Peter Benchley's *Jaws* was a good selection.

They stopped for the night in Billings, Montana. Jeff smashed his finger in the truck door. This ensured preferential treatment for the remainder of the trip. The cab of the truck only fit three comfortably. You can probably guess who drew the short straw and had to ride alone in the rear.

A foray into Yellowstone National Park followed. With her love of nature absolute, the celebrated national treasure was an awe-inspiring place to behold.

For some inexplicable reason her folks let seven-year-old Jeff go into random restrooms alone. One pit stop he failed to return in timely fashion. Jenene was sent to retrieve the impulsive child. At the men's room she saw him come walking out hand in hand with some stranger. Gregarious as ever, he said, "This is my new friend." Jenene snatched his other hand and pulled him to their parents. She declared, "He can't go to the bathroom by himself anymore!"

Nevada turned out to be every bit the gambling mecca of repute. Jenene was surprised to see in Reno there were even attended slot machines in the restrooms. That was their final stop before San Francisco. Just as well they breezed through since it was all a tease when you're underage.

Even if she almost died there California was marvelous. That was the only week their itinerary allowed for rest. Her parents vacationed with a vengeance. From Jenene's perspective lounging on a beach was preferable to being on the road. Bob and Lois seemed to chart success by miles logged.

Of course it would be on a sunbathing expedition that Jenene had a brush with death. Huntington Beach would have been a purely good memory had that exclamation point not been put on her time there.

Sharks were on her mind when it happened. They were on everyone's mind that summer. Not only was *Jaws* a bestseller but the watershed film adaptation released at the end of June had become the first summer blockbuster.

(It should be noted, due to the wholesale slaughter of sharks that followed, Benchley spent the rest of his life denouncing his own book, feeling he had done a disservice since statistically about a million sharks are killed by humans for every one person killed by a shark and the great white he wrote about was depicted inaccurately due to a lack of scientific research.)

The story took place on the opposite coast but that factoid didn't change facts. The ocean on the west coast was no less threatening or full of possibility. A mouthful of sharp teeth chomping into her leg was the worry pervading her mind when the rip current took hold.

There's a certain responsibility as a beachgoer. You stay in the sightline of the lifeguard stations. Jenene had no idea how far she had strayed. Trying to body surf the way her California cousin taught her was a distraction. Also keeping an eye out for shark fins. One thing was certain. She was far enough from shore that getting seized abruptly by the foot was all the more terrifying because she had no idea if she was in view of help. Before she could even scream, she was jerked below the surface.

For a few shaky instants she was overloaded with mortal fear. There was no thought about what had her. Only that she was terrified this was it, the capper to her life was at hand. If her life flashed before her eyes she was too frantic to pay attention. Drowning was one attempted intake of breath away.

As suddenly as she was yanked below a sure hand extracted her from the clutching hands of death.

On shore Jenene saw that a brawny lifeguard was her rescuer. Like Sam Elliot in the movie "Lifeguard." The hunky actor caught her attention for the first time in that flick and determined the type of man for which she would permanently be most attracted. In retrospect, even greater significance would be put on visiting Huntington Beach when she learned the picture was filmed there, the very place a lifeguard saved her life.

Modest like a true hero, the lifeguard brushed off the accolades. Rescues were too commonplace to him to get worked up. Her appreciation could have filled stadiums. He may have spent his workdays getting tan and saving unfortunate swimmers but nearly drowning was with any luck a one-time experience for Jenene. She wanted to show her savior the proper gratitude. Even if he was more intent on moving forward with his day than listening to a teenager profess her thanks.

Since she survived, it was probably better to almost get pulled into the depths than chomped into by a shark, but at the time the experience was no less frightening. An idea that would've seem preposterous to her at the time, prevailing wisdom today maintains that when caught in a rip current the best plan is to remain calm and keep your head above water while the current circulates you out and then back in.

In the future, she would refer to the frozen chocolate-covered bananas she tried for the first time at Disney Land as the best part of her visit to California.

On the long road to Vegas through Death Valley Jenene was delegated to sitting in the rear of the pickup. Injured and unable to hack the furnace, Jeff was all smiles to escape the 106° heat.

Jenene might as well have been in an old style prison hotbox while traveling across the murderous sun-scorched desert plain. She baked like a brisket, cooking thoroughly; by the time they reached Vegas, she was well done. She crawled weakly out of the furnace and fainted on the spot.

Having given her folks a real scare, they rented a room with air conditioning at a motel with a pool, and she was given time to recuperate.

What was it all for? Hoover Dam meant not a lick in her cranky state after suffering heat exhaustion even when her condition was a gem used to get the whole family privileged accommodations. That they were headed to the Fort Hood Army base in Texas, where her former kitchen nemesis Mike was stationed, scarcely meant more. Why? He was a friend, sure, but as much as they argued—he seemed to delight in irritating her—it was hardly worth risking her life to see a major landmark, or a boy she preferred to ignore. If her parents had machinations concerning pairing them up, they would be disappointed.

Texas was muggy. It was impossible to get dry after a shower. After suffering heat prostration, she was none too comfortable and anxious to strike out for home. At least after fainting she got more time in the cab. She was up front when she witnessed perhaps the most profound indications of her dad's feelings toward his siblings.

By then they were on their way back to Wisconsin. Skirting Tulsa, Oklahoma, Lois pointed out to Bob it was the city in which his half-sister lived and wondered out loud if he wouldn't want to contact her. Bob rolled down the window and hollered his half-sister's name. "I called her but she didn't answer—guess she isn't home," he said and on they went.

One final stopover in Illinois and they made it home just hours before the new school year began.

All too anxious to be finished with what was a fun but trying trip because much of it she shouldered playing second fiddle to Jeff, a most revealing bit of news reached her upon their arrival home. If distance makes the heart grow fonder, fondness must not have meant much to her secret boyfriend.

Tempted by all the promises of a relationship, earlier that summer Jenene began dating a local boy her dad deemed a bad influence. They all seemed to have his disapproval in common. Since what is denied always has luster, she had no problem keeping it all hush-hush and had embarked on the trip without worry her fella would stray.

First day of school scuttlebutt was revealing. Confirming everything Jenene had not thought to fear (trust can be blinding), her boyfriend was not only dating another girl, he was "engaged."

Hurtful to be sure, she swallowed the jagged little pill of treachery and used her work to distract her rather than waste time pining or being jealous. On a conscious level she concluded it was better to know the long and short of it before making a real commitment. Yet what we know to be true is no solace when our hearts are caught in the fray.

From then on she would curtail serious entanglements and put an emphasis on fun over substance.

In the next few years she would use men as play things and discard them when she was finished. Most of it she regrets and will never speak to, as is understandable. At that time she had no idea why she was so insatiable, so wanton, why enough was never enough, why she took risks and created regrets. Such behavior was a spin-off of something else she had no idea darkened her life. Attributing it to brushes with death was easier than digging down and finding the lode of memory imbedded in her brain.

In essence getting dumped secondhand, as boorish a method as a dump text today, was more infuriating than she let on, and the rejection touched on something much deeper. At the time she on some level decided the feelings had to be stuffed and ignored…along with many other disappointments, hurts, and regrets. Perhaps not so coincidentally, that was the year she started having gallbladder problems.

That autumn she was unwell. Wracked with pain and vomiting regularly, a trip to a famous clinic would result in disappointment and a wedge of disenchantment toward doctors that would only mature in the future.

The famous clinic's diagnosis: there was nothing wrong with her except in her mind, so she was apparently puking all the time due to an ongoing psychosomatic episode.

As her dad drove them home she felt so terrible. Quite a distance of feeling ill at ease since famous clinics never seem to be close when you need one. Miles of feeling not only guilty but betrayed, because she was sick and now her dad probably thought she was a hysteric or a hypochondriac.

Another clinic would solve the mystery and diagnose gallstones. Validation was a double-sided blade. The prognosis was real. A decision had to be made. A quarry of gallstones could hurt a lot. But would they kill her?

All she could think of was the whopper of a scar her dad sported from the removal of his gallbladder.

An unappealing prospect to a teenage girl as tortured by vanity as any, to avoid such a scar she opted not to undergo surgery to remove the gallstones. At the time she had no idea a scar from stem to sternum would turn out to be inevitable. At the time she hoped for the best, oblivious of what waited some years down the line.

After a few rough if productive teen years, Jenene was already beginning to recognize the dichotomies of life. Whereas her romantic life was unpredictable, uncontrollable, and unsatisfactory, her work life went as smoothly as perfectly performed ballet. Being the subject of a newspaper article praising her accomplishments may not have swelled her head but it did give her a sense of pride she wanted to repeat.

During all the years the Nite Club employed Jenene she was privy to all the inner workings of the business. Bob relished working with his daughter and his welcome never diminished. The closest he ever came to reprimanding her was when he felt she was being obtuse or closed-minded. He would ask, "Do I have to explain it to you in layman's terms?" This was a sign for her to stop and think and an expression, even if used sparingly, she came to despise.

In some family-run establishments blowups lead to quitting and firing even if reunion was eventual. Jenene's job was only compromised one time and it would go up there in the pantheon of funny anecdotes.

Up to some work, she was a little distracted when a movement caught in her peripheral vision drew her focus to a furry varmint skittering across her clean kitchen floor. As squeamish as any teenage girl not known for being a tomboy, her startled reaction was to scream, and to scream loud. Letting off a cry was understandable. Even a shout could be explained, chalked up to a burn or a barked shin, but a blood-curdling scream? Even that could be explained with some fast and witty repartee. What wasn't so easy to cover up was what she screamed. One ill-timed word, yes, but a word too evocative to ignore: "Mouse!"

The first of its kind she had ever seen up close, the teensy rodent shocked the absolute wrong word to use in a restaurant right out of her mouth. The worst part was her proclamation was loud enough the whole bar and dining room heard.

Bob dashed in as if there were a fire, a robber, and a swarm of killer bees all rolled into one, cheeks ruddy with furiousness, and without forethought gave her the boot—during dinner service.

In short order he would relent, repent, and reaffirm her position after she explained and apologized for her shocked outburst. It sure wasn't purposeful.

So many lessons were learned in the Nite Club's kitchen. Like the time a pesky happenstance taught her why broken glass should not be thrown into a trash bag willy-nilly. She had done just that, tied off the days' trash, and hauled the assemblage out to the dumpster. When she returned she got down to mopping only to at every turn encounter blood on her freshly swabbed floor. "Who's bleeding on my floor?"

Deductive reasoning led quickly to her culprit.

Cue suspenseful music…the blood-letter was Jenene all along!

The garbage-weighted bags had pressed into her leg and a sharp corner poked her so painlessly she had no idea she was wounded until she was sopping up blood off the linoleum. She put broken glass in empty milk cartons forevermore.

Working all the time, she saved up a bevy of moola and was able to buy whatever a young person desired. With little to spend money on, frugality came easily. In those years she knew no money worries. She never had reason to learn how to budget. When she got her driver's license she splurged and laid down crisp cash for her first car, a year-old red Camaro.

To her peers she seemed either the height of cool, an idea she never embraced, or the conceited girl, a natural mischaracterization of the notoriously aloof. To her teachers she was a dedicated enough student to sail through with a B average. To the principal's assistant—who would one day be her son's grandmother-in-law—she was a spoiled brat.

None of them knew she drank until drunk every day at lunch. Her parent's were permissive of her having an occasional drink in front of them but they wouldn't allow the sort of drinking she was doing in secret. She could get away with a shot here and there but it would be noticed if she drank from the bar excessively. She solved this problem by buying bottles from the kids whose parents owned the bar a short ways down 12 whom, unlike her, had no trouble stealing from their parents.

Maybe it was that she kept all her plates spinning so well no one suspected, at least not enough to take action.

Sweet cars with powerful engines a real source of interest, the Camaro was showy but not so much it was out of place. It was a fast car. She could take curves so smoothly. When she was behind the wheel negotiating expertly the windy back roads it was obvious she had some of her dad's racing blood coursing through her veins.

Having a fast car made it all the easier to get away.

Chapter 13
School Malarkey

Perhaps it was the perception of Jenene's popularity that got her accused of being the ringleader of a school-wide walkout and subject to reaping the whirlwind of the rebellion.

Everyone was always getting on her case. She hated the attention. Why is it what we want is always dispensed in a corrupted form? The rule of comedy is to set up a fantasy only to turn it on its ear, at which point hilarity ensues. In real life there are no chuckles to be had when noticed for all the wrong reasons. Not when there were plenty of unseen good qualities to highlight. After a while she embraced her status in the places it came into play, such as school.

But that didn't mean she led a rebellious insurgency against The Man.

The superintendent was having an affair with the Home Economics teacher. When the art teacher all the students loved took exception to the fact that the man supposed to be in charge was not only stepping out on his wife but he was doing it with a woman who taught in the very school his sons currently attended, she was dismissed for daring to rock the apple cart.

To display their disapproval, the student body rose up and showed their displeasure by strutting out with heads held high because they believed their protest just and principled.

Jenene was in PE. Had she known the walkout was actually going to happen—it had seemed unlikely—she would have skipped gym altogether. As it was, she only knew it was going down when she saw her classmates spill outside. She left the field to join them, garbed in her athletic wear. Shortly thereafter, she decided to slip inside to change and was denied access forthrightly. Bob was called and when he arrived was informed Jenene had been singled out as the instigator.

Had the powers that be listened to logic it would have been easy to conclude that not only was she not the leader of the pack, her only foreknowledge of the walkout was that it was possible, information known to every student.

Once word of the affair circled, the Home EC teacher was disgraced and swapped for a young upstart right out of college. The art teacher wasn't vindicated. Nothing happened to the superintendent. It was still a man's world.

Not very long after the upheaval usual routine resumed….

There was a bathroom where students went to smoke because it was known to be entirely unsupervised. Looking to make a name for herself the upstart decided to fish around in there and hooked Jenene—the former Home EC teacher likely would have joined her for a smoke. She tossed her butt out the window but it was too late, she was busted and on her way once again to the principal's office.

Tobacco use in some ways was to combat her environment—in those days bars were more often than not smoke-hazed. Smoking went hand in hand with drinking.

In that era it wasn't so much an act of rebelliousness—it was the early 1970's, after all—as an act of fitting in. The cigarette machine was right in the Nite Club—50¢ a pack. Unmonitored. Her parents smoked (until her dad quit), her peers smoked, her teachers, the bar patrons. Seemingly the whole world at large was lighting up, so why not her?

The notion it was unhealthy had yet to gain traction even though in the medical world the writing on the wall was becoming all too readable. Two years before, President Nixon signed the Public Health Smoking Act into law after 1965's Cigarette Labeling and Advertising Act achieved putting a warning on cigarette packs but failed to lead to smoking cessation. Perhaps the second act was made law with an air of tongue-in-cheek since it was signed on April 1 and also failed to discourage smokers.

Had Jenene cared to pay attention to the warnings she would not have cared. She was in the thick of a self-destructive streak that would last until she had good reason to change.

Strangely, unlike the majority of smokers, Jenene could take or leave the habit without the cravings that face many trying to quit.

At sixteen she was brave enough to tell her dad. Even having quit by then after his habit peaked at three packs a day Bob knew it unwise to challenge his headstrong daughter. She was running the kitchen very successfully and with adult responsibilities came adult privileges.

Visits to the principal's office were routine since Jenene did little to conceal any rule breaking she might be up to—other than boozing—because she had discovered she would be sent home without any other reprisal. It wasn't as if she was denied doing her work, a usual downside of suspension, so it in no way affected her grade. Maybe she was treated with kid gloves because she was the girl that missed five weeks not so long before because she almost died. Maybe the perks had more to do with her position in local society. She would soon find out.

The principal was out. "Wait for him in his office," she was ordered.

Nothing new to Jenene, she went on in and bided her time. Out of his character, the principal had always dealt with Jenene impersonally, enabling her machinations to go to fruition many times since he would come in, reiterate what she had done was wrong, and call her dad.

Bing, bang, boom, she was on her way home, homework in hand. It was a nifty system for Jenene because she had better things to do than spend all day at school when she could do the work in short order.

What made the principal's standoffish approach out of character was that he was a little man who made up for his miniscule physique by being the worst kind of bully, one who hid behind his authority.

Besides accusing her of masterminding the walkout—as if—he had completely lost her respect by beating up a friend of Jenene's for little reason other than to display his authority and dominance.

It was true her friend had pulled the fire alarm. But was it appropriate to brutalize him as punishment, proper to humiliate him for staging an impromptu drill, an act another administrator might have chalked up to "boys will be boys" and dealt thusly a more suitable penalty? Jenene felt it was too extreme, even outrageous.

It was a scene that might have been funny had it not been so sad, a man nearly a foot shorter than the beefy boy he was hitting going to town while the boy stood there and took it because he had been taught not to stand up to his elders. She had been fairly certain had he been so inclined one swipe from her friend could have laid the principal out flat.

There was a large round ashtray full of snubbed butts on the principal's desk. There were no bans on tobacco on school grounds, hardly any laws making underage smoking illegal.

Jenene in an instant of absolute defiance decided to light a cigarette. Waited. Smoked. Casual.

Of course the principal entered before she had finished and was furious instantly. "Put out that cigarette! How dare you smoke in here?"

"Put it out in the ashtray full of your butts? The ashtray implied it was okay."

She didn't mean to be saucier than marinara made in an Italian bistro; it came naturally, insolence born of boredom and frustration, and it was impossible to put a damper on her acerbic wit because she just didn't give a damn.

"For adults! You're a student!"

"I don't see what difference it makes."

By then he was looming over his desktop, fists planted on the surface, veins pulsating over his temples. "I don't think you know how much trouble you're in!"

"Bring it on."

Her presentation of an absolute lack of fear incited him. Without terror he was powerless, his authority a fart in the wind. Maybe he had always suspected any bluster on his part would be met with a blasé attitude from her and had avoided the confrontation ignited by catching her smoking in his office.

He was known to get physical with students other than her friend, to beat them up quite badly even. There was no law preventing him from getting as violent as he felt necessary. Even with her. No court of law would waste one minute trying a man for beating a woman, even an underage girl. Not in that day. None of that was looked upon as abuse; it was nurturing.

Although Jenene's exterior conveyed a total lack of fear, under the surface she was a maelstrom of nervous energy. She was willing to use whatever prominence came with being the daughter of a successful business owner to make a point…even if it got her walloped.

Unlike the country boys who earned whippings regularly from their father's belts and their mother's wooden spoons, Jenene had rarely been spanked, three times in total. Once her mom made her dad give her a swat because she thought she fell asleep in church—in truth she was astral projecting long before she had any idea there was a name for the out-of-body traveling she had been doing all her life. Bob apologized profusely throughout the entire interlude.

Once Lal smacked her can for dissecting her alarm clock.

And her mom went a little ballistic when she spilled water on an expensive complete collection of the work of William Shakespeare Lois would one day pass along to this writer without ceremony, as if they weren't so important they once got a little girl's rump reddened.

Jenene knew little of violence; a day would come when she would receive a full tutorial but on this day she was a greenhorn.

"I'll call your dad," he threatened gravely.

Good. They were back on script. She spoke the number. Her eyes dared him to take it further.

Her apparent fearlessness dismayed him. Her angle was one with which he had no familiarity. "I will then." He made the call. "We'll see what he says."

Yeah, we will. Jenene had told her dad about what the principal was up to, the corporeal punishment dealt out with his fists.

Bob disapproved.

After he finished making the call, the principal was far from finished, his rant button having been punched.

"You are a spoiled little girl," he screeched. "You think your daddy will always come along and rescue you. You're nothing but a brat. What gives you license to be so self-important? You think you're the only one in the whole world!"

Yet another person was mistaking her aloofness for self-important smugness.

Bob arrived shortly after that and was met by an angry little man perched behind his desk like a chicken hawk. "Your daughter was caught smoking," he squawked churlishly.

Bob shot Jenene a hard look but only shrugged at the principal. When Jenene confessed to him she had taken up the habit he had renounced, Bob was disappointed, angry…and understanding. "I would rather you do it in front of me than behind my back," he said as he presented her with an ashtray for her bedroom.

The principal was livid. "Aren't you angry? Aren't you going to say something?"

Bob's eyes narrowed darkly. "What my daughter does isn't your business."

"I don't think I'm out of line—"

Now Bob loomed menacingly over the desk, big as can be. All six towering feet and three hundred plus intimidating pounds of him made a battering ram of sorts. He laid down the law in a way that would invite real trouble nowadays. In a cool, even voice registering anger scarcely contained, he said, "Leave my daughter alone. If you don't leave her alone, I will stomp your ass into the ground."

The reversal of fortune was poetic justice of a kind. No law prevented the principal from dishing out abuse to his students and no law protected him from an angry father intent on defending his daughter.

Jenene was shocked. In that instance she would have admitted readily she was in the wrong, since she was in no way denying she had broken the rules. She only wanted to make a point about the principal meting out draconian punishments when he had no business making such harsh judgments.

Bob was a big softy in most ways. Not a violent man prone to tossing out threats. Another father might have put his fist through a wall when his daughter admitted to smoking but Bob only shook his head, expressed his disappointment, and moved on. The most surprising part of Bob's actions that day in the principal's office was that she believed he was deadly serious: if the principal caused her harm he would carry out his threat. It was sort of scary if also in some way gallant, even chivalrous, a manly gesture in a time when such overblownness was still acceptable to express.

Bob said, "Come on," and took her out to lunch; neither spoke of what had happened.

That school year ended on a down note. On the last day Jenene made the mistake of exiting the bus on the way to school. She hopped in a friend's car. She was in class on time. There was still a problem.

As if it were an infraction of nation-breaking significance, the principal, at great risk to his own wellbeing one can surmise, dropped the hammer on Jenene. Facts were made clear. She would not be allowed to begin her senior year if she failed to comply with whatever punishment was levied.

The sentence decided upon was in school suspension—to be served the first three days of summer vacation.

Jenene's natural likeability, prospered when a person actually interacted with her and could see through and beyond the detached bubble she hid inside, helped create an alliance of sorts between her and the principal.

For three days she worked in the office with him and his assistant. They came to understand why her teachers allowed her so much latitude, to the extent it almost seemed like she had something of a free pass. It was just that people who better understood her knew Jenene had her own method. If she were allowed to work unimpeded she wouldn't disappoint.

Never once did she intend to make an enemy.

Chapter 14
Prelude to Escape

In the span of a lifetime six years can turn out to be a less significant piece of time than it seemed while living it.

Jenene would never feel that way about the years between the ages of twelve and eighteen. Unending work, unhappy distances, and unresolved feelings were intertwined with unlimited exploration, uncensored maturing, and unabashed expression. Great times working with her dad, the joke-cracking storyteller, made it all tolerable.

A funnier memory they shared was a Tavern League meeting when highway patrolmen paid them a visit. They came to demonstrate breathalyzers, the first of their kind. The carefree beer-in-the-crotch days were over. The high number of drunk-driving fatalities led to enough public-outcry for legislators to take action—more importantly for police to enforce the laws.

The earliest drunk driving laws were put on the books in 1910. Much like initial anti-smoking laws they did little to curb the offense. In the early days it was at the discretion of the officer involved. More often than not someone who smelled of booze would be encouraged to go home. Only if they were surly would they be arrested and plunked in the drunk-tank.

Jenene and Bob and most if not all the other vendors embraced the new laws. They better than anyone knew what was going on. Even as sellers of alcohol they disapproved of soused drivers taking to the roads. With laws it was easier to turn them down, to deny them that last one for the road.

So the breathalyzers were like a new toy. It was all a hoot. Have a drink, blow, and watch your level of intoxication go up.

Jenene could drink because in the badger state it is legal to serve a minor with in-person parental consent.

0.01…0.04…0.07…right on past today's generally accepted limit of 0.08…and finally up in the neighborhood of 0.15, the limit at the time (considering legislation has gone forward to make 0.05 the limit, they got as lit up as Christmas trees). Oh, it was a total lark…until none of them could leave at meeting's adjournment because they were too drunk…and the patrolmen had watched them get that way.

Good times….

Jenene had no trouble cultivating the relationships she had reason to believe were worth devoting energy to but was never able to fake it, such as with Lois.

If one person made those half dozen years truly difficult it was her mother. Bob would try to play peacekeeper but when it came to picking sides he most often stepped back. In secret he would agree with Jenene and implore her to try harder to get along with her mother.

"Me? She's the one who seems out for vengeance. I can't even call her 'mom'; her ears just won't hear it."

"I don't know what to tell you…."

"I feel like I'm nothing more than a servant to her."

When the time came to begin thinking about moving out, what prompted Jenene to decide the sooner the better was as much to escape the woman who seemed to relish being the bane of her existence as to get away from domestic anguish the woman put on her shoulders.

From the time they landed in Wilson Jenene was the woman of the house insomuch as she was the one charged with cleaning and doing the majority of the household chores.

Lois had a fulltime career that necessitated an hour-long commute each way. That she deigned to help out with weekend waitressing duties but declined to do much else was understandable…to a degree. Jenene had school and worked in the kitchen never less than thirty hours a week. So it wasn't as if there was a lot of room on her plate either.

Once a week Lois would drive Jenene to the laundromat in Menomonie while she went to the hair salon. It was up to Jenene to wash, dry, and fold the household clothes—luckily a company laundered the Nite Club's linens. Doing laundry wasn't the problem; she never minded that duty. The problem was that it was a college town and she was tasked with folding her dad's flag-sized underwear in front of upwardly mobile young people living lives she imagined were so much better than hers. It was embarrassing.

Lois' obvious antipathy bordering on animosity was most likely attributable to the fact that, well, Jenene was willful and impulsive and she could be more stubborn than an oak's root. Putting her to work was probably to teach her a lesson about authority and who was in charge. Had Lois any idea at the time from where her daughter's disinterested attitude derived, she might have found within herself a capacity for sympathy and understanding. It would be years before they had that showdown.

In the intervening time they cultured a mutual disdain that would carry into her adult life. The problem was that so much happened that was unforgettable in a bad way it was difficult not to dislike Lois. Jenene loved her mother even if she had never heard Lois express love for her. She loved her even though she lived under the misimpression her mom wanted to abandon her…wanted to throw her away.

But she didn't like her. They couldn't even have a conversation.

At some point she wanted her mother's approval. When she found it was impossible to acquire she became insolent. If she couldn't achieve praise why not go for indignation? Whichever garnered attention.

There was a period after Lois became so fed up with what she perceived as Jenene's intransigence and disrespect she refused to buy personal products for her underage daughter. Jenene tossed her hair unconcernedly over her shoulder and paid for her own shampoo, soap, and feminine products. In the end Bob interceded on Jenene's behalf. He made sure the items a daughter should be provided by her parents were not held back out of spite.

On February 9, 1978 Jenene turned eighteen. Plans were underway. The date was set. The day after graduation she was embarking on her new life. May 21. Only a few months and she would be free.

As Jenene's son, the writer who has so far taken a backseat to the story I am telling, I am struck with wonder at who my mom was then. So different from the woman I've known. Defiant. Stubborn. Rebellious. I suppose she still has those traits only channels them far more constructively. I once said to her it was as if she was a rebel without a cause only for her to respond, "Maybe I acted out in hopes they would ship me off to the farm permanently."

If that was where her heart wanted her to be I asked why she didn't just move straight back to Minnesota to be near The Seniors. Being that she was put off by the Wisconsin boys, was worried about missing what life Lal, Bill, and Herb had left, and would have been happy to put a continent between her and Lois, it seemed like a no-brainer.

"I didn't want to abandon my dad," she replied. "I could tell just moving as far as I did broke his heart. He wanted me to be happy; he always did. But I could see he wished I would stay nearby. Wished I would stay so he could look out for me. If not for him I don't know if I would ever have gone back. It didn't seem like my mom could stand me. And Jeff, he would accuse me of being the one into the chocolate frosting when it was smeared on his lips."

(Even today Jeff maintains Jenene returned home and in a scheme to set him up committed various infractions, not limited to leaving a mess of food crumbs in front of the TV set, stealing desserts, and getting into their mom's smokes.)

I ruminated on her words a moment. "You told me Lal put a stop to the worst of it but your dad still managed to make you uncomfortable. Like around your friends. You said he'd say things to them like 'You're a lot prettier than Jenene told me,' right?"

"That was one of his favorites," she said. "I would definitely be embarrassed. My friends thought it was funny."

"How was it that his teasing could bother you so much yet you could feel such an affinity for him?"

"I worked on, what do they call it, compartmentalizing?"

I nodded.

"I shut out what bothered me and focused on the good. Besides, by then I had forgiven him. Because I understood: he was a born salesman, and he was always selling himself, looking to cheer people up, give them a laugh. He thought he was being funny, and to many people he was hilarious. I understood that when I grew up. Now I think he teased me because he didn't know how to interact with me. Too bad for us both it went so wrong."

Did she mean him and her…or her and me? Either way, it was no less true.

Chapter 15
Backward Beginnings

Escape was the only option.

Right on cue after graduation, much as her mother fled Illinois, Jenene absconded from Wilson and fled to River Falls, a first step toward getting nearer to The Seniors. Although she promised her dad she would make the thirty-minute commute to the Nite Club, her intention was to eventually live as near to the farm as possible. She didn't want to hurt Bob but she had to live her own life.

Part of living her own life on her own terms was living her life on the edge. Can't take up too much room living on the edge; for some reason she always felt like she occupied too great a space in the world. She took a furnished trailer and got busy making self-destruction a lifestyle.

Why not? She felt haunted by a past rife with illness, regrets, and a darkness she could not yet admit to herself existed, let alone reveal it to the world, because although it enveloped her, the reason why was locked away deep in her psyche. It had so much to do with why she so readily accepted blame, so willingly rejected any sense of self, why she would never cheat anyone else yet so carelessly shortchanged herself in every personal exchange.

    The farm factored in often because it was a place to get grounded in a life evermore lived with her head in the clouds. Her life was increasingly becoming like a movie she was watching instead of living. Nights melted together. She could do it practically on autopilot her work was so habitual. Work, party, and catch a little sleep was the routine. It was burning her out.

    Visits to the farm were respites from living an unanchored life, a jetty to attach her vessel when waters got rough and skies stormy. The flat-roofed old white-trimmed maroon farmhouse and the weatherworn gray barns were sights that arrested her heart and imbued hope even when she felt the worst.

    Jenene discovered young that beauty in motion was a galloping horse. And an unmatched freedom could be found clinging to the muscular backs of such magnificent beasts. Throughout her life much of going there was riding and it continued to be a form of stress relief. Bill and Herb earned income as horse boarders and would buy and sell occasionally. It could be said her great uncles were respected not only for their horse sense but their sense of horses.

    During one visit, a neighbor's horse escaped his pen. He bolted across the field for the farm. He was a magnificent chestnut brown standard bred bay yet too small to ride, little more than a foal.

    Bill explained that out of loneliness the runaway often broke loose from his pen. He came to visit the boarded horses and engage in a conversation of whinnies. Seizing his halter to direct him toward one of the barns, she said, "So you're lonely, huh? Well I'll give you some company."

    A slight upturned crease overtaking the corners of his mouth, Bill watched her lead the young horse. He worried after her, ached in his heart when she hurt, and her joy contented him.

    In the young and gentle runaway Jenene found a kindred spirit. Thereon if he escaped when Jenene was visiting she would brush him and feed him apples before Bill led him home. Her Grandpa Chester until he died promised her a pony every time she saw him. The empty boast was never believed but it stoked a desire she still fed.

Mild and even-tempered, this horse was blessed with a munificent personality. He was unfazed by setoffs such as loud noises that upset most horses. He was too cool. He would have been ideal if she were to have a horse. Only he belonged to the neighbors. And she was in no position to take on the responsibility even if for a price they were willing to relinquish the gorgeous gelding.

Spending time with him was relaxing even if the bonding was unnecessary. Combing his fine smooth mane and the long strands of his tail. Brushing out his soft brown hair. It wasn't as if she would ever ride him after he was grown and had trained. Even if he was still showing up when he was full-grown. It would be inappropriate to ride someone else's horse.

Riding was such a fulfilling release and would be even better with a horse she liked so much. When she was caught up in the throes of riding, she could forget if only temporarily the sense that she was besieged by the ghosts of the past she knew…and the one she knew only as an effect with a hidden cause, a nightmare she forgot upon waking, and a filament of a memory that disappeared as soon as gazed upon like a squiggle in her peripheral vision.

What is a haunted young woman to do? Obviously it was time to search out a prospective boogeyman to rule over her life.

Jenene's expanded social life included mucho barhopping, mingling, and hazardous liaisons. She was the sort of gal who could easily have run afoul of a serial killer; the combination of good looks and low self-esteem led her into several dangerous situations. Activities predatory men detect as blaring call signs.

One dangerous liaison involved a new suitor, a nighttime drive on backcountry roads, and the young man's black Gran Torino.

Before the young couple could go to dinner, her potential boyfriend had to run a friend home from Hudson to Houlton. Everyone had been drinking. They were lit up and in carefree moods and that Gran Torino could burn up the road.

Their ruin was a two-by-four on a curve.

The car went end-over-end.

In those couple of endless instants she was sure she was going to die.

The cliché of life flashing before her eyes actually happened and for her it was the faces of all the people she cared about, Lal, Bill, and Herb safe on the farm, the regulars at the Nite Club whose honest praise meant so much to her, Mary who had remained her best friend, her few close friends, her circle of extended friendships, even that little squirt Jeff, who persisted in claiming his every misdeed was committed by Jenene in a simple yet Machiavellian conspiracy to get him in trouble.

Her dad….

His face was the hardest to look upon, maybe because it was the hardest to face. Her first step in what would ultimately be a greater departure had been tough for him to bear. What would it be like when she strayed even farther? It was only a matter of time before she made her escape complete. What effect would it have on him? She didn't leave because of him or the teasing that so bothered her as a child….

She hated to hurt him, hated to disappoint…

Yet wanted to disillusion him so he just wouldn't have to care about her.

The damaged too often face confusion, confliction…and the results of their poor choices.

The Gran Torino landed upside down and came to a screeching halt, sending up a poof of ditch detritus with a final crunch of glass and a ratcheting clang.

After going 'round and 'round, the whole world was so shaky she doubted it could be shakier.

Pain was immediate. Flares. Twinges. Spikes.

The stink of gas was cloying. They had just filled up. Of course, right. Could the car explode? Who even cares?

Jenene's start point was the front passenger seat. The police found her folded up and crammed in the back window. The three of them were in the backseat, which had been sheared off from the front by the crushed roof when it sealed them in like sardines in a can.

Miraculously no one was killed nor were their injuries, though numerous, life threatening.

"You're lucky you weren't decapitated," a cop spat not unkindly. "Let's get her out of there."

"I'm having trouble breathing," Jenene croaked as they manipulated her disjointed body out of the wreckage.

Innumerable flecks of glass impaled her scalp but that her chest felt crushed was more concerning. She could tell instinctually the damage wasn't bad enough to kill her. The pain of dying would be worse. That didn't change that bruised, possibly cracked ribs were so painful her vitals felt pressed in a clamp and every lungful of air came with an agonizing stitch.

"Emergency units are a ways out and, and…" his voice trailed off as if pursued by a thought; was captured by the thought, re-tinkered, and unveiled as a declaration: "So I better take you to the hospital right away."

The young officer spoke somberly. As if his alarm was authentic and meant, at least to him, she should be as much so or more concerned about the situation. Yet he failed to convince her she should trust him behind the wheel so soon after surviving the laundry treatment. Trusting anyone else behind the wheel would be a proposition long in coming.

"I can wait…."

"I don't think so. Not if you're having trouble breathing."

To her dismay and against her wishes the officers loaded her into the back of a patrol car. She was hurting too much to fight them even with so much as words. Getting into another car so soon after getting flipped 'round and 'round like a load of whites in the dryer was frightening. She was shaken, stunned, and coming out of a daze brought on less by the physical shake up as the unmistakable brush with mortality.

It was one thing to almost bleed out from the anal fissure or get drowned in the ocean or die of heat stroke in the desert. None of those ways to die were courted. To get into such a calamitous accident was a real wake up call. In hindsight it seemed so avoidable. Her priorities had been bent and maybe she needed to straighten them out.

Likely the cop had few excuses to really gun it and used the opportunity. He put the pedal to the metal and scorched the road with rubber.

"I'm not dying," she wheezed painfully. She felt ensnared, caged. "Don't go so fast. If you get in an accident I'm going to shoot you with your gun."

The cop snickered.

The perspective would make her reconsider the recklessness that had consumed her life since she struck out on her own. But there are other ways to be self-destructive than overt wildness. Sometimes pursuing what seems like the safer life can lead to unforeseen jeopardy.

There were dangers so outside Jenene's realm of understanding. When confronted by them she would for a time be stunned into submission.

In the ER the attending physician placed his hand gingerly on the back of her head to help lower her to a supine position for X-ray and only discovered the minefield of glass shards imbedded in her scalp when he saw the damage done to his own hand.

"Hm." He was bleeding. "Nurse, please pick this glass out of my palm."

Soon a nurse was also using a tweezers to excavate her head; several tinks in a stainless steel kidney dish later and the overwhelmed woman threw in the towel. The shards caught the harsh fluorescent light and glowed redly. Even now, like a farm field can never be picked completely clean of rocks, glass continues to surface from her scalp. What begins as a bump sooner or later splits and disgorges another splinter.

Her injuries may have been many and painful but did not require her to be admitted. Jenene was sent home in a fair amount of misery with her glass-laden scalp, bruised ribs, and injured leg. The leg was the worst. Indicative of a break, it had turned black around her knee. X-rays failed to show a fracture. Jenene was dubious.

When she tried to walk she found it was nearly impossible. The way pain flared hotly in her left leg was worse than expected. It was as close to intolerable as it could be without being totally debilitating.

Being sent home without a cast, even though it really seemed like she should have one, made her angrier than worried. They never wanted to listen.

But why should they listen to her outer voice when she refused to listen to her inner voice?

The devil-may-care harum-scarum life she was living had gotten her hurt. What was her life? A deep depression she had dug one shovelful at a time until the hole was over her head and the sides were caving in. Yet it would be some time before she would view this as anything other than bad luck, certainly not a situation she brought on herself.

    A decent guy, the cop waited for her. He insisted on driving her home. Let him play the hero. She appreciated the ride. Even if being dropped off just before dawn by a patrol car probably cemented the more negative aspects of her reputation.

Bonked on the head hard enough to concuss her, she was advised not to sleep. Jenene sat up the rest of the night with her dog, a larger German Shepard mix named Brandy. She sat on the roof of Brandy's doghouse and the dog kept her company. They watched the sunrise together.

Next day Jenene limped exhaustedly into work decked out in a neck brace. Her leg was in searing agony. But it was Friday, the week's busiest night. Calling in didn't feel like an option because it would leave her staff, and more importantly her dad, in the lurch.

    She gestured hello to Bob, who waited behind the bar, and made her way back to the kitchen.

    Bob trailed her, "What the fuck were you thinking not calling me?" That was the one and only time she ever heard him use that curse.

    Not steady on her feet, she wheeled around slowly. "How did you find out?"

    "I have a police scanner," he reminded her. "I didn't enjoy hearing your name and not finding out if you were alive or dead until you just dragged yourself in here."

    Of course he had the scanner. Of course he was listening when her unique name went out over the airwaves. Busted. There was no way to convey her regret so she didn't try.

    "You're lucky to be alive," he continued. "I just can't believe you'd be so disrespectful. I thought you were raised better."

    "It wasn't out of disrespect," she said hollowly. "I was trying to spare you...."

    "Spare me? You come limping in looking like you went through a meat grinder and think it won't have any bearing on me? Go home. You aren't fit to work. You need to heal."

    Wound licking was in order. Her dad was right. She hurt.

Chapter 16
Broken Bone

When the irreducible pain in her left leg failed to subside, Jenene sought a second opinion. Exploration revealed she had indeed broken her grotesquely bruised leg. It was a welcome diagnosis. Without other recourse, the shockingly vibrant pain might have pushed her to explore amputation as an option.

The emergency room crew could be excused from blame for not finding the break sooner: the fracture occurred right beneath her kneecap and did not show on the typical angle of an X-ray. Surgery was necessary to re-break and set the mending fracture, which had somehow not been so structurally compromising as to prevent walking while it still managed sustained pain on a level she would later learn firsthand approached the agony of childbirth.

The process of healing would be arduous and would ignite her questioning of the medical establishment, at least certain players in it, particularly the high-handed surgeon who repaired her broken leg. Orthopedic surgeon Dr. Mack Ernie, a pseudonym because the man still practices today, was likely a narcissist with a god complex. Even fresh out of residency and wet behind the ears his arrogance knew no bounds, even when faced with proof of his own mistake in the form of spilled blood.

Dr. Ernie routinely changed her cast and put her off with his less-than-magnanimous presence. On one occasion he used an experimental process that involved a foam material. When she returned to have it removed, he went to work with an electric saw. Buzz. He made a clean slice down the gauze and plaster.

Pain flared, unmistakably, and she exclaimed testily, "You cut me!"

"No I didn't," he denied sepulchrally, flashing her a look that without chloroform would render dead frogs due for dissection.

Too feisty to back down when she felt irreproachable: "Yes you did."

"You're just being a cry baby," he uncorked his exasperation. "Now be quiet and let me finish."

Buzz.

"You cut me again!"

Shaking his stadium-sized head at her, he sighed. Buzz. Off came the casts and sure enough, there were visibly bleeding slices on Jenene's calf.

"I told you." In retrospect, his self-righteous attitude maybe justified a malpractice suit—for that and other mistakes—but she wasn't remotely litigious-minded at the time and only yearned for when she no longer had to see him.

Demeanor even more chilled, he dressed the wounds, not quite worthy of stitches but close, and offered no acknowledgement that he had been wrong and she was in fact being cut. Apology implies guilt, so even had he not been so high on himself, threat of lawsuit would have prevented any concession on his part since he had to know he was the cause of her injuries.

Why had the misguided surgeon mistakenly sawed too deep? Lack of cotton: when he made the cast the experimental foam so excited him he neglected to place the cotton buffering that would have prevented the bloody mishap.

The whole escapade gave Jenene itchy feet.

Chapter 17
Gestures

Perhaps because she embraced some transient responsibility to Jenene, perhaps because her daughter had been in a life-threatening accident, or perhaps because it was good for appearances, but certainly not out of any sense of sympathy or obligation (or so Jenene believed), Lois seized the opportunity of her wayfarer daughter moving to Hudson to grace her with an unexpected gesture of goodwill.

Lois escorted Jenene to as many garage sales as it took to supply decent furniture for her new pad. With a handful of cash, she paid not only for a sofa, end tables, a kitchen set, and one of those huge console TVs that at one time predominated living rooms across the nation, but also for all of it to be delivered directly to the large house she had rented from a member of the Tavern League with the intention of letting out rooms.

Still encumbered by a cast, delivery was tremendously convenient. Although slightly leery, Jenene was appreciative. Thus she demonstrated her gratefulness effusively.

"Oh, that's fine," Lois replied dismissively, as if such generosity was a matter of course and no thank you was required.

In the coming years rather than express love through the typical warmness shared by families, Lois would gift generously and, if she approved of the purpose, was fast to open her wallet and offer a loan. Perhaps that was a bigger part of their disconnect than anything: Jenene was an emotional person mostly in touch with her feelings even if she didn't necessarily understand them nor know their source. While Lois was chillingly remote when it came to expressing any but the most rudimentary emotions.

One thing Lois felt maybe more strongly than anything else was an aversion for being poor. She worked hard, clawed her way up, not to attain dream riches but only the relative comfort of knowing her bills were paid, her stomach full, and in retirement she would be able to rest and not scrabble for crumbs to survive the way her mother had.

The insufficiencies of her youth permanently influenced Lois. The lacking equated to a driving force to succeed. She never again wanted to live with deprivation; destitution was her nightmare, poorness her bane. She compensated for a lack of childhood footwear with a hundred pairs as soon as she could afford to fill her closet. This writer has found this trait a commonality among people who went shoeless.

Lois may have spoiled herself in some regards. But her earnings allowed her to be altruistic, too. Even if she sought to never need charity, she had no trouble offering what she could for those less fortunate. For her giving what she could was natural. The "good appearances" of giving meant nothing to her.

So it was possible by Lois's reasoning furnishing Jenene's rental was a throwaway gesture. Or it might have been an indicator that Lois considered her daughter—no matter how little she understood her—a worthy cause.

Chapter 18
Boogeyman

Not too long after and still sidelined by the nuisance of a cast, Jenene met the man who would become her first husband.

The mangy rascal who she would marry after a relatively short courtship was a hard-working, hard-drinking, hard-living industrial machinist named Guy. Brutally handsome, he had a dark mop of thick unruly hair, a swarthy mustache, and eyes deeper and bluer than the sea. He was the sort of man who wore a beard and flannels in winter and sleeveless tee shirts and cut-off jeans in summer, would never entertain the notion of piercing his ear, and voted for third party candidates.

He was trim but tough. A man of appetite, outfitted with force and might and persistence. He was from Afton, Minnesota, and lived with his mother in a huge yellow farmhouse plunk in the center of a hilly spread separated from farm fields by woodlands loaded with burdock and ticks. What appealed to her was his intensity, the way he could look right through her…or right into her.

They began dating. He proved to be a touch gentlemanly. Always quick to pick up the check, he had enough edge to keep her interested. He had a problem with any man who even dared appraise her with a glance. At first his jealousy was endearing.

The first time he brought her to his mother's jigsaw puzzle house no one was at home and he invited her in without a hint there was anything wrong with extending the invitation. When he dared show her his room, as if she were a moral crusader tipped off by the possibility of debauchery, Guy's mother had snuck in and was at the bottom of the stairs to bellow, "Get that whore out of my house!"

Jenene's immediate impression was that to possess a roar so booming the woman had to be the size of a silverback gorilla.

Guy's mother stood five feet tall and weighed all of ninety pounds.

With no unacceptable activity underway, no petting or smooching, Jenene was boggled. They were only talking. She had an inkling the relationship was getting serious and figured taking it slow would make for a more meaningful bond if that's what they were incubating. She had a feeling he was more inexperienced than his bravado implied. Guy could be the sort of conversationalist she sought, challenging yet reasonably agreeable, content to listen, unafraid to give an opinion; other times he was more taciturn, almost laconic, but that could have been a reflection of his comfort with her.

At that moment, in a prescient outburst of rage Guy expressed the fierier side of his nature by shouting down the stairs bombastically, "Don't you dare come up here! If you try I'll knock you down!"

He would sneak Jenene out of the house later. Apparently he saw the situation getting more serious too. He wanted his mother's first impression of her to be a good one. A gathering during which the word "whore" was not raised would be preferable.

Guy was like a cornered animal when confronted with an inopportune meeting. Since she neither thought he would literally get physical with his mother nor that it was his usual nature to get so menacing, Jenene chose to see his overheated outburst as proof of his caring for her rather than as a conspicuous red flag.

When introduced under better circumstances Jenene and Guy's mom became fast friends. They incubated a rapport easily. From her future mother-in-law she would learn much about keeping a house, from budgeting to cooking home-style meals.

After seven years in a restaurateur's family, she had no idea how to shop and cook for two people. Her family took most of their meals out. At the time the only items you might have found in her bachelorette fridge were beer and maybe a bottle of mustard. In that way her future mother in-law was a good role model. She better prepared Jenene for a typical family situation.

It seemed as though their bonding was preferable to the antagonistic relationship some in-laws share.

Jenene came to realize it would probably have been better had she distanced herself from his mother. She would come to know just how great was the bitterness Guy harbored for the woman who raised him…and how much his resentfulness would waylay their life together.

The baby of the family, Guy was the substantially addled son of a woman who was maybe more than slightly embittered by a life of difficulty. A single mother after driving out the alcoholic father of her children, the woman devoted herself to tasks. Her life was all work and she expected the same from her children. Even her hobbies were labor intensive: cooking, house painting, and gardening.

Other husbands would come and go. She worked not only the father of her children to the bone but every man who thought he got his claws in her. She was insatiable in the worst way: no number of completed chores turned down her fervency for wanting more done.

With his three older siblings off in college and no other man around at the time, Guy became the man of the house. He was not yet ten. "With Dad gone, Ma had to work," he told me.

"She was gone a lot." He once sabotaged the furnace to lure her home; it was the only way to thieve some attention.

Later he would find out she exaggerated her workday to remain away.

Life outside the house was no easier. Hand-me-down clothes, thrifty shoes, and lack of money marked him as someone to mock, belittle, and terrorize. Friendships were rare, loneliness the norm.

His fine churchgoing peers let him know his status in the grand scheme of the universe and it was a tier below bums. They at least had the decency to panhandle openly and not hide behind the "government assistance" catchphrase. "My family pays for you," they would tell him.

In a confused and ostracized boy resentment and anger were born. Prospered with each taunt and lick and disappointment, mental illness festered. Solitariness fortified the place in his heart where the anger and resentment simmered into fury and alienation.

With little positive male influence after his dad exited, Guy had no guideline by which to measure what it is to be a man. Emotional problems led to an uncomfortable confrontation. He pulled a .22 rifle on a friend who had slept with a girl for whom Guy expressed feelings.

Throughout his teen years he would be in trouble continually and shuffled from home to home, sometimes living with one brother or the other. He was forced into a scared straight boot camp program. Included were two weeks of survival alone in the woods meant to either build character or instill enough fear to straighten up and fly right.

He was a bold bad boy on the outside and a cowering child within. The extent to which he went to elicit the sort of sympathy that would get him invited home after a short banishment was a case in point.

To be fair he was a young man then.

Wet behind the ears.

And he was tired of living in the inhospitable space above a garage.

He used the rifle to wound his foot because he assumed he could take the pain. They probably heard his scream a county over. He claimed the egregious injury was the result of an accidental discharge. He said he dropped the weapon in the gun case and boom! In truth he lined it up very specifically. There were Corvettes stored in the garage below. When the accident story was believed, it was marveled over how lucky it was he was positioned in such a way not one of the restored cars was damaged.

Had he known the extremeness of the pain beforehand Guy would have made other considerations. Though the agony is far in the past, the cosmetic damage is a forever reminder. He was left with a few noticeably shortened toes. A vainer person might have sworn off flip-flops.

Guy often expressed his frustration through self-flagellation. On one occasion he used a razor to slash up his body, covering his midsection and shoulders with long scars.

When Jenene saw the scars, she asked where he had obtained such injury. "The husband of a woman I was seeing jumped me with a razor," he lied brazenly. "He got the upper hand on me and cut me up before running off. It was nothing." Others were told he ran into barbwire fence while dirt biking.

Deception came easy to him, manipulation and mind games, too; he had the chameleonic ability to be a great pretender by hiding his darker qualities while embellishing his better ones. A Jekyll-Hyde duality existed within him to an extent hoodwinked Jenene had never witnessed.

She knew none of that early on. All she knew was what Guy showed her.

He represented himself well. Soon the pair was inseparable, Jenene the jewel to Guy's display stand. Marriage proposals began in earnest. For a time she resisted, not so sure the leap was one she could make without stumbling. The wooing period would be moderately short but it would take a huge event before she was willing to risk the plunge.

Chapter 19
Seeking a Life

Jenene still agonized over feeling like she was abandoning her dad.

Being in a committed relationship offered no solace. Introducing her parents to Guy helped nothing. His unrefined demeanor failed to win over any hearts. Their disapproval was apparent even if their disdain was left unstated.

The accident had forced a wedge; Jenene had been off while recuperating and the kitchen was trudging on without her—better than anyone expected.

The break was welcome, really.

Ambitions to go to culinary school evaporated when she began to figure out she had no real passion for cooking. It had filled a void and provided a purpose. Once she had her freedom, it served only as a way to make a living. She would cook in several more restaurants over the years but the jobs would never be more than a paycheck. It would be some time before she discovered her bailiwick and in many ways she was leading an aimless life to spite her parents, spite the world, and most of all, spite herself.

Wiles on display, Guy privately presented an open and generous personality without being a showboat or overly boastful. He would wryly tell her outlandishness with such cool conviction she would believe his absurdities. He would ante up a crooked smile and look through her with the agile intensity and come hither blueness of his eyes. Guy liked to take the lead. She thought of his assertiveness as a good trait because she was never one for a pushover.

Guy insisted they only see horror movies. His preoccupation with violent imagery was maybe another tip off. They caught triple bills at the drive in, the next movie gorier than the last. Sidling up to a date during a good or even so-so scary movie can be a fun way to stimulate endorphins; but the ladies also appreciate a nice rom-com or historical drama. Many of the flicks they saw were mediocre. At least Jenene got a kick out of the movies based on Stephen King novels, go figure.

Yet she humored her future husband and went to whatever he wanted to see. She was not aware her subservient nature would work against her in the long run. It set a lot of precedents.

The more Guy infiltrated her life the more she found she cared about him and wanted him to stick around.

It came down to the simple fact that elements of Guy intrigued her. He was dark but clever. His eyes were piercing and bright and seemed to see right into her in that overridingly engaging way. He wasn't very social, but it added to his air of mystery. There were times he was short on charm, but he made up for it with caring gestures. Yet he could be very charming too. It made him a contradiction. Which was all the more alluring.

There was also a matter of his devotion. By all indications, his affection was strong enough that he not only wanted a commitment, he wanted to be her constant companion. It seemed like he would do anything for her. He was maybe the first man she wasn't leery of being a cheater because his eyes truly seemed blind to all other women.

The decision to get so close was out of her usual character.

If a man dared to say he loved her he could expect her blip to disappear from his radar screen. Commitment was always scary because she had a perception it was a trap. If men pushed her too much that would also get them the boot. The one she was dating when she graduated made the mistake of insisting she go on a roller coaster at Valley Fair; she warned him she would be done with him and the fool must have thought she was joking only to find out the joke was on him.

In Guy's case she let him get away with floating the idea of marriage. Not ready for that leap, his persistence pushed her to make other serious considerations, including coming to the serious decision to shack up, a move at least in the direction of marriage. With only a handshake agreement with her landlord and transitory roommates who had moved along, Jenene was ready for yet another change and Guy had convinced her she should make it with him.

Unbeknownst to Jenene and Guy, soon after shacking up they became the focus of a police investigation. Hudson law enforcement believed the couple were recruiting underage prostitutes through drug addiction and running them to the Twin Cities.

The raid at the dinner hour was unexpected, terrifying, and baffling; any lawbreaking she may have been up to certainly wasn't of a level to justify bursting in her door and storming in with high-powered rifles. All the furniture so graciously provided by Lois was meticulously shredded during the search and left absolutely destroyed.

As they failed to turn up evidence, the searchers plowed deeper, wrecking whatever lay in their path like barbarians sacking a village. In the end they found very little evidence of any wrongdoing and nothing to validate their accusations. Oh, they were undoubtedly angry when they left, fuming, burning mad even, exemplified by the spaghetti they scornfully left to scorch on the stove.

Jenene and Guy were hauled to jail and questioned separately. The ploy to divide them and root out inconsistencies in their stories failed simply because both were equally perplexed. The absurdity of the claims would become abundantly clear to those making them as their investigation wore on but initially they acted as if they had everything they needed to put the pair away forever and a day.

The timing was just marvelous. It was the Friday evening before Mother's Day weekend. There was no way to get into court before the following week, so even if she could make the price placed on her head there was no judge to set bail.

Jenene had no interest in calling her dad; he would view her current trouble as substantiation of all the misgivings he tried to conceal but leaked through in how he showed his concern. She only wanted to face him when her innocence was proven. She had no doubt her choice of man made him unhappy.

Even if on many occasions such claims can be denounced, she really was innocent, and the aggravation of being accused of crimes she found morally reprehensible—only a truly bad person would be involved in human trafficking—was enough to make her want to scream. Jenene was too busy destroying herself and too soft hearted to begin with to be the head of a prostitution recruitment ring. How proper could their investigation be if they thought she was such a dastardly character?

Jenene saved her phone call for Saturday and used it to contact Lois. "I won't be able to make it because I'm in jail," she reported.

"Jail! What happened?"

"It's not important right now. Whether you believe it or not, we're innocent."

The whole sordid bit of business, no matter how based on falseness, flabbergasted her parents. They didn't know what to believe. Yet the following week Bob and Lois tellingly stood behind her in court and put up the Nite Club to make her bail. It was a safe bet; restricted to the county her only desire was to clear her name. The prosecutor was handcuffed inescapably by a total lack of evidence so all the charges would be dismissed without apology but to her immense relief.

The evidence had to be sparse: the conclusion in court occurred without her attending. She learned the results when her public defender shot her a call with the good news.

Following the dismissal, father and daughter were reclining on the porch in Wilson, watching as the breeze blew and the occasional car zoomed by on 12.

Seemed the time she had been away had added more miles to Bob's odometer than the actual distance traveled. The latticework of wrinkles bracketing his eyes was more distinct; thin fractures had become deep cracks, lines had become fissures. His skin hung looser from his skull, was more pallid, the pores sagging instead of round. Maybe the changes had as much to do with a new weight loss fad—he was developing an obsession with the battle of the bulge—as her. Or so she wanted to believe.

Out of a comfortable moment of silence he set a spark to a fuse: "Your mother and I think you should break it off with Guy and move home."

So Guy was trouble and she needed to be protected (controlled, kept at bay, caged).

Where were you when I really needed to be protected? Wait…where did that come from…protected from what?

A day supposed to be for celebration of a righted wrong was dashed in an instant with a softly spoken suggestion.

Jenene, too aware of the home life to which she would be returning, shook her head imperceptibly and gritted her teeth. Warmth bloomed in her cheeks at the promise of some sort of reckoning. Pressure seemed to mount from every direction, trying to suffocate her into assent. Sometimes breaks have to be made for you to feel like you have control of your life. Grappling with her feelings had taken her around in circles and she was ready to be done with that particular struggle.

Getting hurt was maybe a blessing in disguise. She had been laboring under the misimpression the Nite Club kitchen would hit an iceberg without her but even in her absence the ship had kept on sailing without incident. Rather than act as a blow to her ego, she was relieved because it meant…she wasn't so needed she couldn't sail away on her personal dinghy.

Move home? Really? His suggestion wasn't overtly condescending or pushy or even defensive…only resolute. Yet she felt backed up, cornered, and pressed; putting her in such a position would prove costlier than Bob ever could have surmised.

Boom!

Perhaps the decision was made somewhere back in her subconscious and it took her dad's fabulously undersold words to make her choice bubble up to her conscious mind in an effervescent burst of certainty. Out of cold defiance right there on the spot she made what would prove to be one of the most self-destructive decisions of her life.

"That's funny," she replied. "We've been talking about getting married. We just need to pick a date."

Motives can be abstruse even to the one driven by them.

Maybe it was that she was looking for an excuse to settle down after a near death experience; maybe it was that she was in a weakened state and more susceptible to poor decision making. Whatever the reason, the instant before she decided rough edges and all Guy was the man she would marry. Why not? He was the one she had delved with into the serious zone for the first time ever and it had been going well enough.

Bob's hurt was palpable. Had his aura been visible, gentle light blue would have been in that instant overtaken and enveloped by blackness. Yet he knew pressing the issue would only be seen as antagonism, would only create more distance.

Guy's repeated proposals demonstrated he was obsessive enough she assumed he genuinely cared and there was no ulterior motive; he would be elated that she was finally agreeing.

Her acquiescence would mean he would at last own her. She had no idea saying, "yes" was a submission akin to saying, "I give," or that it would prove far worse than moving home. An unforeseen—no reason was given to anticipate such horror—characteristic, she had no idea just how sharp his rough edges could be, how deep they could cut and gouge.

Even the innocent are persecuted....

In the aftermath of their arrest and exoneration, Jenene and Guy found they had been evicted from their apartment and their local bank accounts emptied.

The Hudson police kicked up so much earth it swirled into a dust devil tornado that whisked the wrongfully accused couple right out of town.

Even without the benefit of ruby slippers, they landed very close to home...her real home (it was also close to Afton and Guy's mother, which would prove disadvantageous). Only a handful of miles from the farm, they took an apartment in New Port, Minnesota.

Chapter 20
The Price of Bad Decisions

June 9, 1979.

The family came together in support of the new marriage, partially because about everyone was convinced Jenene was pregnant—a misconception based on a stupid assumption—and partially because even though she was committing to a man they found questionable, they were smart enough to know it was better to support her rather than estrange her by showing disapproval openly.

The plan was to have the service at the farm. Perhaps a dark omen: it was too rainy for an outside ceremony. Lal made arrangements at her church in St. Paul Park, the town betwixt Cottage Grove and New Port, and the whole assemblage met there. Much of their family encircling them like a band of acceptance, the togetherness helped distract from the specter of actually being married…and an uncertain future. Jenene looked exquisite in her resplendently unassuming gown; Guy was dashing in a blue suit purchased for the event.

Now let's step aside for a moment, away from the happy wedding bubble into a starker place where a future father-in-law pulls aside his future son-in-law to deliver a dire warning.

On that day of nuptials, foreseeing the worst even without all the facts (everyone other than the bride considered Guy sketchy, even *his* family), Bob made one thing crystal clear, "If you ever hurt my daughter, I won't kill you myself. That won't stop it from happening. Fair man that I am, I thought I would give you this one warning."

Guy may have expressed surprise at the suggestion, even shock, but in short order he would ignore the threat. She would explain years later that she believed her dad truly would have had no qualms about carrying through with his threat. She didn't want him to end up in prison. Which was the reason she never told.

Threats spoken as promises aside it was nonetheless a day full of promises, expressed and implied.

If only a few promises of that day had come to fruition.

In the end, they were all broken.

One month to the day after they were married, the abuse began. At first, by all appearances, they were happy newlyweds.

They honeymooned in St. Paul at the Radisson. The first night Jenene was hampered with a headache she attributed to the fizzy champagne that came with the honeymoon suite. While she slept Guy watched *Midnight Express*.

Despite deep reservations concerning Guy and the marriage, Jenene's folks put on a grand reception at the Nite Club for the newlyweds two weeks after the nuptials. They pulled out all the stops: freely flowing gratis beer (or one drink) and a feast of sumptuous chicken and ham. The event occurred a couple weeks after the wedding and in many ways was as much of a send off as a wedding reception. Jenene was disengaging from the area, embarking on a life to be lived elsewhere.

Of all the wedding gifts, the best one given came from Bill and was meant only for Jenene. "I would've brought your present but I couldn't get him to fit in the car," he downplayed.

You know that person who can always cheer you up or impart wisdom, the one person you can always go to when you need comforting and caring? Bill was that person for the entire family. As a little girl he was Jenene's favorite person, even over Lal, a legacy that was passed on first to her younger brother, and then to her son. There was an aspect of him so unassuming, so kind, he was like no one else she ever met. Ever would meet.

"What do you mean?"

"That horse you've been making friends with…he's yours now."

Bill recognized Jenene's affinity for the runaway and finagled a deal so he could gift the horse to her at her reception. Carrying on her tradition of giving pets alcohol names (booze was still as much of a companion as her new husband), she bestowed him with the moniker Cognac. Not only was he Jenene's first horse; he was a testament to Bill's caring.

In the near future such gestures would mean all that much more, would mean the world.

Chapter 21
Illogicalities

Life's brambles present windy obstacles and thorny lessons.

Nursing a fat lip and a gruesome black eye, Jenene waited at their kitchen table for her husband to rise from sleep. She wanted answers. She knew men could be cheating scoundrels, but she had never even heard of domestic abuse.

Still an era when the subject was taboo, no one spoke of such misbegotten behavior. Shelters or support groups were some time away. No help of any kind existed. Because future vice president Joe Biden had yet to aggressively spearhead legislation for the Violence Against Women Act, she would learn even the law had no power to protect her unless she was willing to jeopardize her life by pressing charges.

When Guy stumbled out, hair askew, eyebrows wild, rubbing the sleep out of his bloodshot peepers, she said nothing. Waited. Waited for him to see and assess the damage on his own, draw his own conclusions.

In some regards her life had definitely been a sheltered one because she had honestly never heard about spousal abuse and when he laid the first slap on her she was so figuratively and literally stunned—indignation would come later—that she was overcome by such confusion she could do little else than be his victim. Men hit women? Or was she the only one? If that were the case, what had she gotten herself into?

Sleepy eyes shocked to full wakefulness, horror dawned on his face.

Truly aghast at the sight of her, he sputtered, "What happened to you?"

"You happened to me!"

"I would never do this to you!" he immediately denied. Frowned. Shook his head. "That's crazy."

Guy's genuineness wasn't feigned. He had no memory of the beating he dealt, no knowledge of his actions whatsoever. Alcohol can disrupt the activity in the hippocampus, the part of the brain where autobiographical memories—the minutia of our moment-to-moment activities—are produced, causing a blackout and rendering a person able to function on autopilot while no memories are being created.

Of the two types, Guy displayed more severe en bloc blackouts as opposed to fragmentary blackouts, during which some memories are stored and others can be triggered. Even though he would appear perfectly rational and cogent while being in a state of such deep inebriation, he was in truth so blotto he remembered absolutely nothing.

"The guy who did it was your twin then, your exact double."

Never really admitting he had beaten her, he begged her forgiveness and promised it would never happen again.

Maybe on some level she recognized her and Guy's mutual brokenness without realizing that although both carried the hash marks of difficult childhoods, he was impacted deeper and a force from a darker place directed his true self. He had hidden his demons well. Had he laid a hand on her before they were married, she likely would have said get your caboose on down the road, Mr. Macho, we can't share a track anymore.

What would it look like if she opted out of her marriage straightaway? Like she was an idiot, a fool. Like maybe it would have been wise to listen to her dad, move home, and reset her life from a more stable base.

Married and trapped…or free and by all appearances a failure in the eyes of her family. The conundrum of such a decision is that admitting to being wrong can be more painful than any physical beating. And once the decision was made, there would be no reversal, the label would be permanent—along with another, divorcée—while it was possible the abuse was some odd abnormality, a deviation from the norm.

If only she had known….

Early on it was easier to chalk it up to aberration. The first ten or fifteen times it happened she was left stunned and baffled, unsure what infraction was so irredeemable it required such harsh punishment. In time she would quit wondering. It was just the way it was, the truth of her new life.

More and more often he would get blackout drunk, beat her, and claim no memory. As the frequency of the beatings increased, Jenene grew convinced he did remember…convinced he got a sadistic glee out of causing her pain.

Due to a combination of leeriness, fear, and embarrassment Jenene was disinclined to share her plight with anyone.

Living under the threat of abuse was no kind of life. Believing falsely she was the only woman beaten by her husband she was worried speaking of it would be met with blank stares. Doubt. Maybe even accusations regarding her culpability. She had been made to doubt so much, she had no idea what to think.

She wondered if friends suspected something was amiss. Guy had a way of calling wherever she might end up. Checking in on her. The thing was, even though he made the call, he would always ask, "Where are you?" She learned to restrain her smart-alecky side and answer truthfully. What met her when she got home if she didn't watch herself wasn't worth throwing shade.

The toll of the emotional abuse was far greater than the marks left by fisted hands.

She couldn't tell her family. She was too afraid her dad would fulfill his threat. So rather than seek help she experienced what is known today as a stereotypical domestic abuse scenario. Her every move was controlled. She was subject to cruel mind games. And she was beaten with regularity for small infractions, such as making goulash instead of steak and potatoes. Guy had no trouble sailing a plate of rejected food right into a wall.

At first the abuse was such a shock. He seemed to get a kick out of splitting her lip. Blackening her eyes. Leaving her a mess.

After a time Jenene learned a trick. All her life Lois told her, "Laugh and the world laughs with you; cry and you cry alone." The lesson left Jenene with a deep aversion for tears. This complex meant no matter how hard the pummeling Guy dealt she took the slaps and punches silently. Then one day she hit her breaking point and the levies broke.

She began to cry.

Guy backed down.

It blew her mind.

The waterworks succeeded where all pleas and logical arguments failed. It was obvious: the greater instigator was concealing her pain. He wanted to see her shed tears. He wanted to hear her weep. After all without a reaction how can the authority know their punishment is having an impact?

If crying backed him down, she planned to satisfy. Not one accustomed to emotional outbursts, she needed practice. She worked on her tears in the mirror. If he wanted a show, it was worth putting on an Oscar-worthy performance to diffuse him. And it worked…for a while.

Why did Jenene stay so long under such conditions?

That's always the question that comes up. It is difficult to understand the psychological binds created in an abusive relationship. The constant undermining that erodes self-esteem.

As headstrong and willful as Jenene had been, the abuse had reduced her to a weak, defeated woman.

In the beginning it was a matter of denial. Then it morphed into self-blame. Once she began questioning her responsibility in the beatings, she had given herself over to the sort of defeatist attitude, the sort of doubt, which strips a person of all power.

There was only one person Jenene thought could help her, her mother-in-law. When he would beat her, Guy would say, "You're just like my mother," an inaccurate assessment that gives insight into the root cause of his violent outbursts.

"Put up with it until he grows up," was the advice offered. "He will. You just need to be patient."

Patient? Ludicrous.

What if he kills me in the meantime?

Broken down and crushed, what choice did she have other than to set her jaw and take the abuse?

Chapter 22
Fear Fronts

When there's a turnkey and surveillance, marriage is a prison.

The scope of her husband's control was unreasonable. He expected servitude, deference, absolute reverence, and anything short of that was an infraction justifying his brand of brutal punishment. He was in opposition to her friends and family. They represented outside opinions and ideas. Guy wanted to impose complete isolation.

Because Jenene clung to her loved ones, it was taking time for his plan to go into full effect.

There was little doubt it was only a matter of time until he had his way.

By the end of the summer of 1979 Jenene felt lucky to get to see her parents. As she lay in bed the night before a visit, all she could think of was the uncertainty that had overtaken her life.

Guy was a drunk. He imposed his might too regularly. And he wanted to start a family. What she wanted was to get out yet it was as if she had stumbled inadvertently into quicksand and the only way to slow the sinking was to be absolutely still because pride stood in the way of any effective escape.

Sleep was a proven escape if fleeting.

Drift off and be…elsewhere, on a daytrip to see a house she had known about much of her life and always found compelling. With a gabled roof and a huge tower it possessed architectural uniqueness. Looking through interesting houses had long been a hobby of Jenene's. In this instance she and Guy were evaluating the house. It was for sale. Even if they weren't in a position to buy, it was an excuse to get a look inside a place that inspired curiosity.

Even the realest feeling dreams are differentiated from reality by the inconsistencies recognizable even in a state of sleep.

Even though the whole scenario had all the texture of life, or seemed to, that Guy would indulge in her hobby was absurd. She had no doubt he would look at houses if they were in the market to buy one. But the whimsy required to approach a realtor with the intent merely to view a house to sate curiosity was beyond the man.

In this case the ideal affable Guy was her companion. The Guy so suave and persuasive he talked all her barricades down. Only in dreams was he the man for whom she had fallen in love. Even if in the waking world he would play at being that guy a lot of the time, that man he would never be; the problem was she knew the truth of his veneer, that it was an enticement little different from a witch's candy house or a siren's song.

Along with a friendly realtor it was making for a fun adventure. The woman was explaining the details of the house vibrantly and when she should have been looking to close the sale executed a different tact when she said, "But in all truth, you probably won't want to buy this house no matter how much you like it or how low the price."

"Why not?"

"We've had trouble selling it because, well, people think it's haunted." She paused to take a breath. "I'm inclined to think there's something to the claims. Some really strange things happen—"

At that instant the porcine proprietor of Ma's Roost, Margaret "Ma" Klund, materialized before them out of the magical thin air of dreams and performed an approximation of a curtsy.

"It's okay, you can move in," she said. "I'm the ghost haunting this house and I welcome you."

"But you're not dead," Jenene said uncertainly. How long had it been since she last saw Ma? She lived only a short ways from the large woman for a long time. Not so long ago. At the time she was alive and as well as she could be at her size. But it was possible she had since passed.

"Yes, I am," Ma replied with a smile and dissipated as Jenene sat bolt upright in bed, overcome by a beyond-the-norm feeling of oppressiveness…beyond the norm, but familiar just the same.

Was it one of *those* dreams? Was it a warning? Or as Scrooge surmised of the vision of his deceased former partner, was it all just due to a bit of undigested potato? No guilt was associated with Ma, so there was no reason indigestion should spark a guilty dream.

She lay there and considered if it was even possible to contact Ma. She concluded it would be difficult. She had sold her business, retired, and relocated. Had she moved into a nursing home?

Guy snored beside her. She never even considered confiding in him. He would think she was a weirdo.

Bob probably knew how to get in contact with Ma, so when they arrived in Wilson the next day in the late morning, Jenene used an excuse to pull her dad aside.

"How are you, Cookie?"

"I think I had another dream," she said.

Concern eked through his expression of intentness. "Not about me or someone else close—"

"It was about Ma Klund."

"Ma? Last I heard she was doing fine," he said. "She lives only a couple miles from where you were in Hudson."

"Do you have her number?"

"I could maybe find it. Can it wait 'til after lunch or do you feel it needs to be right away?"

"I don't know," she confessed. "The dream had sort of the same feeling. But it wasn't…scary in the way the others were. Ma showed up as a ghost in a haunted house and invited us to move in."

"A ghost invited you to move in?"

It sounded ludicrous. "Maybe it was nothing."

"After lunch then."

"We better get in there," she said. "Mom might be goading Guy."

"Things…working out with him?"

Could he see the healing marks of the abuse? She nodded, unable to speak a lie, and headed inside before he could ask more questions.

Lunch was well underway when the phone rang. Lois excused herself to answer. When she returned a moment later, her face was drawn and ashen. "That was Ma Klund's son, Andy," she said. "Ma died last night."

Color drained from Bob's face.

In the wake of the announcement Bob was blown away and looked at his daughter speculatively. Guy, mulling silently, and Lois, chattering ceaselessly, remained oblivious as to why it was so amazing that the phone call should have come now. Not only was Jenene coincidentally at home; she had just dreamed of Ma…in a ghostly incarnation.

Once again Jenene was bewildered, bemused, and befuddled all rolled into an indigestible ball she had no choice other than to swallow.

Why did she need to be reminded of Ma Klund in a dream preceding the woman's death? It seemed unlikely there was ever a chance to prevent the ultimate outcome yet the coincidence had to be acknowledged. Certainly the odds of her experiencing a dream in which Ma was a ghost the night before learning of the woman's passing were calculable and maybe not so long yet it was still supremely strange.

Ma was a successful single mother in a time when the odds were really stacked against her as a woman without a man. Perhaps Jenene needed to be reminded of her, to take inspiration from her example.

Perhaps it was a rehash to remind Bob she had a weird sixth sense.

If the dreams were some sort of psychic phenomena, the connection was unreliable and in some ways made her consider the frailty of knowledge and her own powers of persuasion. What the hell did it matter if she dreamed when people died if there was no recourse that allowed her to change the prognosticated outcome?

The dreams would continue throughout the years, some with greater impact. Trying to give them definition, every time Jenene thought she established some tenet, the next dream would in some way dash it, the way the weather stymies meteorologists.

She has thought she would have a dream foretelling the death of all significant family members. She has thought the dreams would only concern people for whom she truly cared. She has thought the dreams always foretold death. She has thought a lot of things.

Jenene wouldn't feel good about the dreams until shortly thereafter. Guy took night classes to advance his career. With free time, Jenene joined him and took a psychology course. She was fairly certain her husband was at least slightly insane and wanted to attain better understanding.

Dreams were discussed. Jenene confided about hers. Out of fear accusations would be thrown around if too much were revealed she played off the phenomena as kooky coincidences with no deeper meaning.

The teacher was very interested in her dreams. She asked Jenene to stay after class for further discussion.

"The worst part is part of me feels I cause the deaths," she confessed once they were alone. "That scares me. I've had crazy dreams about my uncle getting hit by a train for years and every time I do for like a week I'm terrified every time the phone rings it'll be my aunt calling to tell me Herb was hit."

The liberal-minded teacher smiled knowingly, shook her head. "You aren't causing it," she said. "Sounds to me like the dreams are psychic. Like they're warnings. For whatever reason, your antennas are up higher than most and you're being blessed with these warnings."

Blessed? What an odd notion.

"I wish I knew why," she said. "I haven't been able to change anything so I don't know how much of a blessing it is."

"Maybe you weren't meant to in some of these cases. You dream a train clobbers your uncle. Have you told him?"

"He's grumbly and I'm sort of scared of him. But what I worry about is he won't believe me. Like my grandma didn't believe me. Or he'll laugh in my face."

"Is there a reason your uncle is more likely to end up in the path of a train?"

"There's actually a crossing at the end of their driveway he crosses every day."

"Typically you have one dream before an incident, correct?" Jenene nodded. "Seeing as how those are the only dreams you've experienced repeatedly, maybe they're a manifestation of your worry your uncle crossing so much is an odds game and as he gets older the odds are getting longer."

Sort of like my mom commuting to Hartford, she thought. *I wouldn't be surprised at all if I dreamt she died in a car accident.*

Jenene qualified, "He has slowed down a bit and he can't drive anymore because of poor vision. He drove the tractor right into the lake."

"In that instance your subconscious mind takes all the information you have and creates a dream that's perfectly logical. Does he die in the dream?"

"Hm…I suppose I assumed he was killed but the dream doesn't really go that far."

"I can see how it's a quandary. Are you being warned of something imminent you can change? Or is it to prepare you when no preventive measure will stop anything? Wild. I don't usually have such interesting students. I don't envy what you've been bestowed with; but it might be best to look upon it as a gift."

It didn't feel like much of a gift.

Later, when a dream would have been the most important warning, one refused to come.

But a train would hit Herb.

Chapter 23
Steep Prices

The fall of 1979 was a dispiriting one for Jenene.

She was trapped in an abusive marriage and her body was rebelling. It had become impossible to hold down food. Even as she floated the suspicion her gallbladder was to blame when she went to a doctor, her symptoms were attributed to acid reflux. The doctor was persistent if wrong and she continued to suffer.

By Christmas she couldn't even suck on hard candy without vomiting.

She and Guy visited the farm for the holiday. When Lal saw she was so sick, she pleaded and later begged her to get a second opinion.

After riding high as the popular head cook of the Nite Club she was resigned to be back waitressing at a Sambo's. It was better than spending all her time at home. And even if it meant working her way up without the benefit of nepotism, labor was in her blood. She worked the graveyard shift in the heart of Cottage Grove.

Guy was a solid wage earner and would have preferred Jenene not work. His disapproval was palpable. Her refusal to be the proper wife he desired galled him endlessly. He took her insistence on working as a slight against him. A wife at home was a status symbol. If his wife worked, it implied he failed to make enough.

Jenene saw his antiquated thinking as all the more reason to work. It seemed if he had his way she would be like a princess locked away in a tower. Not waiting for Prince Charming because the monster guarding the ramparts would devour whomever might draw near. No matter whom it was approaching.

Fear he would lay down the law and forbid her from working kept her in most other ways compliant.

Guy had proven frighteningly violent. Worse, directing his yen was a streak of jealously wider than a super highway. It was increasingly evident he always felt it mandatory to lay his claim to her. His insecurity was a trait she not only considered less than endearing but repellent. He made a hobby out of accusing her of infidelity. If grocery shopping took five minutes longer than he thought it should she had to be cheating.

Paranoia led to many bruises.

A stroke of bad luck, Guy's job was only a block from Sambo's. He liked to drop in and slay whatever good vibes there were with the spikes of his threatening presence. He would sit at the counter and while she bopped between tables keep his eyes peeled. Any guy who dared speak beyond placing his order got the stink eye. If their perusal followed her too closely they got a sneering grimace.

Guy's behavior was a problem.

Jenene was one to draw friends with her outgoingness and sociability. Even a hermit can be a people person. The regulars as well as several coworkers took a shine to her. Guy intimidated some until they went away. With a few well-chosen words he could be so chillingly undercutting he had the ability to strike real fear. The wiser ones learned not to test him and became lasting friends.

One of her better friends was a self-empowered woman with too much might to fear Guy or consider him a deterrent.

Pookie was a tall, plump black woman. Jenene loved her as a person and for what she represented. For one thing she refused to kowtow to the notion black women should use harsh chemicals to straighten their hair. She wore her hair in a well groomed 'fro at about the length the Jackson Five wore theirs in the 70's. Jenene admired that she wouldn't allow anyone to make her feel as if being black somehow lessened her.

Pookie's husband was a lily-white string bean with dark red hair known either as a bargeman or a river rat depending on where you were asking. Whichever side opinion fell on, he spent much of his life on the unforgiving Mississippi to provide for his family, so he was not only a hard worker but respectable.

For a time Jenene and Pookie were coworkers before becoming good friends. Jenene would babysit her adorable little girl.

One day Pookie observed Guy's stare down routine when she wandered too deep into Jenene's orbit. When his persistent eyes reached hers his were captured, reproached, and awkwardly sent packing. When he left, she observed, "That man of yours is something else, what I don't know, but something else."

"It's a mystery to me too," Jenene concurred. "I know one thing. He's a little afraid of you."

"Oh is he?" She chuckled. "Afraid I'll flatten him?"

"You're probably not far off. I think he senses you're not scared of him."

"Should I be?"

Jenene looked away. "No…it's just…he likes to intimidate people. He feels like it gives him the upper hand or something."

"Insecure, huh?"

There was no need to respond.

There was another buddy who had no reason to fear Guy, in this case because he carried a sidearm and was New Port's chief of police. He told her to call him Fred and showed his approval with good tips and better conversation. A kindly officer of the law was a welcome change after being unjustly run out of Hudson. "You look a little peaked," he observed days before she would seek medical assistance.

The people who seemed to care noticed the distress she worked to hide. Some may have suspected there was more to it than being under the weather. The only way she would ever be willfully deceptive was in denying her life was anything but peachy.

Seeming to exist on another plane, Guy sought emotional separation and ignored her illness. Yet in an instant when he discovered dissatisfaction his mood could pivot and the polarities in the room would seem to switch as the air went flat and the whole world would transmogrify into a nightmare as a sinister transformation morphed Guy into a monster. If only the abuse were as transitory as his mother assured.

Going into the New Year, Jenene could only hope some contingency plan would emerge. As things stood, she was so far from the outspoken open-minded rebel she had been she was a mere shadow of her former self.

1980. It seemed after the malaise of the 1970's, orchestrated gas shortages, endless turmoil in the Middle East, and a presidential debacle of epic proportions, many saw an age of reclaimed prosperity ahead. In fact, on the promise of as much, former B movie actor Ronald Reagan would sweep the nation and first become the Republican nominee for president and then win the office the following fall, a landslide over incumbent and intensely pragmatic Washington outsider Jimmy Carter.

For Jenene the New Year brought only much of the same: pain, frustration, and fear. Even living under the threat of abuse had become secondary to her declining health.

Be that as it may, it would be nine days into the New Year before Jenene broke down and sought a specialist. If not for herself for the people who loved her. The decision came on the heels of her best friend Mary's wedding. Memorable for all the wrong reasons, feeling so awful she was unable to eat, drink, or have any fun at all marked the marvelous occasion.

"Severe gallstones are causing your symptoms," the specialist diagnosed after a hasty but thorough examination. "We need to schedule surgery immediately. There's a procedure we need to do first, though."

"I was so sure it was my gallbladder all along," she said. "The other doctor claimed indigestion."

"I suppose he prescribed an antacid too." Glossy white teeth sparkling charmingly, the specialist shot her a trust-inspiring smile. Captivated, she nodded. "Well that's why he isn't a specialist."

That he believed her meant more than his charisma. The other doctor had looked her in the face crassly and blamed her eating habits for her discomfort. Eating habits? Her diet wasn't atrocious enough to warrant such an assessment. Not often had she felt so insulted. That point had been the beginning of food being more than an enemy due to cosmetic concerns.

Leeriness came as naturally as swimming to a fish even if she trusted this doctor. "You said there's a procedure. Explain it to me. In detail."

"I won't minimize what will be a great deal of discomfort," he said. "This will involve a tube being inserted into one of your nostrils so that I can guide it to your gallbladder and find out what's going on."

Not again. Not more medical deflowering. "Is it really necessary?"

"Maybe you don't understand. If your gallbladder is as infected as I suspect, your life is on the line. From what I see had you waited any longer your gallbladder may have burst before we were able to relieve some of the pressure. Then you'd be in even worse shape."

"Relieve the pressure?"

That charming smile was flashed again, toothy and beaming.

How many people made a habit of going straight from the doctor's office to the hospital and checking in? It was ridiculous.

For what on the surface seemed like a streamlined modern hospital, what came next seemed an archaic technique of cleansing akin to being bled by leeches. Fortunately for Jenene, the procedure she underwent was at least somewhat effective, if gross.

The sterile yet abrasive aroma of disinfectant not quite stinging her nose, she was ushered into a small room and put down on a hard Naugahyde exam table. Positioned on her side. The tube was no wider than a pencil and made of soft yet rigid rubber. As it was inserted into her nostril it felt much thicker and firmer.

As the head of the long cylinder was forced beyond the vestibule just inside her nostril and through the nasal cavity on its way south, the invasiveness of the tube's progression made her shivery: even with the aid of lubricant, without anesthetization the tube making a path through her body felt like a malignant invading parasite.

A mobile X-ray machine was wheeled in so the specialist could guide the tube by sight to her gallbladder nestled beside the right lobe of her liver. Once the tube had penetrated the offending bile storage sac the end not submerged in her body was directed into an old battered bucket that looked more suited to holding a mop head.

Drip. Slow but steady. Drip. Through a trick of physics the bottom of the bucket began to fill with toxic sludge, in the end maybe half a cup worth. Enough fluid was expelled to avoid disaster, so they thought.

Following the siphoning Jenene was rushed into yet another emergency surgery.

The inflamed incendiary that was her gallbladder still needed to be removed posthaste. It proved too late. A mere touch caused it to detonate, rupturing and disgorging a noxious gooey spew into her body cavity. The infectious poison threatened even greater danger.

The specialist would later explain the mess had to be cleaned up as scrupulously as an oil spill because if any were left it could lead to further sickness the way residual petroleum can taint fish and crustaceans. He would also explain that the gallstones they had anticipated, as though having been pulverized by a tumbler, had broken down into a muddy gravel consistency. This prevented the successful siphoning he had hoped would forestall the eventual outcome.

Inwardly directed anger had wreaked havoc on the small muscular sac beneath the right lobe of her liver where bile was stored and caused another close call with death. She only knew how close when she awoke after surgery to find her mother-in-law in the room. Due to anathema for hospitals Guy's mother had told her beforehand she would gladly help her out in any way she could after surgery but not to expect a visit because she wouldn't go to a hospital unless she…or someone else were dying.

In the days after surgery a drainage hose protruded from her abdomen.

The odious task of drawing out some tubing each day so it wouldn't heal in place was a necessary evil. The fear she would pull out too much, that the entirety of the tube would come spilling out too soon if she weren't careful, caused much consternation after she went home. When the day came for the doctor to remove it fully Jenene was shocked to see there was about ten feet of hose coiled like a millipede inside her.

    All of it was a terribly painful and humbling experience…and as of yet she had no idea the eventual repercussions.

During Jenene's recuperation Guy undertook what would be a huge gesture of caring, one of those strange outpourings of love. They were still more frequent than the beatings and tricked her continually into hopefulness.

    To brighten her spirits he brought her housecat Trisha to her hospital room for a visit. There would be other times she was hospitalized he would outright ignore her, but this time he was actually considerate enough to break the rules to make her smile.

    With dishes of food and water under the edge of the hospital bed, Tricia curled up in a chair and slept.

    The nurse, so businesslike she wouldn't even engage Jenene in chitchat, entered and saw the cat without batting an eye, as if she didn't really see her.

    Guy made eye contact, used his eyes to direct her eyes to Trisha, and said with utmost earnestness, "Lifelike isn't it?"

    The nurse bought it, replying, "Sure is," and didn't say another word. The only concern was that she would tip over one of the dishes when she was busying herself about the bed but a moment later she exited without incident.

The chink in her life caused by her illness led to an employment shake up.

    Jenene wasn't given to hastily quitting a job without notice. In the case of Sambo's she was left little choice.

    Ideally her boss would have understood. Yet the manager refused to give her time off for the surgery that saved her life—perhaps she believed not only in reanimated corpses but that the dead could wait tables—and since listening to reason was beyond her, Jenene's concluding words to her were, "I know you expect me to come in, but I'm scheduled for surgery and I just can't make it—so I guess I quit."

    But that wasn't exactly the end of her run at Sambo's.

    The manager would seek to reemploy her, either because she found a heart or simply because she was short reliable staff.

Jenene was willing to listen to her offer. What followed was a negotiation. Bob's voice never far away, she played hardball. All her demands were met, which was how she became a cook again and raised her wage to six dollars an hour.

This changeover would last all of a month and lead to an even better transition.

The other cooks made more, and when she found out, feeling it only fair, she asked for her wage to match. Stating that Jenene had negotiated the pay and had gotten what she requested, the manager refused. No matter how forthrightly she claimed she would be seeking employment elsewhere, the manager was unconvinced and smarmily dared her to go right ahead.

McColl Pub in St. Paul needed a kitchen manager. Jenene talked up her game and convinced the owner, an old-school roughneck, she was worth considering. Right away he called her back in and offered her the position—for a more competitive wage.

"You can start immediately," he said.

"I'm sorry but I need to give notice—"

"I appreciate the sentiment but I really don't think it'll be necessary."

"What do you mean?"

Her new boss grinned. "You want to know why I hired you? Why I wanted you? Your last boss really burned you she was so teed off. Good Lord, the tirade that woman went on! Made me realize I'd be a fool if I didn't hire you. Such a ruckus could only mean she was really sorry to lose you."

The more Guy expressed the opinion she needn't work the more she insisted a second wage helped their finances. Even if Guy remained unsold, Jenene was intractable. A job meant more than money: it was a life preserver. Her time at McColl Pub helped her stay sane. Her moribund marriage seemed like one of those strange experiments in which unknowing subjects are dosed with hallucinogens to see if they would snap, break, or implode.

As always her culinary prowess brought the appreciation so lacking in her life. At work she was not only respected, she was admired; as revenue poured in, her randy and rowdy boss heaped accolades on her and made her glad every day she left Sambo's.

Lunch rush was where she made her bones.

The next tastier than the last, she introduced snazzy new specials. This culminated in what emerged as the favorite among the patrons, her sumptuous take on the classic Monte Cristo sandwich.

Ham, cheddar, turkey, and Swiss are situated between three slices of white bread, secured with toothpicks, and the crust lopped off. The edges are doused in whipped egg before a quick dip in flour, and then the whole sandwich is dropped in the deep fryer, sealing in the juicy goodness. Served with a dash of powdered sugar and a strawberry cream cheese dip, each serving was a mini-masterpiece.

Whether she prepped forty or fifty, her Monte Cristos never failed to sell out, which made for a heck of a profitable lunch service.

Maybe she should have known her source of personal contentment would be taken away. Life was like that. Her health always interceded.

Chapter 24
Worse News Yet

October 1980.

The fever was cooking her alive. Diagnosis was difficult and would only come after enough poking and prodding to make her feel like an alien abductee before such an analogy was vogue. Seventeen days on quarantine in the hospital. In the end the doctor's words were devastating: "You'll never be able to have children. Even if you were to get pregnant, you could never carry a baby to term." She was so matter-of-fact her tone approached icy.

Despite cooking with fever, devastation made her feel frostbitten.

Yet part of her was relieved. Would she really want to have Guy's baby? There had been three miscarriages, at the time called spontaneous abortions. Hadn't the misery of each incalculable loss also come with a strand of guilty relief for the child spared?

The prognosis was dual; two diseases she had never even heard of with exotic sounding names. Count one: endometriosis. A common cause of infertility, it involved Jenene's uterus, fallopian tubes, and ovaries being covered in what were termed chocolate cysts, engorged pouches of blood. Some reached her lungs.

Count two: intrapertoneal adhesions. This involved rampaging scar tissue growth, as if all her organs were bound up in jumbles of rubber bands. Not a year after her gallbladder surgery and the adhesions had twisted her stomach in such a way the entrance and exit were side by side.

"Being that it's unlikely you could see a child through to adulthood," the doctor said in a tone meant to convey solace but served only to infuriate, "maybe it's a blessing in disguise you are physically unable to have a child."

"What caused this?"

"During your gallbladder surgery—"

Apparently back in January when she'd had her gallbladder removed the operation had caused thick fibrous abdominal scar tissue.

"—You were contaminated with talcum powder."

"How did it happen?"

"We don't like assigning blame—"

"Tell me."

"The talcum, well…it's possible the surgeon or some other attendant in the operating theater neglected to wash it off the latex gloves."

It was preposterous. How could one small mistake be so costly?

Perhaps it was a matter of hastiness. By the time she had surgery, her gallbladder was so enflamed, the slightest touch made it explode, filling her abdominal cavity with the poison that too easily could have caused a fatal infection. Afterward, she began having stomach problems, i.e., her stomach would painfully clamp shut when she ate or drank. The pain of having liquid or solid matter pressing down on her clinched esophagus was akin to a heart attack.

"So there's no real treatment?"

"We can fight it for a time. The problem is that the adhesions will eventually crush your organs. No matter what we do, I'm very sorry to have to tell you, but you won't see thirty."

Simmering anger boiled into fury. "You aren't God!" Jenene snapped at the surprised doctor. "You can't tell me I'm going to die!"

The doctor dared to argue.

After ducking the phone, the physician was bright enough to vamoose, probably a little mystified as to why her patient had gone mad: it wasn't as if she was so presumptuous as to give an exact date.

Chapter 25
Fallout

Two weeks into her hospital stay her boss made the pilgrimage to see her; he had to find out if McColl Pub's eminent head cook would be returning.

"Thing is, I need to know," he said. "I've been filling in but I can't keep towing the line. I don't want to but should I find someone else?"

Jenene had once again become the fulcrum of a successful kitchen. Even so she was a replaceable component. Leaving the Nite Club had shown her that.

"Find someone else," she said, allowing herself to sink into the depths. "I don't know when I'll be better."

Who needed a life preserver when you had no life?

If only the tenacity to live she exuded when she launched the phone at the doctor wasn't stolen from her by a life of little hope.

Guy's take on the situation was abysmal. Arctic. Unforgiving. "If you can't even give me a baby," he said with robotic detachedness, as if taking a page of villainy out of a book, "what good are you? Jesus, you're useless."

"It wasn't like I planned for this," she said miserably. "I didn't decide to get sick."

"You are just worthless. I married a useless woman who can't even give me a baby. That's all you have to do and you can't do it."

"Maybe we should just split up then," she suggested sedately. "Go on our separate path—"

The crack across the head wasn't a surprise but was no less painful.

"You belong to me," he chided. "I have a piece of paper that says I own you. You know that if I can't have you, no one can."

"Then we should go back to the counselor," she said cautiously. "We need to fix our marriage."

He scoffed. "Why would I want to listen to some dumb dyke tell me a bunch of bullshit she learned in some prissy school?"

He had made therapy an unmitigated disaster. It had been tense but somewhat productive right up until the counselor leveled her steely eyes at him and said, "You want to control your wife, but she isn't out of control, so she doesn't need you running her life. You treat her like you're Siamese twins…but I'm here to tell you, you and she are not attached at the hip." On the spot he bolted out, putting an end to couple's counseling.

"I can't live like this," she said.

"You don't have a choice. And I dare you to call the police. As soon as they let me out, I'll kill you. You know I will. And don't even think for a second a restraining order will do anything. No piece of paper will stop me from getting to you."

Guy made her see the opt-out factor. She had promised 'til death do us part and she was a woman of her word. Now she had been told death was pending if she could be driven to the point of surrender and embrace the specter. Since the parting she seemed unable to make on her own would also be imminent, death seemed like her best option.

Wound ropes of scar tissue strangled her fallopian tubes; her uterus was a corpse in a sarcophagus of chocolate cysts; her life had no meaning.

To match her gloom Guy treated Jenene as if she were detestable. The constant berating for being a failure as a woman lasted well beyond reason.

As Guy's violence escalated, if she wanted to avoid a beating Jenene had to find ways to escape him. He would follow her anywhere and everywhere, even straight to a police station. She never dared drive to the farm and expose The Seniors to one of his outbursts. But she would find one place he was unwilling to go.

The big scary man was too spooked to go to the place she found.

Why, something out of one of those horror movies he so loved might get him.

Grey Cloud Island is a rustic place with a sense of ancientness; once inhabited by Native Americans, their burial mounds remain among the few homes along Grey Cloud Trail. A lot of superstition has grown not only from the inhabitants of long ago but more recent accidents, such as those at the bottom of Dead Man's Hill where a fast S maneuver called for beneath a narrow train trestle was the downfall of too many to recount.

There are other stories, too, tales of lantern carrying specters and a summer camp where satanic rites were performed. But really the Island was a place where teens went to drink, neck, and smoke pot.

Further on, beyond the actual island, there's a remote cemetery surrounded in shadowy woods. Even today the old boneyard is only accessible via a washboard dirt road one hard downpour away from vanishing. There are markers dating back to the early 1800's. The relic stones look their age, pelleted, gray, and coated in lichen. Newer gravestones jostle to take over. The shiny smooth granite seems out of place, even unbefitting, compared to the stones cut by chisels rather than lasers.

Even on the darkest night the Grey Cloud cemetery was Jenene's sanctuary.

If there were ghosts it was safer among them than at home.

It was fantastic an irrational fear of spooks and ghouls scared Guy away. Jenene found the cemetery to be one of the safest, most relaxing places ever. That the consecrated ground had the power to drive him away was sort of funny. He was scarier than anything she found on Grey Cloud. She never even encountered kids out on a lark.

With her perceptive or psychic touch, she could sense the sort of disruptions some attribute to ghosts, but the graveyard felt clear. It had always struck her as absurd that spirits would remain near their mortal coil.

She spent a lot of the summer of 1980 haunting that cemetery.

Had a miracle not been on the horizon her times there may have been a rehearsal for taking up a plot in the ground herself.

Chapter 26
Powerless Spectators

All too aware of the tedium of small-town Wisconsin for a kid, not so much out of kindness but sympathy Jenene orchestrated little jailbreaks for Jeff.

The kid still accused her of his every crime but he revered her, all the more reason to feel sorry for him. He was an idealistic little chatterer. He was growing up on a diet of "Happy Days" and that's sort of what his life was like. Only he tried to be Richie Cunningham and the Fonz rolled into one.

Did Jenene consider herself a good big sister? Such signifiers never entered her mind because it was never her intention to be impressive. Did it make her a fun big sister that she would spring Jeff from Wilson and let him drive her Camaro around a large park with an enclosed roadway? He sure thought so.

By that summer of 1980 Jenene and Guy had moved into a large brown house on the main drag of the bottom of the hill portion of St. Paul Park. This put them much closer to the farm, which was just down the road. So was the Grey Cloud cemetery.

The accessibility made a real impact. Guy allowed her regular visits to The Seniors, several in a week, neglecting to consider his wife's geriatric family as threats.

Besides, he spent so much time tending his mother's needs he was to an extent understanding of familial obligation. Jenene found mowing the huge hilly lawn and gardening stress relieving, Lal's company consoling, and Bill's wisdom enlightening. Herb still had the power to unnerve but he was such a fixture, removing him would be like pulling a plug on a drain—everything else would sluice away.

By mid-summer Jenene had a hankering to see her lil bro. No starch in his britches to make him the downer so many adults could be, she needed the cheering up. Too much time had been spent sitting on a grave with her back against a headstone.

Having Jeff over for a few days seemed like a good way to give him access to Lal, Bill, and Herb too. Although it would not be deluded for her to opine he most likely only wanted to trail Jenene.

That was fine.

In that last regard she could work as an intermediary. Because Jeff was denied the chance to grow up with Lal, Bill, and Herb the way she had he could be uncomfortable on the farm. Nonetheless he loved his uncles and aunt immensely, even without being particularly close to them personally, and still loved to visit.

His reluctance to go alone was understandable.

There was the misfortunate fact that when he was alone with The Seniors something bad tended to happen. The last time he spent time on the farm without a liaison, he had fallen off a wagon loaded down with hay bales. Like a cat, he managed to land on his feet; only the impact was so great, walking would be absent from his repertoire for several days—he had to be carried everywhere.

The real problem was that on the farm you were expected to be bright enough to take care of yourself. This was due to a generational gap; if you lived during the Great Depression, it was hard to understand that adolescents might not be able to carry on like miniature adults. The rules were set by common sense, so if you had it, you were okay. But if you were a kid occupying rube town USA learning little or nothing, work on the farm presented many dangers because life had yet to offer any starching.

At the magical age of twelve he was straddling the line between boyhood and manhood, which can be a pristine window for the fact he was still boyishly naive yet more mature and receptive. His guileless and innocent admiration made him a welcome digression, first from the men putting the make on her and now from her churlish husband. Had Jenene believed Guy might get violent around Jeff notwithstanding her dad's threat she never would have invited him.

Guy's social degeneration had yet to reach a point where she was automatically worried he would go off when there were witnesses—by and large.

Sure there was the time fairly early in their marriage when Jenene and Guy tried to play matchmakers for their coworkers and things had gone…calamitously.

Guy thought the foursome needed a keg of beer to mark the occasion right. He began imbibing well before dinner. At the meal his mood soured like milk left in the sun. Arbitrarily triggered, he flipped the table, sending spaghetti flying everywhere, leaving red sauce in firework bursts on the wall. He left the room in a drunken huff, the guests left entirely.

The only upside was his restraint: at least he didn't beat her.

Being a spectator to that sort of out of control drinking served to kill Jenene's interest in liquor. Did she look that foolish when drunk? Was she that stupid? The likelihood made her decision. She renounced booze overnight. To this day she only has an occasional drink. Growing up in a bar may have given her a wider perspective of drinking but it took living with a violent drunk to make her see the devastation alcoholism inflicts.

As Jenene cooled her alcoholic ways, another wedge in their marriage presented itself in the form of a reunion. Guy found a new drinking buddy, one who really pushed him to new heights of inebriation. After being out of his life for years, his dad made contact. More on that later....

Another incident of public brutality demonstrated the ugliness not only of violence but jealously. They were eating at the Pannekoeken Huis. The specialty Dutch pancake restaurant was across the Mississippi and was so worth the trip they were ecstatic regulars. An old boyfriend happened along. He made the mistake of saying hello. Guy struck with such predatory swiftness. The poor fellow had no warning before he was punched out. They were asked not to return. Bing. Boom. Banned.

Both events were humiliating. But lacked the deep self-loathing she felt from the humiliation of having hands laid on her. At least that was always perpetrated in the privacy of their home; away from judgmental eyes she was certain would deem her weak, pathetic, deserving.

Even if Guy would clobber her with little instigation, she was confident he would not strike her in front of Jeff.

Guy still wanted to hide the truth of his darker nature behind his intense crass charm. She was sure he would behave himself while Jeff visited. The assessment would prove injudicious. Her brother was changed forever.

The kid was a welcome diversion. He brought a sort of energetic and free vibe into the house.

Jeff's clinginess possibly had as much to do with simple appreciation as anything; since she had been out in the world Jenene invited him regularly for weekends and he treasured the attention from someone he viewed as "cool," whatever that meant. She seemed to baffle and intrigue him in equal parts. He was interested in bombarding her with endless questions. He persisted even if she brushed off many without what he felt were adequate answers.

Maybe Guy was feeling ignored.
Maybe it was cold irrational jealousy.

Maybe he just felt like exerting some might.

Laying down the law.

Assert dominance with aggression so there was no way it could be mistaken for hollow posturing.

Be a man, whatever the hell that meant.

What was a boy pretending to be a man to do? A boy whose only manhood rite was being so bad he was sent away? His own mother felt he couldn't be trusted. Maybe in recognizing reason not to trust her son, his mother estimated him a man. She had reason to believe men were untrustworthy, after all. But her jaded assessment in no way changed facts: grown-up in name only, he had no idea how to conduct himself as a mature adult man.

Tantrums manifest out of nowhere when you have the emotional maturity level of a child.

Sun streaming through a slightly distorted window onto a kitchen table can lend such a sense of serenity to a room that it should have joyous connotations. Three family members sharing company on a warm summer day in such a gentle setting should be a good memory in the making.

Yet violence can erupt out of thin air, even an instant after what had seemed like a happy moment, because in the span of an instant one wrong word can be spoken, a word not even remembered later because it was so random, on the face of it so unlikely to generate such brutal blowback.

The beating may have started with, "Shut your mouth or I'll shut it for you," and the polarities switched, the instant long harbinger before whap, one across the jaw, igniting fire in her cheek. Whap! Right in the nose, blood instantly cascading from her left nostril, hitting the linoleum as dime-sized droplets. Bam! Whap! Boom!

In a suspenseful dramatic movie or novel some form of intervention would have prevented Jeff from bearing witness and being so thoroughly traumatized, a demoralization that would stick with him everlastingly.

Or in a wish fulfillment fantasy the downtrodden boy would have been empowered against the oppressor and against all odds bested the bully, maybe through superhuman strength bestowed by a higher power or maybe through clever ingenuity.

But in cold, hard, obdurate reality, where even children have to face the cruelest, harshest lessons, all Jeff could do was stand there frozen in place until his sister broke the spell of his paralysis by screaming, "Jeff, get out! Lock yourself in the other room!"

With no other option, no action he could feasibly take, he obeyed and vanished.

Once Jeff was safely out of sight, Jenene threw up her arms in surrender and turned on one valve to shut off another.

The wetter her eyes the more doused his fury. Satisfying tears were reward enough for him to lose interest. He seemed to delight in watching her cower for a minute or two, relishing looming over her until he felt he had succeeded in proclaiming his dominance. At which point Guy stomped off to the living room to watch TV as if nothing happened.

Jenene used a dishtowel to clean the blood off her face and wipe up the floor. Then retrieved a shell-shocked Jeff and led him out to the small front porch. Damage control was necessary. What would she say?

Call it horseplay?

Jeff wasn't that naïve.

Lying was about impossible for her so she wouldn't ask her brother to lie, but she would ask him to place the whole event in his classified files and never mention what Guy had done to their parents.

Jenene took a seat in a chair and Jeff dropped to his knees, hugged her lap, and bawled.

"He should never hit you," he cried. "If he's going to do that, you really need to get away from him."

"It's not that easy," she said resignedly.

What did he know of feeling worthless, of being broken? He always had both their parents' love; he was the apple of Lois' eye even if his mischievousness caused her to take the wooden spoon to his derriere almost daily.

She was terrified her husband would kill her if she tried to run. On another level she would welcome the conclusion so long as it was swift, unlike the diseases knotting up and clogging her insides. How could she explain any of these extreme feelings to a boy who had just gotten a ruthless lesson?

How could she make him understand without unfairly burdening and further damaging him?

There was no way. So she didn't try to give him some explanation, only invoked the sanctity of the bond shared by a little brother and his big sis.

"It doesn't matter if it would be hard," Jeff pleaded, "you can leave him."

Jenene was dodgy.

What Guy had done was indefensible. Yet she found herself acting as his apologist. She explained away his actions as best she could, justifying his meanness, because there was just no reason to leave. He had convinced her she was useless, worthless, and totally without value.

Besides, there was no way to know what he might do if she dared break away. She certainly could not guarantee her own safety. But it was the collateral damage that worried her.

Jeff was crushed under the weight of cowardice. Even though as a boy he had no business engaging a grown man in fisticuffs. What did that matter? He was so powerless!

Would Guy have beaten up an underage boy? To speculate further would be unfair because it is entirely possible Guy would have observed restraint. Had Jeff jumped on his back or made some other valiant gesture, there's little doubt he would have been dumped on his head, though, which could have led to any number of even worse outcomes.

What else about Jeff changed? He never again wanted to feel so intimidated and powerless when facing a physical aggressor. He picked up a mantra, large and in charge. It went with his revamped attitude.

He put to good use the weight set Bob bought for him. He bulked up, became a hockey player, and one day worked as a bouncer in Minneapolis before he was even eighteen. Had they met up later, Jeff would have needed little provocation to bounce Guy right into traction. To this day he has no truck with bullying.

Jenene has never witnessed her brother cry again.

Tears were starched out of him.

Chapter 27
Horror Show

During the autumn of 1980, "I am healthy, I am happy, I am terrific," was Jenene's mantra.

Unbeknownst to her affirmations were the first step on an epic healing journey.

If repeated often enough she hoped the words would manifest into truth. She would speak them to her reflection in the bathroom mirror. She would whisper them under her breath when in public. Sometimes they would play through her mind as she lay in bed on the verge of sleep.

The positive affirmation was how she crossed herself against the evil in her life. How she assured herself she had what it took to continue enduring. Yet even as she sought to take control of her outlook outside forces remained out of her control.

Her father-in-law was there to stay. Orville's apartment was undergoing remodeling. They were celebrating their newfound kinship with shots and beers. Orville was the sort of influence that gets a person in trouble. He stoked Guy's bad side, worked him into a tizzy, and set him loose on whoever might be around—all for his own sadistic amusement.

This paired with his automatic rudeness and constant insensitivity left her with little positive feeling for the old sot. He was a mean drunk and there was never a time he wasn't at least half in the bag. He was overbearing and cruel and saw no value in what he would no doubt term the lesser sex.

The family had lost touch with Orville. Jenene and Guy were tipped off a few months before to his bar of choice. They found him in a boozy haze, what they would come to know as his usual state. All boasts and no show, Jenene saw right through him. Guy was enthralled. To humor her hair-trigger husband she joined him at the bar for visits. When they invited the souse to their home he had no problem taking advantage.

Guy loved having him, loved being in the company of the father he had little known in the years after his parents divorced. In their minds they made ideal companions and maybe they were: both put drinking above all else. And they both reveled in playing cruel games, emotional and otherwise.

Fed up with the drinking buddies and their boorish revelry, Jenene bid them goodnight and escaped to bed.

Dead of night and the instigator's plans were afoot.

Jenene was traipsing through dreamland.

Sleep had been and was still her best escape even if Guy made it awkward. When you get photos developed and a pile comes back showing you asleep, things feel weird. Guy admitted to late night voyeur sessions. Jenene was put off but it could have been worse. Creepy may be a far cry from sexy, sure, but dealing with creepy was better than being the recipient of a shellacking.

Waking to camera flashes would have been a painless nuisance. Waking to the sheet and blanket being torn off the bed like a magic trick was terrifying. Exposed in an instant, she popped out of sleep, not yet aware enough to understand what was happening.

The fog lifted quickly when she was descended upon with strikes.

"Making a move on my dad?" Guy bellowed belligerently. "What's wrong with you! I'll teach you!" Seizing her ankle, he yanked her toward him, making her a log drawn into his wood chipper. "You think it's okay to come on to my dad, you whore? I'll teach you good!"

Running on instinct and adrenaline, she thrashed and kicked her way free of his grasp. Rolled. Hit the floor. Dodged. Darted. She was young and in good enough shape to fight to the hilt. She raced out of the bedroom. She felt as if a demon were on her heels breathing scorching heat down the nape of her neck.

The worst part was the unpredictability, the sense that her whole life had become a game of Russian roulette and her every action—every *imagined* action—was a pull of the trigger, and there was no way of knowing which verbal misstep would signal a polarity switch and a blast to the face.

What was the accusation this time? That she came on to Orville?

Ew! What a repulsive suggestion. Such a gross thought! If anything it doused her libido better than the coldest shower. Orville was a cantankerous and disgusting degenerate who stank of drink and wore the extra years accrued by boozing worse than the most beaten fighters wear scar tissue. Sure, she wanted that grinding away on top of her, a hank of sun-beaten leather grittier, smellier, and all around grosser than any previous lover.

Guy so often accused her of infidelity it really shouldn't have surprised her that he believed such a preposterous accusation. The constant allegations came from his paranoia. He would hit her and yell, "If I can't have you, no one will! I'll kill you before I'll see you with someone else."

From whence the idea even sprung was a mystery. Jenene had done everything to assuage his jealously. She cut out male friends, gave the cold shoulder to male coworkers, and made it abundantly clear she was a married woman to any male who came into her vicinity.

There was a time she found jealously attractive. She believed such emotion was misplaced love and all that nonsense. How wrong she had been.

Pausing for an instant at the top of the staircase to orient before descending, she peered down into darkness broken only by the flickering light of the living room television.

She was thinking that jealousy was one of the ugliest things ever, more than a green-eyed monster, it was a hideous hunchbacked, wart-covered, misshapen abomination borne of weakness and insecurity; a freakish thing that thrived on paranoia and fear, which was how it fed itself, creating a circle that could only be broken through a strength she doubted her husband would ever possess.

Down in the living room Jenene could see Orville sitting on the center of the couch like a man observing a particularly exciting sporting event.

Descending the steps heedlessly two at a time, she reached his perched figure in seconds. "What did you tell him, Orville?" she demanded. "Why is he doing this?"

Giving her all the answer she would get, her unblinking father in-law stared at her wordlessly. His stationary and serene disposition was sadistic. There was a little smirk on his mug. He took a drink of his beer. He was enjoying it; he was getting off on his deception and the resulting violence. Being the puppet master was his evening entertainment.

Guy caught up and slapped her.

Knowing there would be no help from Orville, Jenene snatched her keys on her way out the front door. Guy was hot on her trail, the fiery tail of her comet. Faster reaching the car and getting in than he was closing the distance, she slammed shut the door just in the nick of time.

She smacked the lock down with her palm the instant he jerked the handle fiercely, shaking the whole car violently with his effort. Locked out, he had a conniption and smashed off the side mirror in his frenzy.

Before his inebriated brain could decide to try another door, she locked them all with speed borne of terror. Started the car shakily. She would go to the Grey Cloud cemetery, she thought; he never followed her there, fearful as he was of spooks and ghouls and ghosts. To her it was an oasis. A place that, not by virtue of being hallowed ground but simple dumb superstition, was safe when her husband was on the rampage.

Knowing any instant a window could break and she could be caught and dragged out, she knew she had to keep moving.

Where was he?

With the mirror snapped off her visibility was limited. He appeared beside the car. She pressed the brake so the brake lights would be warning enough, shifted into reverse, and began to back down the short drive hesitantly. He kept pace, tapping the window with his fingertips. She had to turn onto the street.

Guy vanished.

Oh no, I hit him!

She shifted into park immediately. Waited for him to reappear. When he didn't she flung open the door. He could be injured. Somehow it would be her fault. The ruse worked. Like a raptor seizing prey in crushing talons, he had her in his clutches. How detrimental compassion could be.

The man who was supposed to love her and protect was the one dragging her out into the street as if he were a soldier and she a suspected spy he planned on beating into divulging all her secrets.

The asphalt rushed up under her back and the collision forced flecks of tar and stone into her skin. It also knocked the wind out of her and she was left gasping. Such weight dropped on top of her chest she was pinned, flattened, and crushed simultaneously.

Clenching the sides of her head, fingers tangled in the long hair he in better times took pleasure in combing, he smashed her head into the jagged blacktop over and over. Constellations exploded inside her skull. Starbursts twirled kaleidoscopically, an array into which she seemed to fall…before coming up darkness.

Flashing lights neared. Cars came screeching up. Headlights lit the man ferociously beating a woman right there in the street…and no one did anything. More arrived. A crowd. The beating continued. Why weren't they helping?

When Guy looked up, realized he was staring down police spotlights, he sprinted into the night, a drunken maniac clad only in a pair of corduroy cutoffs and barefoot as the day he was born.

Woozy and shell-shocked, Jenene muscled to her feet and followed his lead. She absconded from the scene before anyone could get up in her face. She had no interest in answering questions. She drove to a nearby 24-hour gas station, sat in her car, and cried. Would she ever sleep comfortably again so long as she lived with her husband? Can anyone live for long under constant fear?

In short order there was a tap at her window.

The cop was familiar from her waitress job. His name was Johnny Black. He was a friendly, mildly flirty twenty-something. Good tipper. Boyish dimples augmented his handsome face. There was real concern on his face now.

"I had to make sure you're okay," he said. "Do you need medical aid?"

Dreadfully possible but she answered in the negative.

"Your husband got away. Do you know where he would be headed?"

Beyond a doubt but she answered in the negative to that too.

"Are you sure you don't want me to call you an ambulance?"

How bad did she look? Her head was thundering.

"He will show up sooner or later," he said. "When he does, you need to press charges."

"None of you tried to stop him," she said softly so as not to amplify the booming in her head.

"A husband beating his wife isn't a crime," he said regretfully.

"How did you know he wasn't just some guy attacking me?"

"Your neighbors provided information."

"It would have still been a crime had he killed me."

"Of course."

"I didn't know cops could stand by and let someone kill someone else. He might have killed me if he wasn't scared off."

"Press charges and that won't be a problem."

If I can't have you, no one can.

"I can't press charges," she said grimly, hating the position she was in, between the proverbial rock and hard place. "It would only set him off."

The look of pity that came into Officer Black's eyes made her head hurt worse. And what else was it in his eyes? Contempt? Was it because she was too weak to stand up to protect herself? He cared. He also looked down on her for what he perceived as either pigheadedness or weakness.

He wasn't done trying to convince her. "You would have no trouble attaining a restraining order."

There was a simple truth and she stated it, the best and only argument she had: "You think a piece of paper can protect me? You think it'll stop him from killing me?"

As soon as they let me out, I'll kill you.

"If you want this to stop," Officer Black said, as if it were that simple, "you need to press charges. If not my hands are tied."

Henceforth, at least for a time, the cop became a presence in her life. He bugged her with his near-constant presence, dogging her at her job, stalking her during errands, often cruising by the house. His pleas continued to fall on deaf ears. Even if she ignored him, she appreciated his tenacity.

It would take a more drastic set of events to get her out of the abusive marriage.

His words did get through slightly. Jenene began to think, as if it were a sentence she was serving, she had put in enough time. Maybe she should get out before she was anymore broken, anymore a hollowed husk.

Could she though…really?

It seemed impossible.

Jenene wouldn't hear from Guy for two days. She had to call in to his job sick for him. When he called, she hung up. When he called again, she let him talk. He wanted to know what happened.

Chapter 28
Defying Expectation

The zygote journeys to become a versatile fetus bivouacked on the protective uterine wall and from there develops into an inquisitive boy on an expeditionary mission….

The deliverance of sleep would have been the best part of her life. Instead it was when she was most vulnerable. She couldn't trust her husband's alcohol-fueled paranoia wouldn't lead to a late night assault.

Edginess was now a constant state of mind. It was only through always anticipating attack that she was prepared whenever an arbitrary setoff was triggered and wham, bam she was crying and bleeding from her lip.

Guy's behavior was so frustratingly bizarre. For as mercurial as he could be he could be as levelheaded. It was so exasperating. He had an amazing ability to give her hope. Lavish her with gifts. Take her out on the town. Be kind. Then he would snap because she said the wrong thing or a man gave her a glance he didn't appreciate. His mother claimed he would change eventually, that he would "grow up" and shed his abusive habits.

Sometimes the hope felt like rope he was dealing out. That way when he pulled the lever the fall would be worse. The trip through the trapdoor would end with enough snap to break another vertebrae in the spine of her will. The repeat treatment was succeeding in crippling her spiritually and emotionally; before long she was mentally a quadriplegic, her strength of mind paralyzed.

Still recovering from health scares and living with the prognosis that seemed to remove all her value in her husband's eyes, she underwent regular checkups even though she was so depressed her life had zero value. She accepted that death might very well come soon. In many ways she welcomed an end, any end. She just wondered why in the meantime she had to be punished so cruelly.

Any confidence she once had torpedoed, options were few. Dominated and controlled, her only choice was simple; she had to resign herself to her gilded cage. Her arduous path put on a lot of extra mileage. She was older than the sum of her years but felt no wiser. Her decisions had landed her in even worse bondage than the type she always sought to escape. Maybe recognizing as much showed she was getting wiser than she thought.

A most unexpected happenstance, she had no idea the change up she needed would soon be at hand.

The totally unexpected in the course of a regular hormone level check changed all—a series of events would be set in motion that revolutionized her whole life.

Shocking news in a doctor's office usually entails the sort of jarring information that leads to pain, degradation, and a darker outlook on life. This time she would find out that even for the desolate of soul miracles can happen.

Jenene was prescribed the birth control pill not for the usual purpose—she was told she was essentially sterile—but in hopes it would help combat the endometriosis. In that era there was no alternative treatment. To allow the body regular menstrual periods, a usual prescription involves a week of placebo white pills. Her prescription eschewed the off time. Which equated to no menstruating for months.

Avoiding the inconvenience of a period wasn't something to complain about but it was no less a reminder of her inadequacy as a woman.

If you can't even give me a baby what good are you?

The sort of hormone treatment she was undergoing could have less than ideal side effects. Among them was a possible decline in femininity. Her hormone levels had to be monitored closely. Between being on birth control and her tenuous health, she had no reason to think she could be with child.

It began with an excited nurse drawing the doctor's attention so eagerly he hurried to join her. They weren't out of earshot but the nurse took pains to hide what she told the doctor. She shielded her mouth with a hand, whispering hushedly but fervently.

Whatever her news, his reaction was one of abrupt surprise. Oh sheesh, Jenene thought. He whispered back as quietly but there was no mistaking his excitement. All Jenene could do was read their movements as if they were pantomime. In response to the doctor's solicitation, the nurse seemed to indicate something had been done three times.

What fresh hell will this be?

The doctor returned maybe a little nervously. "I have some, um, surprising news," he said bracingly.

"The faster you tell me, the sooner I can start dealing with it."

The doctor smiled charmingly, either to soften a blow or out of genuine happiness. It was hard to gauge. "Apparently…you're pregnant."

Jenene was thunderstruck, unsure in that instant how to feel. Accepting, yes. And happy: so very happy. But could she be hopeful too?

"Oh. Oh, wow. That's such a surprise." She had learned to ask a lot of questions and all she could think to do was try to glean more info. "Didn't you tell me that's not even possible? How can I be pregnant when I'm on the pill? Not to mention the diseases I have."

"We're as surprised as you. But it's true."

"It has to be a false-positive," Jenene concluded. "Run it again."

"It has been run again," the doctor replied, frowning. "Three times. You are beyond a doubt pregnant." Eyebrows upraised wonderingly, he shrugged. "This might be…a problem."

A baby?

Jenene was as shocked as she was elated. Pregnancy seemed like the last possibility. Her reproductive system was so bungled it had been months since her menstrual cycle kicked out a period. Yet here she was, expecting. The aloneness she felt her whole life lifted; gone was that feeling she had even among family and friends that she was somehow cut off and secluded. She wasn't alone, not anymore. She had a constant companion.

At once exhilarated, terrified, over-the-moon, overwhelmed, and eager, what struck her most was the instant hope that permeated her entire being. Suddenly she had value again. She had reason.

A pessimistic voice in the back of her head reminded her there were real setbacks.

Even if you were to get pregnant, you could never carry a baby to term.

The words resonated but had no mojo.

Would the doctor's diagnosis prove portentous?

Doctors aren't God, she thought. *They don't know me. And they don't know my baby.*

Since they had already flubbed part of it, her new hope made it impossible to believe they were right about the rest. She was determined to see her pregnancy through to a healthy conclusion—no matter how long the odds.

The medico's projections were dour beforehand. His mood became even bleaker upon learning there was a definite pregnancy. Despite the grim prognosis Jenene was aware of something he wasn't. She possessed and was possessed of an indomitable faith.

Her belief that she would have her baby was unshakeable, more ironclad than any endearment, truer than any oath of loyalty.

No matter what happened.
No matter how the daddy behaved.
No matter what the future brought.

Chapter 29
Improbable Pregnancy

I suppose the suspense in this portion of the story is undermined by the fact that I'm the storyteller. I don't think that mitigates that it qualifies as compelling reading. For me what my mom endured has never failed to be a source of inspiration. If she could bear what is presented forthwith, what stops any of us from believing we can get through even the toughest situations?

To determine a due date—hypothesis said October 1—the professionals went to the ultrasound. Based on the image of the fetus they determined the baby was about six weeks along.

Mindful not to be overzealous, Jenene went forth and spread the news.

Guy immediately, and to her relief, assumed the mantle of proud papa. Was it possible a child would mend the damage? Cool his fierier feelings? Make her husband the relatively ideal man he could be when he tried? At least a husband who didn't hit her?

Maybe a quixotic notion, upon seeing her husband's buoyant response, Jenene was optimistic physical violence would be prohibited. Time would verify her hope wasn't unrealistic. Not once would he lay a hand on her during the pregnancy. Though that didn't mean there was no abuse. Some real doozies, she would learn mind games replaced slaps and punches.

Lois was severe and questioning, Bob euphoric and overjoyed. Jeff was fearful but good at hiding it behind his natural exuberance. Bill and Lal were happy for her while Herb demonstrated his usual facade of indifference. Guy's family was all good cheer. Their few friends were full of good wishes.

Mary, over a year from the pregnancy of her first child, was kindheartedly envious, her oohs and ahs and words of encouragement meant to be paid forward in the future but all of it genuine just the same.

What mattered most was that Jenene had purpose again. With every chance she talked to her new companion. Sure on some level she was getting through, sure a developing mind was absorbing it all, she told her baby everything.

For all of a week everything seemed wonderful, even blissful. She was happy, her husband seemed like he was riding a cloud, and she felt healthy, at least healthy enough. Of course health concerns would cause the first crack in the facing of her bliss.

Jenene's first prenatal checkup established inescapable realities.

In the seven days since she learned of her pregnancy she inexplicably lost ten pounds. By no means had she eaten less. Such excuses amounted to little. Her doctor chewed her out stolidly. He lectured about how unacceptable it was to drop weight in her precarious condition. She had to recognize how important it was to get the right nourishment.

A period during which most women have little trouble gaining weight, this was the first sign Jenene would struggle to put on every pound.

At some point Dracula must have stole into her room and made a withdrawal. She was anemic. The most common blood disorder, the old sign of vampiric activity in cheap fiction was a sign that her health had to improve or her baby's health would be at risk.

A dietician was added to the lineup to moderate her weight and ensure she was getting the proper nutrition.

Well before the "Do a dollop of Daisy" ad campaign would make a similar case, she was taught about the wide variety of foods that went wonderfully with sour cream. She was introduced to a world in which sour cream was life's blood and should be as readily applied as most employ a dash of table salt. Sure, everyone knows about sour cream on tacos and whatnot. Jenene was taught to put it on items as diverse as pancakes.

Not that she was a calorie-counter. But she had always been overly conscious of being what she deemed too heavy. It was weird getting a lesson in gluttony.

If the baby required her to expand her diet and live altogether more healthily, there was no sacrifice too great. She was onboard for whatever lay ahead, even if that meant many doctor visits.

Every appointment included a blood draw. Poked so much it could be said she started feeling needled, before long Jenene was also feeling bled dry. She was tired of being siphoned.

Finally she asked, "If I'm anemic, how come you keep taking my blood?" She never got more answer than the cursory rigmarole about necessary tests and all that jazz. With little recourse other than acceptance, from this time forth she took the numerous pokes with good humor.

On Thursday, May 14, Jenene and Guy made an exodus from Minnesota to join Bob and Lois in Woodville, Wisconsin. Her parents had sold the Nite Club contract for deed. In the bargain they wound up with a house on Division Street in the sleepy village as the down payment.

The couple was invited for sake of celebrating Syttende Mai. The yearly Norwegian independence celebration includes a preponderance of Lena and Ole jokes, the Stipes Show carnival, and a variety of sumptuous Norwegian delights served up at the American Legion Hall.

Among the confections are crunchy rosettes and golden brown sandbakelse sugar cookies. Sinfully delightful rømmegrøt: a warm hearty porridge to which vanilla pudding's comparatively a distant cousin. And mouth-wateringly flaky lefse: rolls buttered or buttered and sugared, which make for a soft sweet crunch.

A day when they were seemingly a fun-loving couple in love, Jenene and Guy treated the long weekend as a mini vacation. They hit the garage sales pushed by the locals, the carnival, and in the evening wound up driving to Spring Valley. Guy expressed a desire to see her tromping grounds. Jenene was all too happy to oblige.

In the interim since learning of the pregnancy Guy really seemed happy. In some ways he was very happy. Still. She was aware his valves remained; she was oblivious to the crazy pressure accumulating behind them. Even though later on his restraint would be less marvelous, at the onset he could at least hide his anger and resentments. On their trip she was going to get an unwelcome glimpse at the strain playing proud papa to her popular new mama put him under.

From her high school to the country's largest earthen dam, she guided him on a parade lap of the sunken town. She told stories and they made jokes. The culmination of the trip found them at the local playground. They proceeded to have a lot of fun. Flirting playfully they got tickles in their tummies swinging and going down the slide.

They were on the teeter-totter when Guy's dark side reared its monstrous head.

On the teeter-totter what does the meanie do to trick his victim into a vulnerable position? He convinces them that to achieve fluid seesawing they're in it together. He convinces them they're involved in good play. At some point after trust is established he brings his victim up only to slip off the board, removing all counterbalance weight. For the victim the next part involves dropping like a stone onto their tailbone.

When Guy acted out the meanie it was so unexpected the impact knocked the wind out of Jenene and left her gasping for breath. Aftershocks from the earthquake that rumbled up the fault line of her spine recoiled through her body.

Was he trying to make her miscarry? Or was he just a jerk who liked shaking things up by dropping his pregnant wife on her can?

Jenene was furious but given past experience quelled expressing her feelings. The last thing she wanted to do was act as instigator. She didn't want to in any way push him to act with the sort of brutality that would lead to an expulsion of bloody tissue that had been her baby.

One afternoon later that May Jenene received one of those phone calls that comes out of the blue and changes everything. Guy had been "mildly" injured at work. As a precaution he had been transported to the hospital.

Jenene rushed to the ER only to be told he had been transferred. Peculiar. They explained he had been brought in because of a head injury.

There was a fire in the machine shop. A locked gate separated the fire engines from the blaze. To let them in he heroically crashed the gate with a forklift and in the process took a blow to the skull. The problem was the injury wasn't so severe that it prevented his unhinged mouth and addled brain from getting him reassigned to the psych ward.

Whatever he had said or done that had landed him there wasn't revealed to Jenene. Seizing opportunity like a pickpocket an unguarded wallet, she was determined to keep him locked up for his own good. There was obviously something wrong with him. Any man who seemed to take pleasure in beating and subjugating his wife had to be suffering from mental illness.

Sure enough, during his time under observation, he would be labeled paranoid schizophrenic. The only way he would be treated was if it were forced upon him and Jenene felt it was the right choice; his mother felt otherwise and signed him out. This before she brought him home with her, where since he had a little time off work, he took a vacation. He emptied their checking account to stay in pizza and beer while living it up.

It was so frustrating. Guy was her husband, yet because his mother had an unhealthy hold on him, his loyalty remained with her even if he loathed her for all the neglect of his childhood. His mother could exploit him, fire him up, make him seethe, but she didn't have to get abused by him, didn't have to take the blows while he roared, "You're just like my mother," because he would never beat the true source of his rage.

The whole time he was gone Jenene's worry was only magnified. How could she anticipate what to expect from him? Other than to conclude it wouldn't be good. Even with an apparent moratorium on hitting, he made her roil from the suspense of expectation. What might he do next?

Even during ceasefires there are casualties.

Guy came home. Life resumed.

After the injury and confinement, Guy became steadily crankier, meaner, and more unpredictable. A lifetime of paranoia coupled with her inescapable actions, was it any wonder he reassessed Jenene an adversarial traitor?

Of course her doing nothing to see him freed was nothing less than treacherous, not an attempt to save his life and by proxy her own. No, her actions were purely self-serving. Being locked up was bad enough. Being locked up for purpose of assessing his mental stability was nightmarish. She could've worked to alleviate his torment and no motive, excuse, or explanation could change that.

Oh how she hoped he would get the treatment he needed. Instead she got a husband more mistrustful than ever.

It would be long after the conclusion of their relationship that he took mental health care seriously. When he did, he found the psychological stability that eluded him for so long. In his early twenties he was too immature to respect psychiatry or have a perspective open to criticism or judgment. Had he, the accident at work might've proven a positive turning point and not an excuse to wage a psychological war against his wife.

The mind games escalated, became crueler, and stripped away every vestige of security.

One example was when he arrived home from work early and announced he had been fired. Right up until he went to bed he maintained his story. This meant throughout the rest of the night Jenene was on edge. There was good reason for her agitation. No job meant they had no medical insurance. She wept nearly until dawn when she finally cried herself to sleep.

It was only when her duplicitous husband went to work per usual that she knew it was a mind game.

Jenene deliberated over the next several months of numerous doctor appointments, nagging worry, and mental abuse. She sought answers to why she had made such shackling decisions when all she ever wanted was freedom.

Chapter 30
Pregnancy Blues

A burning hot June—the halfway mark.

Being too much of a homebody quickly plagued Jenene with cabin fever. Outside routines were established as a safeguard against forsaking her wits to tedium. She sorely missed working. Her pregnancy was too high risk, so her doctor reminded her regularly. Short a job to go to she still needed outside stimulus.

Eventually she became a representative of Mary Kay. The work was fantastic and required minimal effort for a lot of constructive contact, the sort of networking she always enjoyed.

Never one to let hard feelings put up barricades, Jenene's routine included a stopover at Sambo's, where she still had friends among her former coworkers and the regulars. It was important to be with upbeat people.

Besides good company the indulgence of a layered ice cream sundae with extra whipped cream, made with love by her friends, drew her like a moth to light. If she had to pack in the calories, why not pamper her sweet tooth?

On one such visit what transpired would be another major event of the pregnancy. The New Port police chief, Fred, joined her for coffee. The friendship had prospered and he had proven good for a laugh, some gossip, or a touch of advice. Soft of heart but not character, he was an older gent who wore a glorious thick white mustache and highway patrol silver sunglasses. Thin as a rail and long-faced, his slightness of physique belied a pervasive if subtle personality.

Jenene all at once began feeling ill in that all encompassing way that can overtake you so suddenly you feel invaded.

Fred watched the change overcome her face as color drained from her features. To say the least, witnessing the speedy transition jarred him. His eyes zeroed in on her neck. "Excuse me," he said, seized her wrist, and watched the dial on his wristwatch turn. Shook his head disbelievingly. "I need to take you to the hospital right now."

What now?

"Wait a sec—"

"I can see the beat of your pulse in your throat," he said. "I counted and your heart is running like a jackhammer."

"Do I really need to go to the hospital?"

"You could have a heart attack or a stroke so I would say yes indeed," he replied solemnly. "Now come on. I don't want to have to go home to my wife and tell her I let a nice pregnant lady die today."

Topping out at 160 beats per minute, the impromptu visit to what was then called Ramsey Hospital may very well have averted her heart from going pop like a firecracker. The tachycardia arrhythmia was a dangerous warning concerning the shakiness of her health. Weekly visits to a cardiologist were added to her roster of appointments.

With her life so heartbreakingly full of anxiety was it any wonder she had heart distress?

Another drug on the long list she was accruing, she was prescribed medication to control her heart rate. It came with a warning that it would need to be out of her system when she went into labor. It was necessary in the meantime due to concerns continued tachycardia would cause cardiac arrest, even sudden cardiac death.

Near the end of the pregnancy this would become a concern. She would have to consider each morning whether to take the pill, asking the baby in her womb, "Will it be today that you come?" On many of those days the answer was no as the pregnancy came to far exceed the early October due date.

There was a reason for the importance: with the drug in her system her heartbeat would be too slow to deliver and could potentially lead to terrible complications. Her baby could even die.

Bed rest was ordered for the remainder of the pregnancy.

Maybe it was bad taste to take the opportunity to read *Helter Skelter: The True Story of the Manson Murders*. The bestseller laid out all of the lurid details of how the pregnant actress Sharon Tate died.

That was the summer of *Raiders of the Lost Ark* and the Steven Spielberg blockbuster would be the only non-horror film Jenene and Guy would see together in the theater.

The adventure yarn starring Harrison Ford in the iconic role of Indiana Jones so enthralled Jenene that as her bladder rebelled and the need for a pit stop became excruciating, she refused to go to the restroom.

The reason had nothing to do with missing an important plot element. Indy was going to run afoul of the Nazis no matter what (and triumph in the end), so she wasn't worried missing a few minutes would leave her baffled. The problem was that even as she was getting drawn into the story, Guy was next to her fidgeting, and she feared if she walked out he would be waiting to bar her from returning to finish the movie because he was bored by a story lacking enough gore.

Had they been aware of the astonishing effects driven finale, involving flesh melting off Nazis' bones, Jenene wouldn't have needed to worry. Nor would she have been forced to suffer through to the end, teeth floating and feeling as if she were dying. A credit to Mr. Spielberg, a true maestro of Hollywood and an even better storyteller, and his genius collaborator, Mr. George "May the Forced Be With You" Lucas, it was worth it.

Without air conditioning, Jenene and Guy could agree on one thing, getting out of the house was preferable to cooking inside it.

They spent the hottest days of the summer lounging down on Grey Cloud Island in the tranquil waters. Due to The Seniors being longstanding residents of the community in good stead, Jenene had many connections, including access to the sprawling current-driven lake somehow connected in a roundabout way to the Mississippi.

Beneficent Bill provided a couple of gigantic tractor inner tubes. Jenene would lounge in the cool water while Guy mostly fished between dips. Floating in the water was the only time she found comfort. The baby inside her was a furnace and combined with the summer hotness, she was always overheated and sometimes overwhelmed by hot flashes.

Fishing was enough of a placation Guy would behave and not ruin their outing. It may have helped that they were isolated, away from the rest of the world in a pastoral rural sprawl, where he didn't have to posture like the cock of the walk to feel secure. All his bad behavior, from the passive-aggressive barbs to the outbursts of violence, was a manifestation of his insecurity.

As much as Guy detested her pregnancy while professing to be extremely happy at the prospect of fatherhood it was impossible for his actions to not sometimes reveal his true feelings. This made Jenene certain a fiasco was at all times brewing.

This also made her an involuntary bulimic. Her stomach was a wary traveler headed through hostile territory always prepared to toss its bags aside to seek cover. Since it wasn't like being sick with the flu, when there was no desire to eat, she learned to reload the cannon. Her dietician was always stressing the importance of proper nutrition and how even if she tossed her cookies, she still had to eat.

This led to Guy getting what could be termed sympathy hunger pangs.

For example there was an evening they went to a restaurant to satiate one craving. Each ate a full meal. Jenene needed to visit the ladies room. After her stomach settled following a full evacuation, they hit another restaurant to slake a different hankering. Jenene ordered her second full dinner and Guy followed suit. The thing of it was Guy didn't get sick yet he still doubled up on his intake, which meant putting on weight was not the problem for him that it was for her.

Guy started a solid 180lbs. By the end of the pregnancy he was a fluffy 230lbs.

The Thursday before the Labor Day weekend Jenene was feeding their cats when it happened.

Besides her kitty Tricia, there was Guy's cat Bandit. As she lowered his dish toward the floor Bandit launched himself unexpectedly at her hand. Something akin to madness possessed his eyes. Before she could react he sank his teeth into the index finger of her right hand. The pain was immediate and intense.

After a quick shake, he beat a skittering retreat. She was left stunned and bleeding.

Throughout the day the pain in her finger was enormous. As evening descended and not only had the soreness not diminished but was joined by heat and pulsation, she began to think she had a problem.

On the quest for activities to fill her time, she was a representative for Mary Kay. She liked the products and it was fun to make sales. She was emceeing a meeting that night at a host location. Even with a good excuse to cancel, she went ahead and put the skills inherited from her dad to use. The ladies were enjoying the presentation until they noticed a red streak traveling up her right wrist.

Oh how wonderful it was always having to go to the hospital. Things tended to get worse when she got there and this instance was no different. Before she arrived the worry was bad enough. Her concern was magnified tenfold when the triage nurse gave her complaint one look and immediately guided her back to an exam room without even signing in. You know you're in trouble when the minutia of paperwork is overlooked. It pretty much means you're dying.

A lot of bad times in her life and there was really nothing comparable to sitting there with an IV pumping antibiotics into her arm to combat the serious blood infection caused by the cat bite. It didn't help that she felt she was getting the inquisitor's thumbscrews.

"Where's the cat?"

"I don't know," she said, not sure where he might be, "he bit me and took off."

"Hm-hmm, interesting. Did he show signs of illness?"

"He seemed fine...."
"Does he have regular outside access?"
"He goes out, yes...."
"Did he display any strange behavior?"
"I already told you, he seemed normal."
"Has the cat been vaccinated?"
"No. We didn't think—"
"Do you think it possible he was exposed to rabies?"

Rabies? She had no idea. She suspected the possibility he was infected would become a huge factor.

Next morning she checked into the hospital.

Even as they advised against it she had insisted on going home. They only let her because they took her word when she promised she would return. She had wanted to find Bandit. Find him and see that he was fine, that the whole attack thing was only a feline freak out. Cats can get that dazed yet frenetic look in their eyes and act with irrational disregard; it's a sliver of wildness no amount of domesticity can quite quell.

But Bandit was missing.

Guy was furious. Everything was Jenene's fault. She forced his cat to bite her so she could get more attention because boy-oh-boy was she an attention whore. And then she punished the cat for her dastardly insurrection by driving him away. It was all a conspiracy to drive down Guy's life.

Jenene was told that she was the first pregnant woman in modern times that had possibly been bitten by a rabid animal. Local doctors didn't know how to proceed. At the time rabies shots were injected straight into the abdomen, counter indicated when a fetus in the womb was so short a distance away.

"So the cat hasn't been vaccinated against rabies?"
"Unfortunately, no," she reiterated.

An expert came all the way from New Orleans; he would bring the vaccine and participate in the debate concerning whether to use it. Lying in a hospital bed surrounded by an obstetrician, a pediatrician, a hand surgeon, a gynecologist, and the import from New Orleans, Jenene couldn't speak over the cacophony of overlapping voices vying for supremacy. Did she have something so say? They answered her questions as quickly as they appeared in her mind. Only the answers were in no way definitive nor, in fact, were they even very informative.

Where could the injection go if not the stomach?
Would the vaccine go through the placenta?
If it did…would the fetus be killed?

The incomparability of the case seemed to be the top problem; without some precedent to reference they were blind men traversing a danger-filled obstacle course. Only if they tripped, slipped, or fell, it was a young mother and her baby that would be the ones taking the hit.

Once rabies sets in it is incurable and a horrible way to die, so a decision had to be made.

All Jenene was certain of was no needle should go into her pregnant tummy. The very thought turned her stomach. An IV in each arm, she clutched the stands as she vomited dark green bile, a gross ichor her agitated liver expelled.

The alternative would turn out to be immensely painful and would make her equally squeamish, so there were no easy fixes.

There was also no vote, no real end to the debate: facts were facts and without the cat's brain to study, they had to assume Jenene was infected. In the end she underwent seven injections. One decision was crystal-clear. Rather than abdominal injections the needle was plunged right into the wound in her finger.

Nerve cornucopias, fingers are very sensitive.

To add insult to injury, Bandit's body would be discovered by the police and autopsied. Even though finding the cat dead seemed a sure indication of disease, the post mortem revealed poison killed the cat, not rabies. Suspicion fell on a neighbor who had shown disapproval of Bandit's perchance for wandering onto his property. Without proof, no charges were filed. In the end no culprit was ever verified.

Guy blamed Jenene. "You killed my cat," he proclaimed. "He bit you and he died."

She was poison. Contagious. Typhoid Mary's more pregnant but no less infectious cousin.

Chapter 31
Dovetail

Terrible news came in mid-September.

Bob was in an induced coma. This followed an operation to staple his stomach. He was obsessed with weight loss. In those days the ramifications of the operation were less predictable than today. The surgery was supposed to be easier than eating better and exercising. So what if it put his life in the crosshairs.

Maybe it was his way of reaping all the stress she had sowed and putting it back in her basket.

At the end of each day he remained unresponsive, she waited for Guy to leave for the nightshift and headed to the hospital to spend the night close to her dad. She had to be there to hold his hand. Give consolation. Offer words of encouragement. Sure he could hear. Certain he was listening.

Despite his pitfalls her love for him never diminished even if her respect for him took a couple hits. Even though his decisions placed her in an intolerable environment and largely sacrificed any chance she had of enjoying the latter part of her childhood, she understood why he had made those choices.

At an age when many boys of his generation were concerned about making the team, from fourteen onward he endured a crash course in life. Not many can claim they were the masons of their own groundwork but Bob chiseled every stone, shaped every brick, and laid every single one with determination and perseverance. His foundation certainly couldn't be attributed to any source other than him. He was truly a self-made man, never content to be a pencil pusher, an assistant, or a follower.

Due date less than a month away and brimming with pregnancy, on her way by the nurse's station someone would always remind her half-humorously, half-seriously, "Remember, don't go into labor." Being the Veteran's hospital, since no one is born in uniform, it wasn't equipped with a maternity ward.

During one of those long nights she received a stern message. It concerned the mortalities of the child in her womb and her father.

Clutching his hand as if it were a talisman, Jenene prayed for her dad. All she wanted was to see him better. Alone with him in the hospital room, she heard a voice suddenly, quite distinctly separate from her, report bluntly and dispassionately: "You can't have both. Your father or your son will die."

Son? She wasn't even aware of her baby's sex. Several had predicted a girl for one reason or other. Were all the old wives tales wrong? She was chilled because her intuition told her what she had heard was true. The message struck a chord instantly with a dissonant note that would resound until she gave birth.

Who would want to believe such a communication? She wanted to disregard it, forget it, and never think about it again. All she could do was wait for her baby to be born. If the baby were a boy maybe she would tell her dad…to be careful. What else could she do?

She knew what he would ask.

Did she have a dream? But it wasn't a dream; it was a direct communication…if it was a message. That remained to be seen. Or so she told herself, even if the thrum of that inharmonious note echoed and reechoed on the flipside of her mind.

On the face of it in fair enough health after the crisis, Bob woke and went home.

Chapter 32
Countdown

When the October due date and then Guy's birthday on the eighth came and went the proud daddy became the anxious papa and finally the impatient father.

The due date gathering dust, Jenene secretly felt her unwillingness to release the individual in her womb could be to blame. Once the baby was born, she would not be in so protective a position. Nor would she be protected herself the moment she no longer served as an incubator. How soon before the moratorium on violence ended and she was on the receiving end of a painful reminder of old times?

If Guy's actions were any indication, she had reason to worry. In the final month he was the scariest he would ever be, a veritable madman. What were his motives? She stopped speculating.

One night Guy produced one of the meanest looking French knives imaginable from a kitchen drawer and went searching for Jenene. Whether it was for her or only her goat, he was hunting. No doubt the tarnished foot-long blade could hack or slice. The tip came to the kind of sharp point that ensured a forceful stab would send the blade deep through vulnerable flesh.

He brought this wicked tool with him into the living room.

Stopped and stood there.

Jenene lounged on the couch. She was unaware of what he was up to until his instant of inaction drew her attention. What she looked up into was the wild fixed stare of something she recognized as genuinely dangerous.

Ice water gushed through her veins. The knife tip directed right at her, positioned between those two wide bloodshot eyes, was the most terrifying sight of her life. Adrenaline surged. Harassment, hectoring, and manipulation were one thing. Brandishing a knife was off the charts.

Bursting with mad luminescence, those eyes were the craziest she'd ever seen them, beyond a doubt the craziest she'd ever had misfortune of seeing.

He was smiling too. It was a frighteningly knowing smile. A wide maniacal rictus like a split wound, the sort of unhinged grin that strikes fear due to its mysterious yet invocative nature.

"What's that for?" she enquired hesitantly.

"I'm gonna cut the baby out of you!" Guy proclaimed gleefully.

Holy shit he's really going to kill me this time!

Suddenly she was a girl in one of the horror flicks he insisted on dragging her to; oh how she hated those movies! Not really. They could be good too. It was the lack of variety that vilified the genre. What had she thought when she saw those movies? What everyone thinks. She would be smarter than the players on the screen. In the situation, it became quickly apparent her options were few.

Jenene was up and over the couch in a flash. Stomach pressed into the corner, she screamed bloody murder. She blared so loudly her voice carried through two sets of closed windows. Her scream had to be quite blood curdling. Within an instant they could hear sirens.

Whatever the neighbors told the police, it worked. Maybe they said they were hearing a murder. Maybe history had a bearing. Either way, in short order law enforcement came knocking....

A calm and cheerful Guy met them at the door with a chuckle. When they barged in he had a ready excuse.

All too aware of the sort of violence exhibited on the premises, Johnny Black led the way. "We've gotten reports of screaming," he said. "What's going on here?"

"We were playing Helter Skelter," Guy said as if it were perfectly reasonable to reference the horrific murder of Sharon Tate by the minions of Charles Manson.

"I wasn't playing," Jenene said, once again emerging.

Guy chuckled. "Just a game," he reassured. "She's just looking for some attention."

"Well, keep it down," the other officer advised, ready to wash his hands of the pair.

Johnny Black's eyes bore into her reprovingly, trying to convey what it would be inappropriate for him to say. His dimples darkened his face when his lips were cast in a frown.

"Sure thing, officers," Guy said. "So sorry to cause a problem."

Jenene listened to the exchange and was outraged. Disbelieving yet not surprised, she said, "You're just going to leave me with him?"

"Charges would have to be pressed," the other officer said. "Without that—"

"Your hands are tied," she finished. "Thanks a lot for your help. If he kills me, will your reports reflect that I felt threatened? No. Well, I didn't think so anyway."

And they left.

As she hid upstairs in the bedroom, worrying he would come and she would see the glint of that huge tarnished blade, it was impossible not to speculate about what Guy's terror tactics were doing to the baby in her womb. Game or no game, the fear he was inspiring had to be causing undo stress on the baby. Her anxiety nearly had her pulling out her hair. She could only guess how twisted up he was making her bundle of joy.

As her husband exhibited increasingly terrifying behaviors, Jenene received support from a surprise source. She got a call from her mom every day of that seemingly endless final month. Lois wanted to know how she was feeling, how she was coping. She also wanted to know if she was going to take her heart pill.

The concern was welcome because it demonstrated her mom cared. So often she doubted. In those days so wide did all that was deemed unquestionable make the wedge between them, the daily communication was at once supremely heartening and almost mystical.

Where doubt still lay was in her motive. Was her concern for Jenene…or her future grandchild? Either way it was elevating to see the ice maiden could be thawed enough to have warmth in her heart for something other than insurance claims.

Those phone calls meant more than the priciest gifts. They broke away some of the hardened feelings like plaque scraped off teeth. She always viewed Lois as incisive if remote. When she reached out it meant so much more. What advice she had to offer was welcome.

As the days wore on, Jenene decided to test the credence of various methods of triggering labor suggested to her by friends, family, and strangers. Basically anyone who heard she was past her due date. One bit of advice was to drive around on the bumpy roads. That was sure to rattle loose the baby.

Guy offered to take her for a drive, seeing another opportunity to terrorize her. In no condition to pilot by herself Jenene would come to regret accepting but that was what she did.

There was a patch of backcountry betwixt St. Paul Park and Afton where the farm roads were sufficiently bouncy and remote. They set off in a dusty blue '65 Chrysler New Port they acquired incidentally while they were still living in New Port. The mother of one of Orville's friends finagled that deal; she had needed a winter car and once she had the Chrysler she was able to park her Camaro at the farm.

There were huge roller coaster hills leading to their destination. It was at the top of one of these, the biggest, as they were about to descend, that Guy's crazy needle peaked and he said, "We're going to die tonight," so matter-of-factly she believed the conviction in his voice.

The engine revved and roared as he pushed down the pedal and propelled them down the hill.

Her stomach dropped like a stone as effervescent tickles washed upward.

Guy stared right at her with his piercing blue eyes, once so beautiful to her, and all she saw in them was a consolidated gleeful vacuity, as if he knew nothing of how awful and scary he was being while deriving incredible almost orgasmic pleasure from her suffering. He refused to look at the road. Had a deer wandered out they would have emulsified it without so much as slowing down even if a hoof went through the windshield and staked one of them right through the head.

She couldn't help but oscillate her eyes between his maniacal face and the oncoming road rushing at them with such speed she was plastered in her seat in anticipation of another end-over-end wreck. With her last car accident still visible in the rearview mirror of her life, to apply a car analogy, she flashed back to the terrifying experience and expected it to be repeated.

By the time they reached the bottom of the hill they had gained enough momentum the Plymouth shot up the abrupt incline so fast it seemed there was no way he could hold it straight on the rough narrow road. Not when his eyes were centered on her and the car's alignment was only so-so when pushed so hard. The whole front end was wobbling.

Oh god, what if they blew a tire?

The next guarantee of possible calamity lay just over the hill. A short distance from the summit was an intersection. Not a busy junction by any means but one crossed often just the same. If Guy were still flooring it when they topped the hill where the road became flat there would be precious little time to stop if some unfortunate traveler happened to be in the middle of the crossroads.

Would they be able to stop in time? Even if he locked up the brakes and left most of his tires scorched to the blacktop? Even if they were able to stop and the seatbelt prevented her from shooting out the windshield, would the strain damage her enough to go into shock, compromising her baby?

The summit lay right ahead, then the intersection, and who knew what else. The car reached the apex so fast it almost seemed to leave the road and land with a jerk…and all at once they were decelerating.

"Well that didn't work," Guy grumped and took them home without any more explanation.

What the hell?

As October ticked down and Halloween approached, Jenene thought it would be just her luck the baby would be born on All Hallows Eve. Rosemary had at least labored under the pretense Satan hadn't fathered her child, Jenene wasn't so sure. Was he possessed? Was he a demon masquerading as a man? Was he just a really sick man lacking healthy coping mechanisms?

Overcome by a strong nesting instinct, in the waning days of October Jenene cleaned the house until it was so immaculate the linoleum and countertops sparkled, the carpet was teased and plush, and every piece of laundry folded neatly. Encumbered by a massive pregnant stomach, the task was enormous but the benefit of the distraction outweighed the discomfort.

On Halloween she prepared a pan of lasagna. Boiled the long rectangular and ruffled noodles. Prepped a hearty red sauce loaded with ground beef. Grated mozzarella cheese. Finally layered everything together and put the dish in the oven to bake while she scrubbed the bathroom tiles, washed the shower curtain, and made sure the mirror gleamed spotlessly. Bathroom cleaning was endless because her husband was a hairy beast; she had never seen so much hair in a drain and the speed with which it accrued never ceased to amaze.

With a gutful of Italian food, Guy went to work and Jenene was left alone to deal with trick-or-treaters.

By bedtime she was fairly certain her baby had skipped the Celtic based holiday co-opted into a toothless fun day for little kiddies and adult revelry alike.

Three in the morning by the alarm clock on her bedside table, meaning it was officially November 1, Jenene rose and went into the bathroom to relieve her near-bursting bladder. She had finished and was standing before the sink when a hot gush soaked her feet instantly. The flood of viscous fluid saturated the rug and made a puddle.

With no conclusion other than her water had broken, Jenene dialed Ramsey Hospital for advice.

Once her identity was established, the voice on the line said, "Come in immediately."

"Can't I wait until morning when my husband gets home from work," she suggested. "It's my first pregnancy. I understand I can expect labor to last a long time."

No good. They knew her at Ramsey. Knew her case too well to agree she procrastinate the inevitable.

Jenene's next call was to Guy's factory. "Do I really need to come home?" he asked bad-temperedly.

"They said to come right away."

He sighed. "Fine."

Jenene hung up the phone. Looked around the house. The whole place was sparkling, so spic and span she would be glad to bring her baby here. The only mess she would leave was minor; the lasagna pan. She left it soaking in the sink, too excited to scuff her nails busying herself with the damn thing when she felt better waiting at the door with her bag. She was happy and scared, conflicted but certain, and knew only one thing concretely: her baby meant everything to her.

Having isolated and broken her, Guy probably thought he had all the leverage. He probably harbored no doubt he would own her in perpetuity. Like a fat king secure on his opulent throne, he had no thought of insurrection; no idea how much having a baby would change his servile wife. Or how her new sense of responsibility would force her to regain what strength she once had and multiply it tenfold.

That it would lend to a mutinous state of mind….

Chapter 33
Arrival

Eighteen hours of labor has a way of making a young woman take stock of her life and reassess everything she had thought was painful, hard to endure, or trying.

Born at 8:46PM on November 1, 1981, my father's first words were: "He's too ugly to be mine." Because of his genetics specifically, I will never be what most consider attractive, so he was one to talk.

"Get him out of here!" Jenene screamed, legs up in the stirrups, having just experienced what felt an eternity that ended with a double episiotomy to prevent her from tearing.

A large mirror was situated straight above so she could witness the birth. What she would have rather not witnessed was the scalpel blade going to work on her lady business. Even worse lay ahead. The placenta was still rooted to the uterine wall and would necessitate sectional removal. A painful procedure needed to be performed, and it would be a waking nightmare she would endure without the benefit of a supportive husband by her side.

Another example of archaism in a modern hospital, the crude chop job was performed with a scalpel implemented in a fashion seemingly similar to a spinning blender blade. Had she been one of those new age types into placentophagy who feel dining on their placenta essential, she would have had to be satisfied with a pâté.

Any of the number of cultures that believe the placenta is the deceased twin of the surviving child would probably deem her cursed.

Two nurses and a pair of orderlies were situated like a human four-point restraint to hold her still while work more the forte of a back alley abortionist than a credible obstetrician was executed. Quite involuntarily the pain forced her to twist, thrash, and fight for her life, as if she was an accused witch in the hands of sadistic inquisitors. The restrainers grappled to keep her pinned. At last the doctor ordered, "Give her more gas! She's in too much pain for me to work!"

Instants later she was floating, the ceiling an inch above her nose.

The trauma of giving birth would leave her with a collapsed uterus and bladder. The obstetrician proved a capable puzzle assembler and she was left intact cosmetically and aesthetically, her uterus somehow restored with the deft movements of his fingers and the two cuts to her labia to prevent tearing sewn with such precision they would heal almost overnight.

As for her bladder, it wouldn't be re-inflated for two months, after she had rested up and could again endure incredible anguish. She would learn using compressed air to blow up your bladder like a balloon rates up there with an all-time top pain.

As if experiencing a demonic menstrual cycle, she would bleed heavily for the next four or five days. Postpartum bleeding is expected but obstetrical hemorrhaging can be a life-threatening crisis. After scraping her clean of placental debris, any piece of which could have caused critical infection, all they could do was monitor and make sure blood loss didn't exceed safe levels.

In the aftermath all Jenene wanted to do was hold her baby…hold her son.

This would only happen upon my initial extrauterine appetite, at which time Jenene was asked if I could be given formula. "Absolutely not," she said. "I am breastfeeding my son." The insistence may have been the only way she would have seen me in the first hours of my outside-the-womb life.

People in the medical profession think they know everything.

Seeing as how accusations of infidelity had been one of Guy's techniques of breaking down Jenene psychologically, is it any wonder he would deny his first child?

Of course he has denied such events ever transpired but if there is one thing I've learned about my biological father, he is a master liar and has spent the better part of the last three decades trying to manipulate a revisionist history to shed sunny rather than stormy light on his actions.

His rejection was short lived evidentially. Despite his insulting exclamation, while Jenene was recovering from one nasty and painful emulsification of fleshy matter in her womb, Guy went ahead and forced his name to be my birthright, which made it so that to this day I don't identify with any name.

One of very few schoolgirl fantasies, she had dreamed of calling me A.J. because of Hall of Fame racecar driver A.J. Foyt.

A perk of Bob's racing days, when she was a little girl Mr. Foyt spent the night at their house in Cottage Grove. He made quite the impression. A big surly looking black cricket trundled across the basement floor and gave her quite a start. Playing hero, he dealt with the cricket and won her admiration. Too young to understand the response he elicited, he would remain fixed in her head as a sort of ideal man.

Jenene would not learn of Guy's nefarious duplicity until she went to bestow my intended name and was informed her baby's christening was a done deal.

In the modern age the law stipulates that a child's name is flexible for six months. Not the case in 1981. I was sidled—cursed—with that name for twenty-two years.

There was a reason I came despite all the obstacles.

The educated assurances my conception was next to impossible, that even if a sperm were to miraculously run the gamut and infiltrate an egg the resulting existence would have no chance of reaching a level of maturity that would guarantee life, meant nothing in the end. I was coming…with a mission. The irony is really quite striking. Guy provided the genetic material for the being destined to rescue Jenene from his monstrous side.

I inherited Jenene's light blue almost hazel eyes. To my benefit, blue eyes such as my dad's are manipulatively blue, deep reservoirs too easily mesmerizing; it's only after you have fallen into them that you realize they are abysses and you are trapped and drowning.

On the record, I was born anatomically perfect, every measurement what was at the time considered optimal, and according to everyone else who ever saw me as an infant I was adorable.

After the complication of a retained placenta, Jenene's hospital stay was assured to be long.

The time of convalescence lent to introspection. A son, just as the voice had predicted that day in the Veteran's Hospital. Was it an insight borne out of fear, a prediction that had a fifty percent chance of being true no matter what and was only a coincidence? Her father had been lying there in a coma, after all.

Or should she be truly concerned? Her gut feeling was yes, she should be. Her inner monologue made her acutely aware of the way the voices in her head and more importantly of her head sounded. The voice that spoke those possibly prophetic words was not one of hers. Never before had she wished for a dream but in this case she thought one might act as a guidepost by which she could direct her action.

If you're there, she would think, *tell me what you meant…and why it would have to be that way. Why would either my son or my father have to die?*

Her parents visited to meet their first grandchild. To her delight Bob was ecstatic and ruddy with pride; Lois was all smiles. Later, after we were home, my next visit would be to the farm, where the whole family would gather to greet the new baby and I would experience my first exposure to The Seniors. I was a big hit, apparently. When she was fettered by her shaky health to a hospital room she was certain of as much. Lois visited every day we were there.

The bleeding had cleared up near the end of day four and seemed finished on day five. Jenene took her first bath since giving birth. The soak was revitalizing and relaxing and by the time she stepped out onto a towel her concerns, be they many, were less taxing. Then a blob of matter the size of a baseball fell out of her vagina into her palm. It looked like a bloody chunk of liver.

Understandably concerned, she screamed for the nurse, who rushed in and immediately allayed her fears. A blood clot had been expelled. It was a positive sign. It meant she was healing.

For her taste it was one nasty good omen.

In total Jenene spent a productive if tedious and monotonous week in the hospital. She would be released one day before her baby, a separation she found unbearable.

A poke in the bottom of my tender little heel determined my bilirubin level and what was to be the final test showed I was too low to go home. Connected to the process of the liver, sinking levels can cause jaundice and become dangerous. Jenene had to leave me in a glass container meant to regulate my bilirubin by ultraviolet exposure.

Guy picked her up after work in the morning. He took her to breakfast at a long-gone greasy spoon called Woody's. Separation anxiety gave her what would be the closest feeling to postpartum depression she would experience. Jenene couldn't stop crying.

No sympathy came from her husband. He was too busy rolling his eyes and being annoyed; meanwhile the waitress completely understood and the juxtaposition of the two responses really demonstrated Guy's failings as a human being.

Going home empty handed made her cry. When she saw the house after her time away, she sobbed.

Despite leaving it spotless, the place looked like a frat after a blowout. Ashtrays overflowed with butts. Piles of dishes, including the lasagna pan, were heaped in the sink and everywhere Guy had eaten: the couch, the coffee table, the end tables, and the living room floor. There were enough beer cans to erect an aluminum Christmas tree seven feet tall. And dirty stinky clothes were strewn about as if a missile hit a laundry truck.

Adamant that she wanted to breastfeed, the schedule required her to make a trip to the hospital every four hours. In the meantime she cleaned and cried while her unilaterally centric husband slept.

Having a baby was detrimental to Jenene's marriage for the simple fact that her attention had to be divided and it's probably obvious whom she preferred. Rather than make having a baby a shared experience, Guy chose to view me as a rival (maybe for good reason).

Jenene's job was to care for me and it irked him how committed her focus. This focus was wonderful for a chipper new baby happy to listen to whatever words she would speak or read aloud.

Read to me Jenene did: whatever she was interested in. Subject matter made no difference. All that mattered was her soft voice and the words, the marvelous, fantastic, deeply influencing words. Where does vocabulary begin? Aurally. Our ears suck in words like Dyson's. Our brains sop them up like sponges with an endless capacity for absorption.

Words are indescribably beautiful because they give us infinite bridges for expressing our minds. Through articulation we can gift and achieve understanding, describe a heretofore-unknown perception, or simply express our feelings by saying, "Go away" or "I love you." No more monosyllabic grunting for mankind, language has taken hold and we are blessed to have so many words from which to choose to describe the simplest to the most complex concepts. It's too bad many take language for granted.

Jenene's approach with me was heuristic, prospering my curiosity, nudging my inquisitiveness. So long as I grew up to be self-sufficient and have an opinion, even if I was a virtuoso of nothing and no great success, she would feel successful. A child imbued with resourcefulness, thoughtfulness, and common sense often finds a niche.

Even as she relished absolutely this formative time with me, Jenene was suffering her greatest isolation. Even with so many people stopping in to see us, and even more insisting she bring me to them, she still had a social life where she was given equal standing while in her home she was rendered powerless. Without bringing a check, the balance of clout was tipped, and a new aspect of control was displayed.

Once he became the unquestioned sole breadwinner, Guy became a stingy miser who wanted to account for every penny. Literally. Even a nickel spent was an action that came under close scrutiny.

Food was the only acceptable excuse to open the pocketbook. Restaurant outings were acceptable, extravagant grocery shopping mandatory. As if a baby isn't constantly growing and in need of clothes that fit, groceries called for excessiveness while a quarter spent at a garage sale for a stack of cute baby-wear in great condition elicited a smack. Pack the fridge, cram the pantry, and stuff the cabinets.

The grocery store became a refuge because her actions there weren't scrutinized. Guy expected big filling meals and so long as she met that requirement—the plate of hot dish thrown against the wall set the criteria—she could buy any foodstuff she desired.

Able to acquire food freely, for the first time in her life Jenene sought consolation in the refrigerator. She began packing on the pounds, no longer concerned about the petite figure for which she had yearned. Losing the baby weight was never her goal. She wanted to be dumpy; she wanted to be unattractive; maybe if she disgusted him enough Guy would be driven away.

Quite to the contrary, with his expanded diet he had grown heartier and all the brawnier and a fat wife suited him fine.

At the time making a silent statement, she had no idea she was putting money in the bank for later, when disease was stripping weight off her so fast she was fading out of existence.

Able to control his violent impulses during the pregnancy (mind games were his preferred method of torture, something he would try on me later, at which point I would use words to dissect his brain), the beatings resumed in earnest after I was born. Jealousy drove him to escalate his mistreatment. He was more excitable. The beatings began to happen even when he was sober, and with little provocation.

The abuse culminated in the incident that would ultimately lead Jenene out of the hell into which she had been subsumed.

Before that could happen she had to go endure one of the hardest losses of her life.

Chapter 34
Loss and Gain

Long December.

Another New Year was going to dawn and it was the first in many Jenene looked forward to with hope. Defying the odds had shown her what seems unachievable, even impossible, could happen anyway. It was the nascent of a mindset that would later sustain her.

The first hope she sought to satisfy was convincing her dad he needed to be wary of his health. His obsession with weight loss had prompted him to get the stomach stapling. The problem was, even for that era he wasn't obtaining his weight loss goals in a healthy manner. The sight of him made Jenene worried. The weight had come off him at such a staggering rate it left loose skin hanging off him in sheets.

They spent the holiday at her parents' house in Woodville and the time to talk never emerged. The distraction of a wee one may well have contributed to her desire not to douse the mood. The wonder of Christmas can be lost on adults without a child to remind them, and since Jeff had become a young adult, a baby was just the thing to renew everyone's zeal. It was too good of a time to talk of dire messages.

January 1982.

They were out to the Nite Club when Jenene finally had her opportunity. It was odd going to her old tromping grounds now that her parents weren't the owners but Bob and Lois wanted to show off their grandson and exhibiting me for her extended family appealed to Jenene too. A minute alone, Jenene explained to him about the message she received while he lay comatose.

Like she had with Lucille, Jenene did her best to convince Bob.

Just as she feared he asked, "Was it a dream?"

"No," she admitted. "Maybe this ability, whatever it is, is changing. I don't know how this stuff works."

"There's nothing to worry about," he averred. "My grandson is healthy and I'm getting healthier."

Losing weight too quickly weakens the heart—and the pounds were melting off his broad frame.

Today there are more options than stapling, gastric banding and gastric bypass among them, and a whole contingent including doctors, dieticians, psychologists, and surgeons decides if an applicant is physically and mentally prepared for surgery, including putting the applicant on a restricted diet and intensive workout regimen to show willingness to follow prescribed guidelines. When Bob underwent the surgery, weight loss wasn't as understood. None of these precautions were in place.

Able only to eat one bite of food for an entire meal, Bob excused himself from the table to show off his grandson.

That night marked the last time she saw her father alive.

Bob underwent surgery to remove hemorrhoids on Friday and Jenene talked to him the next morning on the phone.

"I'll be out of the hospital in a day or two," he said, "and I want you two to come stay with us for a week or two."

"That sounds great, Dad." They talked for about an hour. She had no idea it would be the last time she spoke to him while he was alive. Their goodbyes were peaceful and she would always cherish that her last words to him were that she loved him.

That afternoon I stopped eating. I wanted only to sleep. My entire life to that point I had wanted the breast every four to six hours like clockwork and the change struck Jenene as a terrible sign. She called Children's Hospital for advice: a physician informed her that so long as I was still wetting diapers, I was okay, but to monitor me closely. If I didn't resume eating by the following morning, she was to bring me in.

Early Sunday morning the phone rang. It was an unusually frantic Lois. Bob was transferred to United Hospital in St. Paul. As Jenene feared his heart had buckled under the strain. He had suffered what was labeled a minor heart attack. Minor maybe but devastating, they lost his blood pressure and life support was keeping him alive.

I still had no appetite. Nor did I fuss. I was all but listless.

Jenene rushed me to the state of the art emergency room at United and Children's Hospital…and that was how it came to be, that both my grandfather and I were hospitalized in the same building with our lives hanging in the balance fourteen weeks after Jenene received a message one of us would die. A rapid examination revealed I was dehydrated but showed no other malady.

"I need to go to the other side of the hospital. My dad was rushed here in an ambulance and I need to find out what's going on."

"You'll bring your baby back later today if he doesn't improve?"

"I just need to find out about my dad."

When she arrived, Jenene was given some of the most devastating news of her life.

As she listened Jenene felt a part of herself dying…maybe the final shred of her innocence.

A doctor had explained the devastating situation to Lois. Bob's brain was dead. He was still technically alive but would never be able to function again nor even take a breath without artificial support. Two options were floated. He could be kept alive indefinitely in his current comatose state without hope of ever regaining consciousness. Or life support could be ceased.

Lois was unable to make a decision. That was one decision too chilling even for an ice maiden. She turned to the daughter she had butted heads with for years. She needed counsel; she needed advice; she was…at a loss.

The hardest decisions are often the ones we wish we never had to make.

Her son was ill and her dad was dying.

Her husband was a boogeyman haunting her life.

What life?

All she had to cling to was motherhood. With her dad slipping away, did it mean her son would live? Or was the message only half right and she would lose both?

In any case, she knew her father would not want to continue living as mindless breathing meat. One of the many subjects they could agree upon, it was a discussion they had once. Perhaps he had seen injuries of war, soldiers left breathing but for all intents and purposes dead due to brain damage. Whatever it was that swayed him, he had expressed his opinion clearly.

All Jenene could do was advise Lois to order the life support stopped. It was the hardest advice she would ever dispense. Words she dreaded saying even as she knew it was the right decision. Once the brain has died, wouldn't the soul be like a genie in a bottle no amount of rubbing would release, only the expiration of the vessel? Sometimes saying goodbye is a mercy. Even the hardest goodbye can be the right thing…can be the best result.

On January 17, 1982, Bob Davis died in a hospital bed on a cold day in the capitol of Minnesota. In the end he was alone, no one holding his hand, as the machines breathing for him were turned off, ending lung function, and over the course of the next few minutes the lack of oxygen slowly stopped his blood from flowing and his heart from pumping.

With his family there, Lois, Jenene, and Jeff, the question so easy to ask is why weren't they surrounding him, two of them holding his hands? There are no easy answers. But the truth was shock had rendered them too confused to know how to act.

Lois was too emotionally barricaded to even shed a tear. Had she been with her husband as he died, cracks may have appeared in her barricade. Once the shell was compromised, the whole structure may have disintegrated. All that feeling felt all at once may have zapped her catatonic. Or sent her on down the path behind Bob.

A month from fourteen, Jeff was right in the thick of his formative years. Was it that very day the resentment he would carry for years began? Losing Bob may have had the hardest impact on him. He was a teen boy looking ahead at manhood and now he had lost his role model. Not having a figure to emulate can make it a real struggle to gain a strong male identity with the components necessary to be the best man possible.

Jenene would regret forever that she wasn't there holding his hand. At the time it was one thing she couldn't face. She wanted to remember her dad the way he had been, not as a lifeless body on a bed. We always regret our weakness. Some are forgivable in light of the situation.

I'm sure Bob never held it against any of them.

At the elevator, before parting ways, Lois and Jeff heading back to Wisconsin, Jenene headed home to St. Paul Park, Lois hugged Jenene for the first time in her life. Then her mother told her she loved her. It was always "We love you." Never, "I love you." Even with so many emotions swirling inside her head, the significance of that hug and hearing those words didn't fail to make an immediate impact.

As if from a spell, once my grandfather was gone, I woke, hungry and responsive.

Jenene knew a decision had been reached but had no way of knowing how the determination was made. It would be twenty-three years before I would be made privy to how the decision was made, of which of us would go and which of us would stay. I retrieved this information during a Reiki attunement when I was twenty-three-years old, in a detailed vision.

I have always considered visions highly speculative. I believe a strong and capable imagination can build entire worlds. As good as my imagination is, this was beyond the scope of what I could produce, because it was reliving the experience, being there.

The mortal coil is transitory, the flesh but a suit of clothes to don and discard. We dress our souls to go out in the world to learn our lessons, take dozens of faces so we may learn what it is to be looked upon under many guises. We are the sum total of our wardrobe.

A crossroads. Infinite light.

Where souls passing can meet on the precipice of true understanding, when one must go into the white abyss and be drenched in all knowledge while the other returns to the burdens and naiveté of flesh. Where a baby can be a golden-haired full-grown Adonis (a concession when the earliest, truest, most desired form was that of a darksome native) and a fat man can be slender and well built without the scars of obesity. Where there is no vanity or greed or conceit: only naked truth.

Understanding exists even if the flesh is saddled with the ignorance of infancy. In some way we retain the knowledge of our ages even if inaccessible save during a meeting along the spirit thoroughfare.

Mouths need not move for words to be given articulation.

Time is infinite.

Circular.

Nonlinear.

Under the right circumstances minutes can be elongated into hours; our communion might have lasted as long as an empire or was commenced and concluded in the blink of an eye.

Events dictate that there is a future, a past, and a right now yet everything somehow exists simultaneously.

Discussion.

Argument.

Conclusion.

Torches pass…

Knowledge…

Understanding is reached in a way so simple it seems like a trick.

Sometimes gifts can be bestowed, such as the wisdom to look without—and within.

There are paths that must be protected. To be the protector of an important path is to be a savior. Who would the stubborn, pigheaded one listen to, the man or the child? A riddle that can only be solved after a decision has been reached. But sometimes the answer is so plain to see it cries out…like an infant crying out for the nipple after a three-day fast.

For the mistakes he made, Bob proved he was a good father when he went into the great beyond to preserve his daughter's life, a selfless act that to me typifies his existence. Though we went separate directions that day, there will come a time when our paths merge again, as we all ultimately go in the same direction.

Even though my grandfather's death had a lasting impact that reverberates to this day, the ripple of his life still radiating out even though his stone was dropped in the depths of death long ago, all these years later, I can say with complete truth, we made the right choice.

Not one but two blizzards would precede Bob's funeral. Few were able to pay condolences in person. Lois would receive a stack of sympathy cards too large to be contained in a single size-12 shoebox.

Jenene feared Guy wouldn't allow her to go. She was prepared to commit an act of defiance even if it got her body slammed. Let him beat her. Even if she had swelling eyes and a fat lip, she was going to her dad's funeral. He had forbidden her from going to a friend's funeral shortly after they were married and it created an everlasting regret. Not again.

In the end perhaps even Guy realized it would be too draconian to deny her. He would stay away but he wouldn't stand in the way of her packing me up and making the trip to Woodville. Lois would cling to me, forcing Jenene to demand me back so she could nurse.

"I'll give him a bottle," Lois said.

"He doesn't like formula." Even as a baby I knew the good stuff and formula was a poor substitute.

"He'll be fine."

"No, Mom, give me my baby. It's better for him if I breastfeed."

Bob had been so proud of her for making that decision. Lois sooner would have let a hyena take a bite out of her breasts than allow one of her babies to suckle from her nipples.

Lois would ante me up, wait in the wings, and seize me as soon as I was finished nursing.

Jeff was inconsolable. Within so short a time too many hard realities had avalanched in on him to leave him anything other than emotionally buried. For many years he would hide behind a smile and bravado, unable to assimilate all his conflicting feelings, the anger and the love, the sense of rejection and the yearning.

Jenene felt as if she were in a dream. That was what she wished it were, a dream, the warning she had wanted to receive so she could convince her dad to listen. But she suspected he wasn't supposed to listen. It was either going to be him or her son; before the decision was made the only warning was for her, to let her know there was a reason one would be gone while the other remained.

Someone else who wouldn't turn up on the day was Bob's wayward firstborn. To his credit, Bobby tried to make it, had flown in to St. Paul from the faraway place he had relocated to, only to be halted by the weather closing I-94. He would come later, a tall, bearded man with thick glasses and an off-putting manner. It would be Jenene's penultimate meeting with him. The last time would be when a twist of fate placed her in a hospital room with his mother as she lay dying, but that comes later.

Bob's remains were cremated and his ashes released in to the wind.

Chapter 35
Epiphany

February is the most villainous month because it is the grayest twenty-eight days of the year, the grayest twenty-nine days during leap years, and that year's was the grayest of her life.

Jenene turned twenty-two on the ninth. Less than a month after her dad died, she was in no mood for celebrating. Being the first one following the loss would mark the next several holidays. She had no idea how much her life would be different by the first Christmas without her dad, and not just because it would be her second as a mom.

As she prepared to go spend the night at Pookie's, Guy was grumpy. Huffing and puffing, he wanted her to stay home. The only reason she was going was because he made plans to be gone overnight with a friend and she wanted some company—there was a lot of sadness in her life and a luminescent spirit like Pookie's was just the thing to lift her, if only temporarily, out of her funk.

It wasn't her fault his friend bailed on him and he was stuck at home.

"I don't see why you have to go," he grumbled. He had done little or nothing to assuage her sadness. He proffered nice gifts on her birthday and Valentine's Day and figured that should be enough. Material crap meant nothing when what she needed was the consolation of a soft shoulder, the solace of snuggles, and the security of hugs, but such gestures were beyond an unenlightened fool.

"You're just going to sit around and watch TV anyway," she said. "Why do I need to be around for that?"

A gesture of frustration, he turned and stalked away, into the living room, where he plopped loudly—ping, crunch—into his easy chair. If he didn't get his way he either acted like a violent grown-up or a brooding child. Dealing with the latter was preferable; it didn't involve slamming her around. When he went off like that she was left fairly certain she had nothing to worry about violence-wise.

The more time she spent with him, the more she came under the delusion she could read his moods; in truth he was as transitory and unpredictable as Minnesota weather: there could be long periods of sunshine only for a storm to ratchet up out of nowhere.

Jenene hustled out and started her Camaro (she couldn't afford to park it on the farm that winter), leaving her broody husband inside to mope. She had to concede to the dire fact that she was scared of him, sometimes outright terrified, yet in many ways loved and wanted him too. A lot of the time he could be a really nice guy…he could clown around and be nice…he could be so full of apparent love.

Despite all the pain he inflicted he could be a good listener. He bought her nice gifts. He took her out to eat all the time. He always promised to be better. And would he ever leave her? Ever cheat? Would his commitment ever be anything but total? He was committed, generous, and full of promises. Many women feel that's enough. At that moment it was maybe enough for her.

Yet she couldn't make the mistake of forgetting the reverse of all the good: his rough, gouging edge. On some level he would always be the man who could see the woman who was supposed to be the love of his life grieving and not take action to console her.

Back inside, careful of little limbs, she kneeled to strap her baby snugly in his car seat. Eyed Guy in his chair. There was no use saying goodbye. There was nothing she could do to appease him short of giving in. It would be better just to take her baby and go.

On the cusp of exiting, Jenene hoisted up the car seat, turned toward the door, and was blindsided. The clobbering Guy dealt started with a flash of bright pain…followed by darkness. He pummeled her with blow after blow to the head until she slumped to the floor, unconscious against the front door.

Strapped in the car seat, her baby was still clutched in her arms. Screaming his head off, the infant knew terror as his father returned to watching TV, if only abstractly in so young a mind.

Since there weren't remotes back then, I imagine he stopped to turn up the volume.

When usually prompt Jenene failed to show, heroic Pookie, not one to shy away, went to investigate.

Tragedy had invaded Pookie's life. Her bargeman husband was killed when he fell into the rotors and was so emulsified his minced body was irrecoverable. Waiting for deserved compensation, she was in limbo as lawyers quibbled. At the time she was struggling to get by in his absence. She and Jenene with their respective problems forged an even stronger friendship.

Pookie found me to be an exquisite baby and would lavish me with adulation, cradling me in her big soft bosom. Her positive energy in the wake of such heartache bolstered Jenene. Seeing such strength in another woman was the sort of influence she needed.

When Pookie pulled up the Camaro was still running. Suspicious.

Knocks followed by banging on the back door elicited no response. The booming woman was emboldened by righteousness. She had no qualms against letting herself in to check on the wellbeing of her friend. She knew what Guy was about; she had no illusions about what he was capable of. Even if she loved Jenene and had a special place in her heart for her baby, she couldn't bring herself to care one iota for a man who laid hands on a woman.

Inside she saw the bozo plunk in his chair, watching TV and clutching a beer.

"Where's Jenene?"

Taking a lesson from his dad, selectively mute Guy offered no response.

Not deterred, Pookie investigated further. As she journeyed she was drawn eventually by piteous infant mewls. She discovered Jenene slumped where she had gone down, looking like a rag doll tossed carelessly aside by an uncaring child. She was a bloody mess. Lip split, cheek swelling and bruised. The car seat was still balanced precariously on her torso. Guy failed to recover me from there in her arms.

Without hesitance Pookie hustled me out to her vehicle. She made sure I was strapped in and returned to collect Jenene. Lifting her up in her arms as if cradling a baby, she carried her to the car too and got her buckled up. Finally she returned for my diaper bag.

Guy said nothing as she carried out first his child, then his wife, and finally retrieved the bag. Not one word.

Pookie did the only logical thing and rushed Jenene to the emergency room.

She woke at last. In another exam room, in another hospital, feeling the discomfort of knowing she had no power to deceive but forced to try. To save face if nothing else, she had to say there was an "accident," a "mishap," a "mistake on her part," and not the real truth, never the real truth. Admitting it to the doctor would make it even realer than the bruises, the split lip, or the loosened teeth. It would be the look she was sure would come onto his face, part pity, part contempt.

By blaming herself for the beatings, she took the deception out of what she said since she had, no matter how involuntarily, instigated the violence.

Proving she was only ever able to deceive herself, the doctor was no dupe. He took exception to her trying to make him one. "I didn't have to cheat my way through medical school. Who did this to you? I see you have a wedding ring, so I'll assume your husband."

Feeling exposed and on the verge of tears, barely able to speak, she said, "I don't know what you're talking about."

"Deny it all you want, but we both know the truth here. I can't tell you what to do. But I can tell you…I saw a baby was with you, that was your—"

She grinned despite it all. "My son."

"I can tell you, if he'll do this to you, he'll do this to your son, too."

"No, he wouldn't—" She caught herself.

"I promise you he will. And when he does, you'll remember I told you this."

The words resonated in her head: if he'll do this to you, he'll do this to your son….

The bulb of denial that had grown around her was shattered.

Stripped of all self-respect, Jenene would have taken the beatings until he killed her. But the prospect of him beating her little boy was too much. There was no other choice. She resolved to escape him. It would take a plan. So outside her usual line of thinking, it would have to be a clever and somewhat devious plan. So she began scheming.

Like that first smack was for her one month to the day after they were married, Guy wouldn't see it coming.

Pookie was a hero that night.

Without her, Jenene's life-changing hospital visit never would have happened.

Showing the deserving are rewarded too, the woman with a heart of gold would receive a large compensatory settlement that proved life changing. A complete makeover followed; she would lose lots of weight, meet a new man, marry, move away, and to Jenene's regret they would lose touch.

Pookie was one of those great friends who emerge at the right time only to fade away. Even those who make the biggest difference, offer the greatest support, can take up a disproportionately small portion of our lives compared to the huge impact they make. Acquaintances come and go but the true friends hold a section of your heart forever.

If someone else were to deserve kudos it would be the E.R. doctor. He made Jenene see a simple truth in front of her face all along. By this writing she couldn't even remember his name—

there have been so many doctors—but that in no way reduces his contribution. He said the right words at the right time and started a revolution.

The Gordian knot that was her marriage had to be untied, cut, dissolved in acid, or frozen with liquid nitrogen and shattered with a ball peen hammer, anything it took to break that purportedly unbreakable sucker down.

Chapter 36
Justified

"We should move into an apartment," she suggested casually. "We don't need this big house right now and the money we'll save will make it so we can buy our own house."

Reasonable. Commending Jenene for the solid idea, Guy agreed. So the following summer they moved less than a block away, into the Pullman apartments, so known due to the street along which the lineup of blockish brick buildings stands. A single mother on a budget could even cover the affordable dwelling. Tee-he-he....

Once they relocated, all she needed was the impetus to act. She knew once she proceeded with the plan and gave Guy the heave-ho, she would have a good support system. Lal, Bill, and Herb were always on her side and Lois' disapproval of Guy had recently been peaked when he presumed to have a say in her life due to her being a widow—she shut him down so fast his head was left spinning.

It would all come down to timing....

In the meantime all she was doing was biding her time.

Jenene also researched government assistance. Going on the dole, as it was infamously known, was a contrition she never thought she would have to make but between her precarious health, the time she had been out of the job market, and child care concerns, she would be in need for a little while. For her it would be temporary. Desire to work was in the very blood circulating through her unstable but manageable body.

No matter how it turned out in the courts she was prepared to support her child. She knew it would be foolhardy to rely on Guy for anything because it would only be a foothold of control he would use to exert power over her life.

Guy remained oblivious to her machinations. So he saw no need to alter his behavior during a period when every time he snapped at her, every time he acted with disregard for her feelings, and every time he dared lay his hands on her it was a tally against him on a board quickly running out of space.

As the end drew nigh, she tried to engage him in positive ways and found more often than not it would end badly. Even in moments she could mistake for flirty he might snap. This culminated in a broken bone. They were playing a game of back and forth on the couch. Light play. Nothing to get serious about: no reason to want to inflict hurt. Jenene launched her foot in his direction playfully—

He caught her foot in his viselike grip, squeezed, and twisted it a way no foot should be bent.

"Ouch! That hurt! What the hell? I think you broke my foot."

"Oh, quit being a baby."

"It really hurts. I think I need to see a doctor."

"Sure. Whiny baby needs to run and get attention. You're so pathetic."

Jenene refused to go to the doctor. An X-ray taken years later would reveal the bone healed crudely. The bone he broke so callously when she thought they were funning around.

In the past, sound judgment had evaded her and life-altering decisions were made without proper forethought, but after much soul-searching, she was sure this decision was made rationally and more importantly, soundly.

Irreproachability restored, near the end Jenene would be downright lippy because the abuse caused her such outrage. She had taken his best and was still here. The tougher she was the more she could take. If the beatings were meant to keep her submissive and biddable now they were having the opposite effect.

The instant she perceived Guy's hackles going up she would say daringly, "Go ahead and hit me if that makes you feel like more of a man!"

And it would usually work. The dare showing her absolute acceptance of his abusiveness would defuse him and he would stalk off, stymied.

Jenene's defiant words and actions may have been a deflection from me. It was obvious he reviled my baby noisiness

(I rarely cried), detested my infantile neediness (his life wasn't affected insomuch as he never changed diapers, fed me, or bathed me), and really hated that she breastfed (the reason for his aversion remains a mystery); I was a nuisance, an inconvenience, and nothing special.

If she drew his ire she could possibly be forestalling an unfortunate shaking incident everyone would regret.

That was the thing of it, once the idea he would hurt me was planted, she was cursed with an inability not to speculate. When? What for? How bad would it be? How long could he hold off? When would he make her little boy the recipient of abuse?

If there was a countdown, was it years away, months, days, hours, or mere minutes? Not knowing was a huge motivator. The faster she could get me away the sooner she would have some relief and the nervous twist his presence put in her stomach could unwind.

In his every action she saw possible negligence. The lackadaisical way he held me, propped precariously on a knee, was enough indication his concern for my wellbeing was too minimal for her comfort. But the one time she left me alone with him was a real eye opener. She left me asleep in my crib, snug in one-piece pajamas, with instructions to offer me a bottle if I woke. When she got home I was up, stripped to my diaper, and crying.

It was bizarre how he berated her for being incapable of giving him a baby and now he was infuriated the baby he always wanted...what? Stood in the way of his control.

The end came when Guy felt he was defending me and correcting Jenene.

A precocious eight-month-old, I was a born explorer. I would seek to push boundaries, even test limits, in the quest for knowledge. Jenene considered this a prosperous trait. That was, so long as my curiosity wasn't bringing me to danger.

To avoid that end, restrictions had to be established, and Jenene saw the perfect opportunity when I figured out how to get into a cooler designated as the home first aid kit. Packed with bandages, gauze, medical tape, peroxide, and antibacterial salve besides other odds and ends, the only real danger was a mess.

Jenene had to act because figuring out the kitchen cabinetry might be next. That could entail breaching the really off-limits area under the sink: the cubby where all the poisonous cleaners waited to be put to their proper uses. Or in that day, before child safety implements, cause irreparable damage to an unsupervised intensely curious floor crawler. Whichever instance arrived first.

She thought it best to set a limit and teach me "no," a word kids seem to hear far too little of nowadays.

I was fortunate to always have supervision so without fear of serious mishaps I could explore within reason.

So when I infiltrated a place that was off limits, Jenene was there to pull me away and give a corrective no.

I was stubborn, went right back. What can I say? Kids have a rare single-mindedness akin to a dog on a scent.

Jenene removed me a second time with a similar admonishment.

When I went back a third time and began to open the cooler, she took my hand and to get my undivided attention gave it a light smack. Without shedding a tear or experiencing any real pain, the point was made. I got it. A limit was expressed and I understood.

Guy felt what she had done was egregious. He was furious. He hauled off and smacked her across the face, one clean shot. Whereas the light tap on the knuckles did little else than gain my focus, witnessing my mom take a ferocious slap across the face was enough to put me in hysterics.

Guy gathered up his lunch box and departed for work.

Jenene soothed away my tears before she went to assess the damage, pain encompassing the whole side of her face.

The sight of her reflection in the bathroom mirror made her lip want to tremble. She locked it down. She didn't want to weep or blubber or carry on in any way. So she wouldn't. More pronounced by the second, from chin to temple a ruddy handprint was rising. The cookie cutter outline of a hand was perfectly emblematic of all the abuse.

Visible evidence of abuse had always given her problems. Not so much the actual black and blue bruises or the underlying physical pain. It was that signs forced her to be deceptive. She was never a liar and her husband forced her to lie, if only through reassigning blame from his actions to mishaps, blunders, and your common variety free-floating black hole accident.

On some level wasn't that the self-deception she had held fast to for way too long? That the abuse wasn't purposeful? That every time he clobbered her it was somehow accidental? Well, the blows weren't accidents and she was over trying to fool herself.

The temerity…to leave a handprint on her face so clear there was only one explanation…the nerve…to walk out and leave her once again in the wreckage of his making.

That was it.

She was done.

Whatever elixir remained in her love tank soured and curdled. When every feeling you have for someone is tinctured with anger and frustration rounding out the overarching negativity they inspire, what is there to do? She knew. She knew well.

Leave.

Leave because there's nothing left worth prospering.

Leave because no one deserves to live under the shadow of abuse.

Leave because no tomorrow will be as important as the one that follows the decision to escape cruelty.

Just like that she knew it was the time to act. Urgency entered her like a runaway sprite. She burst into action.

Limping on the broken foot she apparently had no right to have treated, every step was a reminder of why, though this was a potentially incendiary decision, what she was doing was right. Today it was a broken metatarsal, tomorrow it might be a broken rib, and eventually it could be her skull that was busted—or her son's skull.

Jenene packed, hauled, and restacked Guy's worldly possessions—clothing, decorations, and personal bric-a-brac—in the hallway. She finished with a little time to spare before his shift ended.

You got this, girl.

The grunt work took most of the night but the work of rebuilding her life would take considerably longer. She had a good start. *One step at a time and I'll get there,* she reassured herself. *It's been a hard three and a half years yet I've survived the worst.* If marriage had depreciated her, having her baby had restored much of her value. Now she was a protector and caregiver, supplier of nourishment and warmth, wisdom-bearer and oracle.

You can do this, she told herself. Scheme in action, she felt she had made the right decision. She was reasonably sure she had taken care of all the loose ends. With a touch of luck (*I know you're looking out for me, Dad*), it would go off without too many hitches.

But it didn't take psychic powers to predict Guy would be furious and likely earsplitting in his loud display. Neighbor relations would probably be tense for a little while. Not the sort of ruckus she wanted to inspire early in the morning so soon after moving in, Guy's probable reaction would be unfortunate. Under normal circumstances she would never be so rude but sacrifices of decorum meant little when so much was on the line.

There is no real exactitude in life: we fly by the seat of our pants and hope we don't land on our rumps.

Chapter 37
Wife in Revolt

Some showdowns are better undertaken at a distance…at least the width of a dead-bolted door.

"Let me in!" Bam! Bam! "You can't do this!" Bam! Bam! Bam! "Let me in!"

"Shut up you jerk!"

"Mind your own damn business, buddy!"

Yep. No regard for neighborliness whatsoever.

Zero need to look out the peephole, she could picture the rampaging Guy outside her door well enough. Chest puffed up. The cords of his neck standing out, thicker than number 2 pencils, and overlaid by networks of twitchy veins. Corners of his mouth transitioning constantly between a malicious sneer and hateful frown. Those manipulative blue eyes saucer wide, bloodshot, and wet with fury. Face red hot as a fireplace poker left in the fire.

"I'm not letting you in, Guy," she said through the door. "Just go away. We're done."

"We won't be done 'til I say we're done!"

Wrong!

"I live here, damn it!"

Not anymore!

"Let me in! I love you!"

Sorry, Guy, like "fair" you've taught me "love" can be just another word in the dictionary.

This was no practice run, no dress rehearsal. Guy was out there on the warpath, throwing bombs and based on the neighbors' reactions, bombing. His one-man show's inaugural performance would be the last. Repertoire of a Raging Husband had entertainment value but Jenene refused to be his anger's muse any longer.

Guy's words and actions didn't surprise or even disappoint Jenene. He had pushed her over a precipice. Once she'd gone over and made that plunge, what was felt for him was reduced to very little, a tidbit so small an ant could carry it around in his wallet like a laminated four leaf clover because it would be better luck to the ant than it would ever again be to Guy.

Sometimes really caring is pushing someone away for their own good.

He kicked and screamed and threatened and cursed like a tantrumy child; the neighbors kept cajoling him unkindly to shut up and he kept snapping right back at them to close their gobs. The hullabaloo may have drawn a lot of attention but surprisingly no one called the police. Maybe they were having too much fun berating the jackass making a scene in the hallway.

Only after several hours did he wear himself out. Finally becoming reconciled to his failure to evoke the response he desired, he collected up his possessions, growling and muttering, and quit for his mother's house.

Run on home to Mom. She can deal with you.
Jenene felt vindicated.
First hurdle jumped. Without tripping. Nice.
It would be a long race and her toes wouldn't clear every hurdle. But the finish line was in sight and she would keep her feet. That was all that mattered.

How sweet what you know to be lies can sound, how tempting, the counter reactionary enticements that are so airy they float....

Their first communication would be a day later by phone and entailed Guy making reformed-man claims. Among them he would clean up his act, he would be a better person, and he would never do the bad things again.

She would want to give him chances, would even entertain the idea of reconciliation and join him on date nights meant to be relationship builders. But those words haunted her: if he'll do this to you, he'll do this to your son, too. Once your eyes are opened to hard truth sightlessness to that light is impossible because it shines through your eyelids even when they're closed.

After Jenene made her final decision and filed for divorce, citing irreconcilable differences, Guy continued to step up his efforts in a bid to win her back. This made the divorce drag on and on.

Knowing it was over, Jenene sold her Camaro; with a baby a sporty car like that wasn't practical. Lois stepped up and gave her a good car. The gesture was almost as good as an "I love you."

In court Guy played the part of a man willing to work things out well, too well, so well he made the judge leery to even grant a divorce. Who was more reasonable? The one pleading to stay in or the one dead set against reconciliation? The judge was unsure.

They went back into counseling. Guy would be singled out for blame and quit. They would return again only for another repeat. It was an endless impasse and a useless gesture he used to stretch out the months. Jenene didn't like watching reruns on TV; she certainly didn't want to live one.

Because she would not cite the beatings in court, the abuse had no bearing on the proceedings.

There was no history of pressed charges. Any claim would be speculative. The judge would have likely thrown out any allegation she made. But it wasn't that legal invalidation would be a blow. Proof existed. Let Johnny Black tell them it was speculative. Let Jeff. Let Pookie. But she would have none of them subpoenaed. She wanted to be away from Guy but she wasn't the type to wish him smeared in a way that would leave a permanent record.

With a court system still skewed in the favor of men calling the shots, Guy's delay tactics worked for a time. It frustrated Jenene to no end because she had made her decision. There was no going back. Yet could she compel the ones who counted to believe her? She felt as if she was being judged a hysterical woman and the setbacks and postponements were meant to force enough time to pass so she would come to her senses.

What was even more galling was that Guy's consent was required for certain medical matters. They were still technically married and that was the law. In her opinion it was no longer any of his business and never would be again. Lacking his signature, medicos denied her a tubal ligation even though it had been determined it would be in the best interest of her health. Since a second pregnancy could kill her, she felt it was a little chauvinistic putting her life in a man's hands, especially when she was fighting like hell to divorce him.

Per usual, her health worked against her, and yet another endometriosis/adhesion surgery in the spring led to a complication when she developed a hernia in the incision. Six weeks later she underwent surgery to have the bulge repaired.

Soon after nature allowed her to have the last laugh on those who thought choice should be taken out of her hands. It was another health scare, one that worked in her favor for once. In this instance a softball-sized tumor formed in Jenene's uterus. A day after she threw my second birthday party, discovery of the tumor triggered an emergency hysterectomy. All was removed but one abandoned ovary bivouacked to her abdominal wall. The baby factory was not only closed, it was gone from the premises. Mua-ha-ha.

Of course the doctor took the precaution of warning her it was a million to one shot she could get pregnant again with the single remaining ovary still in operation but even long odds, in strange cases, could yadda-yadda-yadda. He said if anyone would be that long shot one, it was she, so she ought to be aware. Luckily, no such happenstance ever occurred.

The next few months were emotionally dicey; the hormonal imbalance following the evulsion of her uterus was a mile-a-minute thrill ride she was sick of on day one. Hormone replacements existed. But she wanted to find out if her solitary ovary would kick back in and regulate her body naturally. In time it would but for that block of time she was a wreck, depressed, angry, and desolate in turns.

It felt like she was a failure at life—a total loser.
It felt like she was worthless.
Her marriage ended.
Her dad died.
The world was a realm of little light, less joy.
And another disastrous health dilemma was coming.

The Christmas following the hysterectomy we spent on the farm.

It was during this time Jenene suffered another of the health pushbacks that always seemed to further complicate complicated situations. An outthrust of agonizing swelling the size of an egg grew grotesquely on the side of her neck. So tender even the most minimal pressure sent tear-summoning zings into her eyes, she had no choice but to once again seek medical attention.

What she would learn was an ulcer in her throat—a harbinger of so much to come—had swelled and caused the bizarre growth on her neck.

The pain and discomfort made for a strained holiday; there was a lot of anger caught in her craw. Guy refused to stop fighting for what she knew was too dead for revivification. But her pretender of an ex, so quick for an audience to play the part of a decent guy, was only part of the problem.

On the phone with Lois, splenetic Jenene expressed the funk she was dwelling in like a salamander trapped in a window casement. Not one to coddle, her mother took the tough love approach.

"You need to snap out of it," Lois said as if it was no more difficult than flipping a light switch.

A short fuse lit, Jenene blew; an expletive exploded out of her mouth before the boom of the phone receiver slamming into the cradle ended the conversation.

What at the time felt inexcusable would in retrospect be recognized as the right advice. It takes time for the revelatory cream to rise through the whey of unglued emotions, though, so Jenene suffered the fury time would later deem unjustified.

At United Hospital she was the focus of the entire staff. No one had ever seen such a swelled ulcer in the throat. Two-dozen sets of eyes peered down her narrowed airway in the first hour.

Antibiotics were pumped intravenously. An allergen to natural forms meant a synthetic variation was required.

No way she was getting down a pill. Her own saliva was too painful to swallow. To reduce swelling goopy pink baby Tylenol was the only choice. It was available in liquid form. The dosage was based on weight. An entire tray of the putrid-tasting medication was delivered to her bedside. She choked it down sip by painful sip.

Rotten timing, a close family friend passed away. The impact of the loss was immediate and intense and Jenene quickly composed a note for the nurse to convey to her doctor.

Who turned up? An internist associated with the doctor who removed her gallbladder.

A bespectacled man with a bald crown and a beard, he had serious concerns about discharging her. For any reason, even a funeral. He could recognize her desperateness. He could sense her depression. He took it upon himself to offer up the pep talk it turned out she needed. "What's happened to you could end your life," he said. "But only if you let it. You need to start fighting. Not only for yourself and the life you could have. You need to fight for your son."

If his intent was to settle her horses, in that he failed, but as she fled, his message resonated in her mind. Ironically, for the first time in months she felt hopeful as she made her way to her friend's final farewell.

Not the first time Jenene was forced to go rogue, she acted with stealth and aplomb, even if pulling out the IV proved a bloody proposition.

Determination paid off and bleeding to death was averted. Defiant as ever, there was no way she would be denied paying homage to someone she loved. Not because of her stupid health. The internist said she had to get strong for the sake of a child dependent on her and a life it was up to her to make worth living; part of that was living up to personal obligations as a matter of honoring her own integrity.

Afterward, returning to the hospital seemed unnecessary. With an attitude adjustment behind her and a more positive outlook guiding her thoughts and feelings, she was fast improving. By Christmas day an optimistic future was in her sightline. She had emerged from her rut imperfect but unbowed. Whether her hormones were no longer as wonkers or if mind had triumphed over matter, she felt replenished enough to keep up the good fight.

The superimposition of a livelier disposition over her previous woeful character made it possible to stay upbeat during the slow purgatorial time ahead, while she waited as patiently as possible for our fresh new start to begin.

Conflict, especially when so much was on the line, siphoned too much energy. The battle for divorce was daunting, discouraging, and demoralizing.

Yet every day she marshaled her happy thoughts, said her affirmations, screwed a smile on her face, and hoped her goodwill would propagate the same. She was confident she would be rewarded with a reversal of fortune if she remained true to her sensibilities and consistent in regards to her responsibilities.

Recovering fully from the ulcer took months, a period during which she was robbed of her voice. What little she was able to say was croaked out in a breathy whisper. At least not being able to talk gave her a lot of practice listening. Her skills as a listener would someday factor big in her life.

Forevermore there would be raspiness to her voice some men would consider sexy, a bit like Kathleen Turner. For her the voice change would be a constant reminder of another health implosion presaging the absolution of a divorce she had to fight for tooth and nail.

When all was said and done she crossed the finish line, earning her freedom…and ensured the threat of physical abuse against me by my father was greatly reduced. Five years to the day after their wedding day, June 9, 1984, the judge signed the divorce decree, finalizing the end of a marriage that was three and a half years of wedded dysfunction and a year and a half of one party skirmishing for divorce, the other combating to reclaim control.

What restitution she would receive would be wisdom and her independence.

Chapter 38
Post Time

Custody and child support were the next issue but gamesmanship proved unnecessary.

It seemed much of the fight had left Guy; he made no contestations. He took financial responsibility seriously, enough so he ordered his wages garnished, which meant a lot when times were tough.

Once away from Jenene, he was able to take control of his worst tendencies and exhibited a far more peaceful disposition, as if a curse had palled and lifted.

Granted one visitation day a week and the occasional weekend, Jenene remained restive when it came to sending me off with him. In reality she needn't have been such a nervous wreck when I was with Guy. Even though she worried he would somehow use me to harm her, he cared about me too much to use me as a pawn beyond doing everything he could to win me over. In this quest he made every effort not to flub. He worked on being my buddy. He was better at it than being a father, a position he relished without quite understanding his role.

Even now I remember the Wednesday evenings I would be with my dad as relatively good times and the overnight stays as fun. He would feed me things like hotdog and bean goulash and fried chicken livers. He had two cats, one a huge black tabby named Dudley and the other a smaller white cat with black ears and the evocative name of Zed, an unholy hissing terror if ever there was one.

He had a garage at one apartment complex in which we used pieces of scrap lumber to assemble a wooden cowboy and his trusty dog. At another, he had access to a huge basement space he used to assemble a colossal electric racetrack. We would race matchbox-sized electric cars with the smell of burning components hanging in the air.

He took me fishing and taught me how to tie a hook on the line with a special twisty knot and some spit. Always one to recycle and not sit on my hands waiting, I collected detritus left by other fishermen and made a fishing pole out of a stick, discarded line, a recovered sinker, and a bent hook. I think I even dug a worm out of the ground. I put the line in the water and left it alone until we were going to depart.

"Hey buddy, pull that line out, would you? It's not good to leave a hook in the water."

Lo and behold, what I pulled in was a goodish sized catfish, the first catch of my young life. Guy was elated and praised my fishing skills. A hallmark of my early years, he would clean the fish as I watched and Jenene would fry it for my lunch. A little muddy tasting, it was one of the best meals ever.

It was with my dad I had my first pizza rolls while watching a *Planet of the Apes* marathon. He would introduce me to a lot of movies.

Guy would launch me into the freakish realm of horror films at the perhaps too early age of three. Jenene learned this when word of mouth led her to rent "My Bloody Valentine." In those days the video stores oftentimes put the film box in a plastic case, so the box and the cover imagery went with the cassette.

I saw the tape on the table, the unmistakable image of a coal miner and a heart-shaped box too distinct not to recognize, and said offhandedly, "I've seen that movie."

"Oh, no you haven't, sweetheart," my mom replied. "This is a grownup movie."

"I saw it with my dad," I shot back, and proceeded to describe the film's plot points in detail. I've always had an amazing memory for stories.

Jenene was none too pleased Guy would risk my adolescent psyche. It came out that he had also shown me John Carpenter's "The Thing." Appalled and outraged, she confronted him and advised him not to show me more R-rated films.

She never considered bringing up such a stipulation since she thought such advice was a no-brainer.

There was no way for Jenene to know her fears of detrimental developmental damage were overblown. To her an early introduction to horrific subject matter was a biggie. Much of it came down to taste. Jenene considered showing a child a movie involving an old lady getting cooked in a dryer and the killer escaping into the mines after amputating his own arm while maniacally spouting off his flimsy motive in bad taste.

Guy was just trying to be if not a "good" dad a fun one.

Maybe he thought Jenene vilified him and wanted to create a heavy counterbalance. If he believed that, it was untrue. But it might have pushed him to try harder to ensure we had memorable times together. I was always drawn to the taboo. Horror movies could freak me out a little, sure. But they enthralled my young imagination. Showing them to me built our bond. Even though Jenene disapproved.

Another motivator existed. He met someone with whom he was building a relationship. Displaying a solid connection with me showed he was a standup guy.

He had to suspect Jenene would insist on meeting any new love interest before she allowed me to be around the woman. The truth would emerge. Guy knew how the past cast him. And if his new partner was to be around his son, his misdeeds were going to be dredged up. There had to be a foundation before she learned he had not always been a good guy. The groundwork would pay off.

Jenene's insistence was understandable. After the breakup Guy dated some odd ducks. One woman was proud of her appetite for canned cat food. So there was reason to be wary.

An untimely death would aid him by showing he could be a sympathetic character.

Months would go by before Guy again broached his lady friend.

In the interim he lost his dad. This gave him the impetus to reveal the darker areas of his failed marriage. Why? Due to his loss his new love interest was in a sympathetic frame of mind.

Of course the chance remained his naked honesty would chase her away. But that was his one opportunity to tell her, when she would be most inclined to not judge him so critically it ended their relationship. It would be a lie to say her compassion didn't compel her to be more open and forgiving and it worked.

Hearts big enough to believe in second chances are special. Credit to the lady in his life, she believed Guy deserved a chance to show he had changed. People mature. She accepted his mistakes. She believed him when he promised that was all the past.

But Jenene wouldn't know of his admissions until the two women met.

In the meantime she felt responsible for fulfilling the role of soothsayer. The guilt of knowing she had failed to give some poor woman the proper warning only for her to end up in that hell....

Without a record in the courts she was put in the awkward position of having no official corroboration. The worry she wouldn't be believed upset her enough to put a dull ache in her gut. The fear she would be accused of deceit was an even more dreadful proposition.

On her way out the door, Jenene warned the babysitter, "I have no idea how long this is going to take." She had no idea what to expect either. Denial? Anger? Or would she scare off her ex's girlfriend? That wasn't her intent; maybe another woman could tame him—cage and domesticate the wild beast raging inside him—and prosper his better side.

Over coffee the woman I'll refer to as Lorene made a positive impression. Overweight and freckly, she exuded the air of a woman who took no nonsense and could handle herself.

After making it clear no rivalry should exist between them and her only intention was to make sure I would be safe in

Lorene's presence and offer some warning since she had been given none, Jenene began the painful recitation.

Feeling as if she was in an operating theater with an audience of one, Jenene began slowly, like a medical examiner laying out scalpels, scissors, bone-saw, clamps, cutters, separators, and skull chisels prior to autopsy. Then the dissection of her and Guy's failed marriage began. She pulled out and weighed all the diseased viscera for a veritable stranger.

Performing a postmortem on her marriage—airing the physical abuse, the cruel mind games, and the unreasonable control—was more cathartic than she had foreseen. By putting her in the position of having foreknowledge she would feel guilty not to impart, Guy forced her to speak what theretofore had been too embarrassing to divulge.

As aforementioned, Jenene's worry Lorene would strap on her boogie shoes and tap-dance right out of Guy's life was unfounded.

She never considered that insisting on meeting Lorene would force him to be honest for fear not laying some underpinning would be like sending his girlfriend blindfolded into a room full of mousetraps. Each revelation would be a painful snap if she stumbled into them sightlessly. Warning her of the traps not only accomplished removing the blindfold but also provided a map for her to follow.

This equated to Lorene remaining undeterred. A woman of resolve, she was committed to Guy, and open to his past. It also meant the abridged story Jenene told her was not at all unfamiliar. "He referred to that…yeah, that was mentioned…he told me that one too."

Guy's confession was even more dirt than Jenene thought to include. Evidentially all he speculated she would disclose. She was impressed he had owned up to his worst tendencies; in the real world it's none too easy to admit to villainy. We all fear rejection for our flaws and some bad guys are just regretful and messed up people looking to turn the page on their past mistakes for sake of a fresh future.

All the heavy truth lifting wasn't left up to her. Jenene was relieved. To his credit Guy made it so much easier. Through honesty rather than clinging to lies he freed them both.

The woman's receptiveness was nothing short of a breath of fresh air. It seemed, since she was already aware, there was no reassessing or recasting Guy in her mind as unqualified boyfriend material, which was probably good. By the time the two women parted, an understanding was reached, and Jenene felt good about Guy's choice.

Lorene would probably be a good influence on her ex. She accomplished the imperative of evaluating Guy's future second wife and it went much better than expected. She seemed like the sort of dame who wouldn't take his bad behavior and in that Jenene was right.

Leaving that meeting she had to wonder how it came to pass. How had she been so broken down? How could she allow all the abuse? Why hadn't she been the kind of woman no man would dare hit? In some ways it was up to her to stand tall—when she did he often backed down—but she had been unable. The most she could muster were the tears that would satisfy him and halt the thrashing.

Illumination wouldn't come for many years. Well along an odyssey to achieve good health. At the time she was stumped. She had once been so defiant, so strong, then she married Guy and became a wishy-washy nobody. What happened? How could she have known it was all in a name?

The best advice my biological father ever gave me was to be careful what you take in because it will go with you forever. I extend it to: be careful what you do, because what you do will always go with you too. Be it good, be it bad.

I'm grateful my parents parted even if it meant living in the shadow of divorce. The outcome could have been so much worse.

As a young man I read Gavin De Becker's brilliant book *The Gift of Fear*.

The perspectives offered by Mr. De Becker convinced me my father's weakness for violence very well would have ended with him in prison for my mother's murder. When I told Jenene, she also devoured the fascinating read. The case made in the book of how violence and control motivated by obsession escalate to terrifying crescendos convinced her too.

But that wouldn't have been the best results.

Chapter 39
Putting the Pieces Back Together

Even when you collect up the shattered remnants of your life that doesn't mean it's a puzzle easily reassembled. To Jenene every edge seemed frayed, unable to fit any other edge, so nothing went together seamlessly. What was left in the end was a patchwork at best.

Rebuilding after the divorce was a Herculean task. But after that ugliness, her life leveled out, save for health-wise, and she was busy making a life for us. Since she absolutely treasured motherhood, being a single parent was only difficult insomuch as the duty of tending to my needs was hers alone and she had to juggle my care with her desire to earn a living eventually.

On the health front, pregnancy residuals meant more surgery to repair her collapsed bladder and uterus. A broken ankle complicated matters. Not as much as a surgery to remove endometriosis and adhesions and at twice the bargain her appendix. Because who needs a vestigial anything, right?

Before she was again a money earner, she learned to live on a pittance.

After rent and diapers, there was precious little for food. Braunshweiger became a staple. Making the best of it, she put slices of the liverwurst on bread with mayo and lettuce.

The liver paste was cheap and full of nutrition. Named for a city in Germany, the lightly smoked liverwurst was also heavy on vitamin A, iron, protein, and fat, good ingredients for breast milk, which would be provided to me until I got too toothy and bit her nipple at fourteen months.

The Braunshweiger life hack she had learned years before from The Seniors, who would open their home to us so she could return to work.

Had her priorities been elsewhere, her responsibilities would have taken a greater toll. Since she cherished me, no sacrifice was too great. Even if accidents still happened.

My inquisitive nature would get me in trouble when I exploited an instant of inattentiveness and slipped into the bathroom to explore. This was when we were staying on the farm. I discovered some magic bubbles placed purposely out of reach in the medicine cabinet. Somehow in a matter of one or two minutes I had mounted the toilet and the porcelain sink to recover the pretty bottle and climbed back to the floor.

Maybe deducing such a pretty bottle must contain a tasty drink (very wrongly), I decided to chug the bottle like Stephen King trying to get drunk on mouthwash when he was drying out. Boom. One instant to the next, a life irrevocably changed. Not my best decision. But what can I say? I was eighteen months old and already expressing a wild side. Oh boy was the fallout a bummer. Worst immediate hangover symptoms ever. I blew chunks in a fashion that can only be termed epic.

What was worse, I took a huge breath in media res and aspirated vomit, causing the first of many coughing fits. While I was hacking uncontrollably, Bill threw the pretty bottle in the wood burning stove.

Jenene would rush me to the hospital and the prognosis would break her heart. According to doctors a permanent black spot had tattooed my lung. The damage was labeled chronic bronchial asthma—the worst type. Not a form of asthma you can outgrow.

This meant my childhood was one without sports or much outdoor activity and way too many prescription drugs, sometimes handfuls of pills taken multiple times a day. Countless icky inhaler puffs. And other drugs delivered via an expensive device called a nebulizer. Since debunked as less effective than the simpler inhaler, the loud machine the size of a lunch box seemed to be a medicine humidifier and was like breathing cool steam with a slight medicinal taste.

Jenene blamed herself for what amounted to a lapse of a moment during a time she was terribly preoccupied. Dealing with the divorce proceedings and Guy's faulty attempts to reconcile had her beleaguered and at wits end.

Inattentiveness on her part could be attributed to distraction and my uncanny ability to disappear, a trait that would cause much worry through my life. So much of her world was a seemingly inescapable slog and to lag in the one fraction about which she most cared left her greatly demoralized. It was all about effectuating a better life despite her fear and regret, rebooting and moving forward, and here her morale was sunk because she had turned her back for a minute and her son wound up with a lung disease that would in many ways affect both their lives.

It was a complication that would make things harder. She had to deal with it and could only find solace in the insurance provided by Guy's job. At least her son would have the best medical care available.

What had made her life beyond complicated and arduous was an accident that occurred on April 5, 1984. Ahead of the completion of the divorce, she existed in that state of distraction and that may have contributed to the accident or mishap or whatever you want to call the odd happening that would lead to the removal of her left kneecap.

Moving cars for the auction house—besides transporting cars across country—was ideal because it involved a minimal time investment for lucrative pay. For as chaotic as her life had been, she had established a smooth rhythm and felt more secure in her life than she had in a long time. If not for that fateful day, it would have been perfect.

It was like any other day as so often is the case preceding huge life changes.

Another auction. She had worked several. The odor of exhaust permeated the air. The cars were lined up outside in the order they would be taken into the auction house. She and the other drivers weren't assigned specific cars. Whatever car was next in line was the one they took.

Jenene didn't even pay attention to the model of car. It was nondescript to her, blue, green, or brown with a big wraparound bumper. All that mattered was the task at hand. Her concern was to get it inside on schedule—the auction was coordinated carefully, practically a military operation, and she did not want to be the weak link on the chain.

She slipped behind the wheel. Adjusted the seat so she could reach the pedals. Looked out the windshield. Noticed what should have been a miniscule problem. They left the hoods of the cars open so prospective buyers could take a peek at the engine. No one had bothered to close the hood of the car she was piloting. Not enough to see over, anyway, so she had to do it herself.

Short on time, instead of going around to the front of the car, and without thinking, she leaned over the fender to give the hood a good but measured shove. The objective was to close it enough to see but not so much reopening it would be difficult. A success, she withdrew…only to discover she was trapped.

A most odd circumstance, her left kneecap was caught in the wraparound bumper. Lodged, really. She gave it a shake. It was in tight too. No matter how she manipulated her leg, the chrome refused to release its bite.

Knowing time was slipping away, she gave it a good wrench. Another. Another. It hurt but she didn't know what else to do. Work ethic doomed her sadly. She had to get the car into the auction house, at whatever cost.

With a final heartrending pull, her knee came loose from the bumper…and its moorings. As it happened she heard a sound like packing tape getting ripped off cardboard. The impetus of the pull made her fall straight back…directly into a puddle.

Oh, what have I done! The pain was immediate and intense. *No, no, no!* Tears welled in her eyes. She wanted to cry, maybe even needed to cry, but it was not her nature to allow such exposure. *This can't be happening!* On some level she wanted to shake and wail and blubber—anything to distract from the all-encompassing, excruciating agony in her knee—but it would be in her composure that she found strength and not in a wasteful outburst.

So as she sat there, freezing cold water soaking the seat of her pants, she held it all in…and did her best to remove herself from the puddle. Trying to scramble, it was useless, between the pain and the weakness in her injured leg she was stuck.

When even removing herself from the turbid water proved beyond her, she knew she was in real trouble. Fear engulfed her and needed to be grappled into submission. At the time all she could think was: *What am I going to do? Will I need surgery? How long until I can work again?*

The next driver behind her, a mustachioed man with a crop of curly blond hair, hopped out to help her more to keep things moving than to be a gentleman. Even with him providing most of the support, she could put no weight on her leg.

"I need to be done," she told him. "I can't keep going like this."

"The fastest way out of here is to drive the car in," he pointed out.

"Help me behind the wheel."

So she drove through the auction one final time before learning some of her worst nightmares had come true. Jenene soon learned she had torn the ligaments.

Later, her knee would give out at the apartment complex pool and the cap would be shattered when it collided with the tile.

To make matters worse, after the initial injury, Jenene's boss, the auction owner, was told she had "severe trauma" and misunderstood the word. He took "trauma" to mean psychosomatic. This meant he told the insurance company the injury was in her head. As a result, her claim was denied and she had to fight for her rights in court. Fortunately during the period in-between her car insurance paid her wages and medical expenses.

There would be vindication. In open court her boss apologized and explained that he had misunderstood what trauma meant. But that was two years later.

What also marked the summer following her injury was the lump she discovered on her left breast. Somehow another health scare didn't surprise her. Her life was so jam-packed with them the distinction was coming to define her.

Feeling the fleshy bulge there, solid, palpable, put only one thought in her mind: breast cancer. As much as she wanted to ignore the possibility there was only one feasible option. She had to get a diagnosis. She had to find out if it was just a harmless cyst—oh, please—or the feared killer.

Jenene was understandably filled with worry but far from shocked when a breast examination led to surgery.

Once again she was rolled into a sterile operating theater, IV dangling from her arm. Saucers of light overhead drawing her eyes, the aesthetician kicked things off by counting her down into unconsciousness. She was warned being put under was becoming such a trend the frequency was another danger. The more often you're sunken into the depths the less likely you are to come back up to the light.

Forget about it….

Such immediate concerns weren't as pressing to her as what would happen if the lump were cancer.

Here she was off to sleep so they could remove a bit of material that could yet again shake up her whole life. Knowing if worse led to worse, the next surgery they would try to sell her on would be a humdinger, a lot more than the removal of something smaller than a thumbnail. It would involve eliminating an entire breast. Carrying no more or less vanity than any young woman, such an idea horrified her.

Back then there were far fewer sources of hope for breast cancer sufferers. Certainly not the survivor stories available today. All she knew was it would be very bad. Such terrifying realizations don't sit well when they follow you into drug-induced sleep.

The surgery went routinely. The gob of removed gunk was sent to the lab.

She was left on pins and needles waiting for the results. What would she do if it were a malignant tumor?

Could she hack it, breast cancer on top of everything else? It would be...maybe too much.

She would have to, though, if for nothing else...for her son.

If she had breast cancer, there was only one option. She would view the woman-killing beast as just another impediment to be deflected as it tried to trip her up by nipping and clawing at her heels. She was outrunning other things, why not that? She had no intention of letting it catch her...even if it were to close distance.

Time would tell that the worst-case scenario she so feared wouldn't have to be faced at that point. Caught in time, what was unearthed was pre-cancerous.

Jenene was advised to undergo regular mammograms.

Chapter 40
Fulcrum Points

Between that day at the auction in April and her vindication in court, Jenene's pesky left knee took her on quite an expedition.

After the initial injury, she was shuffled around and once again wound up in the incapable hands of Dr. Ernie. In June he mended her ligaments prior to the operation to remove the lump in her breast. Despite a deep dislike of her surgeon, the operation to repair the damage went magnificently.

Heal up and get on with her life—the recurring theme of her existence.

Rehabilitation was going great until the first accident. The apartment complex we had moved into provided a gigantic swimming pool. Jenene swam daily to rebuild her strength. The kindly older gent who was the head maintenance man would watch over me while she exercised. He was sympathetic to her dilemma. He was also dying of cancer and being around a vibrant little kid can offer rubbed-off energy.

One day in February she was beside the pool when her trick knee gave out. No time to flail or to even know she should flail, she dropped like a brick so suddenly and unexpectedly the impact was unavoidable. Her weight drove her down onto her repaired kneecap. The collision with the tile was like soapstone smacking into granite and the soapstone was shattered.

The pain was instant and overwhelming.

Lying there on the cold hard tile in misery, she salvaged what was left of her dignity. Took back her composure as her knee swelled. In time the insidious pain leveled out and became manageable. She had to wonder when she was cursed. Either she had terrible bad luck or she was hexed.

It wasn't that she slipped on a slick of water or even tripped on her sandal. Rational accidents she could avoid. Her knee simply lost all strength and down she went. How do you avoid that? She was doing nothing and her knee gave out. What would the story be when she had to carry her son? Would her leg just give out then too? What if she had to carry him up stairs? How would this affect her ability to work? Reasonable questions and she was all too sure of the answers.

No amount of denial or wishful thinking would convince her the accident caused only negligible damage. The sort of bruising bloomed that brings to mind midnight skies and hurricane waters. Bad. The pain even after the initial explosive flare of agony was torturous. Worse.

Dr. Ernie would hear none of it, declared, "You're just a whine baby who needs to go back to work," and refused to even look at her obviously damaged knee.

In the reception area of his office, she made a call to the attorney handling her workman's comp case.

"I fell on my knee and I need to see a doctor," she said, biting her lip to distract from the pain.

"What about the doctor you're already seeing?"

"I'm at his office and he refuses to see me. Should I go to the emergency room?"

"He won't see you?" Had he been a mobster the change that overcame his voice likely would have meant some schmuck was going to be swimming with the fishes. "You go home. Wait for my call. Stay right by the phone. It won't be long."

"Thank you."

"Don't mention it. Stay by the phone."

No sooner than she got into our apartment the phone was ringing. Through personal connections—friendship—her attorney saw to it she had an appointment with a highly respected orthopedic surgeon. His secretary listed the details and assured Jenene all would be good.

Jenene had no idea she would be meeting one of the finest men she would ever be blessed to know.

Jenene drove to the Lowry Medical Arts building in St. Paul for her appointment with Dr. Gaither. Maybe the swankiest medical center in town, it was the only one she had visited with valet service.

Dr. Gaither's nurse was a woman in her mid-thirties, attractive but too stern to be pretty, and the curtness accompanying her comportment implied she pigeonholed Jenene instantly as some unrespectable other. Maybe it was her attire; no doubt she was no wealthy snob in an earth-tones skirt, light blouse, and functional boots lacking designer names of account. Maybe the woman had a little crush on her boss and any youngish female patient was perceived as a threat.

By the time Jenene was placed in a nice enough if Spartan examination room after being led brusquely to X-ray for a snap shot of the damage, her expectations were low.

As if propelled by the tail of a comet, a moment later Dr. Gaither entered the room in a flourish and brightened her spirit inestimably. Jenene expected a crusty old white guy with hair coming out of his ears, bushy eyebrows, and a head the size of a globe to contain his massive ego. Instead she was presented with a dashingly handsome black man with a timeless quality; it was impossible to peg his age because he at once looked mature and cultured while also youthful and vibrant.

Jenene was reminded of actor Robert Guillaume who was currently the star of the ABC series "Benson" and would be until 1986. Dr. Gaither struck her immediately as having an air similar to the actor and the character he played on TV.

She would learn Dr. Dan Gaither was a black man who overcame the automatic racial intolerance that existed in the professional world in his day to rise to the very top of orthopedics. He was on the groundbreaking edge and had overseen advancements that resonate to this day. He did this by being a gifted surgeon with hands that could harness magic and make a scalpel into a wand.

"Hello Ms.—"

"You can call me Jenene."

"Very well." His manner was reserved, even formal, but she could see it was a veneer enveloping a being of enormous power. Then he dropped the bad news on her. That it came from him, a man she had known all of a moment but who intrigued her deeply, somehow softened the blow. "Reviewing your X-ray has led to one conclusion, you need more surgery."

"So it is bad? Dr. Ernie treated me like I was a whiny little brat and said I needed to go back to work."

"Dr. Ernie is a bit of a menace to society. I daresay he often does more harm than good. In your case he made a huge mistake." The final line was spoken with such solemnity it was clear by his own estimate if he made such a mistake he could never live it down. "I'm afraid that in being honest I will dash your spirits. I don't intend to but you have to know only so much can be done."

Dr. Gaither's innate caring was so apparent his very manner implied integrity, reliability, and trustworthiness.

"What's the timeline look like? I'm a single mother; I do need to work."

"I don't know if you'll ever be able to work again," he dropped the bomb.

"I don't understand."

"Your knee is completely shattered. Repair isn't an option. The best I can do is clean up the mess and hope you don't lose the ability to walk."

"I had no idea it could be so bad," she said stoically.

Jenene knew not to seize on the downside of all she was learning and get pessimistic. So what if her knee was wrecked. She was already dying, so there were always worse considerations. But it was difficult to imagine any upshot. Well, there would be a lot of time to spend with her son while she was again going through another tough recovery. Reason to read and get lost in distraction while her baby boy listened attentively.

"Don't lose hope. Worst-case scenario your mobility is impaired and you need a brace, maybe a walker to get around. I promise I'll do my best to make it so all you need is a cane for your balance."

"I'll have to walk with a cane?"

"It's going to be a long road back," he concluded. "Walking with a cane is the least of your worries."

Surgery was scheduled before she left his office.

With Dr. Gaither at the helm Jenene had no worries going into surgery.

The one always slow to extend trust, Jenene nevertheless trusted instantly the doctor who would soon demonstrate her assessment was correct by so devoting himself to her wellbeing he would take every setback and failure personally. He was flabbergasted his colleague could be so dismissive of what he saw immediately was a permanent—as in lifelong—handicap. In his eyes she saw a focus she had never witnessed before, as if the gears in his brain were always turning like an eternally wound clockworks.

Even before he became her friend she could sense he was someone with whom she wanted to have a friendship. Her picker may have been skewed when it came to romance, when different criteria based on hormones and pheromones and other causes of temporary insanity applied. But when it came to making genuine friends, Jenene had made several in her life.

In garnering real friendships, sometimes people get categorized in a way that prevents the relationship from breaching certain territory, which would prove to be the case between her and Dr. Gaither.

Before that there was the business of her knee.

Dr. Gaither was disappointed in what a lesser doctor would consider an accomplishment. Like a general following a defeat in battle reporting on the losses, following the operation he went to Lois in the waiting room and admitted he felt he had let Jenene down.

"All I could do was remove as much of the damaged material as possible," he said. "There just was nothing left to rebuild her knee."

Dr. Gaither's surgical assistant was tasked with applying a cast. The focus of the operation may have been her knee but her entire leg and foot were coated. Her leg required bracing to ensure it was held perfectly straight, which would make negotiating her way around with crutches an amusing and treacherous dance.

"I've never seen such a mess," the assistant said. "Your kneecap was *obliterated.* Usually we only see that sort of damage in traffic accidents."

Later Dr. Gaither spoke with such gravity when he described the operation it was worrying. Jenene could see he felt defeated by his failure to conjure greater magic. What could he do? There was no alchemy that could manifest the material he needed out of thin air to restore her "obliterated" kneecap. It was her fault, not his. What he had done was a sort of magic, even if he failed to recognize it. What she had done was bungle on the highest order and succumb to a series of inadvertent pratfalls.

"The patella is sort of the fulcrum of the leg," he explained. "Without it, there's nothing for the series of muscles and ligaments that give your leg all its strength to be affixed. Which means, with the bone matter wrecked and removed, I was forced to stretch the remaining tendon and a portion of the quadriceps muscle and fasten it below. Maybe in the future it'll be possible to replace your knee but that's the best I could do for now."

"Will I be able to walk, Dan?"

"I can't promise you'll ever feel secure on your feet again but you will be able to walk. There's going to be a long period of rehabilitation. Right now the tendon and muscles are strung as tight as guitar strings. They'll need to be stretched, and slowly, before you'll be able to bend your leg."

Dr. Gaither's company during the regular appliance of fresh casts never failed to brighten her day.

In time, as Jenene experienced his generosity, kindness, and expertise, she would come to realize what an honor it was to be Dr. Gaither's patient; he was the man star athletes relied on to extend their careers and wealthy old folks relied on to keep them on their feet. But what typified him most was his humility and devotion. None of the celebrity that came with being a hotshot worker of miracles meant a thing to him. And this highly educated doctor never seemed rushed when he was with her, a lowly peasant who had made about every wrong decision since she finally became a grown up.

Jenene believed helping people was his only concern, all people, not only the elite who could readily afford his unmatched talent. To be so skillful and not to possess a charitable heart would to him be an insult to whatever divine force made him capable of becoming such a maestro of his craft. Or so she would tell anyone who asked about the man she relied on to retain her capacity to walk.

So many doctors had rubbed her the wrong way with their arrogance and god act. Oh, some were brilliant (Dr. Ernie not so much). Yet few struck her as caring in any sense other than clinical. Even if they were lifesavers, without the human touch they could only be rated as fair. Meeting Dr. Gaither showed her the spectrum between a good and bad doctor was wider than she ever expected; she had thought no doctor could be so sympathetic and compassionate, so personable and engaging, so calculated and considerate.

Even though he was a handsome man and her dad was dead (had he a grave, he may have rolled in it, but such a notion never would have stopped her), she never viewed Dr. Gaither romantically even as he began to subtly show an interest she recognized as more than platonic. Why did she think so? The way he listened, his attentiveness. How he acted like there was no one else in the world he would rather spend time while they were together. Why he would be interested she had no idea but it was flattering.

It didn't help that he was married—or so she understood. She concluded he was another man who was a duality.

In January Dr. Gaither experimented with a different method of applying the cast because it freed Jenene's foot from the hot and sweaty prison.

"If you have any problems with this setup, get in touch immediately."

Problems there were. The cast worked loose. Jenene called Dr. Gaither's office and left a message with his nurse. "I'll make sure he gets it," she said neutrally (in her head it can be presumed smarmily).

The looser the cast became, the more of an impediment.
Jenene called again.
"I'll give him the message."
Finally the cast was so loose it slipped right off.

Jenene tried calling Dr. Gaither several more times with the same result.

Caution was her mantra. She was done gambling after the fall that caused her to lose her kneecap. No matter the prognosis, she intended to regain her mobility. If she was ever going to get there, she had to respect every restriction and move forward at a proper pace. To begin with, she needed to recuperate.

Life has to go on. Even though not yet healed enough for it to be safe to traipse around sans her cast, Jenene had obligations. Going out into a world of cold and ice was as inadvisable as it was risky but could she let that stop her?

Crutch slipping on the wintry parking lot of the apartment complex, yet again the hand of the cosmic trickster gave her a shove.

Another of those plummeting falls, this time in a flash she sat straight down on her left heel. The instantly forced extreme bend tore Dr. Gaither's careful work in a split second. There might have been a popping noise like a snapped rubber band when the ligaments and muscles gave way but if there was Jenene didn't hear it over her wails of agony.

Terrific pain was coupled with the oddity of what she saw next; without muscular bracing her leg dangled as if independent of her body.

Lois accompanied her to Dr. Gaither's office. To get around she needed help. Her left leg was as useless as "tits on a tomcat," as Herb was wont to say.

Upon examining her knee Dr. Gaither looked at Lois and said, "I can't make chicken out of chicken salad." The longer his examination went on the more set his face became. "Why weren't you in touch with me as soon as the cast became loose?" he said as if he were asking why she failed to retrieve antivenin after a venomous snakebite.

"You told me to so I called," she said wide-eyed. "Your nurse kept putting me off, saying she would pass along the message."

"How many calls?"

She felt as if she were being asked to tattle. In most instances not one to incur that sort of karma, she thought it was only right to clue him in. "At least a dozen. I knew it was bad. Maybe she thought I was whining."

Dr. Gaither showed uncharacteristic fury when he upbraided his nurse in no uncertain terms right in front of Jenene and Lois. "You never screen my calls! Never! If Jenene calls and needs me, you get in touch! Immediately! Call me at home, any time! Just don't dare stand between an important patient and me! Do you understand? I want to hear you say it."

Shaken by her boss's ferocity, the nurse said, "I'll call you right away...."

"If?"

"If Jenene calls."

"Return to your duties," he ordered. Then turned to Jenene. "I am so sorry she would do that to you. There is no excuse. I promise I will do everything I can to try to fix this."

Dr. Gaither had to again manifest miracles. His success would be proven when she was able to walk. Early on she needed the aid of a walker, later crutches, and then a cane. The handle of her cane is shaped like a hammerhead; it belonged to her dad. Later she could walk without aid. She would get well enough to return to work. What choice was there?

There was a reckoning of sorts when Dr. Gaither attempted to add an element to their relationship. "Would you join me for coffee?"

"I don't think your wife would like that."

"You know about her."

"You are married."

"In a technical sense."

"What does that mean?"

"We're married only in name. She lives in Minneapolis and I live in St. Paul."

"If you're estranged why don't you divorce?"

"She won't allow it. She has a funny of idea of marriage. Even the promise of getting taken care of well won't entice her to sign the papers. So in light of all that, what do you say, will you join me for a glass of wine?"

"I think your wife would shoot us," she said without a glimmer of irony.

"There's no way I can convince you?"

"I'm sorry, Dan. I appreciate all you've done. And more importantly how you've been there for me throughout this ordeal. Meeting you really changed my life. It's just I'm not in any condition to get into a relationship. Not that I wouldn't be interested. But my divorce is right behind me and my son is my whole focus right now."

"I understand," he said without malice. "You can't blame a man for trying."

Dr. Gaither soon after retired from practice to teach. Like Pookie, another of her heroes, he would fade from her life…but unlike the friend that took her to the ER that quintessential time, he would not disappear altogether. Their friendship lingered, a burning ember that could be easily fanned to flame.

Dr. Ernie, on the other hand, *was* a menace to society.

The proof being that no lawyer in the metro area could take Jenene's malpractice lawsuit for one reason: Dr. Ernie and the various offices with which he was associated—there were many, a way to avoid accountability—had at some time retained every law office in a fifty mile radius. This meant none could be retained due to conflict of interest. They all said she had a million dollar case. Such assessments were bolstering but in the end meaningless.

Jenene searched for legal representation until the statute of limitations ran out and she could no longer seek legal action.

Such was life.

Chapter 41
A New Beginning

"Russ doesn't drink at all," her overreaching friend tried to entice yet again, all too aware of Jenene's aversion to drinkers. "He's always bugging me about how much he wants to meet you. He's a really nice guy…and really handsome too."

"I don't think so." Jenene refused to buy into her friend's pitch. She had no interest in set ups.

There was the matter of all that she had gone through in her marriage and the aftermath. If she wanted one she had no trouble attracting a man on her own. It had been a couple years since her divorce and she didn't feel as though she were interested in anything remotely serious. Not when her health was so precarious. Not when she had been so burned.

She avoided commitment even if she didn't altogether avoid men. After taking such a trouncing, her heart needed to be spirited away for safekeeping in a far away stronghold protected by a deep mote filled with sardonic crocodiles ever ready to chomp.

Facing off against spirit-entombing insensitivity takes a toll. Cruelness depletes. She merited better than mistreatment and abuse and so long as she was beset by the aftershocks of her past she couldn't commit her future to any other man.

"What would it hurt to meet him? He sees you around Woodmere and he wants to get to know you."

"I'm not trying to draw anyone's attention."

"Oh, you're noticed. His mom warned him off you because you're a divorcée. You're the forbidden fruit."

Cripes.

"Didn't you say she divorced his dad and remarried?"

By the time Jenene was hoodwinked into meeting Russ—an arrangement made through deception due to the fact she was never convinced to meet him—she had lost her kneecap completely and was looking at being disabled for life. Which, according to her other doctors, wasn't going to be so long anyway.

She was not so needy she was willing to bring someone into her drama for her own benefit. It would be an unequal attachment. She could promise nothing in terms of longevity. Maybe she learned something about self-centeredness from her ex and never wanted to be that selfish.

Unaware she was walking into a setup, she accepted the invite to the private soiree.

Russ proved in attendance. He was embarrassed about the deception. He was nothing but pleasant. She gave him the cold shoulder all night. Yet at the end of the evening she accepted his request for a date. One thing was obvious, he looked a lot like Sam Elliot. She was mildly intrigued and if she were honest about her situation what could it hurt?

You know that strange or even disorienting feeling you get when you think you have reached the last step on a dark staircase only for there to be another and when you think your foot should land on a solid surface it just keeps going and in that instant your balance can save you or you can stumble and fall? That was what it was like for Jenene when Russ came into her life, a misstep and a possible fall…and only time would tell whether she caught her plummeting figure or landed flat on her face.

Even though it began under false pretenses, Russ made a good impression. At first he was cute enough to be forgiven but no welcomer for being bashfully apologetic. Then to his credit he had proven such a perfect gentleman she believed him when he claimed he had also been duped into the meeting. He was so earnest. Unassuming. And open.

So she decided to get to know him better. She would soon learn there were drawbacks. He lived with his mom (a call back to Guy). He was out of work (a major difference from her always employed ex). He had been in the Air Force but had been discharged. The reason he didn't drink was due in part to court orders; his legal troubles stemmed from a past relationship he had put behind him. But he seemed like a genuinely decent guy. Caring. Interested. Engaged.

Despite initial reservations Jenene had her first date with Russ Lehman on July 21, 1985 and so began what would be the great romance of her life.

They played cribbage all evening. After hours of play and twenty-eight games, they ended in a draw. Jenene revealed her health problems. Russ was sympathetic and tried to inspire her with hope. As it turned out he had survived a severe head injury. On December 21, 1979, when Jenene was suffering through her gallbladder trouble, he and a friend were involved in a motorcycle accident. The pair of roommates was out celebrating the holidays…unaware only one of them would live to see the new decade.

Riding bitch because he felt too smashed to drive, Russ miraculously survived…though not without injury. The friends plunged over an onramp embankment. They collided with the frozen ground below. The driver in a car who inadvertently but knowingly ran the pair off the road remains unknown to this day.

Russ's friend was killed instantly, head "cracked open like an egg," while Russ also suffered a head injury. Had he been wearing a helmet his neck would have been broken. Due to the enclosed head injury, his skull required "tapping," a procedure considered a major brain operation when performed on President Reagan but rather minor when performed on your average peasant. The procedure involved drilling a burr hole through his skull to relieve pressure caused by a buildup of cranial fluid.

The accident had a deep impact on him emotionally, mentally, and physically.

Simple skills learned as a child had to be relearned through intense rehabilitation. Impatience a problem that plagued his entire early life, he went back to work before he was ready. The manager of a truck stop, he wasn't able to keep up with his responsibilities and lost the job.

Inspiring the same sort of sympathy she would have felt for an abandoned puppy, Jenene began to care about Russ right from the start—with his sad story, his sad eyes, and his Sam Elliot swarthiness. There was also the fact he presented unmatched listening skills and the gentlemanly habit of anticipating her needs.

Jenene was perfectly fine with all Russ had been through and the fact he was still on his own long road back. It was obvious if they had a relationship his past would have a bearing. But so would hers.

What she saw as a hitch some might consider superficial. Yet it was concerning to her:

"So your last name is Layman?" She was reminded of the expression her dad floated when he thought she was being dumb.

"Not layman, Lehman, L-E-H-M-A-N. They just sound the same."

Sounded the same but the comparison was apt: Russ typified the layman, the everyman. Yet she recognized he was special, too.

His good looks were the frosting on the cake. Appearance was no substitute for substance but when good looks and substance go together it's easier to fall head over heels. She had a type most likely to draw her interest. Russ matched her conception of an ideal man. He had robust dark hair, high cheekbones, and a thick mustache hiding a thin upper lip. He was six feet tall, sleek, athletic, agile, and stealthy. His sleek—slight—build had always been an embarrassment to him but she felt he was built beautifully.

And his blue eyes were so deep and soulful she could look into them all night. When those eyes looked into her color budded in her cheeks, mounting like pink rose petals, and her heart did a hop, skip, and a jump, joyous as the child she might have been under better circumstances.

The power of love never dies; it just lies dormant. The right enticement to return can make all the difference. Feeling irrelevant was torturous. Feeling in love did not so much grant relevancy as show her if another could care for her so strongly she could be persuaded to love as strongly back.

How do you know the one for you? What criteria must be met in a mate? Good conversation factors largely, as does mutual sense of humor. Similar beliefs help avoid fundamental disputes, as does open dialogue about anything and everything to determine where important lines are drawn. What can mean even more? For Jenene the answer was satisfying lovemaking and in that regard Russ was the most competent, ardent, and genuine lover of her life.

Jenene was a passionate, sensuous, and affectionate woman in need of a valve release and Russ was the man with the wrench to do the job. It was as if they were made for each other, two parts of a single organism complete only through fusion. After him she would know all who came before were plain old sex and nothing approaching true lovemaking.

Since this author is the son of his subject, one might find it strange I can speak of these aspects of my mom so frankly and without blushing. The only way to explain it is to say that I view my mom as a human being, one in many ways like any other human being, with the yearnings and needs that impel us all. And because I view carnality as a healthy expression of love or even just a good way to relieve stress with a consensual partner in a non-monogamous tryst, I am in no way squeamish on the subject and would without shame candidly discuss my own love life.

Childhood deification of our parents is ordinary; they are the epicenter of our world, our personal creators, the rule makers and enforcers. But eventually we experience demystification when we recognize they are only human. Part of that is realizing there is universality to the human experience and our parents are as subject to lust and desire as anyone. I think part of growing up and becoming a well-adjusted adult is acceptance of such simple truths.

Because it was a huge change in our life I was a little mystified by the situation when Russ took up residence with us.

By three I was conscious of my own bourgeoning sense of self and the world around me. I was a voracious observer of the peculiarity of people and life. Jenene enrolled me in a pre-school-style daycare center. She thought being around other kids would be beneficial. I remember distinctly finding the other children absentminded and unfocused. Never one to nap, while the other children hunkered in hard-formed plastic floor cots mid-day, my teacher, who I had charmed, encouraged me to sort and reassemble all the puzzles the other children jumbled in a way they found hopeless.

I attribute my early self-awareness to Jenene's attention, affection, and all the reading. There is a stratum of awareness, beginning with self-awareness, and perhaps the final layer is conscious awareness not only of self and family but the world at large, others' feelings, the plight of animals, the environment, everything. Even at that tender age the wider picture was materializing before my hungry eyes.

After the divorce Jenene made the mistake of dating without making me aware. This spared me from gaining an affinity for someone who wasn't going to stick around. Yet it also left me rudderless when her relationship with Russ arose. I was ill equipped to share my mom or accept another father figure in my life.

After a period of adjustment, only months before I was reintroduced to Guy and became aware I had a "dad," whatever that meant.

So at first Russ was an interloper. A usurper. In time we would bond and he would become more my dad than my biological father. There were rough patches, disagreements, but we would become a family. But first Russ had to convince Jenene to counter her conviction that she would never again marry.

Chapter 42
Hard Sell

Floating on the magic carpet that levitates all in the throes of a new romance, Jenene and Russ were enjoying an afternoon at the Maplewood Mall with all the added glamour of feeling in love.

They had been together three months, had been living together for two, and the relationship was going…rather splendidly.

Russ listened. He was there for her. They seemed to have a lot in common. She was recuperating from her most recent bout of medical problems and it afforded them time to talk endlessly. He never seemed bored with her company. And he was willing to defend her and care about her and help wash away the grime of her failed marriage.

They shared musical tastes, particularly power bands of the early '80's. Jenene was enthralled by Steve Perry of Journey and knew every word of the band's albums. Russ attended so many concerts he would become hard of hearing, one of his favorite performances was the stage antics of right-winger Ted Nugent (Russ could not have disagreed with his politics more). Several of the songs of the band Foreigner struck a chord, "I Want to Know What Love Is" in particular. They adopted it as "their" song.

For his part Russ was doing everything he could to woo and wow. She thought she loved him. More importantly she felt she loved him. In her heart and soul she believed he was teaching her what love was really about. As it turned out she had never really known. He was attentive and always willing to listen.

In so many ways he was the best.

Yet in the real world you have to be happy for fairytale elements and expect your happier-ever-after to come with caveats and footnotes. Russ had a gigantic complication.

Russ was besieged by lasting ramifications of that frigid night that permanently altered his life. Even before they married the worst vestige of the motorcycle accident was revealed. A man haunted rather than hunted, Russ like Jenene was always pursued. His diabolical pursuer was The Headache. I treat it as a proper noun because The Headache had a significant bearing on our lives. The Headache was a monster.

The abominable thing never went away completely, not even with heavy narcotics.

Russ visited specialist after specialist. These mavens of medicine could never find a root cause. They concluded it "was all in his head," a rather odd use of phrase when his complaint was a chronic headache. I know what they meant. But they were wrong. It wasn't psychosomatic. We saw firsthand he was in pain, even agony. Seeing someone in that kind of shape has an impact.

Jenene recognized she had her baggage, too, enough luggage for an around the world trip; she was sympathetic to problems large and small. All relationships have trade-offs and when you're in love there are concessions and sacrifices maybe difficult but decidedly worthwhile.

Malls seem to have at least one jewelry store. It was only a matter of time before they came upon one. Jenene would have gone right on by without a second glance. She had no desire to be weighted down with a ring and it wasn't as if she could afford to splurge on emerald earrings.

By Russ' machinations she would end up going into the jewelry store...but not without a fight.

"Let's just check it out."

"I don't like to window shop," she stuck to her guns.

"Just for a few minutes...."

"If you want to go in, go ahead. I'll wait."

Lined up with the reluctant-to-commit guys waiting for their girlfriends to exit the store, she vowed not to be wooed into any sort of entanglement. She knew what he was up to, knew he was going to try to convince her to at the minimum get engaged. Her very reluctance to go into the store stemmed from her fear that...he *could* convince her. Russ had a way of influencing her, of getting his way....

Which was exactly how it worked out. He induced her into coming in, so he could "show her something." The ring was beautiful.

Not asking outright. He had to know that avenue would never work. His only chance was through a back alley. Russ said, "Would you wear it if I got it for you?"

The persistence wasn't so much in his words that time, but his eyes. They were full of hopefulness. She saw love in them...the pure, unadulterated, unmitigated kind, the sort about which her favorite bands like Journey and Foreigner sang. Knowing she wasn't long for this earth, it seemed an incredibly noble gesture. She could die before he even paid the damn ring off, yet he was ready to commit himself to her, to take on the responsibilities that would come with being her husband, which could be many.

So it came down to a decision of the heart. The heart knows no logic, the heart knows nothing of better judgment or fatal diagnosis or what might be right; the heart knows only what it wants, what it needs, and will have that which it desires against any obstacle or complication. The heart is relentless, a muscle that must never stop pumping even if at times it does pitter-patter.

"Yes, I'd wear it."

"Really?"

She nodded. She was happier than she ever imagined she could be. Still, she would take him to her doctor and have it explained in no uncertain terms how ill she was, give him an out. But for right then she enjoyed their moment. "But it has to be a long engagement," she added, knowing, because she cared about him, she would try to talk him out of what she saw as an ill-conceived venture.

There was one thing he did warn her about, the albatross he felt was around his neck. It was a feeling that had beset him for many years. He told her he was certain his thirtieth birthday would be horrible; he felt it in the core of his being. Since it was only a few years off, he thought it was important she should know.

At the time Jenene acknowledged his forewarning, not taking it too seriously. From her standpoint it remained to be seen if they would be together in three years. Even if they had become "engaged" she had no intention of jumping too quickly into marriage. Learn from your mistakes or you're doomed to repeat them.

Guy was Mr. Nice Guy until that marriage license turned her into a possession and he viewed that crummy piece of paper they signed as a receipt of sale. Had they never married, would their relationship have remained stable? Or would he have lost interest before violence ensued? Had they not been married his macho bullshit wouldn't have treaded water long enough not to drown because her heel would have been holding it under.

All in a name….

As for Russ, he was still in a trial period even if he thought he had all the loose ends tied up. The tryout may have lasted for years had events transpired differently. It wouldn't be long before an opportunity arose to prove he could be there for her in a huge way at a time when she really needed support.

When her son nearly died.

Chapter 43
Mystery Illness

My near death began with the mountain of tires.

Recall when I mentioned The Seniors' predilection for assuming a child was ready to look after their own affairs maybe a little too early? Yeah….

The farm inherited by Lal, Bill, and Herb from their parents was in total eighty acres. Once one large rectangle, civilization encroached even before our family settled there. The narrow swath of Grey Cloud Trail and a somewhat paralleling set of railroad tracks split four acres from the bulk of the property.

Legend has it about a century or so before some drama played out over the railroad company's plan, which resulted in the property split. When the workers arrived to lay tracks the previous owner was waiting with an arsenal not limited to a rifle. He had lined up all his equipment and livestock and positioned his likewise armed sons along the barricade. He was holding the payment check in hand and shaking his head.

"This ain't worth spit," he said. "Tell yer boss you all ain't moving 'til I get the eight hundirt dollars I was promised!"

A trip to a bank was too distant for him to retrieve his money up front. So he demanded silver. He didn't trust their piece of paper—once the tracks were laid they were staying whether or not it paid out. Silver was as real as the land he was losing; silver was universally recognized as currency. He refused to budge until they delivered burlaps sacks filled with his treasure.

Rumor was he was quite a miserly stasher and some of that silver may be buried on that land to this day....

But I digress.

The farm stood right at the border of St. Paul Park and the growing city of Cottage Grove.

Where Grey Cloud Trail continued on into Cottage Grove, a right turn onto mile-long Geneva delineated the border and dead-ended at a turnaround. This road was the east border of the four split off acres created by the railroad company, which was shield-shaped and bordered to the north by the vast Sandcastle family property.

A colossal century-old dairy barn stood on the bottom left-hand portion of the shield. Smack on a 45° curve. It was so close to Grey Cloud Trail it's just this side of a miracle no drunk driver ever crashed through the sliding door. Many barn cats met their end on that corner. People loved to abandon their unwanted felines on the farm.

No longer home to cows, Bill and Herb used the weathered gray structure to shelter boarded horses, in the upper holds store the hundreds of hay bales that fluctuated through each year (a long rust colored elevator stood always at the ready), and as a work shed loaded with literally hundreds of tools and knickknacks. There was a sawhorse between two thick beams piled high with horse blankets where they would catch a catnap, hats pulled over their eyes like cowboys on the range.

Another beam, near the door, was graced with four metal tiles, each with a number. They had been there for nearly twenty-five years. They read 1960 and signified an important family birth.

No such other numbers existed anywhere in the barn.

Besides a goodish sized chunk of land right off the road, a rickety looking but secure fence surrounded the spit of land, incorporating the barn and off to the left the concrete pump house that provided all the water for the horses. The perimeter surrounded the horses' domain. A line of broken down equipment distinguished the barnyard, an area that could be gated off. A private corral existed beside the pump house but was utilized rarely.

In the upper left-hand corner of the open grazing area cattycorner to the barn was a fenced off silage pit. For city folk, silage is corn, stalk and all, chopped into chunks and packed together in pits to provide food more sustaining over the harsh winter months. A crust forms that insulates the mulch beneath, which ferments lightly and steams when exposed to the cold.

The land before the silage pit dished down and would often hold a small pond in the spring. In the dry days of summer it would be a sand pit orbited by patches of grass the horses would nibble to nubs.

The horses, as many as eighteen or twenty, were fed hay or silage in long wooden furrows in the higher ground of the barnyard. The lower ground could be swampy at various times of the year, a morass looking to swallow boots and horseshoes alike. The worst spot of the quagmire had to be crossed to reach the steel water trough. The horses never seemed to care.

In trouble was the poor soul who misjudged the squelchy mud and tried to cross the middle rather than skirt the edge.

The region not included in the fence was a grassy space for the boarders to park near the gigantic steel gate where they retrieved their horses and the posts where they could secure them for saddling. It also sported the mass of abandoned tires, against a tall wooden fence shunning Geneva. By mass, I mean a heap that could eclipse the sun.

Bill and Herb put to service a burning barrel in the pump house. Long before environmental and health concerns would prevent such craziness, they burned old tires for heat. Instead of whittling wood, they cut the tires into squarish hunks for the fire. This may have contributed to the emphysema Bill suffered later in life.

Bill's kind nature, the style he used to be friend instead of foe, was often misconstrued as weakness by advantage-takers. Nowhere was this more evident than in the case of the tires. What began as a stack of tires in the 1940's had been added to gradually during the following decades.

Too friendly to post a sign or in any other way deter dumping, folks took advantage. The stack became two stacks, then three and four and five. Soon the stacks blended together into a unified pile. To be ogled over and added to for generations, Mount Cracked Rubber was born.

The problem was that once there was a visible mound of tires, everyone and their brother saw it as an opportunity to dump their old tires and so on and so forth, until there were literally hundreds of them, and not just those in the mountain but many others Bill and Herb had stuffed in every niche, nook, and cranny they would fit in a misbegotten attempt to keep the heap manageable, a feat that proved entirely impossible.

The barn and the horses and the tire pile all lent to what I saw as a sort of wonderland.

Visits to the farm were cherished events. For as long as I can remember Lal, Bill, and Herb were affectionately called The Seniors, which is why they are treated as a proper noun. They seemed both ancient and timeless to a little boy such as myself. Poking around the barn and the pump house, exploring like a free range chicken pecking at seeds, I was happier than a hog in squalor.

I would be Bill's tail and his little buddy. Following him around was a good chance to get another view of the world.

Then there was the permissiveness. It would get me in trouble. But I loved it. Authority was to be respected and when it was absent the lack of was to be exploited.

There was no way my mom would allow me to satisfy my intense desire to go crawling around a greasy, dirty, spiky mound of rotting rubber as if it were an exotic jungle gym. Oh, I'd tried before, when she was around, and bam, denied.

Bill on the other hand was of the let-boys-be-boys attitude and had no objection to my exploration. I would not say it reflected negligence so much as that attitude of a bygone era when kids were expected to be brighter, tougher, and more resilient.

I saw my chance and I seized opportunity, scaling the wobbly mass as if there were a prize at the top. The apartment complex in Woodbury had a wooden jungle gym I was too little to crown so the prize I was seeking was triumph.

Funny how it had begun with a few tires they welcomed because they were free fuel for the barrel stove. By the time I was climbing Mount Cracked Rubber, had they dispensed fliers word-of-mouth could have made it a popular roadside attraction akin to a massive ball of string.

Over the years Bill and Herb had turned a blind eye when people dumped these many unwanted tires, never realizing their passiveness had created the perfect mosquito procreation grounds. Mosquitoes require water for their offspring to incubate and grow. The mountain of tires fulfilled their needs. They were obliged with hundreds of small breeding pools. Regular rain kept them full; the black rubber drew sunrays to keep them warm; a thousand sources of shade kept them from getting too hot.

In victory I would encounter death. Instead of a trophy, I was met at the peak by a mosquito. There may have been many bites—it was a bloodsucker convention, after all—but it was a single poke that made all the difference. For sake of stealing a meal off me, that one particular mosquito left a parting zinger. The little squirt infected me with one of the worst sicknesses encountered by man.

Not one to kill even mosquitoes if I can help it, all things considered, I hope I zapped that little sucker.

Makes no never mind.

Bill called me down. I made my way back as carefully as a little dobber with stubby legs can. What had seemed like steps became a net full of holes. For a brief instant I was afraid I might slip through a gap and disappear into the mound like Alice vanished down the rabbit hole.

I would soon be slipping down a hole. Only it would not be my body that would go. It would be my mind.

Days later on a hot and sunny July afternoon I was given the opportunity to explore a motorboat. Parked at the apartment complex, it belonged to the dad of a friend. He permitted us to play to our hearts' content.

Soon after getting hoisted up, the sun began to get to me. I was flush suddenly. Sweaty. My head felt like it was full of hot air that refused to vent. Unable to release the hot air, I geysered the contents of my stomach and dropped in a convulsion.

Russ was babysitting while Jenene was at work. After regaining much of her mobility despite Dr. Gaither's fears, she had gained a cashier position at a Walgreen's. In some ways a small step, it was quite a leap from being completely disabled.

Scooping me up, he rushed me into the apartment. Made a frantic call. For all he knew his fiancée's son was dying. Summoning Jenene posthaste was the only option. He was aware of her protectiveness. Aware his actions would be judged.

Jenene rushed home to take me to my pediatrician, who checked me out and declared I would need to be kept under close observation. Next morning, I seemed chipper enough and wanted to eat. Jenene made the mistake of giving me one of my favorites, cottage cheese. In the car I had another unfortunate expulsion and thereon out was in a state of illness defined by flu-like symptoms.

This waylaid Jenene's plan to send me with Gram Davis for an overnight visit. She and Russ were throwing a party that night in honor of the one-year anniversary of their first date and to celebrate their engagement. She thought I would prefer spending time with Gram to being around a bunch of partygoers, an absolutely correct appraisal.

Sick in a way similar to how some of their indulgent guests would feel the next day, all I wanted was rest. Whereas the guests could pop a couple aspirin and sleep it off, slumber served as little more than an escape from feeling awful. Things were going to get much worse before getting better.

At midnight I rose with an appetite and joined the party to enjoy some crunchy raw vegetables. Jenene's pride was stoked at the praise that came from her friends.

"Whoa! Your son chooses to eat veggies?"

"That's amazing! I've practically got to threaten my kids with canceling Christmas!"

Enough socializing for one night, I returned to bed. The party went on until the last guests frittered out at around two-thirty.

Exhausted and drunk, after refrigerating the leftovers the beaming couple collapsed in bed. The rest of the mess could wait 'til tomorrow....

No sooner than her head hit the pillow Jenene was slumbering. Yet it seemed no sooner than that happened she was half-conscious standing beside the bed. Weird. A little wobbly on her feet, she had to wonder what compelled her to rise from bed.

What occurred next made her think invisible hands had pulled her out of bed. It was important she was awake enough to listen. Because at the point awareness met contemplation, a voice interrupted and she heard: *Go to your son! Right now!*

What powerful force impelled her to walk out of her bedroom and look in on me right then? Checking in on me was a usual routine, so she eventually would have done it regardless. Upon entering my room she got her answer. There was no time to spare.

Even in minimal light what she saw arrested her for the maybe three seconds it took to turn over what she was seeing and come to full sober wakefulness. In that brief span terror replaced confusion and the total reality of the situation sank in.

Is my son dying?, she thought helplessly. She had to decide to fight or bow in that instant. Such was her love it was never a choice. She broadcast telepathically to whatever forces decided the fate of sick little boys: *You can't have him!*

As if in the clutches of a huge invisible beast seeking to steal me from my bed, I was bent at the waist and my upper half lifted, shuddery chest pushed out. Absent of my senses, my eyes were rolled back in my skull jarringly. I was in the throes of a grand mal seizure but she wouldn't know that terminology until later. All she knew was that it looked as if I was under attack.

The great indignity was that my bladder and bowels had let loose and filled the room with stink.

"Russ!"

Jolted awake and sober in an instant, he joined her as she wrapped me in a blanket. They rushed me to the car. 9-1-1 was not yet common. With no undo recklessness, they sped to St. John's hospital (a choice made by our insurance plan). Meaning no offense to the staff, the facility was grossly ill prepared with my small stature. St. John's was simply unequipped to deal with a child. Without a proper size breathing apparatus to push my lungs to work, if I stopped breathing, all they could do was perform CPR manually.

A better-qualified team was summoned from Children's Hospital. They would bring the right respirator. Even though they were presumably rushing, that was one of the longest interludes in Jenene's life. Only the first of several such periods of unending time she would experience over the next seventy-two hours.

A litany of questions overwhelmed her as she waited at my side. They wanted to know about symptoms. Diet. Environment. No quick diagnosis, they needed information and they needed it yesterday to promise an answer by tomorrow.

What she told them only seemed to inspire bafflement.

Laid out on a gurney, I was thankfully unconscious while they poked me so much I should have pincushion cred in any sewing circle.

Jenene's eyes were on me when my breathing ceased.

When she saw my chest fail to rise, her heart skipped a beat.

Despite all her health scares and being told she would die young, only at the prospect of her child's death did she feel such an all-encompassing mortal fear she was clued into a wisdom she had been blithely ignorant of, that it is in loving others that we gain the greatest capacity to fear death.

She had always known even if not consciously. She had feared for The Seniors since she learned people die of old age. She had feared for her dad because he was wont to say he would not be around forever. But this was different. This was her little boy who had not really lived at all.

"Son, breathe," she pleaded near my face, warm palm cradling my weighty head.

I took a breath.

Then nothing.

"Son, breathe."

Another inhalation. Exhalation. Nothing.

"Son, breathe."

A nurse proclaimed, "Keep saying it! He listens to you!"

"Son, breathe...."

So long as she kept telling me to breathe I obliged.

After an indeterminable quantity of time that might have amounted to minutes as it felt like hours, the convened team blew in as if driven by tornado winds, gusted around the gurney, and drew me up into their whirlwind. Jenene was whooshed aside as they went to work. Less than a minute later I was gone, swept away, and she was left in the dying eddies of their passage.

A moment before she was compelling her son to take breaths—where I had lain was still warm—yet it seemed as if I were gone forever.

"Come on," she said to Russ. "We need to get there."

One of the nurses who had been attending me said, "They won't let you see him right away. We don't know what he has right now and tests need to be done. You should go home, get dressed"—they were still in their night clothes—"and probably eat too."

"Thank you," Jenene said.

At home they dressed hastily. Jenene had contacted Lois from St. John's. She and Jeff would meet them for breakfast; they would eat and then go to the hospital. Family support felt important.

They were in such a rush accidents were narrowly averted. Within an hour they were hoofing it into Children's like a team of galloping horses. Jenene was sick with anxiety. She needed news. For a quarter she should have purchased a newspaper and gotten some. What the staff presented her with was a bureaucratic wall. They expected her to climb before anteing up a crumb.

At first the expectation to fill out paperwork seemed perfectly reasonable. It was only after several minutes—and a large stack of forms—did the rigmarole begin to feel like a diversionary tactic, the runaround. Seeing through the subterfuge, Jenene said, "How is my son? Why won't you tell me?"

"When there's information we will pass it along."

"What's going on here? You can't tell me anything? For instance, can you confirm he's not dead?"

"Please calm down. There's no reason to believe your son isn't alive."

That sounded suspicious.

"I demand to see him," she said. "Take me to my son right now!"

Admitting I had yet to arrive was a chasm too far to cross until Jenene's fury forced the leap. "Your son…is still in transit."

"What? They were heading straight here. We went home; we ate…what the hell's going on here?"

"We don't know. We lost them…."

"Lost them? You better explain right now what's going on!"

"We'll get a counselor to talk—"

"I don't need to speak to anyone," she said evenly. Whenever you get heated in a hospital they want to brush you off on a counselor and she did not appreciate being patronized when she wanted real answers. "All I need to know is where my son is!"

"We've lost radio contact. Right now the ambulance your son is in is silent."

"What could have happened? Were they in an accident?"

"There's been no report of one. Don't believe the worst. I'm sure they'll be here soon."

"You better find my son!"

In a life full of down points, this was one of the lowest.

Soon was not soon enough.

Every second seemed to elongate, stretching beyond reason. Minutes? Hours? What was the difference when everything was on the line?

The ambulance at last made radio contact.

In the dark the monster only existed in speculation. Knowing turned out to be scarier.

The good reason for radio silence was that every hand was needed to grasp my life and not let go.

Around Fifth Street in lower St. Paul the driver was forced to pull over when I went into another grand mal seizure. The whole team worked to resuscitate me. Their efforts ran a medical gamut that meant little to Jenene until they got to the point. What it came down to was there was only one way to snap me out of it and their solution horrified her.

They were forced to put me in a drug-induced coma.

When word reached her that the ambulance arrived, Jenene insisted on seeing me ASAP. They shut her down.

When you are sick with a not easily diagnosable illness, doctors have to become chin-scratching detectives to solve the mystery. The symptoms, contradictory and complicated yet familiar and common, told them enough to narrow the options to two. Both were devastating. What became certain was due to the swelling in my brain I had either meningitis or encephalitis.

Before proceeding with treatment, a determinative spinal tap (a.k.a. lumbar puncture) was ordered.

The juice that makes a protective coating for our spines and brains, cerebrospinal fluid is drawn through a needle popped into the low back. After siphoning me, testing revealed the cause of all my problems was encephalitis. Knowing that much was not enough because my case was so remarkably terrible. Further laboratory testing would confirm I suffered from the dreaded La Crosse strain of mosquito-borne encephalitis, the first case of the life-threatening illness in many years.

Life is strangely circular, a long needle acting as an artificial proboscis pierced me to learn the illness was left in me by a randy female mosquito's natural syringe.

I was put in the Intensive Care Unit or ICU in a sealed germ-free environment.

If I would wake up remained to be seen, or even if I would live.

It was my turn to outrun death.

Chapter 44
No Best-Case Scenario

Encephalitis is the name given to any inflammation of the brain. The affliction is commonly minor with little lasting impact. Discovered in La Crosse, Wisconsin in 1963, La Crosse encephalitis virus or LACV conversely was so dangerous the prevailing knowledge of the day was there was no optimistic outcome.

In extreme cases, such as mine, optimism was discouraged. For good reason: doctors don't deal in false hope. No one had come back without severe brain impairment. To them my case would be no different.

As I incubated in my quarantined ICU quarters, fate uncertain, Jenene was put in an exam room and given a stapled stack of paper explaining the ruthless beast she was told was trying to yank her son away.

Every page supplied worse news. Even minor sufferers were saddled with epileptic seizures, personality unrest, inability to learn, difficulty communicating, cognitive limitedness, lack of social decorum, emotional instability, inadequate concentration, hormone problems, memory problems, pain and sensation problems, and worse problems exhibiting the sort of appropriate behavior that helps a person navigate life.

Then it got really dire. From what was known about my personal condition, the best case offered was heartbreaking. I would remain the mental equivalent of a three-year-old for the rest of my days but would otherwise live a "normal" life. Worst-case, I would be paralyzed and unresponsive. Though death was a possibility, statistically speaking the chances were one in a hundred.

Inundated. Filled with fear. Never in her wildest worries did she conceive of such horror happening to me.

When the doctor strolled in to discuss her view of the situation as opposed to what he saw as the reality, after feigning interest in her opinion, he isolated even the faintest fragment of hope and sought to quash it like a slapped mosquito. His manner came across as coldhearted and inconsiderate. Not so much that he was uncaring; it was more that he exhibited a professional stoicism.

For a man of science and logic, the most caring stance was to let her know in no uncertain terms the son she knew and loved was gone, replaced by a changeling with a currently unknown demeanor—a changeling who at the very least would be greatly diminished.

"I'm supposed to accept that my little boy will stay a child forever…only eventually in an adult body?"

"There are facilities that could care for him. When he gets too big for you to handle."

"He's my son. I could never send him away."

If the worst happened would that prove true? How well could she deal with an adult-sized toddler who might need to wear diapers and could show violent impulses? How long would Russ stick around? Who would help? Homecare nurses? Who would pay? How would Guy factor in? Was the insurance provided by his job adequate? If her health continued to sour and she stroked the doctors' egos in proving them right by dying, who would take up the cause? Was her son doomed to a sanitarium?

Engulfed in the black smoke of blind speculation, one beam of illumination shone through—radiance so bright, resolute, and unyielding it shined on waves of hope. Was it intuition? Was it divine intervention? Whatever it was, instead of being trounced by depression Jenene was overcome with optimism.

The best results would happen.

"That won't happen," she said firmly, resolutely. "I don't care what you say. My son will come out of this. The best results will happen."

As the very words you read prove, she was right, but at the time the doctor must have viewed her as a borderline hysterical woman in deep ignorance-driven denial and he probably thought it was in her best interest to snap her out of the delusional state.

"I know it hurts but your son is going to be retarded. You need to accept the facts in that booklet. Your son will be different no matter what you—"

Jenene pitched the stack of papers and they riffled toward him like a rousted grouse. On the grouse's tail feathers she shouted, "Not my son! You don't understand! He's going to get better no matter what you think!"

My contraction of La Crosse encephalitis was the first such case in years.

The Minnesota Department of Health (MDH) in conjunction with the national Center for Disease Control (CDC) investigated. Fears of outbreak meant it was important to track down the source of the carrier mosquito.

"They need to know everywhere your son has been in the last ten days," the doctor said. "The sooner the better."

In her frazzled state of mind she had to think, so she took a deep breath and concentrated. The problem was even in the long ago land of the early 1980's, people got around and I had been all over. Of course the farm, a couple of times, but also Woodville to see Gram Davis, and Afton to see Grandma, and West St. Paul for visitation with Guy and Lorene. There were other places too. It was amazing how difficult it could be to recollect every single stop along a ten-day period in a relatively active life.

The list set a wider search zone than best suited the authorities. It meant their search could not be focused to one or even two locations. They would collate the data to direct their movement and the farm would be where they hit pay dirt.

In cases of minor encephalitis it is important not to restrict fluids and to keep the patient well hydrated. In the past, LACV sufferers were also given fluids intravenously, which the doctors overseeing me were going to gamble was a mistake. What if too much fluid led to too much fluid accumulating in the brain, the cause of brutal impairment? Their choice would prove visionary.

Jenene's vigil lasted my entire stay.

Russ proved a proficient facilitator, staying with her in the hospital, making trips home, and on top of it all going to his job at a tire shop in Woodbury. Edgier than she had ever been before, he managed to calm her with his subdued and dedicated manner.

Jenene's boss gave her static. He thought her very selfish for missing work. That her son was comatose had no bearing. He called her unreasonable. He even dared to threaten her job. Russ supported her in her decision not to be intimidated and kowtow to his irrational demands. Out of good conscience or simple economics, in the end he caved.

The hospital provided her and Russ a vacant room to catch snoozes. Not that either slept a lot. Too much stimuli, too little rest, and too many big decisions: Jenene felt as if she was on the verge of blowing a fuse. The orbit of her anxiety extended to Russ and they bore the worry together. Suffering such a thing jointly can go far in establishing steadfast bonds and that was their experience.

There was a lumpy cot and an even less cozy chair. Without question he insisted she take the cot even though he had to get up, go home, and get ready for work. He was also responsible for bringing drinking water. St. Paul's water, even under the best conditions, has a rather unsavory flavor. At the time, it was particularly repulsive, ripe with an industrial smell that precluded even taking a sip from the drinking fountain. The bottled water craze being some time away, the best available water came from wells, such as the one at the farm, but the tap water in Woodbury was sufficient.

As for me, I was chilling in a room within a room. The chamber providing a germ free environment was transparent glass. Visitors and medical staff alike had to gown up and wear a mask to enter my personal quarters.

Jenene spent as much time with me as she was allowed. Wanting to believe her voice could penetrate the murk in which my brain was submersed, she talked, assurances and promises and whatever else she thought important to convey. Much more than she might have expected made it in.

How alert and sentient would I be if—when—I woke? Would I be confused? Or awake but absent? Following the trend of trusting the best results would happen, she worried I would come to and be frightened by the totally covered featureless humanoid figures. She hoped to be there to comfort me. All she could do was wait as patiently as possible for that instant. She knew it would come.

Because a ventilator was doing my breathing, accumulated mucus had to be drained from my lungs manually. The process appalled Jenene. A tube was inserted through my mouth down through my trachea and into my lungs and, like a turkey baster sucks up fat, dragged the phlegm out, making a wet slurping noise. As this was happening, my small body went into paroxysms.

The nurse would test me to see if I could breathe on my own. When it became apparent I could, this after the initial dicey slew of hours when my survival was reliant on technology, the nurse said to Jenene, "You need to make a choice. We can remove the ventilator and let him breathe on his own or prevent complications if he were to need further assistance by leaving it on."

"Without life support will mucus still have to be drained from his lungs?"

"His body should return to regular function. But if he were to need—"

"Take it out." The sight of my distress was torturing her. She was banking on her belief it was only a matter of time until I got better.

Thirty-four hours in the abyss while my fate remained nebulous. Soul boogieing nearby but elsewhere while the flesh fought permanence and irrevocability.

Then I came back.

Jenene was by my side when it happened.

I came to with an observation, "Why aren't those doctors wearing masks?"

They were on the other side of transparent glass but I was unable to tell. To me they seemed close enough. My awareness of the surroundings was remarkable. I was so alert I knew being in my presence required a visitor to suit up and shroud their face. It proved that though my body was comatose my mind was not in a vegetative state; instead I sponged up information, preparing myself evidently for reentry into the waking world.

"He's back," Jenene proclaimed. That one instant might be the single best instant in her life, the one when she knew not only that I survived—I was cognitively intact. Nothing has ever made her happier, and some joyous events do lay ahead in a life of inordinate complication.

Once I woke, my immediate recovery was a slow slog for one simple reason: I was thirsty, so thirsty it was one of the most torturous times in my life, and all intake of fluid was restricted.

It did not help that my arms were each equipped with an IV to keep me just hydrated enough not to die, which translated to blood draws having to come from my feet and intense thirst.

Even a butterfly needle becomes an implement of excruciating pain after a bunch of pokes to a tender little foot. I would draw my tootsies up under my butt at the sight of a nurse like a hermit crab sinking into his shell at the sight of an octopus. Unfortunately, the way the beak of an octopus can break into a shell, my feet were in fact unprotected and the syringe always got its drink.

Me, I wasn't so lucky. Another indignity, I was reduced to begging, which broke my mother's heart anew. "Can I please have some water, Mama? Please! I'm so thirsty, Mama!"

Denying me made Jenene feel heartless for doing what was right. That is the lot of the parent, living the pain of doing what is right in the face of the immediate painful consequences. The doctors and nurses laid down the law to her. Then it was up to her to enforce their edict. Being cast in the role of bad guy never sat well with her.

"I'm sorry, honey, but water will make you sick again." Just her being there soothed me and I would be calmed.

Jenene and the nurses were provided with lemon-flavored glycerin swabs to wet my lips and tongue. A poor substitute for a mouthful of cold water, the attempt to pacify was appreciated. But to a child who very well would have traded every toy I owned for a single sip of water, the sweet swabs were little more than a tease. I would have an aversion for sweet drinks until I became an adult, an apparent oddity other parents would praise as their kid expected soda and I demanded water.

Deprive yourself of fluid until your tongue feels like a salted slug in death throes and you'll know what it was like. Even today, because I was totally powerless in the situation, I feel a kinship with anyone dying of dehydration in the desert, any castaway surrounded by a sea of water they cannot drink, and any survivalist with a depleted canteen and no way to make potable water.

My heart goes out to the citizens of third world countries who are forced to drink swill or die of thirst. Easily accessible clean water is truly a gift. Had I a gold bar, I would have gladly traded it for a single swig of water, a concept explored in the classic *Twilight Zone* episode "The Rip Van Winkle Caper."

Diversion by way of well-wishers kept me from absolutely losing it. I learned quickly not to implore my company to sneak me a Styrofoam cup filled with any drink they could acquire, preferably the simplest of all, sweet thirst-quenching aqua. No one would give in and for good reason. Guy did bring me some of the toys I played with at his place. And Russ brought my favorite stuffed animal from home. Alas, no water came my way until fears of brain swelling were past.

Going home meant everything…after a good drink of water.

When Jenene had time to recall the chain of events leading up to rushing me to the hospital, she had to wonder about the force that shoved her out of bed and demanded she go to me.

Ethereal might be a good word to describe the experience. The voice had the clarity and separateness of the one that warned her of her dad's death. Inside her head but outside her consciousness, the voice struck her as distinctly separate from her mind.
The otherworldliness of the incident made her think it had to be a guardian angel.

What were the long-term ramifications of my bout with La Crosse encephalitis?

I have a good memory. I can learn quickly. And I am physically strong. If one drawback follows me, it has been emotional sensitivity. I tend to feel very passionately. I weep for much. Empathy and compassion have hindered me because when others do not share your scruples it marks you as an outsider. Sympathizing with a stranger's dilemma can be mistaken for weakness by the unenlightened. For me caring is no simple undertaking and hating can tear me asunder.

Maybe the most amazing thing is my IQ. In first grade my teacher observed that I wanted to read back and forth in the manner of the Japanese. This led to testing. I thought I was playing games. I don't recall taxing myself. I accomplished the tasks before me leisurely because I was already too aware of the greater worries of life to let school stress me by seeing it in competitive terms. Somehow at about half-speed, I managed to test one point below genius.

Had I only known one lousy point separated me from one of life's most respected labels....

After almost losing me, Jenene would become a bit over-protective. As fate would have it, Russ would factor in my life hugely. Within six weeks of my recovery they would be married. How he conducted himself during the scary ordeal sealed the deal.

Why did I recover against long odds? One word: Reiki.

Chapter 45
Carried Away

After a nine-month engagement, Jenene married Russ on August 30, 1986. It was an ivory and lavender wedding in a time when that was unheard of—they had to send away to California to get half of what they needed. It had all been rushed in Jenene's opinion, but Russ was adamant. After he showed so much support, how could she deny him? He even conspired with the minister to move up the original January date. Who wants a winter wedding he argued.

The wedding present Jenene gifted her new husband was unique and demonstrated her open-mindedness. Despite a fear of snakes dating back to a contest she had with a blue racer as a little girl of four or five, she presented him with one of the slithery reptiles, a yellowtail cribo he named Jack.

And this was after he either startled her inadvertently with the huge snake or took a huge risk by causing her to be startled. They had strayed into a pet store to browse. Eyes concentrated on a display of varicolored tropical fish she failed to perceive sneaky feet Russ sidling up behind her. When she turned Jack was draped over his shoulders and arms like a scaly living stole. Seeing the long sleek reptile so close caused her bones to about jump out of her skin.

Very unlike how they are viewed or depicted, snakes are gentle, even affectionate animals. Jenene learned this by visiting the pet store without Russ to begin payments on Jack and to overcome her fear by handling the smooth-skinned creature. In time, she did just that—even if she could too easily remember the day a blue racer chased her all the way from the barnyard to the back door only to turn tail and flee when she spun to confront the slinky serpent.

As for Russ, he gifted her a brand new western-style saddle. She loved riding Cognac. No longer would her rides have to be bareback.

For some time the wedding day was one I remembered as bad because my rental shoes were too tight, my white tuxedo was too hot, and worst of all I was enlisted to be part of the ceremony as the ring bearer, a task that made me feel like the whole thing was being rubbed in my face. To me I was losing my mom. It would take time to adapt but in retrospect I can see it was a wonderful day because it was when we became a family—not a typical one, or maybe more typical than I ever imagined.

The service inexplicably went perfectly, a nice change of pace from the snags always complicating things.

In a moment that signaled permanent change, their vows were spoken and accepted and they were declared married all in a span of minutes.

In Russ's eyes Jenene saw the sparkle of trueness, of devotion, of all her dreams of humble yet passionate togetherness made manifest.

From that day forward Russ would say it was the best day of his life. His dream had come true. His fairytale.

I had my gripes—a few were alleviated when I was able to switch my duds—but I was soon caught up in the conviviality of the reception party.

Ours would be a family of arguments and hugs, retribution and forgiveness, stinginess and generosity, detonations and neutralizations, want and satisfaction; we would emerge as a unit of component parts stronger for being placed together even if not all the nuts and bolts always fit quite right. We faced many obstructions and impediments—together.

Chapter 46
Herb's Date with the Amtrak

For so long Jenene dreamed that Herb was going to get hit by a train. It came as no surprise when it happened.

One of those menacing reoccurring dreams, it was always the same, the train bearing down, Herb trying to get out of the way, and bam! She was tossed into waking, knowing he was not quick enough, was not able to muster the extra giddy-up to avoid the inevitable, and was hit by the train. Only when it happened…the old boy lived.

Even at eighty-two, Herb would prove just how resilient and downright indestructible he was when bleary vision due to cataracts caused him to mistake the much faster Amtrak for a Burlington Northern, the event that precipitated Bill's request that we move in. He was on his way down to the barn. On that frigid winter day he challenged the train to beat the cold and the train won.

Herb could scoot pretty quickly for an old boy. Hale heartiness defined even into old age. So he made it almost all the way across. It just wasn't his day. The heel of his boot was his downfall. The train caught the lick of rubber.

In an instant the unforgiving force tossed Herb brutally into a pile of jagged rocks. Simultaneously the boot was stripped from his foot and his ankle was snapped.

Bill hauled him up to the house in the tractor's shovel. With no aid and leg bowing under his weight, he hobbled into the house through the basement door. Inside he nestled beside the furnace. He said he would take his meals there. Would entertain no disapproval.

Lal called upon Jenene and Russ. She hoped they could help find a way to convince the old boy to accept medical attention. Jenene had just the idea. She made a call. Waited. Answered the return call. The man she had summoned would come.

The Sandcastle's owned the farm adjoining the spit of land on which the barn sat. The families had an affiliation spanning decades. Out of a diverse brood of twelve kids, it was Dr.

Sandcastle who gained the most respect by pursuing medicine. Bill and Herb had been the older guys the Sandcastle boys had looked up to and they had remained close friends. Dr. Sandcastle was the only physician Herb trusted.

Of course Herb was convinced to get the bone set. But not to get rid of the pain and make sure he could walk again. No. He did it so everyone would get off his back and leave him alone. Dr. Sandcastle would be the one to do it, by pointing out the hassle would only end once he was fixed up.

When the gruff old boy gave in, Russ helped Dr. Sandcastle escort Herb out to the car. Having experienced the pain of a broken bone, Russ was impressed with Herb's reserve. He told me, "When he put weight on his leg it really bowed. Herb barely made a grunt."

Albeit he wound up with some metal in his ankle, getting hit by a train was a blessing in disguise. While Herb was in the hospital the surgeons were advised about the impairment that caused him to mistake the Amtrak for a freight train. Even if he griped the whole time, they convinced him it would be worthwhile to remove the cataracts.

Before the results were evident to him, Herb was grumblier than ever. Then he recovered and miracles of miracles he could once again see clearly. At that he was elated to a degree we thought beyond him. He became a new man practically overnight. When his eyesight became too poor to make out the words on the page he gave up his beloved books after a lifelong love of reading. So reconciled had he become to his poor vision, he was giving his novels away one at a time, a massive collection of westerns.

Vision restored, Herb entered into a new phase of life with a renewed desire to live. Able to read again, able to *see*, he was transformed. His newfound cheerfulness correlated nicely with us moving in.

However, to say his irascibility evaporated entirely would be disingenuous, as Russ, or as he was referred to by Herb every time the old boy was peeved, "Sap Head" would be reminded almost daily. Better mood or not, Herb was a born grumbler, and his space being invaded had a way of souring his mood.

I think it could be said the old boy and I had a special bond.

Chapter 47
A Whole New Life

When we are children our lives hinge on our parents' gambles; when they lose, we lose. Sometimes all you can do is hope to break even.

"How would you feel about moving to the farm?" Jenene asked one day.

"With Lal, Bill, and Herb?" I asked. Life had taken on new hues for me since my health scare and such news fit right into my positive outlook.

"They need help. It's gotten harder for them since the train hit Herb. He's gotten better, but they're struggling. They don't want to go to a nursing home, so Bill invited us to come live with them."

Jenene always explained things to me in a very adult way; she didn't condescend due to the fact that I was a child, the way most adults tend to treat children. Maybe it was because I displayed many adult-like qualities even at a young age. I was one of those kids described as having an old soul, and it was true.

I looked around the dingy basement level apartment, subject to backed up drains and flooding. Then out the ground level living room window at the playground across the street. How I had hoped I would have fun there when we moved in. I had soon learned it was always overrun with bullies.

If I were not such a restrained child I might have yelled zippy!

Nowadays it's popular to send elderly family members to nursing homes. I think there is an inherent lack of respect in this action, but then some parents don't exactly earn the right to be taken care of by their children.

There was a time when there was no question of where a parent would live out their old age except as to which sibling would bear the responsibility. The Seniors came from such a time, only their parents took it further and denied them blessing to marry. The youngest sister, Lucille, was only able to marry and beget our branch of the family tree only because she did it in secret.

Out of propriety, Lal, Bill, and Herb acquiesced to their wishes and were well into middle age before their parents died. An era when folks of their age had limited dating opportunities, they didn't even try. As a result they were robbed of the progeny that may have been there to care for them. Which was where we came in.

"We'll take care of them? Like how?"

"Well, we'll help Lal with the housework and cooking and we'll help Bill and Herb with the horses."

"Can I have a horse?"

"Maybe someday. I can't promise anything right away."

"That's okay. Can I ride Cognac?"

"That could be arranged."

"I can't wait!" Excitement spiraled through me like a corkscrew through a cork and—pop—made me maybe the most open to change I would ever be.

Moving to the farm meant the world to me…even if it was a totally new experience. Much as she instilled integrity, common sense, and a love of reading, Jenene instilled a great deal of love and respect for Lal, Bill, and Herb. Living with them would prove an amazing, strange, enlightening, startling, and gratifying experience; the value of family and wisdom would prove immeasurable.

Jenene was less optimistic. Worries compounded worries. Making one large household eased some concerns and created others. Was she good enough to run a household? Was she capable of making sure The Seniors were taken care of well enough? All she could do was find out by committing herself fully to their care.

Just a hop, skip, and jump away, a Farmall tractor and hay wagon were tasked with transporting our possessions from the Pullman Apartments to the farm. This saved the expense of a moving truck but was a process too easily equitable to molasses flowage in winter. But it got the job done and we were delivered from the workaday apartment complex grind and deposited in a world apart.

Over the railroad tracks and at the end of a fifth-of-a-mile-long gravel driveway, the homestead sat on the main seventy-four acre parcel, an oasis surrounded by fields and enclosed by tall shade trees.

Close to the house were apple trees and raspberry bushes, aspects of an immense well-tended lawn that also included rock gardens. Drawn by the sweet apples so delectable in pies and crisp, deer ventured near for treats, a beguiling buck the most prominent.

In those days there was also an area at the rear of the backyard devoted to storing huge logs to be broken down for burning in the furnace and stove. Beneath the bark the huge logs were laden with carved out networks left by tiny insects like intersecting snail trails on a sidewalk. In the years after we converted to gas the area sprouted a small forest as entropy reduced the logs to mulch and moss; the area took on a woodsy odor and filled with gnats as what started as tiny saplings sprouted a forest.

In its hey-day the farm could have been a candidate for the cover of "Country" magazine. Back when the tiered rock gardens were weeded meticulously and full of flowers, the grass gleamed verdantly, and the perimeter bushes pruned suitably. When there was time and back power to keep up the maintenance. Work worth it when hosting an outside reunion or birthday party. Not all that necessary the rest of the time since the place was so far off the beaten track. Yet done just the same.

The farmhouse sported a huge front picture window. It looked out at an angle on the driveway and the railroad tracks. The fifth of a mile distance between house and tracks did little to dim the thudding rumble when the trains roared by us. The whole house would quake gently. People would sometimes wave from the infrequent passenger trains if we were near enough to be seen.

Whenever Bill sat in his living room chair and a train roared by, he would pause what he was doing and look out the picture window. If the sun were high to shade his squinched eyes he would hold a section of newspaper to his brow. When I asked my mom why he observed this ritual, she told me he was convinced one day there would be a derailment. The notion was a little appalling. Henceforth I too was a watcher.

With the help of neighbors the family erected the house decades before. It was evident they were amateur builders who did the best they could with what they had. The flat roof was a poor choice in a state with a yearly average snowfall of five and a half feet. And the foundation was set in ground so soft the house had sunk several inches over the years, making it prone to flooding.

But, as Lal told us, it was better than the old house. During the winter they had to all sleep around the stove to keep warm in that drafty old dwelling. The foundation still existed in the back yard, overgrown with trees. Part of it was used as an area to dump slop and later another part served as a stoned in pet cemetery.

Three nearby outbuildings were used as sheds to hold tractors, equipment, and whatever else needed storing. Back behind the house, the largest was a tall horse barn used as a Farmall tractor garage and hay hold. Even farther back, the chicken coop, the smallest of the buildings, would become my playhouse. The granary to the right of the house had fallen mostly into disuse and would become storage for much of Russ and Jenene's property, stacked on tables assembled out of sawhorses and lumber.

The rolling landscape made the property hilly and deceptively concise. There were two fields on either side of the house that appeared short but when walked from end to end proved exhausting. I learned this firsthand in those early years when I would "help" Bill and Herb pick rocks in the warm sunshine of spring.

In our family rock picking was sort of a birthright. When Jenene was little, one expedition led to the discovery of a fossil. On another she found an incredible agate that happened to be sawed perfectly in half. She never questioned these finds in childhood, never suspected they might have been planted to ignite an everlasting interest in helping her uncles go picking.

At the rear of the property the fields ended and the terrain sloped up into a lengthy hill. From a distance it looked misleadingly flat, like the side of a pyramid, but also like a pyramid was full of mysteries: pockets and gullies and recesses that made it of a much greater scale than appearances implied.

The hill was comprised mostly of sand and scrub brush yet still supported patches of prosperous woodland. There were two main trails, several ancillary conduits, and many sand traps filled with the spikiest burrs, each like tiny sea urchins. All manner of herbs and berries and animals thrived on the hill, including a small herd of deer, endangered fox snakes, and a feisty old cougar that crossed through, leaving long drag marks with his tail and worryingly large paw prints.

To this day one of the fields sports a boulder of leviathan proportions. My great-great uncles battled it for decades; a party to the final skirmishes, I recall how no matter how much of the buried mountain we exposed we could never get a handle on just how huge that rock really is. I see no failure in that the boulder remains. A testament to its immovability lies in the fact that even when a farming conglomerate rented the field they too could not so much as jostle the rock imbedded deeply where it has dwelled since the last ice age.

In a lot of ways that boulder represents Jenene's will during our time taking care of The Seniors.

Yes, the farm bespoke prosperity. Did it exercise it? Not so much.

Eschewing marriage and private lives for sake of family, Lal, Bill, and Herb continued living on the farm together after their parents crossed for lack of better options.

This created an interesting dynamic since cantankerous Herb and stubborn Lal were like vinegar and oil and the only thing that could marry the two elements was the spice of Bill. The three of them were living quite meagerly by the time we moved in, and Bill and Lal welcomed us with open arms while Herb held an aversion to the situation…and Russ in particular.

"You make my ass tired," Herb would often tell him.

In the beginning, forced by a lack of bedrooms, Jenene and Russ slept on a hide-a-bed in the living room before appropriating the three-season porch as a bedroom. Herb would stay up reading into all hours of the night to guarantee no hanky-panky, unwilling to go to bed before they were both sawing logs. Somehow their new marriage survived this encroachment on their intimacy, but it explains a great deal about why they took to sleeping on an unheated porch in the dead of winter.

Jenene's recollection of that time is less than wistful: "Those were the days when the alarm went off at six-twenty-one so I could have breakfast on the table by seven. We were under a stack of blankets almost a foot thick. I would dread reaching out into the cold to shut off the alarm. I'd coax Russ to go light the stove so I wouldn't see my breath in the kitchen."

At the winter's peak they were up when our part of the world was at its darkest just before dawn, a time of day easy to yield to the notion of bleakness when so much was in doubt. The solution was, naturally, time passing. For as the season languished and spring drew near the sun bursts through the windows crystallized frostily and the porch scintillated with the apricot effulgence of the rising sun, bright rutilated rays offering a suggestion that as the seasons change so do circumstances.

There's an old adage that a light purse makes a heavy heart but that isn't necessarily true. A heavy mind, maybe. But our hearts were filled with helium. We were penniless much of the time but not poor…well, only by the literal definition. I was taught that to be truly poor, we would have had to have a lot less than was available to us at the farm, the warmth, the family, and the history.

The broth may be a little thinner but at our dinner table there was always room for one more.

Chapter 48
The Surly Old Cuss of Grey Cloud

"Look at them go."

"Will they hurt each other?" I asked restively.

Hesitant: "No…they'll be fine."

Much like men, horses can be temperamental beasts.

Recognized for their beauty and strength, people forget horses have a lot of personality. They can be as prideful or as cowardly as anyone. Intelligent, even crafty, horses that possessed the warrior spirit have made fierce soldiers for centuries. Before the world was handed over to the oil companies, albeit slower than cars, horses were the most reliable and green transportation imaginable.

Even as the horse's practical usefulness waned, the desire to own them as a status symbol grew among all classes. Since not everyone could afford to board their horse at an elite stable, a need arose for affordable boarding facilities.

Horse boarding was a hard, thankless business. Passion is the only reason anyone would want to do it; there definitely isn't much money in it when compared to the responsibility. But it was a way to remain a farmer when farming shifted to the large companies and many small family-owned operations faded into history.

The opportunity to be around horses was never to be missed. Even before we moved to the farm, I loved to go down to the barn and stand at the huge steel gate and watch the horses grazing in the pasture.

Temperament often played a role when a new horse was introduced to the population. Quarantined for a time, so they could make introductions from across a fence, the segregation period evidently required more time than was given with the horse we were watching engage in fisticuffs with the other horses.

A cacophony of whinnies, grunts, and clopping hooves accompanied the vicious battle. Rearing up onto their back legs and fighting tall, they threw fusillades of blows.

A figure emerged from the barn and crossed the pasture swiftly to where the fracas ensued unabated.

In well-worn bib overalls, scuffed work boots, and a grease-stained engineer cap, he struck a powerful image as a hard worker, a man with calloused hands, dirt on his sweaty brow, and grit from his skin to his core. From that distance, save for a slight hunch in his back, you would never guess that he was over eighty years old or that he was arthritic or that he had any limitations whatsoever.

Time in the end corrodes the flesh. In some cases, the spirit is deconstructed simultaneously, made piecemeal by the ravages of age. But in those who accept the inevitability of physical frailty, the spirit never dwindles and a strong spirit conquers all…even a brawl between quarrelsome horses.

With all the nerve of a rodeo clown, the authority of a boxing referee, and the vigor of a much younger man, we watched our uncle Herb defuse the horse battle by putting himself smack dab in the middle of it. Not so much a horse whisperer as a horse yeller, he let off a profanity-laced tirade that would make a sailor blush.

A minute later he was leading both of them away by their halters, still cussing up a storm—reprimanding them for making a ruckus. They likely could have torn him apart like a wishbone, but his aura of strength enthralled them into total compliance.

Born on November 9, 1903 (the same year Teddy Bears appeared in the U.S. and Germany and the Wright Brothers took their historic first flight), Herb was the oldest of five brothers and sisters, and the surliest member of the entire family.

A local legend for his skilled handling of the most stubborn horses and for shooting trespassers in the rear with rock salt, throughout his life he had cultivated an image of being the hardest and meanest SOB on Grey Cloud.

By the time he was hit by the Amtrak, his tolerance for pain was legendary.

In his younger days, like some great metal monster the thresher once ate him up. An injury that would render most a screaming insane person, its serrated teeth minced all the skin off his back. When he made it in from the field, did he request medical attention? In a manner of speaking: he had Lal call a neighbor, a retired veterinarian, who came and covered Herb's back with Horse Blue. The salve did its work and within an hour of the injury, he was back in the field to finish out the day.

Herb also told a story about a truck accident he had in his youth. A thread of skin held on his right index finger. I will always remember his words spoken in his hard, gravelly voice. "If I had my buck knife, I would have cut it off for all the trouble it caused me while it mended."

Dentists off his radar as much as doctors, when Herb's teeth began falling out—by 1989 he was down to three—he took to using Redwood snuff medicinally. The tobacco numbed his rotting, sometimes abscessed teeth. If I smell the odor of his brand even now, it takes me back to those days. He always seemed to have a single brown stain marring the front of his bib overalls.

Getting his sight back after cataract surgery improved his mood all around. The thing about Herb, when he was in the mood to socialize the old codger would be the life of the party. This had become a truly once-in-a-blue-moon treat like a restaurant meal, but after his visual acuity was restored, he was much more willing to regale us with stories of his occasionally interesting life.

You could tell they were the honest truth because he always told them consistently, beat for beat, the exact same way, yet so compellingly they were never boring, never stale.

These rare glimpses beyond his rough exterior revealed his depth, his humanity, and his unique philosophy of things. No doubt he was a bit of a quick-tempered old coot, but we began to learn he had a kinder, more tenderhearted side, repressed because he was a part of the John Wayne generation, a generation that believed for a man to be a man he had to be tough and tightlipped.

It was a wonder Bill was so dissimilar, so open and kind. But he was the little brother. Little brothers are often given more leeway in that regard.

Herb had a gift for storytelling.

Imbued with the air of an old-fashioned den by the pine-paneled walls, cream-tiled ceiling, and the shaggy green carpet made of a thousand discarded pieces of cloth (coarse like the hay bales stacked in the barn), when Herb told a story, the living room would be transformed into a magic place. Warm. Homey.

Sunshine streaming into the open space, you could see a strata of gently floating dust pervading the air. From coal and the field. We could never vacuum, dust, or mop enough to get rid of it all until the days of coal and wood burning for heat were past.

It was an informal sort of thing. No let's all gather 'round. It most often began with one of us straying within Herb's gravitational pull and getting sucked in. But by the wrap up the whole household would be enthralled by Herb's narrative. Save for Lal, who would lift her eyebrows in wonder that anyone would care to listen to her blowhard brother.

From his perch in the largest chair in the room, it might start with: "Quite a storm blowing out there today. Though it ain't much of a storm compared to the Armistice Day Blizzard. You know I had to haul milk in that storm?"

Of course, reading it, his words are perfectly clear. Actually listening to him, his gruff, gravelly voice had an accent unique to him, and his words had to be deciphered.

If you showed interest, he would give a wave that was an invite to sit down on the red-topped footstool before his chair. Having found a purpose for the appendage after all, there was always a little snuff stuck under the nail of his right index finger.

Herb had some gnarly, rough-looking hands that he employed for emphasis. A lifetime of farming and, in particular, milking left them sturdy but warped, touched by rheumatism but not riddled with pain. Both hands were bent permanently in the center and there was no curve to the knuckles. His fingers were long, slender, and bony, the nails thick and yellowed, hard as horse hooves.

"I had to get my team from Shakopee to Minneapolis in some of the worst weather I ever saw. That's only about twenty-five miles, but it might as well have been five hundred when the snow began drifting."

He paused to spit in his coffee can. Load up his lip with snuff.

"The funny thing was that day, the eleventh of November, began warm. The weathermen said a storm was brewing but they didn't tell how god-awful it was going to be. A lot of folks thought they would enjoy the warmth and went out hunting; bunch of 'em never made it home.

"The temp climbed all the way to sixty degrees. Then it fell faster than the stock market did a decade before. First came the wind and the rain. As it got colder, the rain became sleet, wet and heavy sleet. And then it began blowing in some of the heaviest, thickest snow I ever saw.

"It began to drift.

"The drifts got so deep I had to get down off the wagon at every power line and use a long stick to hold them up so the horses could pass under. I had to draw 'em along or they would have stopped and froze. It was that sort of storm, the kind that cuts you off at the knees and makes you want to let it win. It seemed like it would never let up. All I could do was take a snort of apple cider vinegar for energy, grit my teeth, and keep going."

Another odor I associate with Herb is apple cider vinegar. Anyone who knows about natural remedies knows about the healthful benefits of this tangy brown liquid, but Herb took his belief in apple cider vinegar to a new level. He considered it a near-magical elixir.

"It took me all day to drive the horses through the wind and ice. When I finally made it back to the dairy, I got to the milking and kept at it right 'til morning. There was no choice. The cows were engorged, hurting, and letting us know. My hands and forearms were beet-red from all the milking by the time I was finished. There was so much to be done. I went out and hauled other's milk until I could barely keep my eyes open.

"All told, I was up three days. By then the blizzard was over. And all we had to do then was dig out."

The Armistice Day blizzard story epitomizes Herb's grit, determination, and stubbornness. To this day it ranks #2 in Minnesota's list of top-5 weather events of the 20th century. The rare panhandle hook storm slashed a thousand-mile swath across the Midwest and crippled communications. It claimed 154 lives.

Never once did Herb voice any kind of complaint about all the work. To him the point of the story was wonder at the ferocity of the blizzard, the incredible power of nature to throw a monkey wrench into the machinations of man.

It is easy to see why Herb has been a huge inspiration to us. From his quaint folk remedies to his tough-as-nails attitude, he demonstrated a rare toughness and self-reliance not often seen today. To him, pain was a negotiable quantity. Once a person realizes that, they are free to do anything.

Another trait I admire about him is that when a lot of older folks are checking out, Herb's mind stayed clear as glass. He could say the alphabet backwards straight through or by two's or three's. Social service workers would ask him and he would show off. He could count backwards from a hundred that way too. Right up until the day he died.

He was also a cancer survivor. But I'll get to that later.

Chapter 49
Our Favorite Aunt

"Out of the kitchen!" Lal would shoo anyone unwilling to take an assigned task.

It was pie day. A weekly tradition since we moved to the farm. With her baking and cooking, Lal made the farmhouse kitchen a magical place long before, so it was only natural such a ritual would materialize.

Lal imparted the notion that pie making is a great art, and she was right. From the flakiness of the crust to the sweetness of the filling, a lot of components combine to make a masterpiece. A life of toil left a hunch in her back and roadmaps of varicose veins on her legs, but it also bestowed upon her a great deal of wisdom, pies being only one of the subjects of which she was knowledgeable.

The bigger treat of baking with her, even though her pastries were delicious, was listening to her prattle on about the many trips she had gone on around the country or living through the Great Depression or her younger brother, Gustav, who had died decades before of rheumatic fever.

We would pull the huge wooden cutting board out of its cubby under the countertop. Lay it down on the kitchen table. I would rub my palms on the smooth clean surface. Then we retrieved the antique tin flour sifter, glass pie plates so old they were foggy, the timeworn rolling pin, and a big mixing bowl.

The kitchen would be warm from the stove, the sort of cozy warm that makes you happy and a little drowsy if you don't keep active. A hint of wood smoke was always in the air. Soon it would be overwhelmed by the sweet smell of baking pies.

Lal would begin measuring flour into the bowl. We had ended her longtime use of a drawer for flour storage recently when we discovered an infiltration of little brown bugs. Bless her heart she had failed to notice the buggers. It was one of the ways she was beginning to slip, why we had to move in and help out.

In those first years, there was no doubting she was an old woman cursed by the onset of senility, but age had yet to sap her vivacity and had granted her a look of eminent kindliness. She wore cotton dresses out of the 1950's and her hair was fine and white and full of body. She had a smile that could soften butter. The small mole on her chin was neither beauty mark nor blemish. The strength in her hands belied their fragile appearance as she mixed the flour and lard. They were so slender and bony, the veins as thick as earthworms and as blue as the ocean.

Then it was time to add the chunked lard. She had taught us it was important to get the right ratios of flour and lard. The lard had to be refrigerated, too. A spritz of ice-cold water was required, and a dash of salt. It was equally important to not over mix it and not overwork it, or else it would turn out hard enough to crack a tooth.

Flourishing apple trees were conveniently in the back yard. Sweet and scrumptious, their prosperous fruit was often our filling of choice. The apples had to be cut to the right size, not too large, so the filling would turn out full, meaty, and adequately juicy but not too moist. The amount of sugar would be predicated on the sweetness of the apples. Some years they were sweeter than others. A tad of tapioca ensured when the slices were cut the filling wouldn't run out.

Topped with a dash of cinnamon and a crust topping, these pies were scrumptious, delectable, and even a little decadent.

Regardless of how frail and arthritic her hands became, Lal was able to begin at the top of an apple and peel the entire fruit so that the skin was one continuous strip; if pinched at the top and held aloft, it fell as a perfect spiral.

The hues and shapes of recollection define those who are the greatest heroes of our lives....

Lal was born on November 5, 1905. As the oldest sister from an early age she was tasked with greater responsibilities but it never dimmed her bright nature. Jenene determined from a young age it was a tragedy she was never a mother or grandmother. In lieu of those roles, she was a magnificent aunt to her; the one person Jenene could trust maybe most of all.

Their bond was unbreakable for good reason.

While her parents were busy supporting the family's lifestyle—to be the first family with an air conditioner and a color TV meant they had to be a two-income home, a rarity in the era—Lal was busy making the sort of memories so good they don't fade. When her parents were still too distracted for her, Lal was willing to give her the one-on-one time and attention so important to a growing child.

Lal was the one who made sure she made good memories. Many of them were the best and earliest, filed away in her mind like treasured snapshots.

Among her earliest memories was thrilling to Lal's homemade applesauce and Lal being happy to teach her the recipe. It seemed Lal's applesauce, created lovingly with her own impeccable hand, akin as it was to ambrosia, defied duplication. For that matter so did her canned crabapples. Comfort food of all variety was her specialty. Maybe it was because she understood that delicious food goes best with a sympathetic ear.

Composed of too humble a grain to match Herb's verbosity, Lal was no less a storyteller. Hers were more like parables, little lessons for living. As a child of the Great Depression, many revolved around scarcity, perseverance, and survival. Through those years she squirreled away bits and pieces of this and that, attaining wisdoms that would sustain her through a lifetime.

But what she really excelled at was taking Jenene to new and exciting sights while expounding her modest philosophies.

When she was a little girl and still open to the experience as something wondrous, Lal was the one who took Jenene to sit on Santa's lap. The day was an event. She was whisked off to grandiosely decorated downtown St. Paul, all aglitter, to be among all the gleaming tinsel and bustling holiday revelers. They would partake in a little Christmas shopping at the lavish Donaldson's. Then catch lunch at the prestigious Woolworth's counter. By then Jenene would be a bit over-stimulated by the bountiful ornamentation, indulgence, and warmth of kindness conveyed by her wonderful aunt.

Jenene is a smidgen Irish. So Lal made a point of taking her to the St. Patrick's Day parade. Herself one hundred percent German (the family immigrated before WWI), Lal thought her Irish heritage, albeit small, should be honored. Jenene never understood why exactly but as a kid she was happy to embrace it wholly. Jenene loved celebrating her Irish blood…with Lal.

Before the family relocated to Wilson, every Wednesday she collected Jenene to take her to the local strip mall. Lal would give her a quarter. Like children do, she would go to Snyder's and spend it all on candy. For twenty-five cents—what would get you one gumball today—she amassed a haul that lasted days (inflation is cruel). If she made the mistake of eating it too fast, say in one or two days, it was so much it would make her sick.

Her parents were too engaged in their grownup pursuits to encourage the whimsy of a little girl. This meant there was little revelry in her life other than Lal's excursions. Bill made good memories, too, not to be beat, sure; and Herb imparted hard lessons, which constitute memories, though often they had a sting. But Lal had a way of injecting an infusion of fun and learning and bonding unlike anyone else.

The memories she inspired were precious as they were being made. Now the most magnificent treasures seem comparatively paltry when weighed against those experiences.

The saddest of ironies, the maker of great memories would in the end have her mind slowly stolen, her own memories dissolved.

Devastation is realizing the mental capacity of someone you love is diminishing. In the years leading up to us returning to the farm, Lal began to show signs of senility.
Little slips. Odd mistakes. Losing her once critical eye. It was distressing in so profound a way it reconfigured Jenene's view of the world; made her realize all the little things that shouldn't be taken for granted. For Lal the small slips led to a rather fast escalation. The sad truth broke all our hearts and maybe Jenene's most of all.

Aluminum poisoning possibly contributed to her decline. A practice that was a depression era holdover, she saved even a single bite of food for later consumption. The problem was she heated this fare in her small personal pan. The pan was unvarnished aluminum. The dangers are recognized today. Lal never knew.

Long before we moved back in Jenene used the pretense of wishing her goodnight to make a nightly call to the farm. Lal was happy to chat for a few minutes. Jenene was happy to get confirmation all was well on the farm. Knowing The Seniors were okay saved a lot of tossing and turning.

Living on the farm meant Jenene was granted an even greater peace of mind. She could oversee the day-to-day trials in general and help Lal navigate life in particular. Bill and Herb needed help as well; only it had nothing to do with their mental clarity. Lal wasn't quite doddering but she was far from the capable woman Jenene always knew. It was her love and admiration for that woman, who Lal always was to her, that made her never doubt the value of any sacrifice.

No matter how hard it was Jenene felt she owed it to her to do everything she could to ease her distress and confusion. Lal earned whatever assistance she needed as her mind dwindled in her nebulous final years.

Even after arthritis stiffened her joints and reduced her ability to contribute to household chores, she would spend hours peeling apples from the farm's trees, never losing her technique. The results baked into pies and crisp and cake, Jenene and I will always cherish the times we convened in our homey country kitchen to bake and enjoy time with our favorite aunt.

Chapter 50
The Family Oracle

"Let up," Bill said. "Won't hold."

"I know what I'm doing!" Herb shot back gruffly. "I ain't no sap head—"

Crunch! Crack! Ping! In the barn, such sounds signaled a mistake and in that instance presaged an unholy tantrum.

At this point, I scampered away, to a place of safety, where I could watch and not be seen. Like many relatives before me, my mom in particular, I had found all the good bird's eye vantages.

My hardworking—and by my estimate endlessly fascinating—uncles and I were down in the barn, where there were about a million ancient tools, jars and jars of screws and bolts and nuts, and the mixed aromas of ancient wood, rust, hay, dust, gasoline, horse sweat, and grease blended into the smell of red thyme. It was a hot summer day but it was always cool in the barn. It was a grungy, grimy, dirty place in all the right ways, a mecca to country manliness.

Having difficulty with the tractor engine only part of the reason he was enraged, Herb rose from the bucket he was sitting on, threw down the huge rusted wrench he was working with, punted the bucket clattering across the dusty floor of the barn, and stalked back and forth, spewing words and epitaphs that would make a pious man's ears bleed. The multiple car pile-ups of profanities Herb could string together were truly epic.

While Herb was having his conniption fit, with monastic equanimity, Bill stepped forward to survey the damage.

Hunched forward slightly, arms behind his back, fingers interlocked, a pose he made definitive, his eyes explored the tractor engine without hurry. I had no idea what was wrong other than some part slipped or broke, and in their vastly different reactions I had no way of deciphering how truly bad the damage was, what with one blowing like a powder keg and the other acting so calmly it seemed as though he had not a single trouble in the world.

Bill cocked up his monkish bald head finally and said, "Ah, shut up," but not in a way that was blatantly mean.

Even though I could tell he was nowhere near running out of steam, it worked: with his square chin, fuzzy with hoary stubble, jutting forward and nostrils flaring like a bull, Herb sucked up his lip and relinquished his tirade.

The quiet, the listeners, are always the wisest and it was his patient quietude and few words that made Bill an oracle.

I think it would be true to say a tiny population cares about no one.

The human capacity for caring is immense and profound and belies all the cruelty evident in the world. But even caring, when misappropriated, can be aggressive, manipulative, and hurtful. Yet there is caring so profound and rich and hope affirming it changes you forever. Bill's caring was subtle but poignant, tolerant but truthful. He read people like others read the newspaper. He liked people the way others like a sunny day: they always brightened his spirit.

Bill was not only the patriarch of the family. He was the glue and the fusion.

The youngest brother, he was born on January 13 of the year Henry Ford began mass-producing Model Ts, 1908.

Most of us have a person who means everything. Bill was maybe that person for the entire family. He could always bring cheer or impart the right wisdom at the right time, could always be relied on for comfort and caring. As a little girl, as much as she cherished Lal and admired her dad, he was Jenene's favorite person.

Jenene's fondness for him cannot be encapsulated in few words. Lal gave her some of her showiest memories; Bill took her on little adventures off the beaten track that opened her eyes to the wider world. There's a story she tells that demonstrates his kindly playfulness:

"Bill would take me to visit friends we would drop in on. As a little girl I never knew this was the plan, of course. We were off on a drive, me little suspecting he had a plan.

"We'd be driving along and he would say, 'Do you know where we are?' I'd say, 'no,' and he'd say, 'I don't know either. We must be lost.' Then we'd pull in somewhere and he would say, 'We'll ask these people.' He'd make me go to the door with him and of course the people who lived there would know him. No matter who they were, they would always give me cookies. Maybe this was because Bill introduced me by my nickname, Cookie. I'd always be a little nervous about approaching the door but it always turned out good. I should have trusted him earlier on. He helped to teach me not to be so shy."

Another story involving Jeff epitomizes Bill's gentle nature. Jeff was only a little squirt. The family journeyed to the farm for Christmas. A sure lead up to tragedy one of his gifts was a dart gun.

Screwing around the way a kid distracted with a new toy will do, he accidentally shot a dart right into Bill's eye.

To this day in all his life he has never felt so terrible. He described it as feeling like the worst kind of bad guy. That there was no penance great enough to make up for what he had done. No way he could be sorrier, he retreated under the dining room table to hide. He refused to come out even for dessert.

Despite a sore eye Bill of course forgave him immediately. It was just his way. He was a strong believer in forgiveness. He was a man who for misdeeds imparted lessons instead of punishments. Jeff's sorrow showed he had learned his lesson, and that was good enough for Bill.

After a lifetime of collecting wisdom, Bill's motivation to invite us to move to the farm was simple. He was willing to admit the onset of old age meant he could no longer keep up with all the responsibility. Ego had no part in the decision. He questioned whether life on the farm was sustainable when his health became a concern. He quit smoking decades before yet suffered from emphysema in his late seventies. Chained to oxygen, limitations controlled his life.

Lo and behold, once we moved in and he was relieved of being in charge of everything, the emphysema retreated. Bill was able to get off oxygen and breathe freely.

Seeing his accomplishment bolstered Jenene. Her own health was soon to spiral. Moving in meant she assumed Bill's stresses. But much like in Lal's case, Bill earned the care he was given. Jenene felt whatever she had to give it was worth the sacrifice to facilitate an easier existence for him.

Cognac was only one of many gifts Bill bestowed upon Jenene. He also imparted insight at no more cost than offering up an eager ear. Aspects of Jenene's life philosophy can be traced back to Bill, to name a few her peacefulness, her level-headedness, and her lack of judgment.

Bill also communicated a lesson that shaped Jenene's way of life.

"Bill's biggest message to me was that what goes around comes around," she told me, "be it good, be it bad. I can't tell you how often he told me that. I wouldn't learn until after he was gone just how significant this point was, how personal. He also warned me about an intersection in Newport, crossing Highway 61"—the one we both crossed with him many times—"he said it was dangerous. I had no idea how precognitive that warning would turn out to be."

Because of Bill this author's life took on new dimensions.

Once we lived on the farm he often invited me to be a tagalong on errands with him and Herb. Jenene encouraged me. I soaked up all kinds of knowledge from my ancient uncles. I was their little buddy. I relished the role. Almost every Saturday morning I joined the pair on their weekly excursion to the grocery store, barbershop, and pharmacy in New Port.

We would roll in Bill's fusty, musty, and dusty old car. At first it was the very Chrysler New Port Guy once used to try to terrify Jenene into labor. The car had been handed down to Bill. Later he would replace the New Port with an overall squeakier, crustier, and dustier station wagon. That relic had a single back seat, right behind Bill.

Herb lost his right to drive when he sideswiped a parked car—later he drove a tractor into the lake and confirmed he had no business behind the wheel.

Lal had a close call with a child darting out from between parked cars. It gave her such a fright she was quick to accept it was time for a change. She never drove again.

Bill recognized that for him to keep driving was contingent on knowing his limits. He wasn't too proud to stick to the back roads. Age dulls reaction time and he refused to let pride cause him to ignore facts. He knew the back way to about anywhere. No one ever suggested he should hang up his license. And he would literally drive until the day he died.

I'm unable to quite convey what Bill meant to us and we would learn the world. A humane, caring man with a kindly face and a cleanly bald noggin, he had stopped aging around forty-five, at the point his mien took on the stature of an ancient marble bust.

I used to imagine that the face of God was Bill's face. He was so kind and benevolent. Not to mention in the dictionary his picture could've been next to the word "wisdom".

Chapter 51
Offshoots

The little sister who fashioned her own comeuppance, Lucille may have raised her family in Dixon, Illinois, but in the summer she sent Lois and her two brothers to the farm.

This tenuous link prospered an exploitable misconception.

Not long after Bill invited us to live on the farm, Jenene and Russ learned aspects of the Illinois family plotted to seize the farm. Uncle Bob was the ringleader of this initiative and maybe the only one truly invested.

Keeping The Seniors in their home was Jenene's mission, her driving force. She cared about them too much to settle for anything less. That Bill said the farm would be willed to her and

Russ in exchange for their efforts was a comparatively small motivation.

To drum up support what did Uncle Bob exploit? The notion he and his siblings were entitled to the farm due to their position in the bloodline. He felt they had earned the farm during those childhood summers. To him it had nothing to do with who was willing to help The Seniors. His idea was to install them in a nursing home and sell.

This despite the fact the value of the farm likely wouldn't fetch enough for The Seniors to live out their lives with quality care.

Jenene believed his actions were part of a personal vendetta against her and by extension Bill. How did Jenene instigate this enmity? What ensured Uncle Bob would always have it out for her?

There was an instance when she was a little girl. She happened to embarrass him and in the process Bill's name was broached. You can sense the cold shoulder once it's there. Based on their every interaction afterward, she was certain he never forgave her.

What set her off? Actually it was two actions on his part. It began with his boast that he was her favorite uncle. She let his false statement slide. Then as she pleaded with him to stop he made the mistake of pushing her on a swing so hard she went backwards over the top rail.

One of those big stomach-dropping scares, Jenene was horrified, angry, and shocked someone would do such a thing to her. As she stalked off she set him straight: "You're not my favorite uncle! Bill's my favorite uncle by far! You're nothing to me compared to him!"

Others were within earshot. That sealed it. Her justifiably angry words were deemed inexcusable.

Cut to years later when Jenene struggled every day to prevent The Seniors from losing their way of life. Her life on the line as her health declined. Then the Illinois family would roll in and Uncle Bob would insinuate she and Russ didn't measure up, as if his alternatives in any way benefited The Seniors.

Of course Bill put up with them good-naturedly; he was a man who would gladly break bread with his enemy, if he ever had one, rather than watch the man go hungry. I wish I had his kind of patience. Lal would wait on the Illinois family as if she was a servant and they had no problem letting her. All we could do was bide our time and wait for them to leave.

Their departure never came soon enough.

Chapter 52
Feeling At Home on the Farm

It was a gloomy Sunday during our first winter. A battleship gray sky filled the house with wishy-washy light.

Jenene and Russ had taken Lal to church and left me at home. I was feeling under the weather. I was maybe four and a half. With chronic bronchial asthma, I dealt with a lot of the lung problems. Bronchitis seemed to follow me around like a black cloud. I always thought it was called "brown-chitis" because of the color of the stuff I would cough up.

Encamped on the couch, I was biding my time until they got home.

Herb had his nose in a book.

Bill was fiddling around with the kitchen stove. Ancient, it had become as temperamental as Herb in its old age. All our cooking was done in and on the antique wood burning goliath, not the easiest cooking implement to control. We also had a colossal wood burning furnace those first years, which meant huge piles of coal and wood were poured into the basement to store for the winter.

Lying there, my nostrils took in the ever-present touch of old person smell, smoke, and the deep-seated aroma of the weeks, months, years, and decades the house had stood upon its knoll. Familiar. Calming. I felt safe on the farm.

I was hungry for lunch. I distracted myself by looking around at all the artifacts of The Seniors' lives, mostly Lal's because she decided the decor. The numerous state trivets she collected on her journeys, hung an inch below the ceiling, spanning the pine-paneled living room walls. The religious iconology: a white embroidered wall hanging of the Lord's Prayer and an antique depiction of the Last Supper that ostensibly lit up but by my understanding probably would have caused a fire if plugged in. The shelves and shelves, darkly stained boards held up by blood red bricks, of old books, many with worn cloth bindings.

The farm looked, felt, and was rustic. In those days, wash water had to be dumped outside because the plumbing was in terrible condition. Years later, when we were able to have some pipes replaced, one section looked like the clogged artery of a heart attack victim. There was always a slop bucket by the back door.

The farm was not so remote it was fifty miles from civilization but it might as well have been. Even as cable television infiltrated the country, it didn't extend to us. Our TV watching was limited to a few local channels. Sometimes we'd pick up channel 45 and I would get to watch old episodes of *Superman* with George Reeves. I would be ecstatic when a program on network television was popular with my peers. It meant a chance at inclusion.

The cable lines could have been extended to include us for a by-the-foot fee. Had we been able to afford it there still would have been a problem. Every time the railroad did work they would have cut the cable like they did our phone line.

There was a knock at the back door. Bill answered. It was a local neighbor he had enlisted to help battle the stove. The man apparently had some expertise in old clunkers. Dick Polk. I got up to see what was up. Following Bill in, red-cheeked and round-featured, he had the dopey smile and shiny face of a ventriloquist dummy.

"Aren't you supposed to be sick?" he said when he saw me.

Bill must have told him I was feeling unwell.

I didn't know how to reply.

"You should be laying down," he said.

I made no move. I did not view him as an authority over me.

In that instant I was struck by his immensity. The man was a head taller than Bill and as thick as a slab of beef. As to why the next sequence of events happened I cannot explain to this day.

Maybe he took exception to my perceived lack of deference. I can only speculate as to motive.

Maybe it was a misunderstanding.

All I know is the man came after me.

Terrified because Bill and Herb were old and I assumed not in a position to protect me and Polk was a gigantic and aggressive stranger, I dodged and ran. He chased me back to the couch. I leapt aboard. Tried to get enswathed in the safety of the blankets. Only to be scooped up bedding and all and carried to the back door. With a heave-ho, he tossed me out in the snow. It was so cold! Freezing! In shorts and a t-shirt, the elements chilled me to the bone immediately.

My lungs seized. I could draw no breath.

I had to get inside quickly.

I rose to my feet unsteadily. Still standing in the blanket, I stepped off. It was so cold the soles of my bare feet felt impaled by the spicules of snow and ice. My nerves were frightened into anarchy. I managed to gather the blankets and raced into the house. Bypassing and eluding Polk, I went and hid in my room.

I took a couple puffs off my inhaler. There was instant relief. But I still had to work on regulating my breathing: in through the nose, out through the mouth. I had gotten so worked up it was harder to catch my breath than warm up my feet, which I was thoroughly convinced had frostbite, a condition I had recently learned about, until the feeling returned and the redness receded to a healthy pink.

When my folks came home from church after what felt like an exaggeratedly long wait, I dared not leave my room. Polk was still out there. Jenene came and found me. She could tell instantly something was wrong. She had a sixth sense about such things.

Trying to restrain my tears I reported the whole incident. "Russ, come back here." Beside herself with anger, she relayed to him what I had just told her.

Russ was up in arms. Enraged, he confronted Polk. Face to face, spittle flying, they screamed at each other. The only component that stopped the confrontation from escalating into physical violence was Russ' respect for Bill. After all, Bill invited Polk into the house.

What was worse was the accusation Polk leveled. "There's some kind of flimflam here. You're using the Wiechman's."

"You have a lot of nerve," Jenene said, "to come here and not only toss my asthmatic son out in the snow, but accuse me of taking advantage of my relatives!"

"I care about these people," he shot back.

"You need to go!"

"You don't have the right to kick me out! This ain't your place!"

They looked to Bill.

"She's right," he said imperturbably, "you have to go."

That was that.

Whatever Polk felt his relationship was with The Seniors—we never saw him before that day, so we can only speculate—he was wrong. Bill always had an affinity for Jenene. He deferred to her in that circumstance as he would in many more to come. He invited us to move in because he trusted her.

Angry as a dog sprayed by a skunk, Polk left that day followed by a cloud of infuriation. He harbored resentment. Later, he would twice shoot our Doberman. Lacking probable cause, police said we were unable to press charges. Butch survived both attempted assassinations, but wound up with a bullet wedged against his scapula for his trouble.

Bill let Jenene know her place that day. Demonstrating his confidence in her made it easier to make decisions for the household. Being in charge was a matter of necessity. Even if on some level she had always known her assistance was inevitable she never envisioned what it would be like when the day came to pass.

Chapter 53
Outperforming Expectation

Jenene accepted Bill's abdication of his patriarchic duties but still sought his advice in many matters.

Moving her small family to the farm was dicey. What choice was there? Supportive Russ deferred to Jenene's judgment. She realized how huge a sacrifice it was for him. The contribution to their bond was immeasurable. The commitment was taxing from the start. But they were up to their necks in it together. What drove them was a deep feeling of being in love limned with the hope they were working toward a better future.

She felt like a trial horse at best and had no choice but to be a show winner. Financial matters made her want to pull out her hair. Bringing home a paycheck was not enough. So much had been neglected. How could she blame The Seniors? They were old and struggling.

With all regime changes come new initiatives. Various cleanups and repairs were soon Jenene and Russ's headaches. The first goal was to see to the elimination of the tire heap. The source of the mosquito that gave me La Crosse encephalitis was determined to be Mount Cracked Rubber. The last thing we needed was a health hazard so near the horses and their owners.

Jenene applied for a grant and it was awarded rapidly. Public health concerns have a way of hastening the process.

The cost of a dumpster contingent was covered but the money fell short of funding a crew to do the work. This left the entire effort of removal on Jenene and Russ's shoulders. Handicapped or not, Jenene pushed to ensure it could never be said she did not do an even share of the work.

Her bad knee was only a problem if she let it be. That was not exactly true. It would be a mindset she held through many hard tasks.

The visible mountain of tires was only part of the job. Bill and Herb hoarded the castoffs for so long they had become inventive in regards to storing tires. The huge barn had many secrets. Niches, nooks, and crannies stuffed from the floor to the rafters with moldering rubber. It was weird how a situation could be discouraging and darkly amusing. It verged on impressive. Just when they thought they were in sight of finishing an additional store was uncovered and another five or twenty tires had to be toted out.

By the time they lugged out the last, the count was astonishing. Eighteen hundred tires were banished from the farm.

The backbreaking job finished, our family did our level best to enforce a no-dumping policy, which brought us to loggerheads with many would-be dumpers. We all had awkward encounters.

This was just one example of how the farm got no respect. Our land was often treated like a landfill. No matter how many "Posted: No Trespassing" signs we nailed up the very next day we would find them torn down.

The perpetuity of keeping the property free of refuse made Jenene wish the powers that be would bring back the crying Indian commercial from the '70's. Maybe redo it and cast an actual Native American. People needed to be taught. Nature is a gift and littering has consequences.

Dealing with the dumping alone made it so Jenene had to muster great restraint not to pull out her hair. A good thing she exercised self-control. Before long the disease ravaging her body would make it so her hair stopped growing. A style of the day, a perm aided Jenene because it looked as if she had a fuller head of hair and was easier to maintain during a period when time constraints drove her life.

Never an instance when we found no refuse, one time recently discarded trash bags offered an opportunity.

Recognizing the possibility of evidence, Jenene and Russ examined the contents. There were beer bottles galore…and a few pieces of mail. The address was local—in Jenene's old territory in residential Cottage Grove, in fact.

A family outing, we paid them a visit.

The man of the house denied he had any involvement in illegal dumping. Which very well may have been the case. But he had no reply as to why mail sent to his name and address ended up on our property.

We began unloading the bags on his front lawn.

A stray beer bottle fell to the street and shattered. The noise of breaking glass garnered attention on a summer day when folks were outside, meaning his neighbors were alerted to watch.

Indignant anger followed, rage that fell just short of combative. He threatened belligerently to alert police. To press charges. Smear us. See our face in the papers from here to Timbuktu with the outraged caption: Misdemeanor Garbage Dumpers Annoy Upstanding Citizen!

Not once losing her cool, Jenene made the suggestion that maybe the man's kids knew something about the trash. Maybe he had better check with them before sticking his neck out legally. We had ample evidence that *his* trash was dumped illegally on our property. It would be his name in the paper. Not the most embarrassing news but embarrassing enough.

Grumpier than a bear roused from hibernation early, seething but closemouthed he cleaned up the trash.

It was one of few vindications.

During our time on the farm tons of trash would cycle through.

Chapter 54
Strays

The first summer on the farm, while I was visiting Guy, Jenene and Russ decided to take advantage of a chance to acquire a puppy. There was one male in the litter from which they had the pick. When they went to choose, they decided the male would be best, a boy for a boy.

In the process of picking Buddy out, there was a snafu, for shortly after I got "Buddy Boy," we discovered Buddy was a girl.

Already partial to the name, we called her Buddy Girl, the thinking being that she was still my buddy. She was a great dog; half golden retriever, half collie, she had a lustrous cedar brown coat and boundless energy.

On the rare occasions I went out in the winter (the asthma hindered outside play in the cold severely), I was covered in numerous layers of outdoor wear. Jenene thought Buddy would make a good companion out in the snow until she noticed that Buddy systematically, in a playful frenzy, stripped me down to my boots, pants, and t-shirt, scattering my coats, hats, scarves, and gloves all over the snowy landscape.

At the same time we got Buddy, a kitten showed up in the horse barn. Another downside to owning a farm, as I mentioned previously people thought it was a place where they were welcome to dump unwanted pets. Over the years, dozens of cats sadly found their way to the farm.

The kitten was a silver and black tiger kitty. We brought the tiny dobber up to the house. Later on, I was back down at the barn…and so was the kitten. I found this odd. Jenene said she was keeping the kitten inside.

Giving me a merry chase, the kitten evaded me and I pursued it all over the barn and pasture. Catching it finally, I carried the kitten up to the house. Jenene was a little surprised. The thing was, the kitten never got out. As it turned out there were two.

It is possible we would not have kept them had Bill not drawn a line in the sand: we could only keep "the dog" if we kept the kittens. The previous generation of cats on the farm had succumbed to that sinister killer, feline leukemia, and Bill missed having them around. Since the outbreak was past, I got to keep Buddy and the kittens also stayed. At that tender age, siblings obviously, they were almost identical save for their sex—one a girl, one a boy.

A couple of outlaws, we named them Bonnie and Clyde.

Before long more dogs came into our lives.

Junior was blind. Black with a tan bib, he was bulky yet agile. Reared by vegetarians he therefore loved bananas. He was older and lived out his few remaining days on the farm. His insistence on coming inside changed the house rules, which had dictated the dogs stay outside.

They were provided a fenced-in area and doghouses. Junior proved a master escape artist. No sooner than he was contained, he was out. Sightlessness hindered him in no way. Sometimes we suspected he saw spirits.

Butch came to us when suburban-bound friends adopted him from the pound and could not contain him. A beautifully constructed red Doberman with a gentle temperament and the sweetest brown eyes, few fences deterred him from going right over, which resulted in return trips to the pound. The free range of the farm suited him better. Russ took to running around the property with him on a leash.

Abandoned in an apartment with an open toilet and a bag of food dumped on the floor, we were told Butch's barking was enough discouragement to keep the landlord out of the apartment long after the tenant took off.

Trustworthy guard dog that he was, Butch made all of us safer. We would learn he was a lover not a fighter but his appearance often made even the meanest looking trespassers reconsider defying even my order to leave. Friendly temperament aside he was the kind of obedient that results in a torn out throat if you tried to hurt those he loved.

Over the years the farm was a refuge for many animals. Our compassion was too great to turn them away even if extra mouths ate into an already strained budget.

Chapter 55
The Vicissitudes of Life on the Farm

The little luxuries most people take for granted were big chores on the farm in those first years, like having heat. In short order the house could become an icebox. A steady inflow of coal and wood kept icicles from forming on our noses.

Or having more than one toilet.

When the toilet is unavailable you most have to go. That's a simple but no less true wisdom I learned young. Even at home Jenene had bathroom troubles due to the disease wracking her body.

The ancient unmovable stone in the field was Herb when he was on the toilet. In the summer he would as soon pee off the back step, a frowned upon practice I can attest. No persuasion or plea, no matter how impassioned, would pry him away sooner than he was good and ready. Of course he was no stranger to being the sort of griper that effectively shuts down bowel activity but I suppose that was Herb's way, to be both the one who could grumble his way to results and in turn be the one no grievance could budge.

Talk of repairing the basement toilet failed to gain traction after we learned the cost would be astronomical.

The only way to approach keeping up, routine took precedence. For Jenene it meant a constant cycle of domestic chores and care; Lal helped as much as she could but senility was limiting.

For Russ it meant rising at the crack of dawn to light the stove and stoke the fires in the furnace before everyone else rose for the day. Like clockwork, Russ was then off to do the feeding and watering while Jenene put together a country breakfast of cereal, scrambled eggs, toast (with choice of marmalade, jam, apple butter, or honey butter), and juice.

They shared the responsibility of Bill and Herb's horse boarding business. In the first year Russ did much of the feeding and watering, maintaining the barn, and otherwise keeping up the physical end of things. At other times Jenene was doing the majority of the work.

Boarding netted no profits. The rate had never been adjusted to reflect inflation. By the time we moved in the business wasn't even breaking even. When Jenene raised the rates to a fee to cover the cost of hay well below other horse boarders in the area, the boarders balked and some of them took their horses elsewhere.

One such boarder took his horse home and fed it grass clippings. The next morning the horse was found hooves up. The owner tried to blame us, claiming a conspiracy was afoot. An autopsy revealed the fertilizer in the grass clippings poisoned the horse, destroying his revenge theory.

The boarders undervalued what they received for their dollar, a big part of which was peace of mind. I suppose having a horse was a novelty to many of them, a status symbol they wanted to pay as little for as possible. We cared about the horses under our care even though they did not belong to us. Horse boarding is taxing work. Many of the owners did not respect that nor value the personal touch we offered.

Those first winters Russ had to chip the ice from the water trough. A mountain would accrue off to the side that would not melt completely until June. When we were able to afford a floating heating implement, to Russ the simple tool seemed like a gift from heaven. Anything that got him out of the cold was a blessing. And he no longer had to risk a pulled muscle by attacking the ice like a maniac with an axe and a steel bar.

There was also horse feed. Multiple wagon loads of alfalfa or whatever hay we could get at a reasonable rate, most often from neighbors, would ride up the conveyer to be stacked in the barns. Supplemented with silage, no less than eighteen hundred bails rotated through each year. This prodigious task was up to Jenene and Russ.

Jenene had no choice other than to push her unreliable left leg to perform. Falling was a three or four times a week happenstance she had learned to mitigate. After losing her kneecap, she had to train herself to roll with it when she began to fall. That way she landed on her keister and thigh. Braces were too cumbersome and inconvenient to help. She was always on the go and she could not afford to be slowed down by clunky technology.

Hefting bales of hay is all the harder when you have no trust in one of your legs. For fear of falling out of the loft, she often unloaded the wagon while Russ did the stacking in the barn.

Times they worked side by side could present dangers, too. Case in point, one year they were on the last wagonload of bails and were stacking together. Jenene swung the bail hook as Russ reached, and the sharp point impaled his wrist in the sweet spot betwixt tendons.

It could have been much worse: the veins were not damaged even though a large puncture mark remained as a reminder. Perhaps distracted by the injury, Russ lifted the very last eighty-pound bail and in the process of propelling it on top of the stack caused a straw to puncture right through his contact lens into his eye. A trip to the eye doctor was required. He was lucky. He avoided the misfortune of impaired vision.

Another source of food came from the silage pit. The mulched corn would lightly ferment. This process kept it piping warm throughout the winter. On a cold day, you could dig your hands in and it would be so warm they would steam when you pulled them out. It had a singular smell, earthy and rich and slightly sour. The horses loved it. Jenene and Russ speculated that it gave them a mild buzz. Besides the thick coats they grew out, maybe that element of the silage helped sustain them through the cold.

Russ was by this time tasked with growing and harvesting the corn. I would watch, jealous because I was too young to drive the tractor or do fieldwork. Why there is such an allure to do work when prohibited is a mystery I still don't understand. The silage chopper between the tractor and walled wagon reminded me of a lake serpent because of the long curved neck out of which the diced corn was expelled.

My folks were overburdened. There was always so much work to do. Her dad would say "you can't fit ten pounds of manure in a five pound bag" and she and Russ couldn't fit twenty hours of tasks into sixteen hours, which would have afforded them a decent night's sleep. Ah, sleep, sweeter than a lover's embrace after a day of so much exertion.

They got so little slumber the running joke was they got to bed early the night before, early in the morning, that was.

Not that Jenene was sleeping very well besides.

On top of it all, although minding The Seniors and the farm was fulltime work, a living still had to be made outside the home.

In stark juxtaposition to the winters, it was miserably hot in the summer. No air conditioning save for what an old-fashioned fan could execute, which was not much, since fans cool people, not rooms, we were left with little reprieve from the heat and humidity.

We may have had a few fans, but that old antique is the one I remember most. The cage was designed before the child safety craze: the fan blade was not only made out of sharp metal, but the louvers were wide enough to emit a fat adult finger…or a small child hand. It whirred like a plane propeller. The fear was the blades would break loose and go flying across the room like something out of an action flick.

"It's too hot to sleep," I remember complaining one sultry night.

"Come with me," Jenene said, getting out of bed. She took me to the bathroom and wet a washcloth. "Hopefully this will help. Put it on your forehead."

The washcloth did wonders, but not only the heat vexed me with insomnia…it was the all-encompassing worry. Aware of mortality, I recognized that Lal, Bill, and Herb were old and, undeniably, were down to their final years. I was proud to help in their care. And I was proud to help my mom. I could see she was sick. I would worry that she did not have that much time left either.

A heaping amount of adult worry was put on my back and I was toting it despite the incredible strain. I wonder if as an adult I could bear it and suffer it with as much aplomb and composure. Children have an amazing capacity for coping. I was a real worrywart…yet I was able to go about my life and play and imagine and devise ways to escape the heat.

During those boiling hot summers, sprinklers became heavenly spouts of relief. We had unlimited free water so long as we had power (one outage lasted six days) and the pump was working. A benefit of the farm was the well water. We should have bottled it. No water is as crisp, flavorless, and refreshing as the farm's water. It came from a spring-fed well and spouted out of the ground refrigerated naturally and so cold it would give you brain freeze if you were not careful.

Our water supply never ran short. Even in the summers of drought that ravaged the Midwest in the late 1980's, when the only patches of rich green in the lawn were where the dog pooped.

On a whim Jenene had a representative from Culligan make a house call to test the water, a prelude to a sales pitch. A man of scruples, he made it clear our water was superior to what he could offer and spared us the spiel.

Maintaining reliable transportation was the curse of my parents' existence.

Low on funds, we limped by on a series of hundred-dollar beaters, the sort of junkers you don't see anymore. Some were decent until they blew a rod. One, a boat of a station wagon, became my playhouse. My folks parked it out back and so long as I kept it from going moldy inside it was mine to do with as I pleased, which involved a lot of pretend driving and sleep outs.

Quite by happenstance, before long Jenene and Russ were driving a monster truck when those things were a whole lot more novel. The lift kit made it so high it was a challenge to the police, many of whom broke out their measuring sticks to double check. It was legal…with about a millimeter to spare.

The truck had belonged to Jenene's little bro. Jeff planned to cut and run to Florida and offered to let Jenene take over the minimal payments. It seemed like a sound investment until the beast of a truck became a monster of a money pit. Jenene couldn't verify this, but I seem to recall the engine was a Frankensteinian hodgepodge of vacuum and other inappropriate parts.

During this time Jenene was working on another goal. If there was even a small probability the doctors were right and the intraperitoneal adhesions could kill her—she was having unnerving symptoms she associated with the painful disease—she had to prepare for the worst.

Before the Affordable Care Act (no comment on the actual benefits), preexisting conditions meant if you were sick you could get no form of insurance.

Jenene's prerogative was to acquire life insurance no matter what. Of course you were out of luck if a pre-approval physical was conducted and a fatal disease was detected. Overcoming such an obstacle seemed a higher leap than she could make.

Foiled too often, Jenene decided to find a way to go through the backdoor. She studied insurance law and discovered a loophole: if you held a license to sell insurance, you could sell a policy to your spouse and make yourself a rider…no checkup required. The loophole has since been obliterated but while it existed Jenene was thankful to take advantage. She refused to leave me in the lurch. Even though it was another sacrifice, Jenene fit insurance classes into her hectic schedule.

"I threw a rod and blew the engine of that damn monster truck on my way home from one of those classes," she reminisced when discussing this period. And added, really revealing her frugal mindset at the time, "At the end of the course, it cost money to take the test so come hell or high water I was going to pass it the first time. I used to have a certificate that said I was one of the three percent that year who passed that test on the first try." A laugh. "I really didn't want to pay a twenty-dollar fee a second time."

In the end she only sold one policy, to herself. The goal then was to live long enough so it would not be contested. And she did. A testament to her devotion to my wellbeing, no matter what financial woes were weighing us down, she has faithfully paid for that policy ever since.

Chapter 56
The Trials of Land Ownership

Not only was the farm mistaken as a landfill, to many the hill qualified as either a walking trail or much worse, an off-road recreation park.

Fearing a lawsuit in the event someone was hurt, the battle against all manner of trespassers was constant and never ending. So long as they did not harm the wildlife or leave litter we were lenient with people on foot. If you wanted to walk your dog and enjoy the scenery, more power to you.

Off-road vehicles were the genuine problem. The enticement was irresistible: all the trails were sand and a large washboard area approximated a motocross circuit. Dirt bikes and trucks would tear through, kicking up hell. We were reduced to guerilla tactics, covering the trails with logs and branches—the impediments were removed so quickly it was as if a crew waited to go into action right behind us.

Trespassers would blatantly claim right to our faces that they had permission when no such consent had been granted. If we asked them the name of the owners, few knew the Wiechman's and even fewer knew Jenene and Russ.

I would do my best to act brave when I was alone on the hill and these people challenged me. Some would intimidate me, sending me running for the house—quite a distance made doubly long by asthmatic lungs.

I felt craven when I failed to stand my ground. In retrospect I cannot fault myself too much: some real oddballs were drawn to the back forty. Who knows what danger standing my ground might have inspired.

It helped when Butch came into our lives. People tend to be intimidated by large alert Dobermans.

As for Russ, to make up for a lack of brawniness he adopted the persona of the black-clad cowboy and looked like a gunslinger of old.

He understood the importance of intimation to intimidate. If he looked scary he got a lot less malarkey when confronting trespassers. Striking quite an image when complete, over time he attained a long black leather duster, black sharp-toed boots, and a black western-style hat he augmented with a rattlesnake band with rattle and a barn swallow feather.

In winter he would apply a bit of mountain man by growing a bushy beard. He needed no weapon to get respect. With a face so chameleonic he could carry a disarming expression for some…or one so withering it inspired nearly immediate compliance for the ones who gave attitude.

There were times trespassers' own tools of destruction were their undoing.

Every now and again someone would come walking up from the back forty, their truck mired in the sand, to ask for help or to use the phone. Fed up with these sort of interlopers, Jenene would tell them we would allow no tow truck on the property, so the only way out was to bribe Russ to break out a tractor and pull out their vehicle.

When they asked him what it would cost, the cowboy would become a highwayman and ask coolly, "How much you have on you?" Not entirely a villain, he would leave them with a couple dollars for gas or whatever, but he took the bulk of their money as discouragement from ever trespassing on our farm again.

We needed the money desperately anyway.

The worst were the trespassers who challenged and even threatened us openly. It got to the point that even with Butch in tow Jenene would carry a rifle with her while walking the property alone.

We lived under the constant fear some yahoo would get himself hurt, lawyer up, and sue. It seems ridiculous that a trespasser having entered a property illegally could hold the property owner liable for damages, but that's the way the law is written.

The rifle Jenene carried had a tale. A .44-40 Winchester, when they were cleaning out the basement Jenene and Russ discovered the powerful firearm stowed away in the wall insulation. There were several boxes of ammunition.

We never got a back-story for the rifle or learned why it was hidden, but even as abhorrers of gun violence, we recognized its usefulness as a tool. On an isolated farmstead you sometimes need an equalizer. It packed a powerful wallop and sounded like a crack of thunder. Between the silent threat of such a firearm and Butch, most people took the message and vacated.

Still…

Sometimes it took more.

One cool fall day Jenene spied a hunter crossing the field. Butch and the rifle in hand, she went out to meet him.

No one could by law hunt the land. Even if we were inclined to give permission, a good excuse to decline when friends were asking, we lacked the required acreage.

Hunters often tried to poach.

She had no idea this one's angle.

When they came face to face, Jenene said, "Butch, watch him." Butch had a menacing way of going back and forth without taking his eyes off his quarry. It tended to make people nervous.

Not this guy.

Unimpressed, the hunter said, "I have a dog, too."

"Well, I have this," Jenene said, indicating the rifle on her shoulder.

When the hunter further confronted Jenene by saying, "I have one too," she looked him dead in the eye and said, "The difference is, they'll never find you."

Even though making such a threat was and remains outside her nature, taking care of the farm brought out her darker side. If it was not conniving family, it was yahoos wanting to shoot off guns. It was easy to feel fed up.

Property ownership is a dream shared by many. But until you experience it, you can never know the hair-graying, wrinkle-etching stress it can involve. It really felt like it was our family against an interloping and encroaching world.

Jenene's eyes were cobalt.

The potential poacher stood his ground for a few seconds.

Then to his benefit and ours, the hunter turned tail and departed.

Land ownership has a way of making people act outside their usual temperament when it pertains to protecting their property.

You can never foresee who might be drawn to your property.

Some years later, a wildfire would reveal a shed concealed within the trees comprising the largest patch of woods. When Jenene and Russ explored the small, surprisingly well-constructed structure they found it stocked. Canned goods, blankets, and tools were enough of a suggestion of shenanigans to alert the police, who suggested it was a gang hideout and needed to be dismantled immediately.

It was easy to have even darker suspicions. We had experience. Some trespassers were not combatable with fierce dogs or big guns.

Coinciding with Russ's prediction his thirtieth birthday would be terrible, an event happened that opened our eyes to terror. Advice to follow: unless spiritually equipped, do not disrupt a black mass.

Sometimes adversaries can seem to brandish the hoodoo of black magic.

Chapter 57
It Begins

It might have been their Sunday night but it was after midnight, which meant it was June 27, 1988.

The interim between late night and early morning was a phase of time they knew too well. It seemed they were living a sleepless life. Even when it got to the point the mere act of closing their eyes brought sleep, they skimmed the surface rather than dive into restful depths. Responsibilities were irremovable floaties.

Were they thinking about Russ's "sure to be terrible" thirtieth birthday? Approaching the end of another long day, they were too tired. They had learned to cross obstacles when they got to them. Relaxing on the back step to chill out before bed, all Jenene and Russ were doing was talking through what lay ahead and the travails of days just passed.

Tragedy had again struck in our life. An aggressive horse kicked Cognac in the head. Apparent at once his vision was impaired, his behavior made Jenene fear the worst: brain damage.

Forced to deal with this shocking eventuality, the last few days had been extra demanding. She persuaded an equine veterinarian to make the journey from the University of Minnesota. The woman had solid credentials. When she determined the injury was not as severe as feared, Jenene was relieved.

The rest of the diagnosis was depressing. Cognac would survive but his sight could not be restored. For the time being he was isolated. He was safer in the pen beside the pump house cut off from the pasture.

In truth he was coping marvelously. Better than she was because as a being of nature he was not sidled with self-pity or doubt or any of the other drawbacks that civilized man lets defeat him. Adapting and adjusting to sightlessness has to be one of the most difficult acclimatization processes—it outright sapped headstrong Herb of a desire to live—and Cognac almost immediately began reshaping his world.

Before feeling comfortable leaving him alone, Jenene watched as he got along. It was evident he was counting out his steps and mapping his enclosure. Soon he navigated his space without bumping into poles or fences. Seeing he had regained some of his confidence, it was clear to her Cognac was not letting his dilemma be a hindrance.

Cognac managing so well was encouraging. But she still had to wonder how it was possible such a dreadful accidental attack could happen. One kick cursed him with permanent blindness.

They had to get to bed but needed the time to unwind. It was a clear, warm night. Enjoyable and calming after so intensive a day, it was a worthy tradeoff. They had to get up even earlier than the usual 6:21 rise and shine. Cognac needed to be nursed. The breakfast routine had to be observed. Then Jenene and I were going on a road trip.

"I wish I didn't have to take him to Iowa tomorrow," she said. "He hates long car trips and I'm hardly up to it." Her ex-husband and his new wife Lorene moved to a town in Iowa so small it did not warrant a dot on a map.

Russ placed a consoling hand on her shoulder and rubbed. "Are you sure you can't postpone? With what's going on and all."

There was only one reason she agreed to a ten-hour roundtrip. Diabolical Guy was still the enemy. The law said he had visitation rights. She would respect the law. But she was still some way from trusting her ex.

I visited with them before. We stayed with Lorene's parents. The town was so small I could leisurely bike the whole perimeter in less than ten minutes. This visit would be my first since they—so they claimed—moved into a house on the same block as Guy's in-laws.

"If I put it off by saying I can't make the trip he may offer to come pick him up. I just…I have to see."

"I get it."

Jenene wanted to know I was staying in a real place. Even before custody abduction cases were vogue in the media, she was tortured by the worry he might kidnap me. She had no idea Guy had no such plan (in fact he felt discouraged by his new wife to even spend time with me). After suffering enough psychological and physical abuse to drive her almost to breaking, Jenene's paranoia was an understandable reaction. After so many threats, how could she not believe he would strike back at her in the way that hurt most?

I have no doubt she would be looking for me to this day. Though I tend to believe my behavior in such a situation would've resulted in my return.

"We should get to bed then," Russ said. "You have a lot of driving—"

So suddenly it was startling, a blast of noise split apart the still night: "Yaaaaaaa!"

"Holy shit!"

"What the hell is that?"

"Yaaaaaaa!"

The gut-wrenching shrieks prodded them to their feet. Fear was as much a motivator. One thing about the farm, they had a lot to protect. Three senior citizens and a little boy would be defenseless in the face of marauders.

The shrieks sounded so close.

"Yaaaaaaa!" Another wail eviscerated what had been so calm a night.

"Up on the hill," Jenene said. The shock of the first shriek made it seem much closer than it was in actuality. "What kind of crazy people would be doing that?" she asked as they made their way to the rear barnyard to investigate. A cordless phone was clipped to her jeans.

"I don't doubt they're sick bastards."

Reaching the rear barnyard beside the woodpile, their eyes searched the hill and observed a source of light amid the thick summertime foliage. Was there a fire? A summer of drought—the first of two, the costliest natural disaster until Hurricane Katrina—there was enough dry grass on the hill a single spark could start a devastating blaze.

All they could tell for certain in the first instants was that on the left quadrant of the hill, near the top in a clearing, was bright enough luminance to cast shadow.

A crowd was up there.

"If that's a fire—"

Projected across the black sky tinged in the yellow glow of the source of luminosity, one shadow figure towered above all the others.

"Look, there's no flicker," Jenene said.

"It must be artificial light."

What they witnessed was the shadow figure's giant arms rise up over his head, reaching high into the clear sky. Between his hands was some sort of bludgeoning or chopping utensil. Without hesitation, he drove down the weapon with unmitigated ferocity—

"Yaaaaaaa!"

Again!

"Yaaaaaaa!"

Again!

"Yaaaaaaa!"

Unrelenting. Remorseless.

Fingers impaired with anxious shakiness, Jenene dialed 9-1-1 and explained the situation hastily to the dispatcher. Explaining an animal was apparently being ritualistically killed on our property was strange to say the least. She was told to hang tight. The cavalry were sneaking in through the back. That way they would catch the crowd—coven—in the act.

Then she and Russ watched and waited.

The anxiety had them on edge. In a world where too much strife is transposed into mayhem, there is reason to be afraid.

The available information being that the trespassers were so sadistic they could torture an animal indicated a lack of empathy that could translate to people dangerous to other people.

If pushed, if cornered, might they be willing to commit an irredeemable act? There was no telling.

The sound of the animal's anguish was nothing short of heartrending and stomach churning.

Russ was desperate to spring into action. Blessed or blighted with a deep sense of compassion for animals, he had to fight his legs not to convey him right into the heart of danger.

Jenene convinced him he had to stay with her to defend the house. She hated hearing the anguished wails too but with the police en route it was possible dangerous people would be flushed in their direction. She needed him by her side.

Aware their hands were tied failed to ease tensions as the seconds ticked off.

They had too many responsibilities to carry out what they both wanted to do, which was to stop what was happening. In the world of fiction a hero can right any wrong at the whim of the writer's ingenuity—or careless plotting—but in the real world good people die for no other reason than they were in the wrong place at the wrong time.

The feeling Russ had all his life concerning his dreaded thirtieth birthday could have been a warning against the very danger he would face if he plunged in the way his aching heart told him he should.

Speculation ran rampant. They had no idea how dangerous the trespassers were, or how many, but if their cruel treatment of the animal—perhaps a goat or sheep—was any indication, there was reason to fear. It was smarter to stay put, play it safe. Jenene watched a lot of horror movies with Guy; she *lived* a horror movie with Guy. She had huge reservations about either her husband or her winding up the stars in one.

She appreciated Russ could repress his heroic-cum-stupid instincts. She felt safer with him there. How compounded would her worry be if he were sneaking around up there? Inaction might have been torturous to him even when it was the right choice but not knowing her husband was safe would have been much worse for her. She could tell his agitation was mounting as they watched whatever dark rite was happening continue unabated.

The seconds felt elongated.

It felt like it was taking forever.

Then all at once there was a total blackout.

The awful wails of agony ceased.

Whatever the trespassers were up to was interrupted. Which had to mean they figured out the police were closing in.

"We better get inside," Jenene said. "They could be headed this way."

"I'll make sure the basement door is locked."

Locking the doors was a rare occurrence in those days. Though it was not so long ago, it was a more innocent time, which is strange to contemplate in hindsight because we lived under the threat of nuclear annihilation thanks to the unconcluded Cold War. Anytime missiles could fall on us in the world's last gasp and that night deranged animal killers could fall on us in what would only be our family's last gasp.

The threat right there on our property was scarier to Jenene and Russ than stockpiles of arms placed strategically worldwide. So far as we knew that stuff was not right in our backyard.

Suspense slew their calm; as tired as they might have been, now they were wired.

Within the hour a police cruiser crept up the driveway. A uniformed patrolman gave them the lowdown.

One of the officers made a mistake. He touched the brake. The trespassers were not about to wait around to be popped; when they saw the brake light flash they scattered like cockroaches. A few were rounded up before vanishing into the cracks. The bugs they were, not a one carried identification.

Tipped off by a lookout, all evidence of the sacrificial animal was successfully removed. A tarp had likely been employed for streamlined concealment. Without evidence it would be hard to hang much of a charge on the captured culprits, the officer explained, but the warning would go a long way.

This point was debatable. Perhaps they would steer clear of returning in the flesh. Perhaps they had other ways of touching us.

"We have had problems around Grey Cloud with these people before," the officer reported. "Let us know if you find any evidence—"

"Do you know if they've hurt any people?" Jenene enquired.

"So far as we can tell, no. Uh, make sure to lock your doors. Just to be safe."

"That's it?"

"Keep an eye out for anything out of the ordinary."

Jenene felt a chill as she and Russ retreated back inside. The surrealism of the night's events left them agitated and a little freaked; where was Roman Polanski to yell, "Cut," and call for the next setup on his new film about unleashed cultists? How could this be reality?

There was a possibility there were other ways they could get to us. People who dabble in the dark arts could summon evil forces, throw hexes, and hand out curses. She had heard and read things about devil worship and black magic and wanted nothing to do with getting on the wrong side of such people. Just in case.

Jenene was curious. "So you think this was all because it's your thirtieth birthday?"

"I don't know," Russ replied. "I just always felt this would be a bad day."

"An early midlife crisis?"

"Other than marrying you, there's nothing about my twenties so great I don't want to go into my thirties."

"Nice to know. We better get to bed. We have another long day tomorrow. Happy birthday, by the way."

"We can only hope," Russ said reproachfully. "I'm just anxious for it to be over."

Had an attack of bad luck begun with those horrible screams, the shrieks of a tortured animal? Seems there had been a lot of bad luck as of late—when had there not been, really? But they had each other and they could get through anything.

Nodding off to sleep, all she could do was hope she was being silly for feeling chilled to her core and reluctant to get up the next morning.

Chapter 58
Worst Birthday Ever

Morning snuck up and forced Jenene out of bed far sooner than her exhausted body thought proper.

All she could do was stretch her achy limbs and achier back before exchanging her nightgown for jeans and a t-shirt. Long days have to be jumped right into or else they are only made longer. In this case she had to tend to Cognac before she prepared breakfast.

The pen was accessible through the pump house entrance to the barnyard. Jenene made her way in that direction after crossing the road. Eyes having not yet relinquished sleep fully, when at a distance it first seemed Cognac was absent from the pen, she blinked, triggering a yawn, wiped away the resultant tired tears, and looked closer, only to confirm what she first thought she saw.

Another one of those times she was snapped awake, shock quickened her pace.

Where was her horse?

Had the gate been left open?

It was unlikely but the first thing to check.

He was in no condition to wander!

Mindful of her bad leg, Jenene rushed into the pen. She figured a search for Cognac should begin where she saw him last. The only gate was secure. There was no glaring opening in the fence. No reason he should be gone. The far side of the pen bordered the pasture and it was there she was given harsh, glaring enlightenment.

Her heart sank

"Cognac, no!"

Somehow Cognac wound up on the other side of the tall fence and was lying in the pasture on his side.

How was it even possible? A healthy horse would be hard pressed to jump that height of fence. There was no sense to it, none, and all she could do was finagle her way through and go to her beloved horse.

Her heart sank even farther upon reaching him. He was so much worse. He was supposed to get better. He was going to be challenged but he was going to survive. Yet it was obvious he was wracked by death throes. Seeing him that way, stuck on the ground and fading, she let out a scream to rival the tortured shrieks from the night before, "Nooooooo!"

Without faltering she took up his large head in her arms and offered what meager comfort she could as he lived his final moment. Had she procrastinated even five minutes she would have found him dead and not been able to be with him as he passed. She heard the death rattle. She felt the cessation following his final breath. Cognac slipped away with his head in her arms, her tears sprinkling his face.

What brought this? The hoity-toity vet said there was no brain damage beyond losing his vision. Why was he dead when she was assured he would recover? Was it a coincidence that the police had exiled animal-sacrificing "devil worshippers" from the farm the night before? In protecting their property...had they been hexed?

Should they have just ignored those agonized shrieks?

The scorch mark indicated there had been huge conflagrations in the past. On other nights before we moved in had The Seniors overlooked the flames visible on the hill? Ignored the cries? Or were they blissfully asleep and hence even more blissfully unaware?

Bill might be up at night in his basement office. If he heard, it would be like him not to incur the wrath of such fiends by remaining tightlipped. Bill had learned a part of getting by was staying quiet. Unless it was a person being murdered up there, it was safer not to challenge the sort of dishonorable folks who would be so cruel.

Perhaps due to a generational divide, such inertia never suited Jenene. Even if it brought trouble, she would sooner step in front of a train than keep her mouth shut when it came to such an injustice. The murdered animal was a life and hearing its agony had torn out her heart. How could she ignore that?

A dream in some way predicting these events would have been welcome.

Had there only been a hint Cognac was in danger....

After enduring one of the worst hurts of her life and dragging herself up the driveway, there was no time for mourning because Jenene had to kick-start her routine.

Life was already wearying; now she felt gut-kicked.

Another Monday. Laundry day. After she made and cleaned up breakfast, she had to basket up all the household laundry, transport it to the St. Paul Park laundromat, and hope there were enough available machines it would not take all day.

Plus she had to pick up her paycheck in St. Paul. Bad leg be damned, she was waitressing at a swanky restaurant where a good attitude drew large gratuity. She could make more hourly cooking, but she did not have full-time availability and the tips often matched a forty-hour workweek.

There was also a matter of delivering me to Iowa.

Before she began breakfast, she put in a call to Guy. She had to cancel the trip. She was not emotionally outfitted to make the long drive. The extenuating circumstances were understandable enough. Emotional wrecks had no business on the road.

Lorene answered.

"Hello, Jenene!"

"Is Guy available?"

"Not right now. Is there something wrong?"

Again Jenene found herself telling Lorene a hard story; this time there was no catharsis, only sorrow.

"I could shoot up and get him," Lorene suggested. "It would be no problem."

It mystifies me that she actually did this since in recent years I've learned how little she accepted my dad's former life. Perhaps she was in some way cleverly extorting him and my visit played into her plans. Who knows? But the offer was there and Jenene had a tough decision to make.

Lorene would not have let my dad take me for the simple fact that I was baggage she would have preferred discarded. Yet for Jenene, the fear weighed on her that they would cut and run. Thinking about it logically, the idea of them abducting me was preposterous because going on the run would have inconvenienced their lives tremendously, but she was going on raw emotion and a dearth of sleep.

Paranoia aside, making a quick decision, she consented: she knew I needed breaks.

Besides, with a less-than-satisfactory relationship with Russ, I was starving for another male influence, no matter how momentary, and looked forward to seeing my dad.

After breakfast, she broke the news about Cognac and told me Lorene was coming to collect me. Hearing about Cognac was a stunning blow. Mortality became real to me that day. Death had come and snatched something that truly had meaning to me for the first time. Stunned into silence, I absorbed the horrible news. Assimilated intense grief.

I paid Cognac a visit and told him goodbye.

Kids have an incredible capacity to accept hard reality, compartmentalize, and continue on. Moments later my state of mind changed in an instant from heartache to curiosity when Jenene gave me a brief account of the night before. She walked straight into a wall of questions.

"They were devil worshippers? The cops chased them away? They were killing an animal?" I was fascinated and for a time distracted from my heartache over Cognac. I was always interested in the macabre, for instance the catacombs beneath Paris, Chinchorro mummies, the inquisition, capital punishment, Druids, and all manner of weird stuff. "But the police didn't find it?" I was disappointed I slept through the action.

I had to wonder why anyone would align with the symbol of supreme evil over the symbol of all creation.

Jenene said, "I'm too busy to answer questions right now. Russ and I are going up on the hill to look for evidence."

"Can I go?"

Since my folks were short on time, we took the field road via car to the base of the hill. From there we walked. Russ went off to search off-trail for any evidence while Jenene and I went up to the area where they had seen the light. There was a huge round scorch mark where there had once been a huge bonfire, probably during a wetter summer. Perhaps evidence black masses had been held there before or only of a party. The devil worshippers could have learned to bring a lantern instead of lighting a big unwieldy fire.

Further on, near the egress that led to a community garden and a tank farm before reaching suburban Cottage Grove, we found a row of animal skulls lined up along a mossy log. Bones fascinated me. I once read an article in an issue of "Ranger Rick" magazine concerning a teenage girl who collected skeletons and had several full animals and skulls in beautiful glass display cases. I asked immediately if I could have the skulls.

"No," Russ said.

Jenene shot a look his way. "You can't bring them inside," she said. "If you store them outside I don't see a problem."

I kept the skulls for a time. I never identified from what animals they derived. They felt like bad hoodoo. I discarded them eventually, feeling they were holding bad luck to us.

Other than the skulls we found no other remnants of the events of the night before.

Back at the house my folks loaded the laundry into the bed of the monster truck.

Every time she climbed into the goliath stomper Jenene was struck by fear. Not fear of an accident. The truck was so huge it would smoosh most other vehicles on the road. No, she feared another gremlin malfunction. She had deep regrets about ever taking over the payments.

They had spent what to our household was a fortune on maintenance. This included putting in seven starters, three flywheels, and replacing a blown engine. It was always something with the damn stomper.

Their first stop was the laundromat to get the clothes washing. Time to sit and peruse a magazine, as others were doing while she and Russ loaded machines speedily, seemed a novel luxury. At least in the mundane chore she could find distraction from her grief.

Their next stop was at the gas station a few blocks away.

Gas was priced at about or only a little over a dollar a gallon. Even in the stomper five dollars' worth should have taken them some ways. By the time they had made the three-mile journey to their next destination, New Port Drug (they had to pick up prescriptions continuously), the truck was down to fumes.

While dealing with a truck inexplicably burning through so much gas a gallon would not equal a mile, trying to get laundry done ate up a lot of time. It was a couple hours before they were able to return home. A nightmare dealing with the truck, frustrations left the pair frayed.

"Yep, pretty much what I expected," Russ concluded.

Heading up the driveway, they were in for another shock. An unfamiliar car was parked beside the house, a nice sedan. It had Illinois plates.

Traveling eight hours spontaneously for a surprise visit was in no way suspicious.

Ahem.

Uncle Bob, orchestrating behind the scenes to take over the farm, greeted them with a wry smile. He, brother Dick, and their wives were in the house. They were visiting with The Seniors. They were casual for people aligned against our family.

Bob spearheaded the initiative like a kamikaze pilot. So intent was he on putting The Seniors in a home and selling the farm he left logic out of his crusade. It never dawned on him that what he wanted would cost him any inheritance.

The facts were simple. The proceeds of a sale would be used to support Lal, Bill, and Herb. Nursing homes are costly. Unless of course you are heartless and have no regard for proper care: even in that scenario it was impractical. Upkeep of three elderly relatives in even the shoddiest home would burn through whatever money existed in short order.

Really it amounted to simple spite. He could not abide us acquiring something he was denied.

Aware Jenene's devious uncles were looking to oust our trio made for a delicate situation. Uncle Bob was hunting for any excuse to prove Jenene and Russ unfit. Testing their resolve, they had to be in top form on one of their hardest days. It was moving mountains not to break into tears. Yet they had to hold it together.

Jenene went straight to the phone, dialed Lois, and virtually shrieked, "Why didn't you tell me they were coming?"

"Who?"

"Your brothers!"

"What about them? You mean they're there?"

"What do you mean, do I mean they're here?"

"So they're there?"

"You didn't know?"

"I had no idea."

"Well, they are here and I want them out. I don't have time to deal with this."

The tension was thicker than Nantucket fog but unfortunately not as blinding because I was able to see too much of my mom's stress. She was tense and angry and on edge. She had to be subservient and kind to family she knew would cut her off at the knees if they got half a chance. But she had to be cordial. There was no use in kicking a hornet's nest.

There was an ally, possibly two, in fact. Dick's petite and attractive younger wife, Diana was opposed to Bob's gung-ho plans. She revealed to Jenene her hubby had his reservations too but felt cowed by his older brother. Diana's assurance Dick was only attending half-heartedly eased tensions. Her support meant worlds.

Diana and Jenene had a special bond, and not only because they shared a birthday. Diana wasn't much older than her niece and when Jenene was a teenager her hip aunt was the "coolest" adult. Dick seemed stuffy by comparison yet he was so smitten by his young bride he accepted her liberal quirkiness. They met shortly after he came home from a stint in the military and seemed an unlikely match.

A gifted artist, Diana had created a portrait of an eighteen-year-old Jenene that captured her essence perfectly. It was the first of what would become a huge collection of Midwest masterpieces.

Even with Diana's support, it would be Bill who provided the brightest ray of light for Jenene and Russ that day.

As she suspected, Uncle Bob had come in an attempt to assert familial control. Bill was sitting in his chair reading the newspaper when Bob plopped down before him and made his pitch. "It's time you wrote a will and stipulated who gets this place when you're gone. By all rights, we deserve it. We came here and worked every summer"—it never struck him his mother had foisted them off and they had earned their keep, not the farm— "and it should go to us. I think you can agree you can't just hand it over to *these* people. It just wouldn't be right."

Because he was a man of low-key deference and endless patience, Bill graciously let him say his piece, observing over the top of the paper, eyes squarely on Bob as he parceled his twaddle. His face, which could look so kind, held an air of indifference that could easily be construed as lack of interest. If Bob mistook it for careful contemplation and that motivated him to press on, he would soon learn he was wrong.

Waiting until he had run out of steam, Bill said, "Don't talk to me. There's a new regime around here. You can leave anytime." With a snapping riffle the paper was again concealing his face and he would not say another word to Uncle Bob. Ever.

Even if in our misery we often fail to look outside our own microcosm, there are billions of other lives being lived and odds are a good percentage are also having rotten days. Case in point, as bad of a day as Jenene and Russ were having, around our lunchtime well over a hundred people in France were forever changed by a devastating commuter train collision. The Gare de Lyon rail accident left 56 dead and 57 injured.

Lorene arrived and I was off to Iowa after a hug and bon voyage session. Jenene struggled to contain her tears.

I felt ashamed. Part of me was just so elated to get away, which multiplied my guilty feelings. I was abandoning my mom when she needed me most. I considered Russ a poor support system. Had I insisted on not going, well, I was persuasive enough I would have gotten my way.

I rarely used my clout as an asthmatic, the one way I could assert my wishes, but it was always available. Using my health as a tool of extortion was an act without pride. I preferred to get my way with quiet logic, a slower but effective process I had no time to apply. But as the gravel crunched and pinged beneath Lorene's pickup on our way down the driveway, I thought I should have staged an asthma attack and got as bright as a cherry tomato to make it perfectly reasonable I stay home without building a case like a prosecutor.

The truth was sometimes I needed a break. Time away, fishing and swimming, freer of worry than I could ever be at home, where all my reasons to worry were ever-present.

It's no lie that whatever fails to kill you only makes you stronger.

"That was probably in the top five worst days of my life," Jenene recalled. "It was the day I lost my horse, dealt with my uncles trying to catch us with our pants down, and feared I would lose my son. After facing all that it would take a lot more to ruffle my feathers."

By the time the scheming Bob and Dick departed, she was so exhausted from walking the tightrope she was ready to collapse. But she was waiting for a call. Only after she heard my voice, recognized no distress, and said she loved me before wishing me a good first night at my dad's could she relax.

While Jenene and Russ were preparing to put the bad day behind them, recognized linear heavyweight champion of the world Michael Spinks was facing a reckoning against history's youngest heavyweight champion Mike Tyson that would see him vanquished in ninety-one seconds, erasing his credibility as a top boxer. Spinks may have been knocked out but Jenene refused to go down even after a long day of pummeling.

Once they had seen The Seniors off to bed, Jenene suggested to unwind they go for a drink. Russ leapt at the idea. Jumpy as a Chihuahua all day, he was still convinced a chunk of blue ice excreted from a plane would flatten him or some other equally awful mishap would occur. Something to take the edge off would help relax his twitchy nerves.

Off they went to an Italian eatery and bar in the very mall that housed the Snyder's Lal took her to all those times as a child.

The friendly woman who concocted their Long Island Iced Teas lived up to the stereotype of the compassionate bartender with an open ear. "You've had one hell of a bad day," she said, toweling a glass and shaking her head.

"That we have."

"I think you could definitely say it takes the trophy for worst birthday ever."

"Yippy," Russ said sardonically.

The bartender chuckled. "I don't have a trophy but your drinks are on the house."

As unworkable as it would have been, Jenene wished so much to bury Cognac beside where he lay in the pasture.

A massive undertaking, an improbable mission, but one she would have made real to honor her loss. If only there was a way to make it practicable. The hard packed ground made it impossible. The spade of a shovel only deflected from the solid crust. Had she been in a position to rent a jackhammer or even better a backhoe she would have gone ahead and dug out a hole big enough.

Not to be, she had to resort to a solution that was yet another blow.

Later I would learn what becomes of dead horses. In those days dead farm animals could be hauled away for free but it meant the carcass would be put to use. It seemed an abomination any horse should be rendered into dog food and gelatin and glue. Even if I admire big cats, they should be in the wild, not zoos, because in zoos due to its leanness they are fed horsemeat.

That the magnificent animal I loved should be…processed, like any livestock, was a thought so repugnant it turned my stomach.

I suppose it was a bittersweet poetic justice it was so boiling hot that June day. By the time they came, Cognac was beyond use in almost every way. His path to dust to dust would not involve being reduced to excrement unless it was through an elementary schooler's unhealthy yen for Elmer's Glue.

Jenene took the owner of the horse that caused Cognac's death to court. When ordered to make reparations, he first offered an undesirable nag. When that was turned down he filed for bankruptcy. There would never be reparation.

For Jenene it was always about the principle.

Not one to close her heart, when a magnificent standard bred palomino was offered at an incredibly low price, Jenene was, to quote an expression, ready to jump back on the horse.

Sweetie belonged to a family friend named Betty. The genteel older woman had come into several acres on Grey Cloud Island and had acquired a stable of horses she needed to pare down. Bill met with her every Saturday in the late morning for coffee and cookies. They were not a couple so far as we knew but there was a suspicion the weekly dates hinted at romance. Or so we like to muse.

Russ acquired Sweetie as a gift. His wedding present would be worthless without a horse to ride. The pristine western saddle would collect dust no more…or so he hoped. Motives being mercurial, there also might have been some discord he was trying to erase with his act of kindness. Unable to afford a rental trailer, he volunteered to escort Sweetie on foot from Betty's to the farm, a hike of several miles.

Palominos are tawny colored and substantially bigger and bulkier than many horses. Sweetie was much taller than Russ's six feet. Leading her by the halter, Russ being in control was predicated on Sweetie being convinced he somehow *had* control. The truth was Sweetie could have run for it and Russ would have been along for the ride if he were along at all.

There was one shaky occurrence.

Sweetie was startled. She reared her head. Russ made a bid to maintain control. Clung fast to her halter with all his might and in so doing was lifted right off the ground. His feet dangled for an instant. His muscles tightened. His heart pitter-pattered. Then Sweetie regained her composure. The bottoms of Russ's boots reencountered the road with enough impact to send shockwaves up his heels.

He guided her the rest of the way home without incident.

As it would turn out, Jenene's health would steal her chance to ever ride her gorgeous new horse.

Chapter 59
Wrecked Lower Back

Every year seemed to bring a new health scare. 1987's was a severe allergic reaction caused by triple antibiotic ointment.

Skin was eaten right off her body.

Whole patches.

Thirty percent of Jenene's epidermis sloughed off. In the hospital she stood over a table in a puddle of her own plasma and tried not to cry.

Laugh and the world laughs with you; cry and you cry alone....

The extremity of her condition was a strong indicator of another health crisis, a disease she may have suffered since she was a child, but that would remain unknown for nearly a decade.

Not knowing was probably better. Dealing with growing back her skin would have been harder had she known she had systemic lupus erythematosus (SLE), another deadly autoimmune affliction that cuts down the seemingly healthy in their youth because it often goes undiagnosed.

1988 started her off on one rocky path only to redirect her to another one that was even rockier. The journey began with a misdiagnosis and an unnecessary surgery.

The pain in Jenene's midsection was so awful she once again groveled at the knees of doctors for succor and found only more hurt.

It began with the verdict her anguish was ovarian cancer. Cancer sounded logical. After everything else, the question was why not? She already had the breast cancer scare. Surgery was yet again sold to her as an absolute requirement to save her life. Twenty-eight years old, so close to that expiration date imposed on her, and she was still trusting doctors.

Laid out on a gurney, rising from the murkiness of anesthesia, Jenene was barely cognitive when the doctor told her there was no cancer, only cysts. Nothing had been removed. They seemed to begrudge her for not having cancer. Before she was even fully conscious she was being wheeled out to the car. Not even with a prescription for painkillers.

She was only there because the pain in her abdomen had worsened so much it made her scared she was dying.

Like a raging ball of fire it seemed to burn right in the center of her core. Because she had ovarian cysts the doctor assured her the pain was caused by ovarian cancer. She only had one ovary left. In such cases a diagnoses of cancer was all but guaranteed...or so she was convinced.

When the word cancer is bandied about, it is impossible not to take seriously. Cancer would explain a lot, actually, so she was open-minded to exploratory surgery. Russ brought her to the U of M earlier that day and bid her good luck as she went in to be dissected.

"If you cough," the doctor said, "hold your incision"—a four-inch-long slice down her middle—"so the adhesive tape holds. A nurse will be in soon to help with your discharge."

"Discharge? Shouldn't I be...kept for observation...or something?"

Without batting an eye, he said unpleasantly, "You'll be fine."

Doctors abhor being wrong. She got the distinct impression from his brevity and terseness that he blamed her for not having cancer.

To hell with him: it was excellent news. The reverse of that, as in what *was* causing her pain, could be pondered over later. Any time you find out you don't have cancer rates as all-time best news.

Then the disgruntled doctor was gone and a nurse was helping her, despite her uneasiness, into a wheelchair. The incision was not even sutured. One false move, one big sneeze, even an unconscious cough, and she would have a major problem—one akin to a hernia but much worse. The idea of her guts falling out was more than irksome. What would amount to even minor disembowelment was terrifying.

Mind not yet clear of post-surgery fog, she was however starting to feel pain. En route to the front doors on her hasty jaunt through the hospital, she was able to put together that if the pain was so bad this soon after surgery, it was only going to get worse. Not one to rely on pain pills—a fuzzy headed Aquarian, she knew narcotics dulling her senses did not serve her immediate and long-term goals—she nevertheless knew she would need more than aspirin to get through the night ahead.

Being shoveled into the passenger side of a car, she asked the nurse quickly, "Did the doctor write me any prescriptions?"

"He didn't," she replied and slammed the door on further inquiry.

It does not feel good when your inner workings are fiddled with and the anesthesia wears off without being backed up with narcotics.

The pain was becoming debilitating. The four-inch incision looked angry. She needed something with more kick than Tylenol. There was only one place she could turn. She contacted Dr. Gaither.

On the phone he heard her out and said, "I'm at Ramsey. Meet me in the cafeteria. I can only give you a prescription in person."

Jenene finagled it so she could get away and zipped on down to St. Paul.

A few minutes of reacquainting were in order before getting down to business. Dr. Gaither told her about leaving practice to teach the next generation. She told him about the grind of farm life and her hopes to soon ride her new horse, Sweetie.

"I thought we were friends," Dr. Gaither said when conversation turned to her current woes. "Why didn't you call me about your pain?"

"I didn't think it had anything to do with orthopedics."

"In this case I'm afraid it does. When you've healed a little and feel up to it in a week or two you need to come in for tests and you'll know for sure, but due to where you say the pain is I'm afraid you have degenerative disc disease."

"You mean, like, my spine is breaking down?"

"Possibly the intervertebral discs. I hate to tell you this but it would be inadvisable to ride horse until you know. And if you do have degenerative disc disease, you'll never be able to ride again without risk of paralysis."

Testing proved Dr. Gaither's worst supposition: her suffering was due to degenerative disc disease.

"I'm not going to sit here and try and give you hope," her orthopedist told her. "Two discs are already gone and another is going fast. At this rate, you'll be in a wheelchair within five years."

The discs in the spinal column are like irreplaceable brake pads; when they wear down, they cannot be repaired nor grown back. Somehow the pain in her back was so intense she had mistaken it for being in her stomach cavity.

"Five years?" she said disbelievingly. "How do you know that for sure?"

"It's just the reality," he said matter-of-factly. "I'm putting you on limitations. No more carrying over five pounds—"

"There's so much I have to do," she said. "Hay needs to be put in the barn. Wood needs to be hauled."

"A fall, even a minor car collision, and you could be made a paraplegic. Even lifting weight will accelerate the degeneration."

Leaving the clinic, she had trouble assimilating all this new crushingly demoralizing news. One of those "oh, cruel fate, why have you forsaken me yet again" moments, Jenene's thoughts were dismal.

The master of the well-timed, marriage-saving gesture, Russ had stepped up, taken initiative, and earned Sweetie—and now she would never be able to ride her. Was she cursed? And what about the simple tasks so easy to take for granted? Laundry. Grocery shopping. Even hauling the slop bucket to the dumping ground would be beyond her limitations.

Limitations? What a joke. As if she had a choice. Chores needed doing. Life needed living. Unless she was banished from reality into a fantasyland, making do would be her goal. That would include breaking her limitations on a daily basis not because she wanted to snub her nose at her condition but because she had no choice.

Horse riding was not the only activity from which she was banned. Parasailing, bungee jumping, skydiving, ATV riding, and water skiing were out of the question. Jumping off the high dive at the public pool? No way. Not that she was involved actively in any of these activities. The point is that she couldn't do those things for fear her spine would fail. The disease proved, besides being horribly painful, very limiting in this way.

The pain had cost her sleep and it was going to be years before her quality of rest improved.

Even the finest clocks can be broken permanently by a single action.

January 17, 1994, Jenene received devastating news while watching the six o'clock news. Dr. Gaither was murdered. Murder-suicide. His estranged wife took his life before turning the gun on herself. Hearing such a fine man's epic work and extraordinary life abbreviated to a couple of sound bytes was tragic.

Their children would hold separate funerals at the same time and chose to attend their father's.

Some people seem to possess a greater spirit. Even if they are humble and modest and kind, their personality is so dwarfing all around them are subsumed by their force. They shine bright and to the misfortune of all can burnout much too early. Dr. Gaither was such a man.

In 2008 Jenene would encounter an orthopedic surgeon named Dr. Comfort who happened to be a student of Dr. Gaither's.

"I've read about your case extensively," Dr. Comfort said upon their introduction. He appraised her curiously. "It doesn't look like you're wearing a brace. I don't see a cane. Am I to take it you don't…use either?"

"Those things aren't necessary," she replied, not yet grasping why the curiosity. "My knee will go out sometimes but I don't let it slow me down. I try to walk every day."

"Really. How far do you typically walk?"

"At least a few miles a day. Sometimes less. If it's pouring rain or there's a snow storm."

An expression of awe made his face shine. "Dr. Gaither would be so proud," he concluded. "His conclusions painted a much drearier picture."

"I know he did the best he could," she said. "Because of him I can walk."

"I don't know if he would think so." That was when Dr. Comfort explained how thoroughly damaged her knee had been; many other structural elements were removed besides the kneecap. So many it was remarkable she could walk without aid. "It was because he failed to repair your knee that Dr. Gaither retired from practice to teach. He wanted to inspire the next generation so maybe others could succeed where he failed."

Because he was unable to repair her knee to an extent he deemed successful Dr. Gaither retired from practice? To Jenene he had done so much for her it was absurd he would feel like a failure in any regard to her. How we measure our failures and successes can be skewed.

Dr. Gaither may not have been able to do all the mechanic work he thought necessary; but he provided so much more by uplifting her spirit, bestowing upon her hope, and offering unadulterated friendship. Was he a success? No doubt.

Chapter 60
Stone Power and Spiritual Protection

It was a warm day in September, a good day for a walk.

Jenene was afraid there would be fallout from the "devil worshiper" incident. Whether they wielded dark magic or not, such people could have too easily made trouble for us. But if it were dark magic they might brandish, no lock would bar them from penetrating our sanctum. So other measures had to be employed to give Jenene peace of mind. Sometimes being proactive is the only way to regain a sense of safety. Even if some would consider the action taken as purely symbolic.

Today she and Russ were walking to the four corners of the farm. They were carrying out a spell of protection.

All this began with a new alliance from which she gained encouragement when she needed support most....

Making the adage it's not what you know but who you know true, people who come into our lives can inextricably act as springboards to greater knowledge and understanding. When we need something new to get us out of a rut or funk, we can be blessed with just such a person to guide us to an alternate path we may not have found on our own.

For Jenene that person would be a lovely and folksy young home healthcare aid named Christel. Dressed in earthy shades, bright eyed, and full of smiles, she brought cheerfulness to our house at a time when we were short on gaiety. With a perchance for natural methods of healing and clay sculpture (she made the cutest yet humorous fishes), she was a fount of wisdom and whimsy.

She also understood the strain Jenene and Russ were under and quickly showed her value not only as a hired helper but as a human being by proving utterly reliable and willing to go the extra mile in her care for Lal, Bill, and Herb. What began as professional courtesy quickly evolved into friendship. They found they were of a mind on so much it was only natural they be chummy. Christel was also intuitive.

Besides the all-but-debilitating back pain, Jenene suffered from many of the Crohn's symptoms she had yet to address with a doctor. In tune enough to see Jenene's distress no matter how hard she fought to conceal it, Christel pried out what to Jenene felt like a confession, and listened with a mind keen to finding solutions without being pushy.

Jenene divulged everything. Opening up to a new viewpoint was liberating.

Christel's reaction cemented their friendship. She was consoling yet brimming with positivity. Unlike others she offered sympathy without pity. Jenene so despised pity. She was sick, not pitiful, and whenever she got dewy eyes filled with pity she was sickened. Pity should be reserved for the hopeless. The hopeful have no need to be undermined.

When her new friend asked her what else she was doing to control her health she had no answer. Doing? Besides going to the doctor? What else was there? As it turned out, there was a whole world of alternatives, and not all of it snake oil, as is often assumed of natural remedies. Every long journey launched with a single step, Christel began by turning her on to the valuable energy in stones.

Jenene's growing respect for Christel lent to her trusting her opinion and she found relief by following her suggestions. Soon she would make other recommendations that improved her life inestimably.

Rather than choose a masseuse at random when her insurer offered massage as part of therapy, she went with Christel's recommendation. That was how she met Lacy. More than a massage therapist, Lacy also believed in the power of stones and other natural healing. The first stone Jenene obtained for purposes of healing, a small polished dark blue sodalite, she acquired from Lacy.

The pixie-like masseuse worked out of a stone-filled room in her small house. Her fingers and hands could work magic and it made the trip well worth the time and miles. She would lie out ranks of stones delicately on Jenene's body and the combined therapeutic effect made the pain bearable without doping her up. It may not have erased the pain but there are times you have to settle for tolerability.

Drawn to stones even as a child, maybe Jenene was predisposed to being open to the women's conviction stones could help her. Everything they imparted was readily absorbed. Soon she had adopted stones as a way to relieve her pain and discomfort. It worked better than the mind-dulling drugs. It showed her the power of natural energy.

Soon, under Christel's advisement, she began to carry a selection of specific stones religiously, a spotted snowflake-obsidian, a purple amethyst, and a clear quartz crystal among a half dozen others. In years to come she has built an immense stone collection.

Doctors had shown her she needed to hedge her bets and find other strategies to hang onto her life. In so doing she would evolve into a new infinitely stronger person. It began with Christel opening her up to the wider world of natural healing and white magic, including Tarot. Jenene's first deck of Tarot cards was a gift from her enlightened friend.

Tarot has often been associated with the darker side of the mystical, linked to gypsies and charlatans and frauds. What most people who dabble in Tarot by getting readings do not understand is that a proper reading in no way involves true divination. Flying in the face of assumption, Jenene learned quickly the cards in no way read the future. Instead, they are a way to gain inner knowledge and wisdom. The reader only interprets the cards; the subconscious mind of the one being read stacks the deck.

Next Christel took her to a solitary building in St. Paul a block or so south off the Wabasha Street Bridge and the Mississippi where she would find salvation.

Like an oyster shell, the plain brick building in no way hinted at the treasure contained within. When it came to pearls of knowledge it seemed more like the goose who could keep laying golden eggs than a single-pearled oyster, though, because she would find so much wisdom there it would change—save—her life.

What was this most amazing locale?

The Llewellyn bookstore had tomes dealing with everything from Tarot to Paganism, the afterlife to alternative healing. The publisher's bookstore, gone now, offered a welcome change of pace from the Western medicine gulag in which she'd been trapped. Jenene glommed on to the alternative medicine section. She was beginning to think that if there's a physical side to everything, maybe there's a spiritual side to everything too. What she found reinforced there was more she needed to do than sign surgery consent forms.

There were so many books she wanted to buy. She could afford very few. She made her choices carefully. She would go back again and again. A period of renaissance and resurgence, Jenene learned all she could. Her knowledge was really only in its nascence; in the years ahead she would discover so much more.

Which leads to that nice September day.

Because of the "devil worshippers" incident, Jenene researched with the intent of discovering a way to prevent any dark magic from further hindering our lives.

In a spell book she found a method of protection that involved burying a quartz crystal at each of the four corners of the property. The tip of each crystal had to point inward. Beyond that requisite, intent was the most important aspect of what they were doing; there was no incantation to say or symbol to draw in the dirt, just the conviction to believe in the protection.

Even if it were only an act of personal reassurance, from the day she and Russ walked and walked some more to bury those crystals onward, the place did *feel* safer. Although we still had the occasional trespasser who would try our patience and even intimidate us, so far as we know, no one ever performed any black magic rituals on the farm again. In the years ahead the spot where the "devil worshippers" were up to their shenanigans would return to nature.

This signaled another footstep in Jenene's progression into the realm of natural healing—and the beginning of her awareness of the need for spiritual protection.

As we would soon find out, practical protection was still necessary too.

Chapter 61
Our Nightly Near-Death Experience

I cannot reiterate enough how much morning always seemed to come too soon.

"Come on, it's time to get up," my mom coaxed.

Rising out of sleep was like climbing a cliff wearing a backpack full of weights. Luckily falling back into sleep is no worse than falling off a climbing wall wearing a harness. Good thing. Down I went.

"Come on, it's been ten minutes, get up!"

It was always hard to wake up in the morning, torturous toil, and we would learn why. We had the furnace inspected our second winter on the farm. As it turned out, there was a crack all the way around…which had lent to us being asphyxiated slowly but surely. The oxygen deprivation left us all exhausted, which was why it was so darned difficult rising in the morning. The housing inspector said it was lucky we survived and condemned the house pending the installation of a new furnace.

Discovering the furnace was killing us led to a smidgen of good fortune.

Previously, a wheelchair-bound friend, knowledgeable of the system, suggested to Jenene that she seek state assistance to pay for home care workers. This would allow her and Russ to earn a living while ensuring The Seniors were taken care of while they were working. Since they were in desperate need of money, it was the only option. Bill and Lal had a small social security income while Herb had never bothered to apply. This lack of funds resulted in the three being malnourished when we moved in, a state Jenene rectified immediately and fought valiantly to avoid and always succeeded.

The family was assigned a social worker who saw to it so many hours a day of assistance were paid. When we learned the furnace was out of commission, we were in no financial condition to replace it or update the house to gas heating. The social worker came through for us in a huge way and helped us receive the Alternate Care Grant, given for sake of improving living conditions in run-down or antiquated homes. This meant we were able to update the house to gas, get a brand new furnace, plant new insulation, and winter proof and direct heat to the porch.

Bill was resistant to taking aid. He saw it as charity and Bill was far more comfortable giving than receiving. Jenene told him, "This could really help us." Never one to stand in another's way, he knuckled under begrudgingly, recognizing she was right even if he did not want or accept it.

When the new furnace came, it won him over the first time it began blowing heat into the house. "He was tickled," Jenene told me. "The furnace kicked on and he practically did a jig. After all those years of collecting, cutting, and stacking wood, it was the height of functionality and luxury."

"It turned on and I didn't have to do anything," he declared. "Not even kick it." He was truly elated.

Two weeks later, he was dead.

Life can be cruel.

A week before the accident that would take his life Jenene had another funeral dream, this one with a closed casket. She was so sick she mistook the message. She was convinced she was the one in the box.

Chapter 62
Bill's Death

October 20, 1989.

Isn't it strange how days that irrevocably change our lives can start off so prosaically? Just another day like any other?

In those days I was always up with the sun. This aided me in going with Bill and Herb on their errands or watching the Saturday morning cartoons. That Saturday I was forbidden to go to Newport with my uncles because my room was a mess. So I was watching cartoons on my bedroom TV, procrastinating cleaning up.

There was commotion outside my bedroom door. I went to see what was the matter.

My mom rushed by first one way and then the other. I caught her on the way back. I could tell by her frown there was something wrong.

"Bill and Herb were in an accident," she said shortly. "We need to go to the hospital. If you want to come, get ready. We're leaving right away."

My heart sank. "Are they hurt?"

"I don't know. They wouldn't tell me anything."

There was good reason for her agitation. My folks had already been up early to get their morning chores done. On Saturdays, they had a little time between breakfast and lunch to get in a catnap. In their clothes, they'd lie down on top of the blankets and catch a couple precious moments of sleep.

That morning when they laid down, Jenene heard Bill pull the car out of the garage. She looked out the window to see if I was with them since I was forbidden from going. Had I cleaned my room, I would have likely been with them, in the backseat on the driver's side because the other backseat was removed.

It seemed no sooner than she fell asleep the phone rang.

"Is Lila there?"

"There's no Lila here," she said.

She hung up and began to drift off, only for the phone to ring again.

"Is Lila there?"

"There is no Lila here. Why do you keep calling?" She was getting frustrated because this woman was robbing her of sleep.

"We have a gentleman here. He says this is the number. There's been an accident."

"There's a Luella here."

This was another instance of Jenene coming instantly to full wakefulness. She sat bolt upright and began shaking Russ as she plied the woman for information. She told her Bill and Herb had been in an accident on Highway 61 but would say no more. That's ridiculous, she thought, Bill only drives on back roads. The woman told her she needed to go to Ramsey Hospital in St. Paul immediately. Stunned, she hung up and was able to shake Russ awake finally.

They had only been laying down a few minutes, but he said, "I had a dream. About Bill."

Right away Jenene snapped, "Shut up," because she just knew, and the realization crashed down around her like a cave in. If he had dreamed about Bill, Bill was dead. All the way to the hospital he would pester her to let him tell his dream. She didn't want to hear it. But he has always had a way of pestering until she gave in. In the dream he and Bill had met face to face…and Bill bestowed upon him the gift of patience.

It hurt her that if Bill would visit either of them, it should be her, but I pointed out, "Bill knew you were strong enough to live up to your responsibility; he wasn't so sure about Russ."

The ride to the hospital was frenetic and fast.

We used the St. Paul Park onramp to enter Highway 61. As we approached New Port, we could see vestiges of the accident at the first intersection crossing 61, the very one Bill warned Jenene about so many times. Workers were tending to a large utility box beside the center stoplight. A cop was directing traffic because the light was out of commission.

"Maybe the accident happened because the lights were out," Jenene speculated, not realizing Bill's station wagon was bulldozed into the utility box, resulting in the lights being out.

Even though not so long ago the asthma often brought me to the ER, as we were rushing in it was like going into a funhouse. The noise. The lights. It all added up to insanity. Never before had it been such an inhospitable place.

I'm sure because I was a child I felt that much more powerless and at the whim of a cruel and arbitrary world. I can remember with perfect clarity that we were led to a small room where Russ and I waited while they pulled Jenene aside. We had gone past a room with Herb laid out on a gurney, lips bloody, and I was in a state of shock and terror. His eyes looked glazed and absent. The sight of this man I cared about so much looking so frail and vulnerable broke my heart. I felt very scared and very minuscule.

We had also seen a woman who was also in the accident, just a flash. We did not know her name then. Did not know the part she played in the accident. The extent.

Did not know she was a killer....

My mom returned a moment later with the worst news I could imagine. "Bill is dead," she said resignedly.

Time might as well have stopped that day, or so I thought at the time, a little boy facing a stiffer introduction to death than I had theretofore faced. Cognac was a horse I loved. But this was Bill. Bill. The face of God: the bearer of all wisdom, the oracle. When we're kids, maybe we labor under the fantasy certain people just can't die. If he could be taken...anyone or anything could be lost, snatched away in one crummy instant when everything changes.

That was the first time I realized that in the span of a minute, a few seconds, maybe even a split second, the final turn of a life can be decided.

The force of the collision caused Bill's aorta to burst. Such a catastrophic injury to the main artery carrying blood from the heart left him with no chance. Sure there are arterial grafts, but Bill was old and he would have needed an immediate transfusion of blood, a lot of blood. It just wasn't to be.

As my young mind worked to philosophize away my desire to sink out of existence, Jenene was trying to organize her thoughts and found her mind too cluttered. She had to make calls. Let people know. Oh, goodness, Lal had to be told! There would need to be a funeral. Where? There would have to be planning. How would they afford it? Was there a will? Her mom had to be called. Jeff. So many others had to be contacted, too. So many calls had to be made.

Standing at a start point, Jenene was daunted before taking one forward step.

In the first days after she would find ways to mitigate being overwhelmed, such as putting reminder Post-its all over the kitchen cabinet doors so no call would go unmade or task unfinished; but right then all she knew was grief and remorse and worry because not only had she lost one of the most important people in her life—she had been put in the position of having to call the shots when it came to final arrangements and the whole razzle-dazzle that follows a passing.

Lack of understanding gave her a sense of emptiness. It felt as if a giant scoop had hollowed her. Amid the clutter one question stood out. Why did this happen? He always warned her about that dangerous intersection…only in the end it got him. Why Bill? Why did he have to die that way? Why?

Later we would learn Bill died within an hour of the accident, before Jenene had even been woken by the initial confusing phone call. The paramedics said that he knew, that in his awareness he accepted his fate, and he died reconciled and at peace. He was at peace? Was there solace to be taken in that? Really?

Maybe. But it wasn't fair he had to die like that. The notion that "fair" is just a word in the dictionary was never more applicable. It was not fair and to the majority of the world it mattered not at all. The sun would still rise. Commerce would continue unabated. No matter how much it felt like a sign of the apocalypse to Jenene and I, in other words life would go on even if Bill were no longer in it.…

Our only comfort came from the fact that Herb was expected to survive.

We would learn Bill's head was driven into his chest with such force his ribs were broken. Grotesquely, the paramedics were forced to use Bill's ears as handles to pry loose his dome from the cradle made of Herb's ribcage. In the urgent aftermath of the accident what was straight away apparent was Herb had broken ribs and suffered a heart attack.

Worse damage—a collapsed lung—would be overlooked until later. Whether the miss could be blamed on justifiable distraction or negligence would hinge on how it was responded to when brought to the medical staff's attention.

After learning Bill was dead we exited in a strengthless daze. On the way out we heard a nurse exclaim that all Herb's teeth had been knocked out. Since he only had three left to begin with we were quite worried for him. It turned out only one tooth was lost in the accident. There was so much blood the nurse was mistaken as to the degree of the injury.

The door we left through was beside a helipad. There was a red helicopter. It was limned in glowing white haziness, as was every object in my purview. The whole world had taken on the dimension of a dream. It was all so surrealistic. The urge to cry was irresistible yet shock allowed me to hold my composure. Maybe it was that I was walking through an illusion. It had to be. It had to be nothing more than a nightmare. Any instant I would wake up and none of it would have ever happened.

For months I would wonder when the nightmare would end.

Wonder when I was going to wake up.…

I never did.

About that time on Grey Cloud Island, Bill's lady friend Betty was setting out a plate of cookies in anticipation of Bill's weekly visit. After tending to her horses on a cold autumn morning a hot cup of coffee joined by good company sounded perfect.

She would have her coffee alone.

She waited as minutes of tardiness turned into an hour. It would not be until after the lunch hour she began to worry. Bill was never late. Not without a call. He was a considerate man. Even before news reached her, it was easy to deduce there was something wrong—really wrong.

Chapter 63
Down But Not Out

We paid the old boy a visit after Herb had been admitted and placed in a room.

Not much for company, he was lethargic, listless, and disengaged. We attributed his disinterest to all he had endured. We understood if he had no desire to talk. He lost his brother and was dealt a world of injury simultaneously. In such a long life it was maybe the worst day he ever lived.

Jenene began to worry when she returned a second time and Herb still had none of the vim and vigor that defined him.

For one dire reason or other she needed him to sign a form, at least mark it with an X, and he was unable to do even that.

Flinty eyes wishy-washy, watery, he winked in and out of consciousness, not able to stay awake, listen, or respond. Jenene knew such enervation was not typical of her ornery old great uncle. After recuperating from his broken ankle, and with his vision quality restored, Herb was full of boundless energy and vigor for life. Without so much as breaking a sweat the old boy could still swear up a storm in a way that would leave a younger man spent.

A woman who would prove appearances are not always misleading, Jenene tracked down a shrewish nurse with a witch's nose and beady little eyes.

"There's something wrong with him," she said. "You need to check him out."

"Well, he's an old man," the nurse replied blithely.

Boom. Negligence.

"You don't understand," Jenene pleaded. "This isn't how he is."

"I think you need to leave the diagnosis—"

"Do I need to go over your head? I know my uncle and there is something wrong with him! Do I need to take him to a different hospital?"

A good thing for Herb, and the uptight neglectful nurse, Jenene got her way. The problem was soon discovered. Herb perked up literally within instants of being equipped with an oxygen mask.

Within a couple minutes he was his old self.

Listlessness and lethargy were clues he was taking in too little oxygen. The collapsed lung had been missed because the evidence was ignored. I hope honestly and not out of a faulty assumption old people are lifeless slugs.

While recuperating in the hospital, Herb refused the hospital food. To make certain he ate Jenene brought him at least two meals a day. His aversion seemed to have less to do with the quality of the food than his disapproval of the staff.

On another front, Herb's bibs and coat reflected the horror of the accident and were completely ensanguined. Seeing the bloody ware, Jenene wanted to throw them out. Herb felt differently. When it came to his bibs, well, Herb had a stance similar to the late great Charlton Heston's stance on guns. In that particular case, they were his favorite pair and parting with them just was not going to happen lest we accept inciting his loud and boisterous fury. He adamantly demanded they be cleaned and returned to him in the hospital.

Jenene was put in a bind.

After losing so much, damn it, she just couldn't deny him.

After repeated washes, one small stain, perhaps imbedded grease from before (they were a hardworking farmer's bibs), remained, so Jenene felt they were good enough to pass his muster and in that she was correct. The shrewish nurse was the one who deemed the bibs unacceptable.

She claimed we were unfit for bringing such ratty, dirty clothes to Herb per his request, not understanding we would gladly have thrown them out had Herb not been so insistent. She also took exception to the fact that my folks brought him no underwear, as he would not wear them (for Herb it was commando or nothing), and did bring him a brand-new pair of shoes that had been altered with cuts to fit his feet, a state of affairs she apparently found deplorable even though alterations were necessary to tailor shoes to his oddly-shaped feet.

The thing about Herb, he got what he wanted. The man made obstinate adamancy a profound part of his character. Still, the nurse saw to it that we were investigated by the state. Funny how people have a certain idea of things and those beliefs will cause them to go against the notion people are free to choose to not wear underwear or alter their shoes.

Herb was the sort of man who would laugh at the notion of political or any other kind of correctness others might want to impose; no censure held his tongue, no conventionality informed the way he chose to dress, and no one else made his decisions.

The investigation led nowhere because Jenene and Russ were good caregivers and Herb was too sharp to say anything that could be construed negatively.

Herb, too gruff, stubborn, sturdy, and plain bad-tempered even in his mid-eighties to give ground without battle, recuperated from the broken ribs, the collapsed lung, and the heart attack. He came home. There were ups and downs along the way; the road home was a long, bumpy, and trying one but the old boy persevered nevertheless.

When Herb finally made it home I became his preferred caregiver. He still held a deep distaste for Russ and would not have felt comfortable being aided by Jenene. I was enlisted to bring him his meals and help him out of his bib overalls before bed. We got very close, me this fresh-faced little boy, him this wrinkly-faced old man.

I remember that first Christmas after the accident, Herb wouldn't take a shave nor, due to health concerns, could we take him to his barber. Thick and bristly, his beard grew out. Not fat enough to be Santa, he looked like Old Man Winter with his puffy gray whiskers. The first holiday season after losing Bill was mournful, but we were joyful we still had Herb…no matter how cantankerous, dare I say Grinch-like, he had a knack for being.

Chapter 64
Mourning

For as much as he meant to me, Bill meant that much more to Jenene. Suddenly she was forced to be the matriarch of a fractured family. In the first days after, she operated in a state of total shock. All the same questions kept swirling through her head. Why did it have to happen? Why now? It was so unfair, so baffling, a twist in a particularly hard to stomach episode of the *Twilight Zone* it was so outside what she wanted to recognize as reality.

That was the thing of it, though; it was reality. Inescapable reality. Jenene had to face her feelings, hit upon acceptance, and move on.

We even went to the place where they transported Bill's car.

The wreckage of the station wagon was a crushed and twisted mess. Seeing it hurt deeply. Not only because it had been involved in an accident that snatched away Bill. The deep down pain came from all the good memories I had in that car…all the Saturdays I rode along with my never boring uncles. Having those images in my mind juxtaposed against the sight of the wreck showcased how much life can change in a matter of seconds.

The hardest one to break the news to was Lal. It broke her. Lal's fragile mind fell to pieces. The senility she suffered as she aged went into hyper drive. Almost overnight she became heartbreakingly enfeebled.

We all took Bill's death like a hard punch in the gut. But there is no doubt Lal took it the worst. She was the least able to cope.

Bill was her best friend of decades, her companion, her confidant, and doubtless the only man in the world she felt she could trust entirely.

Jenene decided it would be good for Lal to see Herb. She and Russ transported her to the city. Frailty of mind distanced her from reality, erasing the loss for the time being, and she was in sociable spirits. In the hospital she lit up and became a goodwill ambassador, visiting cheerfully with strangers. It took several minutes to navigate her to Herb's room.

She had kind words for everyone.

The reunion went unexpectedly.

Shattered by Bill's death, dementia enabled her to shut it out. Once Lal saw Herb it all flooded back.

Spitefulness toward her grumbly older brother emerged like a snake from a hole. As soon as she saw him her mood soured and her fangs came out. She went straight to him and slapped his face with her small arthritic hand and hissed, "Why did my favorite brother have to die and not you?"

Bill was the brother she loved, Herb was the brother she detested; the accident did not change that.

Russ guided her out of the room. Removing Herb from her sight restored her good-natured mood.

That day in the hospital was the only time she acknowledged Bill's death without the devastating news being new to her. Thereon her mind could never grasp that he was gone. She would ask, "Where's my Billy?" At first Jenene made the mistake of telling her about the accident. She would begin to wail as if she were never before told. To her it was the first time.

Powerless to deceive, Jenene still had to find a way to obfuscate the truth. Bill had taken many trips to Montana in his younger years. So Montana became an analogy for the afterlife. When Lal would ask, Jenene would tell her he was on a trip to Montana. She would be placated without replaying her intense sorrow.

Lal's rapidly declining health showed how cataclysmic losing Bill was for her through thinness and wrinkles. In the weeks and months that followed, the years stacked up on her and her memory began to slip drastically. We worried about her wandering off. I would often go with her on the walks she so enjoyed. The fear was that she would go somewhere and suffer amnesia, forgetting where she had come from or even whom she was, leaving her vulnerable and at the mercy of whoever might be around.

It's easy to understand why she would flee into senility to evade the truth. Alzheimer's was an escape from the painful truth she couldn't face.

Watching our favorite aunt's crushing decline would strangely make Bill's quick death seem merciful. Of course that bit of wisdom would only be revealed in hindsight.

Chapter 65
Saying Goodbye

The official mourning began with three scheduled visitations. Because one bled over into another despite scheduled interims, it became one long session, hours of uninterrupted mourning.

Bill's choice of cremation was a blessing to me. To see him motionless in a coffin would have been too much to bear. The thought of his ashes in the ornate wooden box on the table at the head of the room was far less troubling.

In his place was an absolutely beautiful charcoal drawing. Diana was the artist and it was one of her masterpieces. It was such an eerily perfect rendition it seemed to embody Bill's soul.

She referenced a photo taken when Bill was in his mid-fifties. He was sitting on the tractor, looking back over his shoulder. Remarkably, the face it showed was the one he carried until the day he died. If like the picture of Dorian Gray some magic made it so Diana's truly incredible drawing aged for him, its faultlessness as it sat on the easel that day reflected his unblemished soul.

We would learn later our presumption of Bill's untarnished karma was misguided.

The day of the funeral was the gloomiest of sad days yet the sun shone brightly in a crisp blue sky.

A universal tribute and a record that stands to this day, even before we set out for Bill's funeral early that October day the temperature had climbed to an unseasonable and balmy eighty-one degrees, the age Bill was at the time of his death.

We had just breached the St. Paul Park residential area when Jenene was the first to see a squirrel flit out into the road and stop dead in our path.

Jenene said, "I think that squirrel"—she squinted through the sunshine—"is totally white."

"It is," I confirmed from the backseat as we drew near.

Displaying an odd and trenchant obsequiousness, the white squirrel planted his sleek ivory body and would not budge.

The tiny beast refused to make a move even as we closed the distance.

Jenene had no choice other than to brake to a stop. The white squirrel met her eyes with nothing short of knowingness. The message was obvious: even though Bill was no longer of the mortal coil, he was still with us and in some way always would be.

At Jenene's acknowledgement of this simple fact, the white squirrel vanished into the woods and allowed us to pass.

If the value of life is measured by the number and variety of people who come to your funeral, Bill was worth more than a fist-sized diamond, his weight in gold, and a lifetime supply of Hershey's chocolate put together.

Hundreds of people came, all races and creeds and denominations, men and women, most of them strangers to us, many not, people Bill had touched, people who had been impacted by his presence in their lives, people who mourned as much as we did even though he was not part of their daily lives. The outpouring didn't end after the wake or even the funeral. Bill was so impactful we received letters for weeks from those who were unable to make an appearance. Those were some of the most heartfelt letters imaginable, filled with stories of Bill's wisdom and chivalry and kindness.

Even the minister choked as she spoke of the great man Bill had been. I have been to funerals where not everyone is reduced to tears. That could not be said of Bill's funeral. There was so much crying that day we could have filled a quarry with a lake of tears.

Bill meant so much to so many people. He with the clean-shaven head and the gentle, kindly, deep-set eyes always seemed to know how to make a friend even when he could have made an enemy. For a life so honorable, his death was anticlimactic, but the mourning that followed was epic. We never knew just how much of an impacter Bill was until he was gone.

It is in the distinctions defining our loved ones we find the memories that help us mourn our beloved while clinging to who they were and what they imparted to us. In that we are enabled to be happy for the noble, unique, intriguing life they lived and person they were rather than be sad for their departure. Bill left enough memories to smile every time I think of him, even if my eyes mist too.

With the suggestion they remain unseen the funeral director returned the clothes Bill was wearing the day of the accident. We decided to burn them in the pump house stove along with letters that served as our last messages to Bill, our goodbyes.

In spite of the warning, Jenene opened the bag. She was prepared for any horror. Herb's bibs had looked like wardrobe left over from a horror flick.

Bill's clothes were miraculously perfectly clean.

Burning Bill's clothes and those letters was a step toward catharsis, but we were all far from recuperating. In the wake of Bill's death there was still a vehicular homicide trial to endure.

The unquestionable cause of the accident was a woman named Roxanne Holmes. Coming down from a three-day cocaine binge, the party girl fell asleep behind the wheel, ran a red light, and T-boned Bill's station wagon while he and Herb were crossing the very intersection Bill had warned Jenene about so many times.

A resident of St. Paul Park, Ms. Holmes was practically a neighbor.

In many ways merely procedural since her guilt was not in dispute, during the trial Ms. Holmes would still test boundaries. At times she was able to make a farce of the proceedings. Her flippancy and remorselessness would gall Jenene incessantly and inspire her to come the closest to hate she would ever journey in her life.

Chapter 66
The Trial

Stillwater, the Washington County tenth district courthouse.

I had to concede the courtroom was far duller than I had assumed, having seen many on TV. Once I was seated in the gallery, there was no denying the facts. My disenchantment had begun outside when I saw the building. Showing no architectural artistry whatsoever, not even a hint of the baroque or neoclassical, the building looked like a hospital. Without a single column or arched window or dome to be seen, I was disappointed thoroughly even before I saw what amounted to a huge disappointment because it did not match the conception of a courthouse in my head.

With the pew-style benches and the judge's bench hardly raised more than a teacher's desk, the courtroom was a cross between a church and a classroom. There was no stained hardwood. There was no statue of blind justice. The judge didn't even have a classy wooden gavel.

Jenene went to every court date. Even though Roxanne Holmes skipped out whenever she could get away with it. There had been a hard-as-nails woman judge in the beginning, one who took none of her malarkey. For undisclosed reasons, she was taken off the case and replaced by a man who evidently developed a crush on Roxanne because she was henceforth treated with kid gloves. Pregnant with her fifth or sixth illegitimate child, she would call in with morning sickness and the judge would let her off the hook as if she wasn't on trial for two counts of vehicular homicide.

When Roxanne was in court, she wavered between smug and indifferent. When I saw her, the first time since I caught a glimpse of her in the hospital, the impression I got was that she believed she was far more glamorous than she was, better looking, classier, basically above all the trouble her poor decision-making landed her in. She had that manner, the air of someone who felt they were above criticism.

And that day Roxanne would show how little respect she had for the court, for Bill, and for us when she went so far as to say, "He was just an old man." The judge had taken away her license and she was unhappy she should lose the right to drive simply because her actions led to the death of some anonymous old guy who, in her mind, was on borrowed time anyway.

To hear Bill's life trivialized so carelessly, as it was taken so carelessly, ignited a combustible pot of rage in all of us, but to Jenene it was a breaking point. A powder keg waiting for a spark to explode, Roxanne supplied the incendiary that made Jenene blow. Shocking the judge, the court reporter, the court clerk, the others in the gallery, and especially the bailiffs, who were put on edge immediately, she rose and galvanized everyone with the shrapnel of her words.

"Bill was more than an old man, you murdering bitch!" she uncorked. "He meant more than you could ever know! He was everyone's friend! He was—"

Jenene had to be removed—wrestled—from the courtroom, her flare-up ringing through the chamber.

Later, when all the black powder had burned off, she wouldn't regret her outburst. She wouldn't apologize for her feelings. She wouldn't apologize for being so insensitively provoked. The judge was apparently sympathetic: Jenene was forgiven and not held in contempt.

Through it all Roxanne had a dumb look on her face, as if she could not understand why Jenene would freak out. It wouldn't be until an odd coincidence—synchronicity in action—gave Roxanne a whole new perspective that she would understand just what she had done.

During this period early morning Tarot readings started the day.

To Jenene the practice was no more than a way of accessing inner knowledge. She made a habit of reading her own cards every morning, rising at a quarter to six so she had time before implementing her routine. She needed answers. This practice was giving her a great deal of experience and she felt confident her readings were getting ever more accurate.

The cards were certainly showing her, without exception, her foibles and faults.

One morning the message hit her hard. The cards gave her a view into what she was becoming and it frightened her, embarrassed her, and made her determined to not allow it to happen.

The Queen of Swords had come up and from its placement the message was clear. Others viewed her as a spiteful woman full of wrath and fury and rage—if she didn't put a stop to it, the assessment would become her. The insight was hard to swallow but she could not deny it was true. It was how she felt. In time she may have learned to conceal it, to hide those true feelings, but that would have only created lessons.

The only thing she could do was find forgiveness. That insight would elude her for some time, though, as it was not within her to forgive Roxanne Holmes at that point. The wounds were too fresh. Too infected.

Since the cards didn't predict the future, there was no way they could show her the next stunning development to come.

Another day. Ongoing. Survival was the name of the game. Keep the bills paid, keep food in the cupboards, make sure Lal and Herb were comfortable, ignore the symptoms of an illness she was beginning to suspect was much worse than she wanted to believe.

The crackle of rubber rolling over gravel that always signaled a visitor sent Jenene to the kitchen window to see whom it was before going to the door. To her surprise, the face behind the wheel belonged to her nemesis.

Roxanne Holmes had driven up our driveway.

Came right on up as if she belonged there.

It was crazy.

Jenene had to blink her eyes, make sure they were clear…make sure she was seeing correctly, not mistaking someone else for the woman she despised, hallucinating due to the intensity of her hatred.

It was Bill's killer, all right.

Jenene had to take a breath. Calm down before she did something irrational. Part of her was thinking there was a lot of land around, plenty to hide a body. She was not a violent person. Vengeance was not for her to inflict. The justice system was dealing with Roxanne.

So furious she was shaking, Jenene dialed 911. She demanded the police come and get Roxanne off the property immediately. "She killed my uncle," she snapped. "I know her license is suspended. If you don't get her out of here, I don't know what I'll do, but I can tell you I have a Winchester .44-40 I'm pretty sure will take her head clean off."

"Ma'am, don't make threats."

"This is no threat! Get her out of here!"

I am so thankful the police were expedient and took care of removing Roxanne. Irrational from grief and stress, my mom may have killed her that day.

Amidst chaos there can still be poetic justice.

The following court date, Jenene stood and requested a restraining order.

Roxanne was genuinely puzzled. The police carded her away without explaining how they came to know where to find her or at whose residence she had been pinched. So her confusion was understandably legitimate.

"I don't get it," she said when able to defend herself. There was no mistaking her bafflement. "I don't even know where she lives. I was going to see my friend Billy."

All at once Jenene understood. The barn right there on the corner, many people stopped to see the horses. Drawn like moths drawn to a lantern. One of them was Roxanne. Like so many, Bill had befriended her. Of all the people Bill impacted, one was the very woman who cost him his life.

With far more ammunition than she had the last time, Jenene confronted Roxanne with words that would crush her. She looked her straight in the eye and exclaimed, "You killed Billy!"

Roxanne visibly paled as the blood and moxie ran out of her face. The nameless, faceless old man she was responsible for killing was suddenly a real person. Someone she had spoken to, who had amused her with a fact, who had made her laugh with an anecdote, who shared moments with her she had taken pleasure in and maybe even cherished. Was he just an old man? Not to her. Not anymore.

The rest of the trial Roxanne was humble, quiet, and subdued; in the end, she was sentenced to twenty-two months in prison, a paltry amount of time compared to a life. Bill may have lived another twenty-two years. After dealing with emphysema, he had weaned off the oxygen and was in good health again. There's no telling how long his natural lifespan would have been.

There was no vindication in the minimal sentence and Jenene went away from the situation with a spiky ball of resentment in the pit of her stomach. She refused to forgive Roxanne. The "murdering bitch" had cost us too much to let bygones be bygones.

The day of sentencing would not be the last time we saw Roxanne Holmes.

For one thing she would haunt Jenene's dreams. They were not like *those* dreams, no, not when she would have welcomed—no matter how small it made her feel—forewarning of her nemesis' death. They were dreams that would make her reconsider everything.

Chapter 67
No Surrender

To compound our troubles Bill died without a will.

Not only did we lose a man who was important to us, it left us vulnerable to vultures. As a result of no will, Bill's third of the farm automatically went to his siblings. Somehow, it worked out that this included his dead sister Lucille, meaning each of her kids were awarded a third of her portion.

This was just the foothold Uncle Bob was looking for to launch an attack. His siblings and he each inheriting a portion of the farm gave him all the incentive he needed to go on an all-out campaign to maneuver the farm out from under us. His greed was insatiable and he did not care whose life he destroyed to get what he wanted. His hopes were to be dashed at every turn, from attempting to hire Bill's attorney to coaxing his siblings to fight beyond reason.

In the wake of Bill's death, Lal and Herb attained wills to name Russ and Jenene as the beneficiaries of their property. This meant the others had little chance of ever obtaining enough of a stake to decide the farm's fate.

Through the aid of a terrific lawyer, Jenene was able to arrange to pay Lois, Uncle Bob, and Dick for their shares of their mother's portion. Uncle Bob was reluctant to take the money, salivating over the prospect of acquiring the whole farm. Lois stepped in and insisted he do the right thing. Once we had their signatures and they had their money, we no longer had to worry about losing the farm.

Each share in the ballpark of twenty thousand for a grand total of sixty grand, attaining the payout meant another painful decision. The four-acre parcel of land across the tracks and road had to be sold. The barn the family boarded horses in for decades had to come down, the land put on the market. Prime real estate, it sold quickly. It was sad seeing the century-old barn come down piece by piece. It was even harder watching a new owner take over the property.

All the barn's wood was transported across the road via hay wagon and stacked up beside the granary. People were drawn by the timber and paid or traded for it, intent on using the aged boards as paneling for their cabins and home dens.

Jenene collected the old but well-preserved cedar roof shingles for herself. Like children's paper snowflakes, each was individual, some whole, some with nail holes, and some broken into unique shapes. She saw another way to make a few shekels. Each shingle became a base she used to paint on sayings, quotes, idioms, poetry, and draw pretty things like butterflies and flowers. Expressing her soul artistically was relaxing and soon proved as profitable as she hoped.

She pasted a placard with a brief history of the barn on the back of each piece. Then she stained them with polyurethane. This crafty hobby, done in her fleeting spare time, produced some beautiful keepsakes that were snapped up quickly for five to fifteen dollars by the customer base she cultivated simply by giving out a few as gifts.

The issue of money never lost prevalence. Even after assorted settlements and selling the land, money was tight. Another source of income besides the shingles was the garage sale we ran for the entire summer following Bill's death.

The garage was beneath the house and wasn't exactly ideal. The house had sunk, which meant the garage opened at the bottom of a decline. If it rained, the garage automatically flooded, the drains all but useless, likely overgrown with tree roots. Big black wolf spiders took up residence in the window wells…and there was a dank, moldy smell that couldn't be scrubbed out.

On makeshift tables, doors placed on milk cans, boards on fruit crates, two card tables expanded with a piece of fiberboard between them, we made the best of it. Among the items for sale were antiques we hated to part with, the stuff with less sentimental value mostly, old lamps, Vargas calendars, and other little gems.

The rest of our inventory was supplied by Russ, who had taken up robbing local houses…kidding, he had gotten a job as a trash collector, and it only seemed like he was stealing—people threw out good stuff. They even tossed brand new items. Even expensive items, like the ill-fated video disc player. He could take whatever he wanted and was able to supply the sale all summer.

During this time he garnered the large Buck knife that would become his sidearm; the owner tossed it because it had been in a house fire and insurance supplied a replacement for the largely undamaged blade. A little spit and polish and it was good to go. Saber on his hip, Russ was all the more intimidating when facing off with unruly trespassers intent on insisting they "had a right," whatever that means.

Russ scored toys, books, knives, swords, figurines, and in one case several boxes of frozen lobster and steaks. The woman of the house watched for the garbage truck. She brought out the food and explained she and her husband were leaving for a month and she wanted to unplug the freezer. Not wanting it to go to waste, she insisted Russ and his crew take the food, which they divvied up gladly.

Such delicacies were to us nothing short of gifts from the universe. We lived so frugally; the only way we would get such treats was if they were given to us. Those were hard times, but after we got Uncle Bob off our backs, we were able to enjoy one less major worry.

Jenene was committed to providing a happy childhood despite much adversity.

Even if I have in some ways grown into a jaded, dour adult (the state of the world causes me great vexation), I appreciate her efforts.

Although Russ and I were often at odds he could still show he had a good heart. Even with money tight, he supported the idea when Jenene wanted to see to it I got a horse. They worked hard for me to have what rates as one of the top gifts of my life.

They did get me a horse, too…in a manner of speaking. Cupcake was a pony. This meant she was short and stout whereas the other horses were tall and slim. She had a coat of black hair that thickened and frizzed out in the winter. A sassy tuft of mane stuck up between her ears. She had a real attitude. I loved her very much…even if she tried to nip me occasionally.

When Cupcake was in an elevated state of feistiness she would try to buck her rider by rearing up. Fancying himself the sort of man who could be a rodeo rider should it be his desire and taking advice from Herb, Russ set out to break her of the habit—by staying aboard no matter how hard she worked to unseat him.

Mounting rapidly, the skirmish was on. Cupcake shot onto her back legs with a furious lack of reservation, front hooves shadow boxing frantically. Momentum developed with each rear up.

Long legs clamped, Russ held fast.

Hard to tell what knocked her off her axis, maybe her franticness, Cupcake lost balance. She fell backwards—directly onto Russ's slender figure.

This happened on the unpaved hard packed gravel driveway. We feared he was killed. Cupcake rolled and hopped up. Her brown eyes were leveled at him, a blaming gaze. Smooshed flat but not to death, Russ peeled himself off the ground.

The impact was enough to propel a meteor shower of small stones through the denim of his blue jeans. Jenene spent the next hour picking gravel out of his hind end as Russ shook and swore.

Several years in a row Jenene threw me huge birthday soirees. A feast of my favorite foods aside, I was uncomfortable with all the attention. The limelight not for me, I was the quiet kid. Sulking in my room, I could be snottier than I like to remember.

I have never felt comfortable accepting gifts; I have learned all I can do is set discomfort aside and be gracious and grateful.

As a kid I was all for winning prizes, though, and Jenene was tireless in her efforts to help.

To that end she put together costumes based on my preferences that often won me prizes at the church basement party we attended on Halloween.

The best costume was the year I went as Swamp Thing. Christel helped with that one. First by crafting a mask out of oven bake clay that went over my eyes and the top of my nose. Then by working with Jenene to dye a bodysuit and a bagful of leafy lace green before sewing it all together. I got all sorts of accolades for that one. In a position I was more comfortable being noticed, hidden behind a mask.

Another way Jenene helped me win prizes was through my channel 9 Fun Club membership. There was a daily call-in contest. Be the ninth caller and win a t-shirt and a couple of medium Little Caesar's pizzas. Jenene helped me win not once, but twice, re-dialing repeatedly.

Both times my last name was spelled wrong in the crawl announcing the winner at the bottom of the screen, but since my initials were distinctive, the kids at school were aware. Winning was oddly a feather in my cap to my arbitrary peers.

The second time around the prize was two tickets to a Billy Joel concert being held at the then-new Target Center in Minneapolis. Even though a gorgeous blond horse boarder offered to be my date, I gave the tickets to my parents. All the effort Jenene put in to help me win those tickets, it seemed only fair.

They were good to me so I wanted to be good to them. They got so few diversions. Vacations? Not a chance. Going to that concert was a short but needed respite from the grind.

Parents play such monumental roles in our lives and all the good stuff they do pays dividends when we become caring, generous people.

I will always remember how Jenene sprung me from school on my birthday under the promise I would make up my work promptly. The year she took me to the magic and costume shop on Seventh Street in St. Paul especially. I was able to acquire a much sought after plastic Freddy Krueger glove.

I will always remember that she and Russ sacrificed to give me Cupcake. How they worked side jobs to ensure I had the status symbols of my day, videogame systems such as Nintendo and later Sega Genesis. How they made my birthdays and Christmases and New Years grand events full of joy and cheer.

We were broke but not busted, and from that may spring one of the greatest lessons of my childhood.

Chapter 68
The Value of Slumber

By the winter of '89 Jenene had accrued quite a sleep deficiency. The back pain muscled in the way of everything. All she had learned about stones and meditation coupled with massage helped to a point. But it was clear. More was needed if she was to find lasting relief.

A period of trial by ordeal tested her resolve before she could make the next step in her healing ascension.

A typical night involved sporadic dozing.

Jagged chunks of sleep were broken by a need to continuously move around.

So exhausted she would fall asleep as soon as her head hit the pillow, a mere twenty minutes to half an hour later she would snap awake. Her back would be throbbing and her legs, asleep, would be tingly. This sensation of pins and needles forced her rudely out of bed.

Avoiding creaks in the floor that could go off like knuckles cracking and shaking off the uncomfortable sensation jangling her extremities, she wove through the dark house, a pained figure in a nightgown and robe. She alternated from bed to chair to floor to couch; the circuit had much variance because no order assured relief.

After a while her feet would carry her to Bill's chair. That would only work temporarily. The couch served for a few minutes. The carpet made of Lal's collected scraps was poor padding but the solid floor could better serve the need of her spine, at least for a short time.

From there she would warm Lal's rocking chair.

In her bleakest moments she would even curl up in Herb's chair, which was preposterous. That was one big, hard, uncomfortable chair. But his footstool helped.

None of these spots were comfortable. The different positions were what counted.

"I just kept moving around," she told me. "I was never able to get settled. It didn't help that we had a waterbed. That fad was really terrible for my spine."

Hearing her tell of her plight, it is easy to see why this nocturnal routine left her fatigued. She was so depleted and tired she had bags under her bags.

As her health declined so too did her mental state.

Jenene began to experience horrible flashes of what would prove to be fragmentations of appalling memories. She had no idea where they originated, why they were flashing across her vision now, or what she could do to stop what made her mind feel invaded, tweaked, and stung.

Often triggered by scents, the visions—they would consume her head like floodwaters gushing through a cave—were ghastly. A hulking figure hovered over a shuddery little girl. Acts of ghastliness perpetrated in a subterrain. Pain. Hip displacement. Shame. Fear. Confusion.

At first they seemed like fluke flashes.

Soon enough they would become more pronounced.

Sometimes she felt like her mind was falling apart, crumbling like the house they couldn't afford to maintain.

There was a conspiracy in Jenene's mind to shield her from maybe the worst abuse ever done to her.

The problem was her subconscious had gotten fed up with bearing all the brunt of a great hurt, went rogue, and was spritzing the flashes into her conscious mind to let her know it was time to throw open the door to her top secret memories so she could grow as a person and overcome newer hurts literally burning holes inside her.

Chapter 69
Revelations

Life is a tapestry with many strings, some unimportant; others so important if they are pulled the whole thing will unravel. I can only hope the mosaic is as colorful, vivid, and compelling as a Turkish rug in writing as it has been told to me.

I have collected and arranged the fibers, twine, and thread that make up the embroidery of my mom's extraordinary life carefully and in so doing have discovered dark patches she has found ways to conceal with the brightness that surrounds them, dark spots I had to pluck at to learn of their existence for sake of those who can be helped. Ahead I am going to relate the darkest patch of all....

So aptly demonstrated by the story of Bluebeard, when there's a locked door, people want to know what's on the other side. Jenene had such a door in her memory, only because it existed in hint and insinuation, she had no reason to be tantalized until it was too late.

It wasn't a collection of severed heads that awaited her. What was behind her door was even worse. The horror of Bluebeard's beheaded wives was over while hers, like Bluebeard's curious current wife, was only beginning.

Following a marvelous session with Lacy that by then gave nominal relief, Jenene was open to suggestions. When a magnificent massage that once worked magic imparted no lasting relief, it was time to look for some fairy dust elsewhere if elsewhere it could be found.

"Your pain seems so persistent it has to be connected to an injury," Lacy said wisely. "I'm convinced there was an incident in your past. Because you don't know what it is, it means you've blocked it out."

"You really think my back problems could be connected to something I don't remember that happened in my past?" Jenene asked. The notion intrigued her instantly. For some time she had been plagued by those pesky repulsive flashes. They derived from somewhere in her psyche. That much was obvious.

"Our minds have an incredible ability to repress what we don't want to know. The problem is learning can be really important to get over trauma from the past. It's the basis of rebirth therapy. If I led you through a rebirth you could find out for sure."

Their fast bond led Jenene to confide much in Lacy. The bird-boned masseuse had many ideas. They had discussed how old injuries could linger. Other than the health history heretofore lain out, Jenene knew of no situation during which her lower spine was harmed. She supposed it would be residuals of her car accident maybe. What else—*it hurts*—was there?

"So I would relive my birth and early life?"

Lacy shrugged. "It depends on you is what it amounts to because if you're not open to the experience I can't force you to do anything. The past can hold pain to us if we don't recall it and confront it. Some people choose the pain."

There was no way Jenene would "choose" the pain. About to lose her mind from lack of sleep and too much hurt, she needed to pursue any option that could help her.

"I've been experiencing these"—so afraid—"weird flashes," she confided. "I don't know if they're"—shameful—

"memories. But it seems there"—a bulky silhouette crushing…someone—"are gaps. They seem like"—such confusion—"gaps anyway."

There was no doubt she was hazy on her earliest years at this point, confirmed by the photo albums she was looking through on the farm. There wasn't one photo of her mom and dad until after she was the age of two. Only one photo from that early in her life showing her with Lois existed. Years from learning the truth of her origins, all she could do was speculate.

"Not surprising," Lacy said. "With others I've had a lot of luck leading them through a rebirth. I think it would benefit you, too. You could relive your memories, fill in the gaps."

For real relief Jenene was willing to try any idea that could be sold to her as a reasonable option. "Explain a rebirth to me."

"First I would create a comfortable environment for you in here. Lay you down on the massage table and wrap you in blankets. Then I would act as a guide and talk you through the whole process. I would return you to your birth and direct you forward through your life from the very beginning. That way you can relive everything that's happened to you."

"Where did you learn how to lead a rebirth?"

"Oh, I took classes and became certified. It's really serious therapy. When it works, it's better than psycho analysis."

Jenene was sold. "What could it hurt?"

Maybe not so much of a trend as its detractors would have you believe, what Lacy was suggesting, Primal Therapy, would work for Jenene. Had she known going in how successful it would be, she may have better prepared herself by bringing along a Valium.

Lacy's credentials to perform this form of psychotherapy seem dubious.

But as a minimally yet sometimes successful fad it seems likely many in the world of natural healing would recognize the benefits and adopt the practice. So her claim to have gotten certification, likely from a fellow amateur, seems believable. Arthur Janov's book, *The Primal Scream*, is readily available for professionals and laymen alike.

At the onset, Lacy swaddled Jenene in blankets and arranged stones around her form. Then with a calm, lulling voice

Lacy guided her back to the womb, where the journey of recollection would commence.

The rebirth took her forward through her infancy and her time as a toddler. The passage to what they sought wouldn't be far beyond those first few years. Each event was like a hopscotch grid she had no choice other than to land on if only for a second before hopping to the next.

On the way she relived Lois' seeming rejection only for the pain to turn over into joyfulness at being on the farm with Lal, Bill, and Herb. Meeting a stranger she was told was her daddy. Losing the place that was so dear to live with the lady who hurt her and the daddy man. Meeting the other big man. The younger one who stirred no trust the way the daddy man managed because his spirit was dark....

Had she approached the memory that tore the lid off Pandora's box through regression all she would have found was the locked door. By going from her earliest memories to the important gap, she snuck up on feelings and memories too terrible to believe...except it was real, it had happened, and it was always in her to know.

Not intended to spark visual and aural memory so much as a journey through emotional history, Jenene re-experienced the event with such clarity it encompassed all her senses and proved a horrific form of time travel.

What it began as was seeing/experiencing Bobby, the half-brother she had not seen in years, taking her forcefully down into the basement. Then he was a giant looming over her, wish-boning her legs after taking down her pants.

She was so small, doll-like; a paper-thin child, not some blossoming teen, but a little girl; and the monster was doing horrifying, unspeakable things to her (*It hurts!*), bad things in this loveless, incestuous, pedophilic context; the sort of things that would make him a pariah even among criminals who make killing secondhand; and as he bore down he crushed her and ground into her and it hurt so much!

Snapping back to reality, Jenene hurt so deeply and forcefully the immediacy of it took her breath away.

She was physically reliving the event. Feeling compressed under immense weight being driven into her body…it felt like her pelvis was going to implode. She began to sob uncontrollably.

Crushing via rocks chiseled into huge bricks was an interrogative form of torment once used on suspected witches and she never felt more sympathy for anyone who ran afoul of such a dire state. At least they were spared defilement beyond the search for marks of the devil.

I was molested by my half-brother, she noted, acknowledging what she now knew. The repulsive realization beamed her on the head like a ball peen hammer. *How could you, Bobby? How could you? I was just a little girl! I couldn't have been more than three! How could you do that to me?*

Overwhelmed emotionally. Hurting physically. She had no idea what to feel. There was so much, a dizzyingly kaleidoscopic maelstrom of churned emotion. Fury. Humiliation. Defilement. Betrayal. All laced and churned with such confusion.

Jenene had given little thought to her wayward scofflaw half-brother in the intervening years beyond wondering if he was even alive. By the end of the 1980's his own actions had long made him an outsider to the family. He had often dropped out of sight for longer periods even before he departed after their dad's death, perhaps to never call or pay a visit again.

At the end of his last go-round, the manipulator was manipulated since he asked Lois for a loan and she handed over a few dollars gladly under the agreement it be repaid upon his next visit, as it turned out guaranteeing he would never return. She saw it as an inexpensive way to be rid of what she saw as a trashier person than she wanted in her life.

To Lois' credit, in her way she tried to make an honest go with Bobby. Yet her interactions with him left her no alternative save for to view him as a liar and manipulator since, well, he often was a liar and manipulator. She had no idea how to deal with an angry young man. To this day she does not quite comprehend the emotional complexity of other people even if she has empathy. With little intricacy to her own emotions, she has little baseline to judge the emotionality of others. Nor could she distinguish easily bad behavior as cries for help, for affection, for love.

Lois' way in those days was always to show caring monetarily. In Bobby's case, he was charged rent after he graduated from high school, an action meant to teach him responsibility yet probably inspired little more than ire.

Unbeknownst to her stepson, Lois deposited the payments into an account. When he moved out, she turned the account over to him with her best wishes for the life he was embarking on. This is attestation of the fact that she had no true ill feelings toward him even if she harbored a resounding distrust.

But you didn't ever trust him, did you, Mom? He always seemed off, didn't he? Yet somehow he was able to get me alone!

Jenene wondered how her parents could remain oblivious. Where were they? She had been such a slight, almost frail little thing. How could such a large man do such awfulness to her and not leave a mark? How could they not notice a change? Wasn't there a time she was happy and open only to become sullen and distant? Signs of such trauma had to be evident in so many ways yet every one of them was apparently missed…or ignored.

What was worse there was no way she could ever broach any of this to Lois. She was a woman who refused to talk religion, politics, or any other taboo subject—she was all about maintaining a no-wake zone.

So Jenene had no choice other than to confront what she was feeling without sharing with the very person who could shed light on what happened. Lois may not have known any specifics, but she could explain other details, add brushstrokes to the picture.

And confront she would have to, the facts, the feelings, and the repercussions, an undertaking that would take her far beyond this first cascade of tears.

Lacy was at her side without delay, sheltering and consoling her in a way her mother never could. Her friend, therapist, and masseuse would be the first to offer her council. From her she received all the assurance needed to reject the notions of the victimized: that she was at fault, possibly deserving.

Even then she knew if she shied away from confronting what happened the hard truth would certainly shred her psyche.

I am again a biographer in a position of relating events that are sensitive and perhaps not the usual domain of a son. Aforesaid, I feel that only in coming to view our parents not as somehow deific as our personal creators but as individuals with all the wants and desires shared universally can we master adulthood.

In any case, coming to terms with being molested and how that entwined with Jenene's healing is too important to omit due to any discomfort on my part.

The sum total of all the events of her life, dividing her reality as an individual person from her reality as a mother is impossible so it is up to me to chronicle as many of the important events as I can no matter what they might entail. To a casual observer my mom is a person who might seem on the surface to be of simpler makeup than, say, a business mogul or a brain surgeon. In reality she is as immensely complex as anyone driven by ambitions, goals, and red-hot desires.

After healing the remnants of the abuse and coming to terms with her feelings toward Bobby, Jenene had no interest in reliving any of these events. The only reason she let me relate this part of her story is to offer hope to other victims.

Even though she felt crushed reliving her trauma following the revelation, she refused to allow the knowledge to be a weight that would continue to crush her. She had a suspicion she had been bearing it unknowingly most of her life. So she set about a personal quest to understand, accept, forgive, and heal.

That makes the process seem cut and dry when it was not at all; stirred emotions wind up churning into a thick gruel not easily swallowed or stomached. Jenene had a lot to digest before her system would be cleared.

Reassessing her entire life under the newly surfaced knowledge of abuse, Jenene realized why she had always felt so isolated and alone; she had been marked, if to nobody else to herself. Even though on one level aloneness was preferable because it meant not having to expose herself, on another level there was an intense need for closeness, intimacy, and the love for which she had always felt undeserving.

This leads to addressing another problem Jenene had to conquer: sexual addiction. In relating her younger years, I chose not to record whatever dalliances might have occurred because I do not think it is a son's place to chronicle his mother's sexual escapades. As such I do not intend to go any further than necessary to get across the points I seek to make.

There is speculation as to whether sexual addiction is real. In Jenene's case I think her actions might be an example of Freud's writing in *Interpretation of Dreams* about "return of the oppressed," particularly "Dynamic Unconscious," the process by which repressed memories are hidden from consciousness and manifest in adult life as symptoms that in theory could include impulsive promiscuity. Despite the DSM not recognizing sexual addition as of the fifth edition, counselors have expressed that with the prevalence of such behavior and difficulty treating said, Jenene's ability to conquer her compulsion for sex would be of interest to many.

I include this information for the most part to show cause and effect. Jenene was molested, repressed the trauma, and wound up suffering hyper sexuality she did not understand until she realized she was rebelling against, hiding, and circling away from powerful emotions.

This also explains why she would stay in her soul-crushing first marriage beyond reason. Why when he was beating her regularly she would conceive a child with him. I never understood that. Why stay with a violent man? Why sleep with him unless it was outright marital rape? It made no sense until I knew she was battling powerful urges and hoped being in a marriage would win the war, sort of amateur therapy to deal with the guerilla warfare going on inside her body and mind.

To that end, no matter how often he accused her of infidelity, she never cheated on my father. Many sex addicts have no trouble jumping beds and little qualm against breaking hearts even if they feel awful about causing so much hurt. But Jenene took her first marriage perhaps more seriously than she should have in remaining unfalteringly true.

Marriage was an institution Jenene took seriously, a truth that factors hugely in this story because it was her commitment that forced her to renounce the urges that reemerged after the divorce. It can be argued that the desire to remain true even in a serious commitment takes more than just wanting all to be right. So what else helped Jenene overcome?

The answer is a solid mate, an endeared husband, a complete lover, an undying love, and the security of a marriage always worth fighting for. In that she was blessed.

Had Russ not shown his unique and special devotion, stepping up efforts whenever necessary, it is very possible their relationship would have floundered and she may have sought comfort in the arms of others. But for them there would never be a lull, never be a lack of passion, even if that passion was expressed in arguments as often or more than lovemaking.

Absolute trust and security in a relationship frees the mind and spirit from the shackles of uncertainty, where energy can too often be wasted on pointless speculation and attachments trivialized until former meaning has vanished. In her first marriage she had no fear her husband would stray but the abuse removed all trust and security, so his faithfulness meant nothing when the majority of what he inspired was uncertainty. Russ's faithfulness meant everything, his unquestioning loyalty. Even if their collaboration could be a volatile one, they were stronger together.

They accepted each other warts and all in a way few couples achieve. Commitments are made and broken all the time, endearments dashed with insults, professions of love revoked with cruel acts. Neither would ever repudiate their love for the other, no matter how angry or frustrated they might be. Their love was white-hot fire between respites of intense smoldering. With Russ she was no longer alone or lonely, she no longer felt unloved, and most of all she was no longer unsatisfied.

Sustainable love is attainable through reciprocity.

Love should not be a bridge that carries you to one location; it should be a spiral that takes you to new places forever. Love should be feathers that lift you into the sky and shelters you when it rains, the light that warms and comforts, and the moon that shines through the clouds and illuminates the darkest night. Jenene had the poetry of true love in her life and with that on her side anything could be healed.

Others suffering from such tendencies may not be so lucky as to enter into the kind of fulfilling relationship that helped Jenene. For them she advises seeking to understand the causes because had she known all along what had happened to her it is likely her life would have gone very differently.

With one demon born of the abuse behind her, Jenene meditated and used other forms of natural healing to reclaim what Bobby stripped from her: true self-esteem, true self-worth, and true self-love.

By concentrating and descending into the catacombs of her subconscious she was able to unearth the undead corpses representing all she had meticulously hidden. They were not rotted. On the contrary, they were porcelain vampires that for too long had been draining her of life. She had to stake them one by one and drag them into the light; once she had done that, their power over her powdered into dust.

It was another lesson in never underestimating the value of introspection. Looking within to where the secrets she kept even from herself were stored and tearing down the walls so nothing was hidden, she discovered the answers she needed. She also found herself.

Illumination can come at the cost of innocence but her innocence had been stolen long before. Sometimes it is only in walking through the fire and feeling the lick of the flames that we can burn away the weakness that hinders us from true enlightenment and perhaps come as close to apotheosis as mere mortals can without offending the powers that be.

Jenene had to come to terms with what had happened on a multitude of levels. With failings on the parts of her supposed support, with herself, with the brother who betrayed her in one of the worst ways possible. Truth can be like pinpricks. In retrospect it was obvious her social problems, tendency to isolate herself, and general malaise could be traced to the abuse. Was it why she took the negative aspects of her childhood so personally, why she was so temperamental and unhappy? Likely.

Then there was her willingness to endanger herself. Smoking. Drinking. Seeking dangerous people to fill out her life. There was wanton promiscuity driven by an ostensible sexual addiction, too, a symptom of sexual abuse she attributed to a mysterious insatiability. The abused often have trouble distinguishing sex from love. Sex can be a temporary balm but without the triple antibiotic ointment of love can never altogether heal the emotional wound left by rape. No matter how many times the act is repeated.

There was also her tendency to run away from good guys while she ended up married to a bad guy, continuing a cycle of abuse she had no idea she was living.

When looked at as a whole all the behavior and feelings dovetailed neatly. Taking it all into account helped her achieve a greater self-understanding than she had henceforth attained and she for once and all felt like a complete person.

Within months a reckoning came serendipitously out of the blue that proved helpful to Jenene's eventual complete enlightenment.

Lois was given the first news concerning Bobby put forward in years. The unexpectedness was enough for Lois to pass along what she learned expediently.

Word was his estranged wife had leveled accusations of sexual abuse against him. The rumor of indiscretions had led to him dropping off the grid and his whereabouts were unknown.

Jenene was appalled any other child had to suffer. She regretted so repressing what he had done to her she was unable to tell. Then when she recalled the time before the memories were concealed she knew that her telling was unlikely in any event because she was too afraid the grownups would dismiss her or worse label her a liar. If only she had not been so bricked in and detached from her parents. Had she been able to talk perhaps the revelation would have prevented further victimizing.

Even then she could not speak.

Her silence prompted Lois to ask, "Did Bobby molest you?"

What a heart stopper. Jenene lost strength in her fingers and the receiver slipped out of her hand. It clanged off the kitchen linoleum and the dangly cord flopped around like the tail of an insolent housecat.

"I'm sorry about that," she said unsteadily after retrieving the receiver. "I never thought you'd ask that."

Lois was adamant. "Did he?" she pressed.

Had deceit been in her composition, Jenene may have avoided this pristine opportunity simply because actually facing it was far harder than she anticipated. It was easy to be full of bluster over what seems like the impossible and quite another thing altogether when it suddenly becomes reality.

"Yes," she said simply.

"Why didn't you tell me?"

What an absurd question.

"I didn't think you would believe me."

"Why not?"

Another absurdity.

"I was little and he was big."

"How little?"

"Three."

There was a long silence.

"I'm so sorry. I...I just didn't know," Lois said finally. "I tried to never leave you alone with him. I didn't...trust him. But I didn't ever think he would do that to you. Had I even suspected...."

"I never thought we would discuss this. I repressed the memories. I only recently found out myself."

An outpouring followed.

Lois expressed regret, sorrow, and even anguish. Jenene was touched. Her mother came short of tears; she was still a ways from the day when she would wear her emotions on her sleeve. But one thing was obvious. Jenene concluded learning of Bobby's abuse was as hurtful to her mom as it was to her.

In that Jenene was granted a farther-reaching consolation than she ever imagined. Because of it she was better able to find forgiveness for the lapses that allowed abuse. Better able to understand.

In seeking to understand Bobby's motive it becomes clear what he did could in part be blamed on family dynamics.

As a very little boy, his former model mother put Bobby to work as a child model only to cool toward him when his cuteness wore off. She never forgave him for robbing her of an hourglass figure and summarily her career. A boy rejected by his narcissist mother long before the definitive rejection when she outright refused custody of her only son in open court ("Why don't you want custody?" "He makes me look old!"), he was without doubt an emotionally complex individual by the time he landed in his father's sole care.

He was a teenage boy who felt hated by his mother and little more than tolerated by his father. Then he was suddenly brought into a home situation with a woman eleven years younger than his father who was the mother of a little girl.

But who was the little girl's daddy?

Bobby was told her father was killed in Viet Nam when he was first introduced to Jenene. But he never believed that, no; he was perceptive enough to even in the toddler see his father's features and hear the falseness in their lies.

Tell a young person a lie when they know it is a deception and the imparted lesson is that lying is a tool okay to use. They also learn to disrespect the dishonest authority.

Rape and molestation are not so much about sexual stimulus or satisfaction as power. I suspect the power Bobby sought was over his father's much younger wife.

Lois made no bones about her position as an authority. She was too young for him to take seriously. There was less age difference between her and him than between her and her husband. He had no respect for her. She was nobody to him and she dared to think she was his parent. Much wrath can be inspired in a young man in a difficult and confusing situation.

So who had to suffer?

The tiny three-year-old child only Lal and Bill had time for, the little girl who would have maybe been traumatized for the rest of her life had she not grown into such a strong person. Growing reservoirs of strength and eventual catharsis aside, she didn't feel strong in the initial days and weeks following the life-changing revelation.

Luck or fate or maybe nothing more than coincidence had brought her to Russ and for it she was thankful because having him in the aftermath of reliving the trauma of her past meant the world. He was furious on her behalf, outraged, fit to be tied. Jenene was afraid that if Bobby were to intrepidly make an appearance on the farm he would wind up buried in the back forty. Even if his devotion was a little scary, her husband's genuine need to make her feel safe was touching and reassuring.

All told, she was better and wiser for surviving the worst experiences of her life and coming to terms with the abuse.

Now that she knew why she was damaged and was working to repair the damage, did it at last free her to care about herself? Damn straight. It was time to make her life matter, even if she still contained intense bitterness toward Bill's killer and was sick and getting sicker. The future seemed suddenly real because now she could look forward to moving toward it without carrying the monumental weight of so much invisible baggage.

What Jenene ultimately reserved for Bobby was the thing she hated most of all, pity. He funneled his rage into her in a skewed gambit to spread his pain. Who but a pitiful person would feel that kind of abuse was an answer?

She was able to forgive him for many reasons attributable to her own illimitable capacity to grow and understand. But most of all because she had deconstructed him and recognized there were many ways he was a victim too. It was even possible he was sexually abused. He was a child model in the 1950's with a mother prone to negligence, which opens the door to speculation.

Besides, the way you can smell the rain before a storm or feel the moisture in your joints, she sensed retribution awaited Bobby no matter what consequences he faced in life. Whether she was a participant in his comeuppance or not had no bearing on her, her life, or anything for that matter, so long as in her heart, mind, and soul she felt healed and whole. Withholding forgiveness would only chain the depravity and pain to her at a time when she needed to be strong.

Two people, Roxanne Holmes and my wayward uncle Bobby, made me know a vengeful core of ichor resides in my heart. I recognize for whatever wisdom I hold this makes me in some way small. Yet it also makes me seek to never inspire that feeling in anyone else. It drains away a person's humanity.

Ahead in these pages Jenene has reckonings with both people who gave her so much opportunity to grow.

Chapter 70
Herb's Change of Heart

Shortly after we moved in Herb had been diagnosed with melanoma on his arms caused by years of unprotected sun exposure.

The worst of the three types of skin cancer, early detection is vital. True to his nature, Herb had kept the ugly purple growth to himself. When he was diagnosed, the doctor felt it was too advanced for him to survive. Herb shrugged off this diagnosis. He treated himself with ample applications of apple cider vinegar. The melanoma disappeared.

This was not the only time the old boy went to battle against cancer, nor the only time doctors were sure it would kill him. Even if he disputed that he even had cancer. By the time the prostate cancer was detected, he was peeing so much blood they could not detect any urine. They scraped his prostate and put him on female hormones.

Jenene would set him up his pill daily. One day, she caught him flicking the pill on the floor in front of the big gray tomcat Clyde. Much to her surprise, Clyde ate it. We had noticed his voice was getting a little…high-pitched. That was the effect the hormone pills had on the tomcat: his lion-like meow became marred by a squeakiness that stayed with him all the rest of his days.

Aghast, she told him, "You can't feed that to the cats—that's for prostate cancer. You need it."

Herb replied, "I ain't got no cancer!"

Jenene took him back to the doctor, so he could explain to him why he needed to take his pills. Herb would not have it. And in the end, he didn't die from cancer—nor did he ever believe he had the big C.

Still, after the car accident, Herb developed a small cancerous growth on the upper helix of his right ear. The doctors wanted to remove the crinkly brown spot, but Herb refused. Since it itched, he scratched at it…with his snuff finger. Pick, pick, pick until it bled. He never gave the wound a chance to mend. Years later a similar situation would lead to a bad infection in his leg.

One morning he shuffled out to the kitchen table and the whole right side of his head was tomato red.

"I need to take you to the hospital," Jenene gasped. "There's something wrong."

With a gesture of dismissal, he sat down for his corn flakes and prune juice. Noticeably ill, he forced down his breakfast as Jenene worked on convincing him to seek medical aid. He scarcely paid attention. Which was Herb to a tee. It would have been odder had he not been dismissive.

Herb had never quite accepted our presence in the house. He didn't appreciate my folks' efforts. He had never felt comfortable with Bill abdicating the household to Jenene. As in all other avenues of his life, he was uninhibited in voicing his disapproval. He would shout, "I don't want your help! I didn't ask you to move in here!"

Russ got the worst of it. Herb's love of reading often meant when anyone would approach him he would have his nose in a book. Therefore, whoever it was had better impress him with what they had to say. Because if he didn't like what you were telling him, he had no trouble letting you know.

Nothing Russ had to say ever seemed to impress him, and he also had no trouble telling him to "go shit in the river and watch the bubbles come up" or "go piss up a rope" or simply not give him the respect of lowering his book from in front of his face. When he was most annoyed he would say, "You make my ass tired."

I was the only one he seemed to accept.

Even as Jenene and Russ invested in the farm and it became more our home, we were careful not to infringe on Herb's sphere. This was for no other reason than deference to him; it was also better not to get the sharp side of his tongue. Much hardship had befallen him, so we felt his tetchiness was understandable and therefore tolerable, even if hurtful. Aging is expedited by loss and injury and change and he'd had a heaping helping of all three.

The old man needed his space. Proceeds Herb received after the accident meant he was able to afford what was at that time a big screen TV. Funny how time and technology change perspectives because that dinosaur TV—which weighs a ton— seemed like a real marvel. Today flat screens three times the size can be easily carried by one person. Because his TV was the centerpiece of the living room, during the hours he was awake we gave it over and treated it as his unquestioned domain.

Solitude to read his westerns seemed to make him if not happy at least not in the mood to complain. Watching *Family Feud* and *Wheel of Fortune* offered diversion. Being fed in a timely manner on a tray brought to his chair was an unacknowledged but cherished routine Jenene observed religiously.

That day, perhaps out of some small respect for her services to him or just because he recognized how sick he was, Herb agreed finally to see Dr. Sandcastle. Early in the morning, they had to wait for his office to open. Herb went out to his chair to pass some time while Jenene cleaned up the table.

Stacking bowls and juice glasses in the washtub, Jenene felt an intense urge to check on the old boy. Heeding her feeling, in three quick strides she crossed the kitchen to the opening to the living room.

Only minutes before she had observed as he lowered into his chair. Now she saw he had collapsed forward onto his footstool. He was pressing down on his chest so hard she was afraid he was suffocating. She raced to his side. Seized him under the armpits. And struggled to pull him back up. He was just too heavy. All she could do was drag him aside onto the carpet. Make sure his airway was not obstructed. Then she went for help.

She called 911.

Regardless of how antiseptic, sterile, and well meaning, the odor of hospitals will always make me think of gloom and doom.

Shoes squeaking on the linoleum floor, trying not to glance in the open rooms but too curious not to peek, I felt chilled to my core as we made our way to Herb's room. Losing him so soon after Bill…I did not want to even entertain such thoughts. Yet there was a chance we could lose him. We would soon find out the medical establishment had already counted him out.

But then Herb had pick, pick, picked his way to cellulitis, a dangerous bacterial infection. A dose of penicillin wouldn't be enough. Such a severe infection, which was also that close to the brain, was dangerous enough that he required the sort of care only available through hospitalization—which he hated.

Even if it required bending time and space we made a point of visiting Herb as often as possible. Whenever we had someone to care for Lal and even if that in no way changed the limitation of time, all three of us would make the journey. If not I would go visit with one or the other.

The visual of any one of The Seniors in a hospital bed was heartrending but the way Herb was particularly miserable made it that much worse. It was so discouraging seeing him confined, looking all of his years and then some—so out of place, so far from home. In their accepting way Bill or Lal took hospitalization good-naturedly. Herb looked as if he just didn't understand how it could come to this, all hope gone.

We at least got the pleasure of seeing him perk up at the prospect of home cooking since it remained true he would rather starve than eat the hospital food.

Except acknowledging the food, for the remainder of the visit he might act indifferent toward us. His poker face could have fooled the devil because I believe he was gladder to see us than he ever let on.

It wouldn't be until later that he truly appreciated my parents.

One visit in particular forced Jenene to step up as Herb's caregiver.

We got to his room and there he was, looking frail and dejected under a white blanket. We came in and greeted him. Sat down. It was just as likely he would read a book during our visit as talk to us, so we were prepared to sit there and watch whatever he had on the TV.

A positive sign, he wanted the food we brought right away. Good appetite was important. It doesn't take long to waste away once you get old.

Jenene asked him, "Have they been walking you?"

With a mouthful of fried potatoes, Herb shook his head no.

"Have they had you out of bed at all?"

He shook his head again. Without exercise, elderly bodies atrophy quickly. The doctor told her so. Jenene was shocked they had not walked him at all. She went down to the nurse's station to ask why not.

She confronted his nurse. "Why haven't you had him up and out of bed? You need to be preparing him to come home."

The nurse smiled uncomfortably and shook her head. "Oh no, he's going to die," she said assuredly.

"He's not going to die," Jenene replied coolly.

"This would kill a much younger man," the nurse persisted.

"You don't know him. He's not just some old man waiting around to kick the bucket. I promise you he'll live."

Having come up against this sort of medical skepticism before, Jenene tried not to let it faze her even as she was galled. She knew they were wrong…and Herb would prove it, but you couldn't tell them that, they would have to be proven wrong.

Incredulous to a fault, all week the nurses neglected to get Herb out of bed. Then the day came that they wanted to discharge and send him home. The cellulitis had cleared up miraculously, lo and behold, and Herb had regained his mental robustness if not his physical vigor.

Not one to take pleasure in gloating, it was for more important reasons that Jenene pointed out their obtuseness.

"You want to send him home and he can't even walk," she said, pointing out a huge problem they failed to see since they were so certain the undertaker would be picking him up. "I can't lift him and we don't have room for a second wheelchair—"

The stress put on her, the constant need to negotiate obstacles, forced Jenene to her wit's end and made her want to retreat into a cave. But what you want to do often doesn't coincide with what you have to do. She took her responsibility so seriously it was eating her alive. She had no choice other than to keep zigzagging and hopping.

"He needs rehabilitation," she said. "I don't think I can trust it will be done well here."

There was only one choice. Herb had to go to a nursing home if only temporarily. Jenene made arrangements. He needed to regain his strength before there could be a homecoming.

Herb was furious. As well as she hid it, so was Jenene.

Obstacles…

1990 was a hard year for a number of reasons. Fallout from Bill's death was still exposing us to the radiation of hate. Lal would suffer a stroke in September (to be elaborated on later). Herb got sick and had to go to a nursing home. And in the midst of it all, Jenene suffered that year's illness, a real humdinger called rheumatic fever. Yet another autoimmune disorder, caused by streptococci or strep throat bacteria, she became deathly ill.

Sore throats had become so regular Russ once observed, "You seem to get strep throat over the phone," which is not possible technically. Yet the notion fit Jenene's growing conviction her health was predicated on more than random exposure. The truth was she carried the bacteria for so long it evolved and reoccurrences of emotional distress caused several separate appearances before she was really walloped.

Rheumatic fever included all her joints swelling to ponderous proportions. Russ was forced to cut the wedding ring off her finger. Yet it was her heart that was in the most danger; oftentimes rheumatic fever is not even discovered until the patient has symptoms of heart murmur and heart failure years later. The damage is described as "insidious" and "permanent" and "progressive."

Oblivious of all that, all Jenene knew was that she felt rotten and had no time to be sick. Not when it separated her from the people for whom she was caring. Exposure to her could be fatal for those so old. The immune system only weakens with age. Her devotion had grown to almost obsessive proportions for the simple reason Lal and Herb had a limited number of tomorrows and she wanted to forge no regrets. The days away from them were worse than the intense pain in her swelled joints.

Treatment of rheumatic fever involves a course of penicillin or another antibiotic that can go on for months or years to avoid resurgence. Herein laid a problem. After so sickly a childhood, Jenene had developed an allergy to penicillin and most other antibiotics. Few worked for her, some caused horrible side effects, and those that did have a positive effect were very expensive.

In a bind, Jenene sought the counsel of Dr. Sandcastle because he was a family friend, knew the situation, and could be trusted to offer cost effective aid. Kindly and quick to assist, the doc listened to the mitigated circumstances. He thought on it and decided he would administer a course of what had to be uber antibiotics over the next five days.

Each day she made the expedition and took the shots genially. Dr. Sandcastle did not even charge her.

The injections were a bit painful. The fluid forced into her muscle was thick. What was pain? So long as she was improving, she had no problem gritting her teeth and taking it. She had watched her son when he was just a little boy good-naturedly endure a long-drawn-out allergy test that included first many "owie-owie-owie" pokes in the back followed by several "ouch-ouch-ouch" injections in the arm. Five shots were nothing compared to that, nothing compared to the rabies shots when she was pregnant. Still, each was one big "Ouch!"

Jenene was lucky. The course would work and the rheumatic fever would go away. Yet in the meantime her life would remain inconvenienced by another damn illness.

Because she was contagious Jenene was quarantined from the nursing home.

This meant only Russ and I could go to the nursing home. Those first visits were torture. The old boy was beyond miserable, disconsolate in the truest definition of the word. Never one to hold it in, he let rip with his discontent and had no trouble assigning blame. He had a list of demands. His ire was epic. I was scared for him. Fearful he would anger himself right into the grave.

Then from one day to the next there was a monumental change. Herb was suddenly…afraid.

This might sound like a bad thing. There was a good reason.

After we left the day before he made some aside about Russ. I'm guessing something really snide. At which point some friendly soul overheard what had to be a biting comment. Whoever it was recognized what Herb failed to see and laid bare the cold hard truth: my folks had no obligation beyond their caring for Herb to bring him home.

This good deed changed Herb's perspective and reordered his outlook.

All at once Herb understood. The sorry fate of scores of seniors, many who do not even get visitors, it meant something that we were committed to not leaving him to languish in a nursing home. Despite his ire toward them, my folks made it steadfastly clear their intent was to bring him home.

Dawning realization sparked fear his harsh behavior might make my parents reconsider.

The old man's eyes were wide and a little watery as he made his plea: "If you bring me home, I'll make my own meals, I'll do my own laundry, I'll make my own bed, I'll, I'll…"

Seeing him beg was a travesty.

"As soon as you're better, you're coming home," Russ told him. "All you have to do is get better. If you can do that, there's no reason for you to be here."

Herb did get his strength back. He did come home. And he never again bemoaned Jenene and Russ. Some old dogs can learn new tricks. He learned to be appreciative. He learned to be grateful. And he learned it was within him to befriend Russ, someone he had sold short for no other reason than he couldn't handle the upheaval in his life and needed to lash out at those he would learn stood between him and even greater turmoil.

Getting old robs us of many things. What it doesn't rob us of is our younger loved ones—if we don't push them away.

Jenene was able to miraculously and lastingly heal the rheumatic fever after a lengthy convalescence. Years later, testing of her heart would show none of the damage and scarring she had been warned could affect the rest of her life.

A couple months later on May 16 news broke the incomparable Jim Henson, creator of the Muppets, died from an illness borne of the same streptococcus pyogenes that cause rheumatic fever. She had known she was very ill. It was only then she knew how close she came to living up to her hypothesized expiration date.

Even if her downfall were to be by a sickness different than the one sure to kill her, that was one prediction she was determined to prove wrong in every direction.

Chapter 71
Lal's Stroke

A temperate September followed a hot summer.

I was out horse riding on a perfect day for riding. On the back of beauty in motion, you become an extension of something much more powerful than yourself. Clinging to a galloping horse, the hooves clopping rhythmically, the muscles working in tandem like well-oiled gears, there is a sense of incredible potency and freedom. Unable to be very athletic due to asthma, I was granted the sensation of running, the sun in my face, the wind in my hair, without risking an asthma attack...even if I took a header occasionally.

To truly enjoy the ride there has to be mutual respect between you and the steed. "Control" is only a toothless word when on the back of an animal so powerful. One that can choose to be defiant...and if not treated properly, will rear up; will buck; will even bite. Cupcake was an ill-tempered exception to the rule. Winning her over was next to impossible.

I had outgrown my volatile pony. Now I rode the more equable Heidi, a beautiful brown quarter horse with the capacity to outrun the wind.

When Jenene and Russ acquired her she was with foal. A birth was not to be however. Heidi developed a devastating infection in her withers aptly called *fistulous withers*. The hump above a horse's shoulders is the withers and an infection there meant she needed more care than we could give. Jenene sent for a vet.

The lady vet who came was young and wittier than you'd expect. She lanced the pus pocket above Heidi's shoulders. A discharge of pus-laden blood shot out when she plunged in the scalpel blade. The flood continued to spray for several minutes. The vet said in jest, "Go get an ice cube tray and some toothpicks. We'll make Popsicles."

Losing the foal was a sad event for us all. Heidi's recovery was all-important.

Once she regained her health I took Heidi out daily. I would ride and brush her, feed her apples and carrots. To some, horses may be little more than handy animals to bet on or walking dog food, but I learned that they have distinct personalities and, as

I pointed out earlier, can be temperamental, sensitive, really all the emotions people feel. We all wanted to help her get over her loss and this was my way.

Heidi liked to gallop uninhibitedly. Taking her out, saddling her, and clinging to her back as she set fire to the trail made her day and mine too.

After another exhilarating ride I was nearing home from a distance down Grey Cloud Trail.

Blessed with keen vision, from quite a distance I noticed what was soon revealed to be a collapsed figure lying prone at the foot of the driveway.

Intuition or simple deductive reasoning, I knew the truth even before my eyes confirmed it was Lal. Such a sinking and weakening feeling overcame me one jerk could've unhorsed me.

I pulled myself together and spurred Heidi into a full gallop. Her hooves boomed thunderously on the hard packed sand on the berm of the road, kicking up plumes of dust torn asunder instantly by our impassioned passing. With the alacrity of a racing horse Heidi closed the distance quickly.

Even though it was a cool day sweat sprang up on my brow. I veered Heidi toward the gate of the horse pasture beside the barn, dismounted, and sent her through the gate without taking off the saddle or removing the bit and reins.

I ran to cross the road and was almost taken out by a car making the curve. I stopped short, feeling the buffeting breath of the car's passage, mere inches in front of my face. The surprise of it stopped my heart for an instant. I had to blink kicked up dust out of my eyes to look both ways before crossing.

When I reached her, Lal looked so vulnerable and frail lying in the gravel the harsh sight made me feel sick to my stomach.

Even when I was unavailable to go with her, we could not stop her from going visiting. We tried to deter her but she was insistent on having her freedom. She had made many friends among the neighbors, so we could only hope she was with safe company and it had always been true.

Life became a slog for her after losing Bill. So much so her mind retreated more noticeably all the time.

I had no clue what was wrong. But I knew old folks have brittle bones. Just being on the hard ground could mean serious injuries.

"Lal, are you okay?"

As if she was not connecting she stared up at me dumbly. Her eyes were deep watery fissures. I could see she had no awareness of my identity; who she was; or why she was lying in the gravel. Viewing her that way, totally lost and adrift, permeated me with such a feeling of powerlessness I was stunned into inaction for the first and hopefully last time in my life.

I had no idea what to do because my mind emptied like a punctured basin.

Drawing my attention, crackling gravel signaled a car coming down the driveway. I looked up. Squinting, I did not recognize it as it thudded over the tracks. Jenene was thankfully inside. I had no idea why. As it turned out a passerby also saw Lal. She heroically drove up the driveway to raise the alarm.

When Jenene saw us, she said to me, "Go call 9-1-1!"

The obedient son, I snapped to and faster than I ever had before raced up the driveway.

Aforementioned running wasn't so much my thing. With asthma, the action gave me a lot of trouble. I often found myself wheezing and coughing whenever I tried. I guess being juiced on adrenaline contributed to why I wasn't out of breath in the least when I reached the garage phone. I wouldn't recognize the small miracle until later.

If I had a tail it probably would've gotten spinning so fast I took flight.

The adrenaline triggered by plain necessity made my hand shaky and my extended forefinger vibrate like a tuning fork as I dialed those three magical numbers that would summon help.

"9-1-1, what's your emergency?"

"My aunt, she's an old lady, she fell down and she isn't able to talk," I reported. I'm amazed I was able to stay so calm, cool, and collected under such pressure. Maybe losing Bill had tempered me.

To the 9-1-1 operator's credit, she never doubted the veracity of my call; I suppose I was so staid and serious it was easy to believe me.

"Address?"

The information spilled out of me in a torrent. I was a kid who knew my address, my phone number, my parents' names, basically everything I would need if I were to ever get lost…or worse, kidnapped, a fear that seemed to be a preoccupation of Jenene's.

I stayed on the line while paramedics were dispatched. Even stuck in place I could hear the approaching sirens. It seemed to take an eternity for them to reach us.

Lal survived but the stroke was disastrous.

Later on we can gain greater perspective and the hard truths can get easier to stomach. Now we know had Lal not pulled through her death would have been a mercy. At the time we were so thankful not to lose her. Despite her increased need for care, we were willing to make the necessary sacrifices.

This meant Jenene and Russ had to intensify their care, what was already more than a full-time job required even more of them and the toll taken would take years to recover.

Before long we knew the truth. Lal might not have lost her life but she inarguably lost something more. And we lost one of the finest, most superlative personalities we ever knew. The woman with whom we had conversations and baked pies and played cards was all but completely gone. Lal had vanished. There would be flashes. But for the most part the woman who lived with us after the stroke was a stranger.

Adulthood was lost irrevocably, as this stranger in many ways had the mentality of a quarrelsome child. She would have those moments of clarity infrequently and there would be a glimmer of her old self. She was mostly in a childish haze.

The lasting physical impact resulted in her left side being so weak those limbs were nearly useless. She had to be diapered. Even though she was incapable of walking she never quite understood why she had to be in a wheelchair. This meant at night she had to be restrained in bed because she could get up, try to wander, and collapse…or manage to get up to shenanigans.

In the wheelchair, she would pull herself around with shuffling feet and spread discord. Not only was she like a little kid, she was a bully. She would lash out and pinch. She would shut off Herb's TV and spirit away the remote. She would hide the remote and other things her grabby hands could grasp.

Once a home health aid doing an overnight missed her sneaking a paring knife. After a lifetime of use she was able to cut her way out of the restraint without causing herself injury. From there she managed to get her hands on a pan of brownies. As any out of control child might, she ate the whole thing. The diarrhea was horrendous.

Witnessing the rapid decline of such a respected and beloved family member, reduced to a doddering and mean old woman unable to care for herself, was the zenith of devastating. As Lal's body became shriveled and etiolated so did our spirits. But we refused to allow her dignity to be lost. We remembered Lal and recognized she earned our care. We will always remember her…even if in the end she could not remember us.

As upsetting as it was for Jenene to witness the assiduous ruin of a woman she loved so dearly, what was worse was being powerless to help her beyond seeing to her needs and comfort. All those who have watched a beloved family member get cut down by dementia has experienced the same feelings of frustration, sadness, and powerlessness, never knowing which moment of clarity will be the last glimpse of the person they knew.

Jenene would ask her every day, "Do you know who I am?" In the beginning, more often than not she knew; later, her responses became heartbreaking. She would say, "I know you're someone important," and worse, when she was really lost in the miasma of senility, "You're my mama."

In her final weeks she was confined to bed. The magnificent person we cared for so much, the woman who had always been dependable and full of love, was cut down cruelly to a grotesque shell and emaciated caricature of herself. She thinned so much, became so bony, her appearance frightened me. I feel guilty admitting it, but watching age despoil her mind and body gave me nightmares and might have given me a phobia about getting old.

Aforementioned, Bill's passing was more merciful for him and us; watching Lal languish pushed me through a hurried maturing process as I gained an ever-better understanding, changing me profoundly.

I realized wealth, prestige, and fame mean nothing even if in life they distinguish our individuality and grant real or imagined popularity. Because the billionaire Koch brothers won't be able to buy their way out of what they are quickly approaching. Because today's movie star is tomorrow's nobody. Because it won't matter who was elected what, who slept with who, who won the big game or the prestigious award. In the end, we all end up the same. Age is the great equalizer. All of us, if we live long enough, will be weak, frail, and vulnerable.

August 5, 1991 was the day Lal was freed from senility and old age by shuffling off the mortal coil. Jenene was out gathering products to make her more comfortable. She had been confined to bed for weeks. Time was running out. All we could do was offer soothing gestures.

Russ and an aid were with her in the final moments. A death without fuss, she passed quietly. After all she had been through, widespread loss so overwhelming it robbed her of everything, it means some fairness exists that she could die at peace in her own bed.

Even if we could not be there right at the end for Bill, it means everything that we were there for Lal and later for Herb.

I don't think I could face myself in the mirror had they died alone in some nursing home. Two decades later I sometimes have dreams in which I learn they have not passed away after all. They have been living in a home all these years. I am stunned and infuriated—at myself for abandoning them. I wake in a cold sweat. Those are my nightmares. Monsters and bogies and mind-bending psychedelics are the stuff of my sweet dreams.

There are no spotters and nets in life unless we prosper others to want to fulfill those roles for us. Lal spotted for us long before we understood what that meant. I'm thankful we were able to spot for her right to the end.

Even now every time we bake an apple pie, hang a sheet in March or April (those are the months she taught Jenene were best for sun bleaching), or lay out a quilt Lal assembled stitch-by-stitch she might as well be standing beside us.

Lal was a wonderful person with a first-rate heart, inarguable integrity, and boundless compassion. Sorting the possessions she acquired over her entire life bummed out Jenene.

The process reduced Lal to a bunch of stuff a mourning niece felt uncomfortable inheriting.

There were little surprises. Lal had kept diaries. Curiosity got the best of Jenene and soon she was reading.

That was when we learned Lal was a family record keeper. It would take some time for Jenene to get through the compact tomes. Lal wrote in a next to indecipherable chicken scratch.

Some of it was day-to-day routine of a young woman on a farm. Some of it contained fascinating and illuminating details.

Lal wrote about Gustav, her youngest brother. Sometimes not being forgotten can be the most important thing of all. In many ways, I feel the best way I can honor The Seniors is to immortalize them in words. The rest of the family seemed content to let his memory die, but not Lal. She had a brother, she loved him, he was special and unique, and he didn't deserve to be forgotten because he died tragically young. For her, I honor his life now.

If not for her diaries we never would have known about the man Lal loved. Jimmy was everything. The love of her life, the man she was going to marry. Then one day all she wrote was "my Jimmy went away." This was her way of writing he had died. It is safe to say she lived an abstentious life.

Lal never got to have romantic love after losing Jimmy, which means she was denied many aspects of life that can be so fundamentally fulfilling. Deprived of her own children, Jenene and I were blessed to be her surrogate kids. She deserved more. Losing the contribution of Lal's simple wisdom impacted us greatly. The diaries were a glimpse at how she came by her genuine kindness and devotion. And even greater revelations waited in Lal's diaries.

Chapter 72
Accessing Inner Knowledge

After working extensively with her personal deck and studying every book on Tarot she could find, Jenene decided to make a side business of readings. People she knew showed a lot of interest. For five bucks she would read your cards and do her best to answer your questions.

Giving readings helped her cope with the stressful and painful time. She "saw it as an opportunity to get some insight into what is coming, to help be prepared and possibly avert disaster." She also saw it as "a warning to take a different route if an accident was foreseen. Or make a different choice if jail was foreseen." She hoped she could help others to avert disaster while honing her skills and acquiring much-needed funds.

Jenene learned early that honesty is the best policy when giving readings.

To me this is what separates her from many card readers, who seem to want to tell their clients what they want to hear regarding romance or job prospects. In such a case, card reading is reduced to a parlor trick no different than a magic illusion in that it is a deception bought into for sake of entertainment. Jenene offers serious, truthful readings.

The experience that taught the importance of honesty to her has remained seared permanently in her mind. It was one of her earliest readings, for the mother of a friend.

Not long after Lal's death Jenene and Russ moved into her bedroom, freeing up the porch. After first using Bill's basement office, where he tucked himself away at night to pay bills or read, she moved her office out there.

The basement room was cold, gloomy, and spider-ridden. The porch was pine-paneled with two walls of tall windows. Bright and sunny during the day and the stars and moon visible at night, it was an environment more conducive to healing.

The porch was also better for readings.

An antique blonde-wood dining room table served as her workspace. On it she set up a layer system of bricks and boards to display the stones she had acquired, everything from citrine to amethyst and geodes to Lake Superior agates. The sunshine made them gleam and sparkle and even glow in the case of the mica or sunstone.

There were all shapes and sizes of clear bottles in which she had mixed stone elixirs; with windows on two sides, when the sunshine poured in, light would heliograph in the glass and crystals, lighting that whole end of the porch in prismatic rainbows.

There was a large granite ashtray on the table she used to burn sage that grew naturally on the farm. She had learned that "smudging" sage smoke cleared negative energy. She always burned some before doing a reading. The area was decorated not only with all types of stones but also Mandalas, dreamcatchers, a mauve moon made out of clay (a gift from Christel), sea shells, and other objects associated with what she had been learning…including the feather of an American bald eagle.

One of these grand, majestic birds had soared over our fields and left a feather as a gift. Collecting such a feather is only legal if acquired this way. When stores sell "eagle" feathers, they are selling dyed turkey feathers. The real thing was much longer, with a solid white quill pencil-sized at the thickest part where it tapered into a rounded point.

Jenene laid out the cards for her friend's mother. What she saw was terrible. Her husband was unfaithful. Jenene didn't want to be the one to tell the woman what on some level she had to know for it to end up in the cards. So she sugarcoated, and because she sugarcoated, the reading was inaccurate.

The oblivious woman was blindsided with the obvious. In no uncertain terms her man's infidelity was revealed and she was emotionally crushed. If Jenene had told her what the cards showed, the intensity of her pain might have been lessened. Even had the woman declined to believe her, the warning would have put the possibility in her conscious mind.

Jenene felt terrible. To appease her guilt, she knew there was only one solution. She could never sugarcoat again. Such deception, even a lie by omission, was too much when someone's wellbeing hung in the balance.

Honesty garners all types of reactions. Some absorb the truth and want to know more. Others want to be deceived; the truth only makes them uncomfortable. Before she was better able to read people, being truthful could put her in scary situations. Still, whether the cards showed good or bad, integrity dictated how she proceeded.

Even now she gets goosebumps recalling the night she feared her honesty would put her danger.

She was doing quite a few readings. Gaining confidence. This time she was in for a challenge. She was reading for a complete stranger for the first time.

All the research proved an asset because all but one of the cards has some negative aspect. About half have a duality. Some are just bad, even terrible. Like you never want to get The Tower. Death on the other hand, even The Devil card, is not necessarily terrible. But to what degree are some good and others bad? That's where interpretation comes in; she worked hard to finely tune her perceptions, so her interpretations could be as accurate as possible.

A regular referred her to a bingo friend. She knew virtually nothing about the man. He came to the farm one night. At the door she saw he was an average-looking guy in his late-thirties with a face not quite movie star handsome but quite good-looking just the same. Nothing about his appearance justified the instant bad vibe he imparted. Despite her reservations she perceived—hoped—he wasn't a threat. Nor was he hostile. Just off. Soon she would see there was good reason.

In case Herb or I needed attention, after bedtime she performed readings in the kitchen instead of the porch. So she invited him in. Guided him to the kitchen table. It was just the three of us that night. Quite a defenseless group if the unnerving man did decide to go berserk. Yet she felt strongly we would be safe. He came for answers, not to cause harm.

As it would turn out he was doing enough harm already and knew as much.

Jenene sat him down. Took a seat facing him and unwrapped the cards from a purple 'kerchief. She put them in his hands. Asked him to shuffle at will, explaining that the one being read handles the deck so they personalize their reading by subconsciously stacking the deck.

Jenene smoothed out the 'kerchief on the table. He handed her the deck. Making small talk, she laid out the reading he had selected from her small repertoire. When the reading began taking shape it became a struggle to keep her voice even.

Like seeing an oncoming tsunami wave, the message the cards presented wasn't good at all. The man manipulated and lied to avoid work and was spending up his wife's money. He was younger and she was desperate for love. He was able to extort anything from her and had thus far had no misgiving about taking every advantage. He even resorted to stealing her money and pawning her jewelry. Some real trouble could be coming his way.

Her foreboding was right. He was a bad guy.

Would calling him on his mischief set him off? His misdeeds were all over the reading. She had to make a decision right then and there. Her previous experience showed her she couldn't live down giving a dishonest reading.

A voice in her head told her to proceed.

She had to trust the outcome wouldn't be bad for her or us. She was no less scared of what sticking to her scruples and telling the truth might provoke.

"If the reading is accurate, it is," she said, hoping to defuse him before she began telling him that the cards painted him as a manipulative advantage-taker. Such an implication was in no way misleading because it wasn't for her to judge the truth of the cards. Letting him know she didn't necessarily believe what she was telling him served to make her a neutral entity.

That much less likely to be a source of blame, she felt secure to continue.

It was important to her he not think she was judging him because she truly was not—Jenene has always felt it is not up to her to legislate how people choose to live their lives unless they are a student intent on healing and give him- or herself over to her direction. "I'm new at this," she added, to feign a note of personal skepticism to sell fully the illusion she did not trust the cards entirely.

"That's fine," he said. "I understand."

So she told him everything. He was silent as she rattled off the entire reading. He had an overarching poker face—not a crease, not a twitch. The less he reacted the more nervous she became. She kept watching him, waiting for a crack in his veneer. But he took it all in calmly and spent a little time assimilating everything read. He enquired finally, "Can I ask a question?"

"Go ahead," she said.

"If I tell my wife I've been pawning her jewelry, will she forgive me?"

"Turn another card," she told him.

To her relief, and perhaps to his poor wife's ruin, the card said she would forgive him. In his heart of hearts, that's what he believed.

When he paid her, he said, "I've been to a lot of readers"—when he said "readers," he did the quote unquote gesture with his fingers—"and none of them told me the truth."

The bills were folded. She had no idea how much he had given her until after he was gone. She could tell it was a five and another bill. Oftentimes people would give an extra dollar or two as a tip. In this case, it was a ten. It made her feel good. Fifteen bucks at the time made a world of difference. She had been honest, told undesirable information, and she had been rewarded.

The subconscious already knows the answers, so all she can do, all she has ever done, is interpret.

Chapter 73
The Path to the Future

Stone energy and Tarot were perfect primers for the next step in Jenene's journey. After Bill and Herb's accident her health plummeted; when Lal checked out mentally it hit rock bottom.

Bob always told her it's not what you know but whom you know. Christel proved him right. First she introduced her to stones, Tarot, and Lacy. Then she took her to Llewellyn's bookstore for the first time. By the time Christel introduced her to Frank, an astrologer and healer, Jenene was ebullient with hope even as recognition of the illness sneaking up behind her approached.

Too much evidence was mounting to ignore.

Frank possessed the stoic mien of a Native American. I believe he had to be at least partially native, though we do not know for sure. He was a sinewy man with leathery brown skin and deep-set, darkish eyes. When we updated to a gas stove (boy was that a luxury, a controllable flame), Jenene traded the wood burning stove to Frank in exchange for astrology readings for the three of us.

Since the clunky old eyesore would have likely become a permanent fixture in one of the barns had she not traded it this way, a little rustier each year, you would think we got the better deal until you consider the value of safe heat. Ultimately, as to the value of the trade, another quantity would come to bear, namely that Jenene's reading would plant a seed of belief in her subconscious that flourished into an entire rain forest.

In the end the real exchange was one of life, heat for faith, and in that swap Jenene came out with an immeasurably valuable gift while Frank got a clunky old stove, so it may well have been the best trade she ever made.

Words that would prove clairvoyant, Frank said, "You will heal yourself…but not only yourself…you will heal others."

Unsure of his assertion, Jenene listened skeptically. It was a lovely vision, certainly, but could it ever be reality? When he got to the part where he claimed someday whole groups would come to learn from her, at the time an idea verging on laughable, she thought he was a little crazy.

Sitting there with Frank, Jenene shook her head and laughed disbelievingly. She didn't even have a name for the disease currently gumming up her life. All she knew was that how she was feeling was worse than the intraperitoneal adhesions, which seemed to loosen up after escaping her first marriage. Or maybe it was that the adhesions had worsened so much it was endgame time.

She said, "Frank, the doctors say I'm dying."

He looked her square in the face, deep into her eyes, and said, "They are wrong. You cannot escape…your destiny."

Frank's unbelievable predications have all come true—what he did next very well fulfilled his prophecy.

Frank was a practitioner of Reiki. A form of healing Jenene heard of but had yet to explore. To help her better understand this method of energy healing, he offered her a hands-on Reiki treatment.

Reiki is a form of healing that utilizes the healing energy all around us. In some parts of the world it is described as having "hot hands" because the flowing energy often causes the hands of the conduit to become hot and even sweat—without there even being direct contact. Some have described this as a form of stigmata.

"I couldn't feel it as he laid his hands on me but afterward I could feel the effect was great," she recalls. "I felt genuinely better for the first time in ages. I hoped the adhesions accounted for my escalating symptoms but I was afraid there was more to it. I was still dealing with degenerative disc disease too. Even then I was aware of variances in my body and I was worried there was something else going on."

The experience—the relief—would remain on Jenene's mind.

"Reiki hadn't gained any mainstream exposure, so it wasn't easy to find a Master to attune me. There was no World Wide Web back then to help me search. I doubted I could afford it even if I found a master. I knew Frank would probably introduce me to his but why ask if I had no way to pay?"

Jenene would bet her bottom dollar Reiki would help her with the overhaul and renewal she needed to undergo if she was to keep her life. Reiki prospered the best results no matter what they were and required no Faustian deal, no heretical bargains.

The notion of healing energy with no misapplication, no ambiguity, was heartening. It was effortless to imagine her best results, good health, steady incomes, even lives of light and color and humility free of disease and pain. She supposed the trick was to live in a way that precluded death from being the best results.

Reiki was a tool she needed to acquire…at some point.

In the meantime her bottom dollar was for the household; she felt it was not hers to bet.

More than a fellow traveler, Christel had become one of those fast friends easy to confide in because she had a level head and good advice. A trouble shared is a trouble halved, after all, and the young aid was quick with solutions.

Christel's influence diversified Jenene's exposure to so much, for instance introducing her to another oasis that would play a large role in her quest to attain Reiki. The Shop of Enlightenment was a joyous place where natural healing classes were taught, stones and crystals sold, and more hope could be found with every visit.

As wonderful as the Shop of Enlightenment could be most often Jenene was regrettably left window-shopping.

Differentiating them from regular rock shops was the unfortunate happenstance that they sold stones based not on weight and gemstone qualities but instead on healing properties, making their fare far steeper and largely unaffordable. The difference between the monetary worth of a crystal based on weight compared to properties can be literally hundreds of dollars. It may not have been daylight robbery but it was no less misfortunate the prices were so steep.

If there was no bargain route, in those days Jenene wasn't reaching the destination. When you live on a budget consisting of dust and cobwebs, instead of straight out buying the expensive healing stones you require, a less costly solution must be found. Jenene was prompted to become skilled at what distinguished crystals and stones as having healing energies and which ones were most suited to her purposes. That way she was able to obtain the best pieces wherever she might find them for prices far easier to absorb.

Fantastic stones can be found everywhere. Jenene has discovered some beautiful pieces, from mica to amethyst, at pet stores, curio stands, and in one memorable instance a butcher shop. Natural history museums often sell stones for a fair rate, too, Lake Superior agates and what have you, including fossils, which can run a little higher. We have even found beautiful stone beads at dollar stores. You can distinguish the real from the plastic by how they feel rubbed against your teeth or how they reverberate when tapped on a solid surface.

Perhaps Jenene's greatest acquisition was a gift from the universe and a lesson to always keep an eye open for incredible deals. In this case it would be at an estate sale that luck would shine a bright beam on her. She conveyed the story this way:

"I was walking around and noticed a box sitting under a table. I looked in it and what should my eyes see but a big piece of amber. It was huge, almost the size of a baseball. It was surely very expensive. I'd seen such pieces go for over two hundred dollars. But there was no price tag. In fact, looking at the other parcels it was with, I realized I had gotten it from what looked like a junk box.

"I took it up to the woman collecting money and asked her the price. She looked at it disdainfully and I realized she mistook it for plastic. Amber is very light and to the untrained eye such a mistake would be easy to make since the piece wasn't polished. After her negative appraisal, she smiled and said I could just have it. Knowing the value of the stone, I insisted I should pay something. She settled on twenty-five cents. I doubt she would've believed me if I told her what she had sold me had any value at all. The look on her face said she felt I was too naïve for my own good."

The priceless piece of amber would be instrumental in Jenene's healing.

So keep your eyes peeled.

Stones will find you.

Reiki will, too: as Jenene would soon find out.

When she learned there were going to be Reiki classes held at The Shop of Enlightenment Jenene assumed she should just forget it. The dang budgetary constraints running—ruining—our lives prevented her from doing something so "selfish" as shelling out hard-earned moola on herself.

Bills had to be paid.

The farm needed to be maintained.

A vehicle had to be kept on the road.

Each school year meant I needed new clothes, shoes, and other supplies.

And what unexpected expenditure would crop up next may have been up to speculation but with past experience as an indicator, it could be a lulu.

With bill collectors breathing down her neck and never enough money to keep them at bay for long, when Christel insisted she take the class with her, she tossed up her hands in frustration and said she couldn't afford the moderate expense.

"I'll pay," Christel said. "You need this. I won't let you turn me down. I insist."

Like Bill, it was always hard for Jenene to take what she viewed as charity. She wasn't even in a position to call it a loan. Steamrolling any opposition, Christel gave her little choice with her insistence it was an important gift, not a handout.

Taking Christel up on her offer was maybe the best choice of Jenene's life. She will be eternally grateful to her friend for bringing her to the path that would save her life. But then according to Frank, it was fate that Jenene would heal herself…and heal others. Such was a nice notion but not real when caught up in the realm of practicality. She was not yet ready then to accept that she could attain the ability to make herself healthy.

On a conscious level, Jenene may have found Frank's prediction—nay, assertion—laughable, but I think it is clear it made a strong impact on her psyche. When people discount or dismiss Reiki and other natural methods, I point out that if nothing else, Jenene's remarkable healing proves the incredible capability of mind power. Because what else can her healing be attributed to if not the methods I'm describing or her mind? Either way, her results are undeniable.

Though he was perhaps instrumental in Jenene's healing, we were unfortunately unable to know Frank better. Working on a roof, he fell and was knocked unconscious. Unable to provide himself with spiritual protection, from that point on, he felt haunted by a dark spirit that invaded his unprotected body while he was conked out. Plagued by the possession, Frank chose to take his own life.

People have questioned whether Frank was mentally ill. I don't think so. He did not endure a catastrophic head injury. Hauntings are real. Spirits can drive even a strong man with a strong spiritual connection and moral fiber to suicide. Which is why spiritual protection is so important.

Chapter 74
The Bridge to Health

On February 20, 1990, Reiki Master and fabulous lady Dee E. Millard attuned Jenene, signifying perhaps the most important step in her healing.

Reiki has gained popularity in recent years, even become a source of humor for cartoonists. Once obscure, Reiki has taken a foothold in the cultural zeitgeist and has become a subject that may not quite border on common knowledge but it will soon. That nowadays people often don't need an entire primer has made talking about it much easier. Back when Jenene was first attuned it was still largely unknown and mention would be met with blank stares.

The class had gone so fantastically Jenene and Christel emerged as if riding a wave of exultation. Jenene felt so invigorated it was as if she were literally lightened. Upon being attuned she was also filled with a sense of calm she had not enjoyed in so long she had almost forgotten it possible. It was as if the storm had calmed and the waters mellowed. She enjoyed the cathartic release not provided by her experience with primal therapy.

She may not have had a profound vision as some describe but that calmness was more than enough to validate the incipient experience.

Christel was behind the wheel on the highway home. The friends were sharing an animated discussion. They had learned so much and they recognized it was only the beginning.

"Thank you so much," Jenene said. "I never could have afforded it and I can already feel the Reiki helping me."

"You staying alive makes it worth it."

Their excitement was palpable but not so much of a distraction a sudden irresponsible occurrence went unnoticed. An aggressive merging car veered recklessly in their direction. Surrounded on all sides, and with no place to go unless a portal opened before them, Christel's knee-jerk reaction was to put both feet on the brake pedal.

The car kept going.

Christel steered with conviction. Somehow slinked through an automotive melee. Hanging on for dear life, Jenene saw how close they came to hearing the screech of metal kissing metal. Saw wide eyes belonging to those who were also aware of the proximity to danger they were in. They came mere inches from disaster, only just snaked through, yet emerged on the other side unscathed.

The amazing thing was that the car was a manual transmission. Hitting the brakes should have killed the engine. Yet the engine kept running…until they were beyond the ghost of a fender-bender that by all rights should have happened yet in defiance of physics was avoided. Had the brakes worked they almost certainly would have been in a serious collision.

Pulling to the side of the highway because her nerves were frayed, Christel said, "That was a miracle."

"We got through that by the skin of our teeth," Jenene concurred.

Mutually shaken but relieved, the friends headed for the farm.

To Jenene the close call was an omen of confirmation that she had done the right thing.

An experienced and wise Reiki Master, Dee was very intuitive. She sought out Jenene after the first class and told her, "You have a son who would also benefit from Reiki. I feel it's so necessary I'll come to your home and attune him for a reduced price." That was how at eight years old, I became a Reiki practitioner.

I recall vividly meeting Dee and liking her instantly.

It was in the safe familiar sanctum of the basement room that Dee told me the story of Reiki. I listened raptly, hanging on her every word:

Reiki has always existed but has not always been accessible to mankind. Through war, enslavement, and any number of human moral blunders, the knowledge of Reiki has been lost at different times. But like the Phoenix, the knowledge is always resurrected. Dr. Mikao Usui recognized that Reiki existed and through the mid-1800's researched tirelessly to learn of the mystical healing energy. His journey culminated in a twenty-one-day fast, during which he intended to learn the secrets that had theretofore eluded him.

Usui ascended Mount Kurama-yama to attain isolation in which to meditate. He gathered twenty-one stones into a pile. At the end of each day, to mark the passage of time he threw a stone, determined to stay no less than the twenty-one days.

Feeling as if he had gained no enlightenment, on the final day Usui beseeched the universe to grant him the wisdom he sought. Looking toward the sky, a ball of light appeared. Usui's first impression was of fear. Then, mustering his courage, decided it was better that he should be struck down on his spiritual quest than shy away as a coward. Upon proving his heart was pure, the ball of light engulfed him in the untainted radiance. The colors of the rainbow flashed across his eyes.

An authoritative voice inside his head but separate from his thoughts advised him to memorize a series of symbols.

Once Usui absorbed the gift the ball of light brought to him, blackness descended on him. Death? Eternity? Usui only knew of his fate when he awoke the following morning, reinvigorated, renewed, even reborn, as if he had been tempered into a new man by the events of the day before. After twenty-one days without nourishment, he was surprisingly in good health and felt no ill effects of the fast.

Usui threw the final stone and rushed down the mountain impetuously. In his haste, he stubbed his toe on a sharp stone. Felled, blood soaked quickly through his footwear as he held his hurting foot. The pain receded gradually as his hands warmed around the injured area. After the pain was negated, in fact conquered totally, Usui removed his bloodstained footwear and discovered there was no wound. In a few short minutes, he had used the energy directed through his hands to heal what he had feared would be a huge impediment.

When Usui reached the bottom of the mountain, he came upon a bench covered in a red cloth secured in the middle by an ashtray, which in the mountains of Japan signifies a place of food service. The server recognized that Usui had come from a fast and implored him to eat lightly, so as to not shock his starved system. Laying his money on the table, Usui ordered a veritable smorgasbord, an entire feast.

"You will harm your stomach," the server rallied.

"I know what I am doing," Usui assured. "Please bring me what I asked of you."

While he awaited the meal, Usui noticed a child connected to the home of the server. The girl's swollen face was wrapped in a rag. Usui called her to him and asked what relief she might have from her pain. The girl explained that the journey was too far and the price too steep for her to see a dentist, so she would have to live with the pain until the rotten tooth died. Suggesting it possible he could help her, Usui asked if he could place his hands on either side of her mouth. Willing to try anything, the girl allowed him to lay his hands on her.

Soon the intense but pleasant heat he had felt when holding his foot returned to Usui's palms. Before he had taken his hands away, the girl's eyes had grown wide. "The pain is gone," she said gratefully.

The server was so appreciative for what Usui had done he insisted on giving him the feast *gratis*. Usui thanked him. And commenced eating a meal that would give even the stomach of a sumo wrestler trouble yet gave Usui no indigestion, bloating, or pain, despite his long fast. Once he was satisfied, Usui resumed his journey home, to his monastery.

At his destination, Usui immediately requested a meeting with the Abbot to discuss his newfound illumination. The monks informed him the Abbot had been immobilized in bed for several days, suffering through a particularly taxing arthritis flare up, and would only see him if it was truly important.

Believing he had the perfect opportunity to show the Abbot what he had learned, Usui convinced them his reason for seeing the suffering man was worthwhile. Usui was able to relieve the Abbot of pain with his healing hands, proving the success of his fast. Enthusiastic about what Usui had learned, the Abbot encouraged him to figure out who would most be benefited by his discovery. Together they concluded the poor and destitute could gain the most from what Usui would soon call Reiki, for they could not afford medical care or even to be ill since their entire livelihood depended on the ability to earn a living.

In the shoddy raiment of a beggar, Usui went out into the world to teach the impoverished Reiki, intent on showing the have-nots how to better their lives with healing. He devoted years to his quest only to be confronted by failure in the form of students returning to begging rather than growing from and spreading Reiki. "Why?" he asked of them. "It is easier," they replied. How could they view the great power he had bestowed upon them so frivolously?

The futility lay in giving a valuable gift for nothing. Even a trinket can be valuable if desired, but even the greatest gift will mean little to one who does not earn it in some way. The physical side of the healing meant little if it was not built upon a foundation of spirituality and enlightenment. Usui decided he would never again give Reiki without an energy exchange, whether it were food or money or service. This way the gift would not be underrated and carry the value it deserved.

The Reiki lineage goes from Mikao Usui to Chujiro Hayashi to Hawayo Takata to Phyllis Furumoto to Dee Millard to us, so our roots are grounded firmly in the soil Usui sowed.

With the story of Usui swirling through my mind, Dee performed the first attunement of my life.

Radiance resonated in my being so enormously I felt immersed in warmth and love.

A long way from the kitten I chased around the barn, Clyde had grown into a tough, grizzled tomcat. He never purred. With a squeaky meow and a surly disposition, you were more likely to elicit a growl or hiss. Yet he was equable so long as you avoided agitating him.

When I laid my hand on him after my first attunement he responded instantly. I heard him purr for the first time ever. Not just a purr, a rumbling throaty reverberation radiating through my hand. Never before had he wanted to be loved up so much.

Clyde's reaction validated that something about my touch, especially from my palm, was now different. Then I went and took one of the most rejuvenating naps of my life.

The way Jenene utilized Reiki to tame her illnesses I utilized it to control the asthma robbing me of a childhood.

In a span of six years I went from taking handfuls of pills daily to needing no medication save for the occasional puff on an inhaler. At sixteen I learned second degree and, despite the assertion of my doctor, a well-respected and somewhat famous pulmonary specialist, the asthma would only degenerate, I outgrew the damage caused that day I aspirated vomit.

Reiki gave me a life.

It gave my mom a life too.

One month after receiving first degree Reiki, on March 22, 1990, Jenene was taught second degree Reiki and received two more attunements.

In most cases it would be inappropriate for a new Reiki practitioner to move on to second degree without first utilizing and becoming very familiar with first degree. When the person is very ill like Jenene, it becomes necessary to hasten the process. In Jenene's case, it likely saved her life.

Second degree involves learning three symbols and a formula that allow for absentee healing. Assembled correctly, the symbols can be used to send healing to any time, place, person, animal, inanimate object, or anything else under the sun. At the time she was attuned, Jenene had no idea how to maximize on this useful tool, yet incorporated the absentee healing in an attempt to control her symptoms.

One of the first events she sent to was my bout with La Crosse encephalitis.

Sending healing brings about the best results. This should not be confused with the results the sender hopes to bring about. Reiki does not allow for motives to play a factor in healing save for the decision of whether or not to send. Some students have grown weary of this distinction, not quite able to grasp that what is the best result is not always plain to see.

For instance, if someone were sending between them and a potential mate the hope is that the healing will foster the union, since that is clearly the best result from the perspective of the sender. Instead, the Reiki may work toward causing the relationship to fizzle out because it is not the best result. This can be difficult to appreciate, especially for the lovelorn.

At home Jenene found little support from her indignant husband. Even if it was someone else's money, why was she wasting it on some stupid scam? And why was she spending time away from home when he was stuck looking after *her* relatives?

The Headache could make him act like such a jerk.

"This works," she said. "I can feel it working. You'll see. Maybe you'll be ready to check it out yourself then."

"Yeah, we'll see."

Jenene explains how she coped and found solace:

"So thankful I was attuned to Reiki, degenerative disc disease was my first big healing success. It wasn't conscious. I wasn't putting my hands on my back, but on my solar plexus, which is a nexus for energy distribution. Within weeks of being attuned, the pain and tingly sensation had faded enough that I was able to sleep through the night again. And that was just with hands-on healing."

Had she gotten Reiki a year, or even six months sooner, it is possible she would have been able to stave off the next health hurtle. Reiki is an incredible panacea, but by the time she was attuned, Jenene was too sick and unknowledgeable of the power at her disposal to do anything but forestall the inevitable: she would need medical attention, evidenced that day in the restaurant bathroom when the white porcelain was stained red.

As if she had dug herself into one of the deep sand traps up on the hill, she was buried, unable to dig her way out, every attempt only making more sand fall in on top of her head—without help, she feared she would suffocate.

Chapter 75
The Real Enemy Outed

After seeing all the blood in the toilet bowl, Jenene was quick to make an appointment.

"Your symptoms," the doctor informed after a course of invasive testing, "are attributable to Crohn's disease."

That the doctor supplied a name to a disease she had never heard of before inspired feelings of déjà vu.

The denigrating day in the restaurant may have been the eye-opener Jenene needed to seek diagnosis. The haunting image of a toilet full of blood was powerful. But now that the cause had a name, it was somehow worse than the nightmares she feared. Not that she had much hope. She just thought she would recognize the disease this time, that there would be an established course of action even if it were radiation or chemo.

What was Crone's disease? She did not know the correct spelling and thought about old crones automatically, the sort of women who had big ugly warts growing out of their noses and hunched backs. Would her future entail warts and growing a hump and this would somehow kill her? How did that relate to her digestive system?

No beating around the bush, not unduly blunt but blunt just the same, the doctor explained the prognosis straightforwardly:

"Other than steroid treatment"—he failed to mention the hundred or so side effects, including psychosis—"there's little we can do other than to closely monitor your health. I won't give you undo hope; your odds of survival aren't good. With the number of ulcers in your digestive tract, you're a ticking time bomb. If any one of them perforates, you would likely die before you could undergo emergency surgery."

She felt like asking, "Is there any good news, doc?" But he wouldn't have gotten the dry humor.

Perhaps what was most offensive was his matter-of-factness, the assuredness in his voice when he made the claim she had heard before—that her days were numbered. He was so sure. They were all so sure. And she knew they were right. Her days were numbered…like everyone else's from the moment of birth.

"Since it wasn't my first death sentence," Jenene related, "I took it a lot better than when I threw the phone. They had already told me the adhesions would make it so I wouldn't see thirty and here I was thirty-one. I knew doctors could be wrong. And I had Reiki on my side."

Hearing her recount the day she would prefer forget I was struck by how immediate it was to her even after all these years. Such events are scarred into the psyche so deeply they always feel close.

It's hard to imagine what it would feel like to be told by a highly educated professional that a disease would end my life. Being told I would never be able to compete in sports or even participate in athletics due to asthma had been a blow even before I was old enough to truly understand the ramifications (in the school yard the asthmatic is often singled out as weak and gym teachers didn't give a squat).

"I guess I have another challenge," Jenene said.

"You don't seem to understand the gravity of what I'm telling you." Doctors need to remain in bleak reality. They see a lot of tragedy. If they give hope it can be proven false hope. I suppose it's really a trust issue: doctors want to avoid compromising their credibility by offering an outcome over which they ultimately have precious little control. That's why it's up to the patient to embrace positivity.

"What's not to get? I'm sick, really sick, and I need to do a lot of healing." I respect Jenene all the more for again looking a doctor in the face and telling him in no uncertain terms she was a survivor and her plan was to disregard his professional negativity.

"You seem less affected than I would expect."

"Am I supposed to beg and grovel for help you can't offer me? Either I will survive this or I won't."

"I think it's possible you're in denial," the doctor presumed. "I think you should consider therapy to deal with your feelings."

Therapy was an option but in her case she knew it was unnecessary. Her up attitude would only convince a therapist she *was* in denial. She understood the prognosis and its ramifications. She wasn't depressed about it, even if she was stunned she had accrued yet another devastating diagnosis.

Not that she was against counseling. She sought help for depression before. After Bill died and the bills were mounting, she needed to talk to someone and it would not hurt if a magic pill could soften some of the sharp edges in her life.

She approached Dr. Gaither. He listened to her story and agreed it was rough. Then he dashed expectation by telling her no magic pill would help. He told her she had real reasons to be depressed thus antidepressants would be unhelpful. Antidepressants are for people who have no reason to be sad and down, not those who are living a truly depressing life.

"Thanks for the advice," she said, knowing there was no point trying to explain her feelings.

With Russ at work and not at her side she felt totally alone upon departing the doctor's office. Brain a-buzz like an agitated hornet's nest, her conscious mind retreated into a sort of autopilot daze that got her home safely without the trip parting a lasting memory.

As soon as she was in the door a young home healthcare worker named Renelle asked concernedly, "Jenene, what happened?"

Not long ago her cherished friend would have greeted her but circumstances in Christel's life changed and she no longer worked as a home healthcare worker. Another of those situations where the impact of a newfound ally was huge compared to the short time they were in her life, Jenene missed her friend but understood life works that way, some relationships are destined to be transitory.

Other home healthcare workers rotated through, but not surprisingly none would approach the closeness of Christel or her immense contribution to Jenene's life. Meeting such a good friend under such circumstances was fluke or fate; either way it was immensely beneficial if fleeting.

Each new aid offered a fresh viewpoint but many were only interested in the most obligatory contact with our family. Some were even detrimental. One had an impulse control problem when it came to raiding the freezer for day-old doughnuts snatched from the hands of bear baiters. She binged so gluttonously she was asked not to return. We were sure each would remain a detached outsider until the current day aid, the cheerful Renelle, was assigned to our home.

Through Renelle's eyes and the eyes of the other aids we were able to see what we were doing was right—at least right enough.

Jenene was so disheartened by the elderly relative caregiver support group's lack of advice. It gave her that rudderless, free-floating feeling that accompanies being at a total loss. Not that she and Russ were doing a bad job. It was more a desire for experiential hints. Ways to make things easier and lighten the crushing load. With no such suggestions it was becoming obvious there were no shortcuts to lessen anyone's discomfort.

Due to what she had discovered was her "authority" on the subject, Jenene received an interesting offer but I'll get to that later.

Renelle had fallen in the quasi-friend circle of acquaintanceship: she was kind and willing to listen but in no way inserted herself in our lives the way Christel had. Maybe Jenene was leery to commit to another friendship. But having her there the day of her diagnosis brought her up a notch in Jenene's estimate.

"Jenene, are you all right? Tell me what you found out." Bespectacled, a little dowdy, and full of youthful vibrancy, Renelle was one of the pleasantest personalities who came through the house and I thought she was fantastic.

"The doctor said I have Crone's disease," Jenene unburdened. She was not looking for pity; throughout her ordeal, the one thing she absolutely did not want was pity. What she was looking for was understanding, maybe some information. "I know next to nothing about it and the doctor had nothing to tell me. Somehow I have to deal with it."

Renelle's reaction was less than promising. "From what I know about Crohn's, it's an autoimmune disease that ravages the body," she said somberly. "Besides ulcers on the inside, it can cause infected lesions on the skin. It can get really nasty."

"Wonderful. What else do you know?"

"Not much. All I know is that it's a difficult disease to deal with, very inconvenient."

Not boosted or bolstered, Jenene did what she always did when she needed more information, visited the library. What she found there was even less promising. In all the available medical books, she could only find one mention of Crohn's disease, which gave her the correct spelling but little else.

"It was like two sentences," she told me. "And there was no information Renelle hadn't told me. That was disconcerting. If the library didn't have any more resources, where could I get information? Now you can go online, type Crohn's into the Google search engine, and there are an infinite number of websites connected to the disease, from informational sites to online chat groups. Back in '91, there were none of those options. I wasn't comfortable going it blind, but I had no choice."

The one bright side for Crohn's sufferers today is that the disease is much better understood than it was even a decade ago. Diagnosed with Crohn's disease in the spring of 1991, there was virtually no literature on Crohn's available in America, nor were doctors very knowledgeable. It was often an automatic death sentence comparable to stomach cancer and remained that way for many years.

Instead of researching the disease as a whole, she broke it down into components and learned everything she could about ulcers and autoimmune diseases.

"I had to better understand just what I was facing," she reported. "I had to learn how to back down the ulcers. I learned jalapeño peppers were good for ulcers because they cauterized the acidy internal sores, so I began eating a lot of chips and salsa. That was one thing the doctor really hammered home, I had to keep my weight up. Every pound lost was a pound lost forever. They wanted me to only eat foods high in calories and to eat often. Suddenly it was like when I was pregnant again."

Easier said than done, food was a boon and a bane. There were several foods she simply could not eat without vomiting, especially pizza and chilidogs. She would eat candy because it was high in calories and not too hard on her system.

"Overweight by a number of pounds great enough I considered it a bumper, it seemed strange they would be so concerned about weight loss. I would learn why when I was shedding pounds a day with no way to slow it down. Even without medical confirmation, I knew I had the Crohn's in remission when I was able to gain weight back. That was another thing I was never supposed to be able to do, put on weight." Then she added with a self-deprecating smile, "I hate to admit it, but I put on more than I would have liked."

From the onset the Crohn's quickly progressed, Jenene bore the brunt, and as always life wore on. Sick or not, she had to be up at 6:21. Sick or not, meals had to be made on time, money earned to pay endless bills, and all the little needed tasks seen through to completion.

You might think buying a lemon sucks but consider if you had been bestowed a used body that was a lemon; she thought that wittily sad declaration of her dad's uncannily accurate considering her track record. Too often she felt in need of an overhaul: if only it were that easy; a quick stop at the mechanic, a little time on the lift, and she would run optimally.

All she could be was inexhaustibly strident in mind and spirit because her muffler was connected to a wrecked exhaust system and there was no way of installing new parts. What she learned quickly was she had to envision refurbishing her shot system because short of that there was nothing else to do.

She was beginning to have tooth problems because Crohn's stripped her of needed nutrients; many teeth would get pulled after infection set in. Her hair thinned even more: she continued to wear a perm because curliness always helped her get the most out of what she had.

Living with illness had its ups and downs and I imagine it was during a down, when the worry lurked right at her back, that she decided to tell me about the Crohn's. I had to be forewarned, prepared, given a chance to assimilate a possibility I found unbearable instantly. There were also the impending possibilities. Such grim ramifications made my ears recoil and my heart stutter.

"The doctors have told me I have a disease that could kill me," she said. "But I'm going to try really hard to stay alive at least until you graduate from high school, when you're old enough to take care of yourself."

The news was apocalyptic. I was shattered. I wanted to believe her when she said she would live, but I had seen the effects of the disease. Even as a child I had tracked its progress. The many trips to the bathroom, the inability to eat, the weakness, I had been seeing her decline at an alarming rate and I was terrified.

"What will happen to me if you die?"

None of the possibilities my mind manifested in any way consoled me.

"Russ and I have talked about it and he would like to take care of you."

Better than the other options, I asked what we would do and he suggested we might buy an RV and travel the country. Why not?

Just hit the open road and go where the wind blew us, the next locale as unknown as the previous one was before we got there, strangers wherever we wound up, nameless passers through, vagabonds, close with few other than each other, drifters ready to kick out the blocks and tie up our awning at a moment's notice, wandering ghosts haunting the highways and interstates, lost souls on an endless journey nowhere.

We would be wraiths of the roadway, on no quest but one of escape, fleeing desperados for the purpose that our pursuers would be regret, resentment, and anguish, and we would have to get a good head start and make a lot of distance. It sounded coldly, frostily, frozenly romantic; chilly consolation for hearts packed on ice.

Fearful as I was I could lose her at any time, from that point on it became a mission to be near my mom.

Bill's death was a lesson. Don't squander a moment. I could not remember my last words to the man I cared for deeply, which angers me even now because my memory is usually very good, and I made an oath to myself I would not be so unobservant, that I would always remember the exchange that was the last one I shared with my mom. To this day I memorize every possible last exchange with those I love—just in case.

I tried to be sensitive to my mom's pain. I tried my best to make life easier for her in any way I could. Around five years old I had shown an interest in learning to cook and, to her credit, Jenene started lessons immediately, beginning with scrambled eggs. Learning was all the harder because all my lessons were on an unevenly heated wood burning stove. By the time Jenene was committed to battling the Crohn's I was helping cook meals and feeling grownup for pulling assistant duty beyond washing and drying dishes, a task first incurred due to getting caught in a lie, an old family punishment.

Also to her credit, Jenene kept up a braver front than I ever realized at the time.

With hindsight I can put together a clearer picture than a child's mind can construct and can recognize keenly that never letting the Crohn's impede on her responsibilities was an incredible achievement. She ran herself ragged. Kept it up. Refused to slow down. For years we could not watch a movie as a family without her falling asleep, invariably at the big climax.

We couldn't blame her. She was overworked, tired, and fighting constantly.

So long as she was still kicking Jenene felt her failing health gave her no excuse to evade her responsibilities. At her sickest she never shied away from hard work.

Always questing after money for bills, Jeff hooked her and Russ up with a job cleaning vacated apartments. By now he was the general manager of several complexes in St. Paul. There were almost always turnovers in need of thorough cleaning. The pay made the hard work worthwhile.

On one of these jobs Jenene met a book editor named Mary R who Jeff had briefed about our life. Mary R suggested Jenene write a book about caring for elderly relatives. At that time it was an unfilled niche with a lot of potential. Our family had gained attention for that very reason shortly before Lal's passing when an article entitled "Caregivers Alter Lives " profiled our story in the Cottage Grove *Bulletin*.

Mary R claimed she would see to it the book was published. It just needed to be written. Jenene made a brief attempt, scribbling out about forty pages in a notebook.

Then the project was abandoned. She wanted to believe it was because she did not have time to write. Also that she had little to say other than to outline the mostly mundane, sometimes revolting, and infrequently rewarding life in which she was bogged. It seemed disingenuous to act like an expert when all she was doing was relying on common sense and her capacity to love.

Because what else was there? Did it make her a hero because she diapered Lal? Consoled the old woman in her aunt's body because her aunt had earned such caring even if it seemed she was long gone now? For Jenene it was just being. It did not distinguish her as in any way special. She was doing what she felt was right. Writing about it would make her seem high-minded—worthy—and she was far from that.

The truth was purer. Jenene felt too inadequate to write a book.

Had she the nerve—courage—to write the book and accept her value—and love herself—she would have been saved so much difficulty. But more growth was necessary before she could throw off the shackles of self-doubt and procure the freedom of self-empowerment. Feelings of inferiority are a universal plight.

So they kept cleaning, menial labor. The fast cash eased tensions while sometimes putting them in scary situations. One building included bathrooms in which the medicine cabinets could be removed creating conduits between units. Jenene never felt safe in those units; they were creepy enough to stir heebie-jeebies. Not too many years after, a popular horror film with a similar apartment situation would validate her trepidation.

Round about that time Jenene received a medical settlement payout, which was always a blessed event even though it meant some malfeasance had complicated her life. Investing much of the money back into the farm was pertinent to prepare the smaller parcel of land for sale.

To keep the money in the family, she hired Jeff and his friend to do an assortment of jobs, from painting the house to razing the barn.

Hiring relatives can entail problems. Familiarity bred laxness in so far as no task was completed before the next pursued. Jenene was fed up. No job was left unfinished when she worked for Jeff doing turnovers.

Confronting a family member can go any number of ways. A calm, objective conversation was preferable to a kerfuffle but either was possible.

Was the latter option inevitable? Two headstrong people facing off can lead to no good end when neither is amendable to bending, so it seems likely the instant Jenene called Jeff on his lackadaisical approach to the work she had paid him for the situation was going to devolve into chaos.

They were in St. Paul. She was there doing a job for him. A job she had finished, per their agreement.

Jeff offered some flimsy justification.

"My doctors tell me I'm dying and I still live up to my obligations," she snapped, for the first time revealing the extent of her health concerns. "No matter how sick I am I do what I have to do every damn day! What's your excuse?"

Jeff's reaction was a perfect example of how not dealing with death leaves a person unprepared to absorb the prospect of loss in a mature manner. Rather than be consoling or hopeful or even showing dreaded pity, all of which would have been preferable, he was furious. A smooth cat with no brook for wasting energy on anger, his personal ethos undertook a pole shift and he snapped at her, "So you're going to die on your son the way dad died on me!"

Turning his back on her, Jeff leapt into his 'vette and scorched rubber as he ripped out of there. Jenene jumped into her recently acquired Bonneville and pursued. No matter what evasive maneuver he employed in his high performance vehicle she paced him all the way to the farm. If his plan was to arrive far enough ahead so he could disappear into the barn before she caught up his plan failed. She was right there to take it to him.

The outburst turned into a rift; Jeff saw to it some of the jobs were completed while quickly arranging a supposedly permanent move to Las Vegas. Rather than face the possibility his sister was dying he chose not only to hide from it; he fled like a coward escaping a battlefield.

There was a valuable lesson about being guarded; also the circumstances under which she revealed her dilemma. Not her intent to scare off her brother, the words had spilled out in the fieriness of the moment. In such a turbulent instance, it could be construed she was using her challenge for maximum heft to win the argument. That was not her intent. A point was being made but not one about treating the sicky with kid gloves because she was "dying."

Jeff did move away…for a time.

Thereafter Jenene was more guarded. About opening her big mouth when it came to her predicament. About trusting even those to whom she felt closest. Life went on no matter what was going on in her world, after all. Burdening others served what? If they were not ready to listen, it meant nothing. Such things had to be gauged. Besides, maybe it was unfair to throw it around if she wanted no preferential treatment.

Hard for some to understand—there was a difference between being treated special and simple respect.

As a young boy with the mind of a child but the sensibilities of an old soul, understanding was fragmentary but there were enough pieces to assemble a workable representation of what was going on with my mom.

The warning of her possible demise resonated in the way few things do. Never knowing when the life I knew would go away made for a lot of uncertainty. Today I would be a wealthy man if I got a nickel for every time I worried about her.

Even if I was a little besieged, I was bolstered by my mom's ability to maintain a positive attitude. Even if her life was in threat of being dragged down by the inconvenience—and humiliation—of enduring painful evacuations, events that burbled up with no warning other than knowing the next impromptu blastoff was inevitable, she strived to live her life on her own terms.

Never was that more difficult than before she began taking control of her bathroom issues.

One story clearly emphasizes her dilemma. With a speed limit of 45mph, folks often zoomed around Grey Cloud Trail. This led to a tragedy when a neighbor backed out of her driveway and was T-boned.

The woman's car was turned over in the ditch like a bested tortoise. She died almost instantly. Before help arrived Jenene came upon the accident. Because she desperately needed to get to the bathroom, she had to pass without stopping to offer aid. She would put in a 9-1-1 call but would always wonder what might have been. To this day she regrets being unable to stop. No one wants to mess his or her shorts and it was a fear she had to face daily.

Constant witness to Jenene's battle, my hope was growing, pesky setbacks that would crop up aside. She had gone out and come back with a treasure trove of ways to heal and once she knew what she was facing the disease was more beatable. Some days she made strides; others she lagged.

There was a reason her gains were smaller achievements than she wanted.

She had her suspicions….

Guiding her, there were messages difficult to face….

She had to find out for sure.

Our subconscious ticks away in perpetuity and has figured out more than we could ever conceive of in our waking life. We are all reservoirs of untold wisdom if only we can make it accessible, which was where tarot cards came in…and pendulums.

Jenene had taken to asking questions of a fluorite octahedron attached to a chain, a simple but effective pendulum. It was a way to get fast answers from the subconscious without having to perform a reading. She began by programming the stone to speak; spinning clockwise would indicate yes, counterclockwise no. Then she would ask what she needed to know, such as: "Do the dreams mean I have to forgive her?"

Clockwise.

Of course….

It would take wisdom to heal, the wisdom of mercy.

As it would turn out a large part of her healing would involve doing something she had resolved not to do: forgive Roxanne Holmes. In the months since the conclusion of the trial, Jenene's bitterness toward the woman responsible for Bill's death had grown exponentially. Her anger was eating her alive, a living entity, like a swarm of fire ants, pinch, pinch, pinching her all over, never far from her thoughts.

Some breakthroughs, like pulling teeth, are torturous.

Chapter 76
Facing Death

If you come face to face with Death, is it better to stare into Death's face or shy away?

Jenene was so sick she had no alternative other than to face her mortality. There was no getting around the possibility—her doctors wouldn't quit reminding her. Everyone dies. We are mortal. Yet few truly accept that they are going to die. The concept is too unpleasant. When you face a life threatening disease, you no longer have the luxury of denial. When the Crohn's was at its worst, Jenene had to come to terms with her fears regarding death.

Do you fear dying? Does the thought of your own death bring tears to your eyes? A majority of people will face feelings of anxiety and fear and maybe even terror when diagnosed with a disease that could kill them. It makes sense because there is so much more that you want to accomplish and, of course, thoughts about other concerns such as what will happen to your children or your spouse or your pets flit through the mind and intensify the fear by dramatizing the importance you bear in the world.

What most people don't realize is that if we fear something, we are giving energy to it and the energy that we are giving will very likely draw our fear to us. But if we face our fear and conquer it, death no longer has energy and thus no power over us. Death and dying are pretty intense fears to face but only by facing them do we gain the strength to beat them.

If you are diagnosed with a disease such as cancer, don't ever claim ownership to it by referring to it as "my" cancer. Instead say "the" cancer. Claiming ownership makes it more difficult to shake that dog off your leg. Claiming ownership gives cancer energy.

"We waste valuable time and energy on either being worried or fearful," Jenene suggests. "What are we really afraid of? I learned to take the time to discover what my fears really boiled down to when it came to death. It was the only way I could face and conquer them. For me, my concern wasn't myself but my son. I wanted to make certain he would be nurtured in my absence. So I could leave him with some security, I found the life insurance loophole so at least there would be money. Other than that, there was little I could do…other than strive to survive."

I cannot laud my mom enough.

Dealing with her feelings tempered her into a stronger person, one that saw depression as pointless and nothing short of detrimental. How many people given an appointment with death the way she was meet it right on schedule? A simple answer is too many. To her it was as if hearing the hypothesis preconditioned their minds to cause them to self-destruct. The mind is powerful and suggestions from authority figures can root deep.

Denial can be an awful thing that leads people down painful paths. But it can also be a tool. Acceptance would have been death. By choosing to believe the doctors were wrong, that even if she had a deadly disease, it would not claim her, Jenene was able to survive what they assured her she could not. By choosing to see Crohn's not as a death sentence but an adversary to be defeated, she also chose not to buy into the concept of dying even as she faced her mortality. She accepted the inevitability of death and it freed her.

Even though there were many times she felt like she was dying Jenene chose to stare Death in the face and showed Death can be backed down.

What can be even harder to face down is the need to forgive. Especially when the face of forgiveness was Bill's.

Chapter 77
Facing despair

How much easier it would have been to give in, just give up and quit. Constant pain weakens even the strongest will; death would have been relief, liberation, and freedom, her spirit unloosed from a shoddy vessel.

It didn't feel to her like she was indulging or wallowing in a quitter's mentality; what drove her darkest thoughts was a last resort state of mind. When your body put you through prolonged rounds of torture, well, there's a reason the thumbscrew inquisitors got the answers they wanted even if they were lies.

In sports athletes push themselves to the breaking point. Marathon runners collapse feet from the finish line, boxers get stopped in the final round, basketball, football, and soccer players choke in overtime. It happens. No matter how prepared, how mentally together, or how great the desire to win, breaking points are reached and tripped over.

There's an edge we all ride at some point in our lives. When we're driven to the farthest reaches of what we can endure. Jenene rode that edge so long it became an effort for her not to let herself fall….

All of her anguish revolved around one character flaw. What it came down to was her inability to believe in herself. She couldn't believe she was good enough to do all that was required of her. Her foil proved to be her righteous sense of what was right.

Accommodating the needs of the Seniors was daunting but she refused to short them. Just keeping up with everything she needed to know was overwhelming. Their dietary needs and likes were individual. Feeling like at a certain age it becomes possible every meal could be the last, she wanted them to get what they wanted. That nugget in mind, foisting a meal upon them they didn't enjoy was something she wouldn't do, even it meant she felt like she was running a restaurant kitchen again.

Some nights the undulating pain in her core would reach a point it was so bad she would pray for death. She wouldn't ask for sweet release. She refused to beg for death. What she would do is say to the universe and any interested spectators, "If this is all there is, if this is how it will be until I die, just take me now."

Whoever might have been listening possessed greater faith in her prospects than she did.

Chapter 78
The Reward of Forgiveness

It was a gorgeous and perfect day, an ideal day to visit the beach.

The sunshine made the crispness of the scene vivid and clear; everything in the distance was limned in light, shimmery, granting the whole world a limning of brightness.

The blue-green water was lapping serenely on the shore, a sound easy to imagine was like fish making kisses. The sand was baked hot, but not so hot it would burn soles nor bottoms so long as a towel was laid down. The breeze was gentle and warm and insinuated with the marvelous scent of barbecue, burgers and hotdogs sizzling over red-hot coals, smoky and pungent.

On the edge of the beach up in the softest grass, Jenene lays down a colorful blanket, wary of ant mounds and dog piles. She looks down onto the stretch of sand and can see her happy son, frolicking with a group of equally blissful children, tossing around a beach ball, playing hot potato. She glances over and Roxanne is setting down a picnic basket, opening it to take out sandwiches and macaroni salad and potato chips.

Once all the food is exposed, they call for the kids at the same time and looked at each other, sharing a moment. They exchange a smile…and only then does it strike her exactly who it is she is with, as the kids fill up the blanket and begin gnashing. What is she doing here with Roxanne Holmes and her family? What could possibly have possessed her?

Then she sees Bill as he always was…standing beyond her enemy, there in the middle distance. He is in his pose, bent slightly and arms held behind his back. His all-knowing eyes look right into her with such gentle conviction. The universal wisdom of the ages resides in his eyes like embers in a furnace. Seeing him here, in appearance like he always was, a hint of a smile on his lips, chokes her with emotion. Then he tips her a nod, and in that nod his message is clear.

Forgive…or be devoured by anger.

Forgive…or risk forfeiting life.

Jenene snapped awake, restless and exasperated. Again. She had one of the dreams again. She took a deep breath. Let it out. She wanted to fall right back to sleep—all slumber was precious—but her whirled mind had been spurred into reflection.

The dreams had been plaguing her since she was diagnosed with Crohn's. They were recurring, always her and Roxanne doing some enjoyable activity, shopping together, horseback riding, and now picnicking at the beach. And Bill would always be there to give his nod.

Laying there in the dark, unable to reclaim sleep until her mind had time to cogitate, she recognized what Bill wanted. The sudden need to rush to the bathroom suggested she had to at least think about why it would be so important to Bill she forgive his killer.

On the toilet she conceded to herself that the dreams had been wearing down her resistance. Why was it so important to Bill for her to forgive Roxanne Holmes?

All she could think of was the lesson Bill imparted: good or bad, what you put out comes back to you. What goes around comes around. This meant he likely believed Roxanne's reckoning was certain. And Jenene's anger was wasted emotion.

Was she ready to make such a concession? Even wounds on the way to scarifying can be too fresh not to hurt. Life was too full of reminders of the absence left by losing Bill. Such reminders gouged into the healing wound. The more she hurt, the more she hated on Roxanne.

Why did it matter if she forgave the murdering bitch? She just couldn't do it. No matter how much Bill wanted her to, there was too much pain clouding her mind to grant forgiveness to someone she despised so much. She wiped and got the first clue of what she would see when she rose from the toilet.

The toilet bowl was full of blood.

It may have remained that way had Jenene not found Lal's diaries.

In her free time Jenene would do her best to decipher the chicken scratch. Too much of it was a chronicle of Lal's cleaning routine, sad insight into the monotony of her life; but some of it was interesting insight into the family.

Then she found an entry that would send her on the path to discovery that would end with a much deeper understanding of Bill's message.

Reading on the porch, she sat up straight in her seat and reread the passage she had just completed. The diary read first that Bill and Gramps were not back from a trip at the time they were expected. It was the next entry that perked her interest. It said Bill and Gramps were in an accident and two men were killed. That brief sentence was it. There was no other information. Not even in the forthcoming pages. She scanned several ahead, trying to glean more, but there was simply nothing else.

Jenene made a point of hitting the public library, intent on learning more. To the microfilm reader she went. She scanned many old newspapers. By the time her search hit pay dirt her eyes were beginning to blur every time she went to the next page.

The accident had happened in the dead of night six decades in the past. There was some object hanging off Bill and Gramps' truck. They were passing. The two young men were decapitated.

According to the newspaper, Gramps was driving, which Jenene knew was preposterous. The man never drove. He was incapable. He could not coordinate the shifter and the clutch. There was one reason he had a license. To obtain one only required paying a fee.

They had lied: but why? What were they covering up? All she could do was speculate that Bill was maybe drinking. A veritable teetotaler the rest of his life, preferring a Classic Coca Cola to a beer, it seemed improbable, but maybe there was good reason for his preference.

Shock could only explain part of what she felt. Bill was likely responsible for the deaths of two men. One revelation can make you reassess everything you ever felt about a person. She realized Bill knew his day of reckoning was coming and had known all along. After living the rest of his days as a resoundingly good man, to strike karmic balance he still had to make up for his misdeed.

Thus he forgave Roxanne immediately. The label killer and savior in this case walked paradoxically hand in hand. She freed him of a huge karmic debt, at the very least paid down his tab. And he was all too aware that she would now live with the brand he carried for the majority of his life.

With so much more of the big picture revealed Jenene recognized the smallness of her anger compared to the transference that had occurred.

Why couldn't she forgive?

Why couldn't she dig into her humanity and see Roxanne was a human being who had made a terrible mistake and was likely the sum total of an unenviable life? Her blasé attitude in court, prior to learning of her victim's impact on her life, was a reflection of immaturity and maybe a lack of coping skills. Maybe she acted that way out of denial. Who wants to face that their negligence took a life?

Jenene was taught a powerful lesson of mercy. In her heart she found compassion for the woman whose bad judgment cost us Bill. Why? It was the right thing to do. It was not for her to judge Roxanne. Bill had worked hard to show her Roxanne was a person too; a human being, and all humans are subject to quarks, foibles, and even mistakes. Besides, doers of harm are entitled to forgiveness if for nothing else than to free the grudge holder of hurtful emotions.

Since Roxanne remained incarcerated, serving her twenty-two months, Jenene knew where she could reach her.

In the letter she wrote, she expressed that she knew Roxanne had not set out that day to kill Bill—or anyone, for that matter—and that her life had also been destroyed. She wrote that she forgave her because she was only human and, remembering her reaction when she found out Bill's identity, she was the one who had to live with the guilt of her actions. She also wrote that she hoped Roxanne could forgive herself and move on with her life for her sake and the sake of her children.

It would be several years before she received a response.

Chapter 79
Talent Borne of Tragedy

Fall, 1991.

An unseasonably warm month preceded the record-breaking Halloween blizzard.

When the snow began to fall that October 31, it was wet and heavy. As the hours wore on and the snowfall continued, the temperature dropped and the sodden snow stiffened to solid ice. Because the plows had worked hastily and sloppily, large islands of what had been the consistency of slush became hard as concrete. This made the streets and roads slick obstacle courses. A car's alignment could be shot with one wrong move.

The blizzard raged, until the snow fences were not high enough to keep the snow from drifting across the driveway. The farm became a winter wasteland, all the trees coated in a thick blanket of ice, along with the powerlines, and the fields were rolling mounds of endless stark whiteness.

During and after the blizzard school would be cancelled for days but there was no fun to be had even after the snowfall tapered off. There was a hard crust on everything coated in fluff. It was too cold to make snowballs or dig forts. The loose snow was like powdered sugar, wispy and dry. If you tried to crush the snow into a ball it sifted through your fingers like granulated sugar.

In the midst of this a call came out of the blue from an old friend. After she and her family relocated to another state, it had been some time since Jenene had spoken to Dina. What should have been a pleasant surprise was revealed to be a plea for help. There had been a horrible disaster and Dina's parents were in grave peril.

The blizzard smashed the Dakotas before hitting the Twin Cities. Dina's parents lived in a mobile home in North Dakota. The storm blasted their area with such ferocity events transpired that caused their trailer to explode.

There was little detail at that point. Later it would be learned that there was a problem with the gas line. It had become encased in ice; the whole trailer was covered in hoarfrost. When the storm began it was above freezing. When the temp dropped all the wetness solidified and sealed them in a tomb of ice. Icebound like that, gas had accumulated over time. When the stove was ignited—ka-boom! The spark made the whole place go up in a fiery column. The blast shoved Dina's mother out and sucked her father Jethro in, nearly taking both their lives.

When Jethro staggered out of the inferno, he was a pillar of flame. He wobbled and reeled away from his burning home before falling in the snow. So thoroughly scorched, when his sons lifted him up out of the snow, his skin was left behind, frozen to the glacial ground.

Jethro was airlifted to HCMC in Minneapolis and his wife was taken to Fargo.

Dina knew about Reiki but was not herself attuned. "Jenene, can you send my dad healing," she pleaded, "just so he'll live long enough for me to make the trip? Please, can you try?"

"I can't make any promises," she warned. "But I'll send." She could only hope the best results would mean her friend got what she wanted.

Before this Jenene had largely sent healing to herself and those in her immediate circle. She could only expand her sending so much with what little time she had. She had never even met Jethro. She had no idea how sending to a stranger would work but after all Dee had taught her she had no doubt Reiki would help.

Not only was Jethro the first stranger she sent to, he was also the first person other than herself whose life was so jeopardized it literally hung in the balance. The notion she could help him cling to life never entered her mind.

Healing crystal clutched in her left hand, Jenene wrote out the symbols, treatment-by-treatment, hour-by-hour, covering a span long enough the sending wouldn't lapse before Dina arrived.

Jenene had no idea the effect the Reiki was having until after Dina was at the hospital and called with an update.

Just short of miraculously, Jethro clung stubbornly to life, though ninety-eight percent of the skin was burned off his body. Only his scrotum and the soles of his feet were spared. Dina had been told there was no way he could survive. The damage was too severe.

Yet his vitals were stable.

"Can you keep sending?" Dina requested sorrowfully. "Long enough my brothers and sisters can get here?"

There was so much going on in Jenene's life. She was overwhelmed constantly. And writing out the Reiki hour by hour was time consuming. But she agreed because she knew what it felt like to lose her father. Every free moment she could squeeze she would do more sending.

She promised her friend she would do her best. A mission of goodwill and learning, she was committed to living up to the obligation she had accepted even if it meant spreading herself even thinner. Sometimes she felt like a jelly packet divvied between every slice in a loaf of bread.

Despite her limitations, Jenene sent faithfully. When she said she would do her best, it wasn't an empty declaration. But the strength of one's word cannot always be lived up to, no matter how important, when so much impedes.

The blizzard made even the simplest tasks extremely difficult; made for a lot more work all around. About thirty inches of snow fell in two days. Wet heavy snow that froze solid. Russ was tasked with using the tractor to pull cars up and down the driveway lest they remain moored. The Twin Cities were veritably shut down. Jenene was amazed Dina was able to make the trips to the hospital and back without a ditch sucking her in.

Of course, Herb watched through the picture window and concluded the storm had nothing on the Armistice Day Blizzard.

In that he may have been right, but from Jenene's perspective the blizzard of '91 was making its own legend. The farm was slammed with such ferocity she was humbled by the unleashed power of nature. It would be in the aftermath, during the epic undertaking of digging out, that an oversight would happen. In a life so busy and tiring, slips can happen. She learned what it means when necessary Reiki lapses…and the lesson was harsh.

On the third day Dina made a frantic call. Her dad's temperature was spiking and his blood pressure was plummeting. She had one question: "Did you stop sending? My dad's dying!"

Jenene looked in her notebook. The healing had lapsed the hour before. She wrongly thought she was farther ahead. You can't always keep everything straight all of the time. "I'm so sorry," she said. "I'll sit down right now and send more. Let me know what happens."

Jethro again stabilized.

A few days later, a similar lapse occurred. When she already had a demanding life this sending was an intensive regimen. She reestablished the link and again he stabilized. Dina later told her that that second time, when his blood pressure improved, a male nurse in the room actually commented that someone had to be sending him Reiki. Jenene realized the Reiki was truly keeping him alive. Because she was sending, by extension *she* was keeping him alive.

Such a huge responsibility was more than she could handle. She had to do some big soul searching. She contacted her Reiki master for guidance. She explained the whole story to Dee and beseeched advice.

"It's kind of like you're playing God," Dee observed.

"I know," she replied. "I don't feel it's my place to be doing this."

"Your feelings are right," Dee told her. "You need to tell him this is it, this is the last you're going to send, so he had better use the healing to cross."

It was the eleventh or twelfth day after the explosion. The doctors and nurses were saying they had no idea why Jethro was clinging to life. There was no medical reason for him to remain alive. Recovery was impossible. His entire body would have required skin grafts. If not kept in an unconscious state he would have been in excruciation.

She went to the hospital and she used the symbols to connect. She sent it in an attempt to connect psychically, to let him know what she had decided. She went in the room but didn't get very close because he was in horrific condition. She tried to convey that he should use the Reiki to cross, there wouldn't be anymore.

Dina wanted to stay, so they hung around the hospital. A cop brought in a drunk who had been beaten up and Jenene unexpectedly blurted out, "I guess I won't be doing any more of that." She felt like a ventriloquist's dummy. She didn't even drink, not for years.

Dina looked straight at her and said, "That's something my dad would say."

So began the flow of messages.

For the next several hours, one-liners kept popping out; tidbits meant for his various children. Dina was paying attention and jotting notes.

Afterward, Jenene would remember little or nothing of the specifics. She learned while channeling she was a conduit, no more aware than a radio picking up waves. A totally new experience, she just went with it and let Dina gather the pearls Jethro was conveying through her. It was a long night. They got home in time to make breakfast at seven the next morning.

Later that day, with family nearby, Jethro crossed. Due in part to the Reiki, Jenene would learn later he ascended to the level of spirit guide.

After this enlightening experience, in the coming years Jenene learned not only how to channel at will using Reiki to forge a connection but how much more she could do if presented with a similar situation.

Jenene went away from her experience with Jethro profoundly aware of the amazing power of Reiki. Such insight meant a lot because she still had many healing obstacles of her own ahead. If a body so horrifically damaged could cling to life well beyond reason, why couldn't she heal an autoimmune disease like Crohn's?

"If only I knew then what I know now," she told me. "I think I could have helped him heal."

"Totally?"

"He would have been scarred—"

"You think?" I interrupted. "The poor guy would have looked like Freddy Krueger."

"But I think he would have lived," she continued. "I think he could have been functional again. Had somewhat of a life. If I had the information I have now."

"You would have been better able to connect to his spirit and communicate with him."

"Definitely. I would have been connecting with him and telling him to visualize growing back his skin, visualize putting on a wet suit of his own skin. I would have taken it as a challenge. Herb was able to grow back the skin on his back when the thresher stripped it off. I grew back my skin when that allergic reaction made it fall off me in sheets. Amazing healing is possible."

"That would have been a huge challenge."

"But not impossible, I think."

"After such an experience, it's surprising we didn't hear more from Dina," I said.

"That might've had to do with her family," Jenene said resignedly. "They were Catholics and they were calling me a witch and not being very nice."

"How did they even know about you?"

"Dina must have told them. It was wounding. It hurt because I was putting a lot into helping and it *was* helping. I sent to their mother, too. Thirty-five percent of her body was burned. This sounds crazy, I know, but I heard they were only using Crisco on her in the hospital up in Fargo. She wasn't out in time to see her husband before he died, but her recovery was so fast she was able to attend his funeral."

Chapter 80
Nature's Medicine

With today's best-selling drug Adalimumab (Humira) years from release, doctors had few pharmaceutical choices when it came to treating the Crohn's. Jenene was prescribed Prednisone, a corticosteroid. The drug controlled the ulcers by stopping the bleeding. The problem was the terrible adverse effects, including steroid psychosis.

Jenene was certain the steroids were physically helpful. The problem was that the sort of large dosages she needed played hell on her mentally. All of sudden she was deeply depressed. The long-fought battle was useless, pointless, and not worth waging. She was ready to lay down arms and surrender.

For this to happen to a spirit that had been so strong, a spirit that had been so unwilling to relent, demonstrates the deleterious effect of the steroids.

One night Russ pulled in the driveway after work to find her sitting on the railroad crossing.

"I'm waiting for the next train," she informed him.

The steroids did what the disease could not, sapped her of hope and made her court death. Russ had a hard time convincing her not to take her life. It's impossible to convey just how out of character this attitude was other than to say it was tantamount to the Pope renouncing Catholicism.

In the end, Russ used me as a lynchpin to convince her to leave the tracks without force.

Jenene weaned off the steroids immediately. This left her with only the little purple pills, which had no noticeable effect. This meant she was at the whim of the Crohn's—constant vomiting, sharp pains, and dehydrating diarrhea. Notwithstanding that there would often be blood in her stool and vomit.

After the attempted suicide, a doctor I will not name because they are due their right to confidentiality, suggested Jenene consider trying medicinal marijuana. He or she thought it might help her eat and keep down food. Later, after Jenene testified on behalf of medical marijuana, this doctor went so far as to say if it were legal to do so he or she would prescribe ganja gladly.

Jenene took the suggestion graciously and went about her life. What lingered in her mind was something the doctor told her about HIV/AIDS patients. Marijuana helped them get an appetite. Murder keeping food down, the notion of having an appetite again was more than appealing; it was imperative if she were going to survive.

Had she not met Darrell through a mutual friend it might have ended with speculation.

Darrell had severe cerebral palsy. His legs were small, shriveled, and useless; this meant he was confined to a motorized wheel chair. He required an aid to help him with all tasks, including getting him in the loo. His mother was an alcoholic. With her unable to care for him, he was left to fend for himself at sixteen.

A firm believer in the benefits of medicinal marijuana, Darrell smoked to alleviate appalling fits. Much later he would get a prescription. Tremors could wrack his entire frail frame and go on for hours. Marijuana helped him keep control. Without herb he was left to endure unrestrained shakes.

In those days, when his dealer was out, he was like an infection sufferer waiting for antibiotics. Getting sicker by the day, by the hour, sometimes by the minute. His life was tortured without marijuana. It did not grant him euphoric highness; it granted him a measure of normalcy. Allowing him to live his life, even to start a business geared toward helping the disabled.

Of course Darrell agreed with the doctor's assessment and suggested Jenene try a trial run to see if smoking helped her. It was not as if Jenene was unaware of marijuana. She had smoked recreationally in the past and preferred the buzz to alcohol. The problem was the illegality and the expense; it was not exactly covered by insurance.

"Had it not gotten to the point it was all but impossible to hold down food," she insisted, "I never would have went that route. It was a risk to my family. I really didn't want to do that."

Darrell's experiment proved fruitful: Jenene was able to eat and hold down her meal. A rare feat, the marijuana's effect was almost miraculous. In the days that followed, eating only to vomit, an involuntary bulimic, it was difficult not to yearn for the relief she had when she smoked.

She made a hard decision.

She would use marijuana as medicine. Smoke only to perk up her appetite and avoid nausea. Like Darrell, it did not get her high. What it did was calm her tumultuous stomach. Able to eat, she could slow the weight loss.

Marijuana in no way healed her (although evidence has emerged it fights cancer), but instead acted as a palliative that awarded her with enough serenity and tranquility to heal.

Without it, the process would have been much harder.

We in no way encourage or advocate marijuana use without prior consent from a doctor. This is merely an honest account of Jenene's healing process and I would be remiss not to mention it, especially since it led to her testifying before the state for the legalization of medical marijuana, a fact easily attained by a hard nose willing to dig around.

Jenene was honest with me about the marijuana. She told me it was illegal but it made it so she could eat. She told me if anyone found out, it could be used as a reason to take me away so I must never tell anyone if I wanted to stay with her.

I asked her why it was illegal if it helped her.

She didn't have a good answer.

I would learn it was unjustifiably vilified when it could be used to alleviate the pain of people sick like my mom because the government had arbitrarily decided it was bad. She told me it was not appropriate to use it as a recreational drug because it has a tendency of causing indifference and laziness. Yet she also floated the opinion that alcohol also wasn't a very appropriate recreational drug since it tends to make people violent and quarrelsome.

I asked why one was legal and one was not. Jenene said she didn't know how it worked out that way.

Due to Darrell's connection to the movement to legalize medical marijuana, Jenene was asked to testify at the Minnesota state capitol before representatives of the Food and Drug

Administration. When she asked why, it became apparent it came down to her coming across as a good poster girl for the cause. She was articulate, a mother, and a caregiver.

Jenene recognized the importance of the push for medical marijuana. Ganja helped her so much. But she was afraid exposing her use would open her up to ridicule and trouble. It was a hard decision. What if it put up red flags and the police began watching her? Foremost and above all else her biggest fear was that the information would be used to take me away. There was always a fear my dad would contest the custody status and use of an illegal substance would be just the fodder he needed.

In the end she took the risk because she truly believes in marijuana's benefit to the chronically ill. Without marijuana facilitating her healing, allowing her sporadic but well-used relief from pain to devote to meditation, visualization, and targeted healing, it seems too likely she wouldn't have had the reinforcement necessary to keep overcoming obstacles and winning battles.

"Testifying at the capitol was one of the scariest things I ever did," she reminisced. "It's hard to even remember it very well now. It was sort of like a nightmare and I was up for inquisition. I do remember I was in a lot of pain that day, one of the few times the pain could be used to my benefit because I was clearly sick. I looked pale and worn out, which was exactly how I felt."

Fear besieged her when she entered the capitol building. Her only conciliation came from the fact that she was one of three testifying, so some of the attention was deflected off her.

As soon as she was allowed to speak, she asked if she would be arrested after testifying. Assured she would not be, she was able to calm down but not so much as to diminish that the experience was in some way traumatizing. This was due primarily to one figure. "I don't remember his name. You could just call him Mr. Scary. He loomed over me, this large, robust man, and really came down on me with questions."

Mr. Scary's first question was whether or not Jenene's doctor would prescribe marijuana.

At that point her doctor had counseled her to self-medicate as needed, but had never specifically said he or she would prescribe it. If a legal option, I think this indicates that her doctor would have prescribed cannabis, but Jenene wouldn't assume anything and sought clarification later, realizing she should have beforehand.

Under immense pressure, she found the question tricky. Maybe it was nervousness that made her feel on the spot. She is a woman who values herself based on integrity and ethics. Those who know her feel her word is gold. She rightly holds herself above reproach—I know her to be incapable of spinning a lie, even the white ones most of us pass off frequently. She couldn't say yes even if no was not the correct answer either. All she could say was that her doctor would do what was appropriate, but that marijuana was suggested as treatment.

Jenene was asked a litany of questions.

I do not have a transcript of what was asked and answered; all I can go on is Jenene's memory, which is somewhat fragmented. During that period of time she was only beginning to get a handle on the Crohn's and was still under tremendous stress.

All she could do was answer honestly. And hope her testimony was beneficial to the cause. There were several severely ill people counting on her to make positive points in hopes that a victory would be won and marijuana would be legalized for medicinal use.

There were several inquisitors. Of them all, Mr. Scary asked the most questions. A pervasive presence, his questioning unnerved her continually because he seemed antagonistic in tone and manner. She began to feel like he was hammering her with questions, trying to break her down, to trick her into saying something harmful to the movement.

Under his withering gaze, she kept her stride and answered forthrightly and with the conviction that was keeping her alive. Equate keeping bleeding ulcers under control to a car tire holding air despite a visible hole and you have an idea of what she was dealing with every day of her life. Her conviction kept her from losing her cool or misspeaking.

Here's a recreation of some of the questions Jenene was asked and her answers:

Inquisitor: Do you get marijuana from people you know or strangers?
Jenene: Both. It's a catch as catch can sort of thing. It's all about availability. If your regular person is out, you have to get somewhere else unless you're willing to wait. When you're sick,

waiting isn't an option. Not when life goes on whether you can hold down food or not.

Inquisitor: Can you name someone you get it from?

Jenene: No, I cannot, as that would compromise the person's right to anonymity.

Inquisitor: How did you come to use marijuana medicinally?

Jenene: After my doctor first broached the subject, a friend who also smokes for medicinal reasons suggested I experiment with him to see if it brought me relief.

Inquisitor: How far would you drive to get it?

Jenene: Within reason—I have a son and I do not like taking time away from him. I've gone pretty far, though. And to places I probably shouldn't go, bad neighborhoods, where there are dangerous people, people with guns. I don't want to and wouldn't choose to, but when you need medicine, you go where you have to go to get it. Sometimes I get there only to find out someone is trying to rip me off by selling me oregano. Usually when someone tries to con you that way, they won't take no for an answer and get threatening. It can get very scary. It makes me wish it were regulated, so I wouldn't have to expose myself to danger just to get relief.

Inquisitor: Do you go alone?

Jenene: Usually, yes. I don't want to take my husband with. What if we were caught? Who would take care of my son?

Inquisitor: Where do you get the money to buy marijuana?

Jenene: It isn't easy. I won't take food out of my son's mouth. If I can earn extra money, I spend it on marijuana.

Inquisitor: How much do you pay?

Jenene: It's inconsistent. The price goes up and down the way the price of fruit does. It's all supply and demand. If there's a good grow season and not too many busts, the price goes down.

Inquisitor: How much would you pay?

Jenene: It depends how reasonable the deal. I wouldn't pay a high price for poor quality marijuana. I would pay more for better quality marijuana, but prefer to pay as little as possible for marijuana of good enough quality to achieve what I buy it for.

Inquisitor: Is the quality consistent?

Jenene: Not at all, it would be wonderful if there were regulation. Sometimes there are a lot of seeds and stems, other times it's bunk picked off the side of railroad tracks. There are a lot of people who try to rip off marijuana users. Sometimes inferior marijuana is dusted with chemicals to give it value. If I were to receive such marijuana, it wouldn't help me at all even if it would cause a buzz. I don't do it to get high. I do it for relief, from pain and from vomiting.

Inquisitor: How is your life with it?

Jenene: I am able to live. Life doesn't stop because I have to get sick or have pain or need to frequent the bathroom. Whether I lose no weight or five pounds a week, life goes on. I have many responsibilities and none of them go away when I need a break. Smoking marijuana grants me a little relief because I'm able to eat without getting sick, sleep without getting woken from pain, and most importantly back down the Crohn's disease.

Inquisitor: How is your life without it?

Jenene: A misery. If I can't eat without getting sick, I don't retain nutrition, and the weight melts off me at a startling rate. My doctor always reminds me that every pound lost is lost forever. The malnutrition has weakened my teeth and caused some to fall out. I feel weak all the time and can never seem to catch up on sleep. Without cannabis, all my problems are worse because I retain less food, get even less sleep, and get constant Crohn's flare ups.

Jenene was relieved when it was over; it drained and exhausted her, but she had made her point and felt validated. Maybe in the end the cause would be vindicated.

She was surprised when Mr. Scary approached her and no longer presented himself as a combatant. In fact, he thanked her. It was pointed out to Jenene later, and in hindsight she was able to see it, that his piercing and seemingly critical questions coupled with her honest answers made a progressive and persuasive argument for the cause. He thanked her and said that he thought her testimony would help make changes.

Lifted up as if onto a cloud, Jenene felt she had struck a blow to those who outright condemned marijuana without understanding the natural benefits. Of course medical marijuana was not at the time legalized in Minnesota—despite Jesse Ventura's endorsement—but it was still a victory for Jenene. She stood up and spoke out for her beliefs and felt empowered.

And today medical marijuana is legal in Minnesota to a degree.

Boosted, she was all the more inspired to speak her mind and gave a speech before the FDA outlining many of the points she made at the capitol. It didn't matter that medical marijuana wasn't legalized. The personal victory was good enough.

When Jenene gained total control over the Crohn's and the symptoms receded like waters after a flood, she quit using marijuana for many reasons, among them the expense and the illegality, but primarily because she no longer needed it. As she always maintained, it was medicine.

Of the three asked to testify that day at the capitol, Jenene is the only one alive today.

Chapter 81
Jenene's Daily Healing Routine

Jenene developed three daily routines she religiously followed after assembling her healing toolbox. This is how Jenene described her routine to me:

"Weekday mornings I would get you off to school and go lay back down. My life at last afforded me such a luxury.

"That was the best time of day to suit my purposes, a calm, quiet time. I would smudge with sage to cleanse the room of negativity, as I always did in advance. Then I attached my piece of amber to my solar plexus with a bandage wrap.

"First I would totally relax my body. I would say over and over, 'I am happy, I am healthy, I am terrific.' I had been saying this simple affirmation since my twenties, when I was first diagnosed with the adhesions disease; it was almost a personal prayer, a mantra. I treated all affirmations as a mantra, saying them repeatedly to really drill them into my subconscious.

"I used hands on Reiki and bumped up the energy by sending symbols through my palms. Sometimes I would just rest and let the healing flow. But I would often visualize.

"The main visualization I used was simple but powerful: I would see myself as a worker inside my digestive tract—my stomach, my intestines—and I would have a paint can full of Reiki and a big brush. And I would just picture myself painting all the ulcers with healing. I would spend a long time visualizing that way. A doctor had given me a photo after a scope of some of the worst ulcers, so I could target them specifically and picture painting them with healing. I would meditate and concentrate on seeing this happen, and of white light spreading through my being and healing me from the inside out.

"On a physical level, another way I sought relief, as mentioned before, was by eating corn chips and salsa. I had read jalapeños were good for ulcers and decided to take it further with visualization. I visualized that they actually cauterized the ulcers. It was one of the few foods my stomach was generally willing to accept.

"The next routine I liked to get done before you came home from school. I needed to be standoffish and isolated to properly concentrate. I would drink a mug of tea, a healthy tea, usually green tea. I was not as knowledgeable about tea at the time but I knew that it was good for what ails you. I would sit up, in Lal's rocking chair. I would concentrate on being calm, on being healthy, on being healed. I would say another affirmation: I am pain free. I would send symbols and visualize.

"The last routine came before bed. At night I would do more affirmations because I felt like they pervaded more deeply into my subconscious. 'I am pain free. I am ulcer free.' It felt like my guts were being ripped apart. I would do this for long periods of time, until I felt relief. Then I would meditate myself to sleep.

Amidst all that I would also take a daily shot of apple cider vinegar.

By being faithful to my healing, I was able to stave off the Crohn's while dealing with major stress and begin winning the daily battles for my health."

Chapter 82
Another Goodbye

"The ulcer is right now perforated," the surgeon reiterated, in some respects browbeating Jenene yet doing it in the interest of his patient. "We have limited time. We need to operate or death is imminent."

Herb's most recent hospitalization began with another infection, this one in his leg, only to reveal a graver emergency.

Since he was obstinate as ever, the precipitator of it all was his insistence on keeping his extremity too close to the space heater. He was warned repeatedly. But the old farmhouse was drafty and old bones chill easily.

Of course he had scratched at the burn sore when it tried to heal…with the fingernail he used to dig around in his snuff, opening up the wound and once again creating the perfect place for a brooding infection to take hold. After the whole lower part of his leg reddened and swelled to twice its normal size there was no choice but to hospitalize him again.

The stress of the ordeal caused an ulcer in his stomach to perforate. He never complained about pain. Although he must have been agonized for some time, we had no idea he even had an ulcer. So in one respect it was a blessing in disguise since the ulcer could have perforated at a less opportune time.

But there was a problem....

Since he was by no means a doddering old man, although she was his proxy, Jenene could not say—would not say—Herb lacked the faculties to make his own decisions. And Herb, as cantankerous and headstrong as ever, was refusing surgery.

"I can't just make the decision for him," she persisted.

The look the surgeon gave her would sour milk. He didn't understand what a demonstration of disrespect it would have been toward Herb to say he was mentally unfit.

"Then you need to convince him," he said. "I cannot stress enough how little time he has."

"I already tried—"

Standing back quietly, Russ said, "I may be able to get through to him."

Hard alliances can make solid friends.

Russ' income was paramount to our fiscal situation. Between the stress at home and The Headache, he struggled to keep employment. After gravitating away from trash hauling, he went through a long transitional period during which more often than not he was out of work. After Lal's passing, he crawled out of the employment rut to apply for a job as a home healthcare worker. He won a position.

The true benefit of the new job was that he was assigned to our home. For the best wage of his life up to that time, his job was to take care of Herb. He was doing essentially what he had been doing since we moved in—only he didn't have to work outside the home to bring in a paycheck.

Russ taking this assignment coincided with Herb's epiphany. To our surprise and his, Herb's newfound positive outlook meant the two men were able to develop a deep bond...a true friendship based on mutual respect. They found common ground. After all both could be stubborn. Inflexible. Even mean. They could also show the rare moment of tenderness.

Building a rapport with Herb as he cared for him day in and day out, Russ was in the rare position of being close to the old boy in a way that fostered insight and wisdom. Their improved relationship put Russ in a position to reach Herb in a way Jenene never could. He had an idea of how he could appeal to him on a psychological level.

He approached Herb in the hospital bed. Pulled up a chair. Sat close enough that he could lean in. This put him on an even plain with the mulish old man.

When he sensed a figure hovering above Herb's eyes fluttered open. His toothless mouth was set in a stubborn frown. Pain glazed his eyes. The perforated ulcer in his digestive tract was so painful even heavy narcotics couldn't dull it completely.

"What do you want?"

"You told me you wanted to die at home," Russ said simply. "Is that true?"

"I wouldn't have…said it…if it wasn't," Herb said gruffly.

"Well you're not going to," Russ declared as if that was it, there was no way around it, the decision was made, all letters had been sealed and mailed.

The old man's eyes widened. Little struck anything akin to fear in Herb—after all the man had been manhandled by a thresher and flung through the air by an Amtrak—but the idea of never again going home came the closest to terrifying him.

"What do you mean?"

"If you don't sign this piece of paper so they can do surgery you're going to die right here in this bed," Russ clarified. "Because they won't let us take you home in your condition. You understand? They won't release you. You'll die right where you're lying right now."

Herb signed.

That's the thing about friendship; once you know someone on that level, you can find the words to break down their barricades.

Waiting rooms during surgery are chambers out of time, existing in some other where, realms of interminable waiting, every minute elongated and stretched to a point of absurdity. When the surgeon came in and said, "The patient is doing well," the relief was indescribable.

Although it was a touch-and-go operation, Herb recuperated enough to come home, achieving his final goal, so he could die in the place he had worked so many years, where he spilled his sweat and his blood, and the place he loved in his way. Within a week of coming home and despite a miraculous recuperation, he was dead.

The thing of it was, Herb always claimed he was going to live to ninety, a ripe old age that would beat out the rest of the family he had watched die off like flies in the fall. He was eighty-nine when he passed in bed quietly. No matter how many times we told him, he simply would not believe his age. I think his insistence had to do with his desire to reach ninety and his tiredness after losing his siblings; he was ready to die then, not in another year. He had already outlived everyone from his time.

Other than that quark, his mind was sharp as a tack until the day he passed—December 1, 1992.

With him we buried his copy of *Dan Patch*, a tin of snuff, and his favorite wash brush.

Chapter 83
An Amazing Moment

Russ was still the master of the occasional gesture, the act of kindness or charity—an unexpected foot rub, the gift of a rose, doing a difficult chore—that reminded Jenene there is something more between them than a legal document sporting their signatures.

The lesson I have taken from witnessing this is that when someone loves you, even the small gestures have a huge impact. In my marriage, I'm going for a record accumulation of small gestures so my wife will never be discontent.

In early 1993 the band Foreigner was touring in honor of their fifteenth anniversary. The tour brought them to the Twin Cities. Anyone who graduated in 1978 was entitled to a ticket for a mere five dollars, in honor of the year the band kicked off. Since Foreigner was one of their favorite bands and Jenene graduated in '78, they took the opportunity to see the St. Paul concert.

They looked forward to hearing their song. When the concert concluded without "I Want to Know What Love Is" being played, they were disappointed.

Always one to whoop it up and to get others to join in, Russ led an initiative to coax the band into two encores. During the second, he yelled out his request.

"Play 'I Want to Know What Love Is.'"

"Sorry," the band's lead singer Lou Gramm replied. "We don't have an orchestra tonight. We can't do it without an orchestra."

"It's our song," Russ yelled right back. "Can't you do it for my wife? It would mean a lot."

"I don't know," Lou Gramm said. "It's really not the same—"

"It will sound great to us."

"I guess I can't argue with that."

Foreigner played the song.

Chapter 84
Back to Work

You ever hear that expression, from the fry pan into the fire? It seemed like there was too much of that in our lives.

I cannot verify that the big dude who charged out of his house brandishing an electric screwdriver and a maniacal expression of infinite disbelief that we would dare violate the sanctity of his mailbox was crazy. All I can say is that I moved as if he was an escaped mental patient intent on using the electric screwdriver for more than tube removal. He roared, "I don't think so, [expletive]."

A twelve-year-old softie (or fat wimp as my peers loved to point out), the sight of this man thundering toward us triggered a fight or flight response.

Opting for flight, I looked at my mom in the driver seat. Eyes wide, she said, "Take off the tube!"

Moving like those people you see in videos escaping avalanches, the ones in which their legs actually seem to blur, I did my best to defy physics as I reversed the screw I had just planted. Even as I tried to conduct supernatural energies to aid me, the world switched over into slow motion and the image of my hands trying to guide the Phillips head into the screw slot was an instant of intense suspense. In the scale of time, it only took seconds. In the scale of the moment, time ceased to exist and it felt like it took far too long.

I dared not look up. Even from a distance I had seen the dude's eyes. Violence was far too evident for me not to at least be a little afraid.

Pulling the tube back into the car, I shouted, "Go!"

We screeched away as the disgruntled homeowner reached the street. Waving his arms passionately, as if conducting an orchestra, we were spared his tirade by burning rubber.

This man was ready to have a coronary over the idea of a free press newspaper attaching a tube to his mailbox. Crazy. Now I understand why he might be perturbed but at the time I was boggled.

The next address was only a short distance ahead. Jenene kept going. Turned the block. We would return after the furious grizzly bear returned to his den.

"That was close," I said. "I guess we were lucky he had a power tool and not a gun."

"Better cross him off our route list," Jenene said without a hint of irony.

Jenene had to work despite the ever-present impediment of Crohn's for one reason. The impact of Herb's death coupled with her illness was too much for Russ to endure. He spiraled as The Headache took control and the pain prevented him from having what it took to hold a job.

Drawn to delivering papers for ADX because they offered latitude other jobs did not, she required a job with flexibility. When she needed to use the bathroom there was no debate. Struggling with Crohn's symptoms was a brutal slog.

Carrier of a short-lived free press newspaper, ADX was trying to wheedle into magazine delivery. Besides being mildly amusing and gratis, the paper was sometimes accompanied by cereal samples.

What many discerning readers might be wondering is how Jenene, after losing her kneecap and learning she had crippling degenerative disc disease (not to mention a medical five pound weight restriction), was capable of delivering slings full of papers on foot. The answer she gave was simple: you do what you have to do to mind those you care after. Wow. Based on her level of caring, she had no choice other than to ignore her supposed handicap.

Besides, by her way of thinking Jenene's health was beginning to improve. Despite—or due to—shying away from the walking talking depressants known as doctors. Did that mean she wasn't throwing up most mornings? No. But she was seizing control; she could feel it in her bones, her blood, and her cells; she was improving all the time, if only minutely. Momentum was on her side even if the day-to-day achievements were sometimes imperceptible. Nothing could convince her otherwise.

Her positive outlook made it possible to hold her head up high even if possible humiliation waited around every corner.

Meanwhile I still lived under the fear that she could at any time drop dead. Not because I did not believe in her. I did believe. But because I was a kid scared of losing his mom.

The idea of her out delivering alone, when I felt her health was in such jeopardy, was simply wrong. Russ may not have been in a position to help, but I could. I had my own job, walking dogs for a local kennel and doing lawn work. I still made time to help as often as I could.

At least we did not have to be out before dawn like the deliverers of major newspapers.

We would do several routes, some on foot, some driving. The driving routes were better. We didn't have to approach homes. Although when we were doing a driving route for the first time, such as we had been earlier that day, it was incumbent upon us to attach an ADX tube to everyone's mailboxes. The dude with the crazy eyes and the electric screwdriver wasn't the first displeased homeowner we had encountered.

Much to both our relief delivering routes out of necessity turned out to be temporary. The coordinator of the warehouse in Woodbury recognized Jenene was capable of more than schlepping papers. In short order she was promoted to a warehouse position. A born climber, it was not long before she was coordinating her own warehouse in Little Canada, then the area's largest depot.

Diseased or not, she was as Herb might have said full of "piss and vinegar" and determined to excel. Being in a managerial position offered better wages without restricting the autonomy she required for bathroom breaks. Jenene was in her element in the position. From her time in the Nite Club's kitchen she was an able manager. And from her time with her dad she knew how to talk to people, how to deal with them on a level of understanding.

The majority of her employees were loyal to her if not the company. She took the time to know their names and what was going on in their lives. Knowing them certainly made her better able to convince them to take unfilled routes, less she feel responsible for delivery herself. But she liked many of her people genuinely. Many were illegals that could fake their way in, and not only the stereotypical Mexicans either but many Russians too. This meant the occasional INS sweep could decimate her crew.

For Jenene's part, she took good workers at face value.

Soon after she was promoted to the larger Little Canada depot. Something about her always made it seem as if a reputation preceded her. Because she took no guff she was known as the "Dragon Lady" well before she arrived.

She learned of this descriptor from a subordinate—while he took back the notice to quit he tendered to avoid the "Dragon Lady," explaining he enjoyed working for her after all. As it turned out they got along so famously they are friends to this day. Being the "Dragon Lady" was a distinction she was proud to hold. It meant her employees knew she was no pushover even if she was personable.

Employees who did their job got the kindly Chinese dragon; those who did not got the fire-breathing European dragon. Either way she tried not to be too scaly. If you got the fire she wanted you to know it was for an understandable reason.

Even supposing she only delivered the occasional unfilled route, Jenene still found herself out in the field when suspicion arose that routes were getting dumped.

When people failed to deliver, it meant product was being disposed of…somewhere. If we were dishonest, we could have stored years' worth of papers in our barns. Once all the tires were hauled away room was ample. We even knew the secret: if you delivered the magazines you could probably get away with paper dumping since no one was ever clamoring for the free rag.

So Jenene would put on her investigator hat and find the discarded papers. Which led to me traipsing through the woods—shovel in hand, regretting the choice of shorts because dang near every ankle-level plant had thorns or spines or needles—on the quest to solve another not-so-great mystery. On this occasion, there was a tip to check a patch of woods in a particular public park.

The refuse littering the ground seemed to lend credence to the claim. The place was a dumpsite one way or another. Jenene took the lead. She had a good nose for sniffing out "misplaced" papers and worse, dumped magazines. Customers miss what they pay for and that was flack Jenene was adamant to avoid.

In short order we exhausted our search. It seemed we were the victims of a false lead. The wooded area was not very large and we had covered the entire space with a grid search. There were no obvious dirt patches indicating a recently dug hole or stacks of hastily discarded papers.

Led by a feeling, Jenene said, "We'll check one more time." That trek through Jenene noticed a difference in a patch of ground. It was pliable, almost squashy. "Give me the shovel."

There in the ground Jenene unearthed the mother lode. Someone had gone through a great deal of trouble to camouflage the place where they buried several routes worth of papers. They might as well have done the routes for all the exhausted effort. Others took the easy path usually and ditched their routes in dumpsters. Note: it was always preferable to catch them there, before we would have to dig through the landfill.

I took a lesson from the situation. It stunned me what someone would go through to avoid earning an honest buck.

It would be over her loyalty to her employees that she left the company. Management decided to make the deliverers independent contractors, which effectively cut their wage and benefits. Fit to be tied, Jenene refused to convey this message and gave her resignation. Fearing a revolt, her notice was preempted and she was paid off to leave the premises immediately and have no contact with her former employees.

Despite the inauspicious end to her time at ADX, the job showed her what she was capable of, how much she could endure. It was also the period during which she was able to gain a great deal of control over the Crohn's. When she began as a deliverer, she had backed down the pain but still needed close access to a bathroom at all times. By the time she left, she had few symptoms and felt strong enough to pursue another career opportunity.

As for Russ, the Headache became a constant excuse to disengage from life. The only thing Jenene could do to help was to encourage and offer him the knowledge she had learned.

When he complained, she would say, "When you're sick and tired of being sick and tired, come to me and I'll help you. Until then I don't want to hear about it anymore because it isn't constructive. I'm sick and tired of watching you suffer when you won't take my help."

Even though he was witnessing firsthand what had become her amazing convalescence, he remained resistant. His stubbornness derived more from fear than doubt. The agony of The Headache was terrible, debilitating even, but was it worse than facing the reason for The Headache?

A known pain can be less hurtful than one unknown. Solving the mystery of why The Headache plagued him would mean facing immense emotional turmoil. On an instinctual level he knew such a reckoning would be necessary.

It took the thundering pounding in his head reaching a crescendo before he was ready to face up.

The day he reached the point he could set his reservations aside Russ called Jenene at work and said he was ready.

From there he became a Reiki student; getting attuned changed his life forever.

Jenene stood by him for every step of the journey, equal parts counselor and cheerleader. She was tickled at his change of heart and direction and the fast results that followed only validated her techniques. Russ had a difficult lesson to learn. The pain stayed with him for nineteen years because he was too stubborn and afraid to learn the necessary wisdom.

And his sense was right.

There was reason for his evasion.

The Headache was a manifestation of survivor guilt. It was not the lasting physical impact that caused the pain; it was the subconscious belief he had no right to have a life since Corey lost his. What did the pain do? It robbed him of any kind of life. There was always that nagging voice in the back of his mind suggesting all would have been different had he chosen to drive.

Different had he made any number of decisions.

That it was his fault—his fault his friend died.

The constant underlying feelings of guilt left him a shell of a man, wracked by ruthless pain. Even though the ongoing ramifications controlled his entire existence, in his day-to-day life he infrequently thought of the event.

Once he accepted the unchanging nature of what had happened, how it was decisions made by them both that led to the accident, absolving him of feelings of sole responsibility, the acceptance lifted The Headache, never to return.

Sometimes you have to fumigate your mind and soul of damaging thoughts, unhelpful patterns, and destructive misbelieved personal untruths before moving forward with a productive life.

Postscript by Jenene

By climbing my way up the ranks in ADX, I was able to find my stride in the world at the same time I was finding my stride with my health.

At a time it meant a lot to me I was offered a field coordinator position in the warehouse. It meant even more when I was promoted to distribution warehouse coordinator. I wrote the job description. It all happened faster than I expected. It restored confidence. Maybe gave me confidence I never had. It meant more money. More responsibility.

I made myself do more than I thought I could.

The distraction and the exercise were good. I couldn't be as faithful to my healing routine, but I always tried to make time to meditate, to visualize. Working really helped me feel better about myself at a time when it was extremely important that I learn to trust I was good enough to do what needed to be done in any situation I might face. Had I not learned that, the Crohn's probably would have killed me.

In my next job I would learn a lesson about compromising my integrity.

Chapter 85
Full Circle

I spied the pair first.

Making their way up the driveway on foot in the wavy haze of heat baking off the driveway, they began as dark silhouettes dashed with sunshine. Strange visitors were usual enough I was not surprised at their appearance. I watched from the front step as they approached and became visible. Realized they were women. Closer yet I saw both were svelte and had blond hair. One was older, in her early or middle thirties; the other was a teenager flirting with adulthood.

I did not have the foggiest idea who they might be.

Maybe their car broke down and they needed to use the phone. Cell phones had yet to reach the prevalence of today so such visitors were common out in the boonies.

I waited for them to close the distance.

"Is Jenene home?" the older one asked upon reaching me.

Interesting. Should I know them? I wondered. Recognition was just outside my grasp even if they did seem...familiar.

I nodded and said, "Just a minute." I went inside to retrieve her. "There are a couple women here who want to talk to you."

"Who are they?"

"I have no idea," I replied.

I was curious to find out and followed her back outside. We were both in for quite a shock.

"Roxanne," Jenene said the instant she saw the woman who had spoken to me.

Realization was instantaneous and my interest increased exponentially.

"Hello, Jenene," she responded, hesitantly. "I don't want to take up your time but can I talk to you?"

Jenene invited her to stay and they powwowed right out on the front step.

I stuck around but acted disinterested. I still could barely believe the woman was Roxanne. I conjured her face, captured in court, and compared it to the face of the woman sitting on our step.

The years, including her prison sentence, had aged her. Her face looked plainer. Lacking the luster of cosmetics. Her hair was shorter and courser. It was as if she shucked some vanity and accepted she was past her preening days. Seeing her again, I wondered if her children had hated her when she went to prison.

I listened with vested interest as Roxanne explained what Jenene's letter meant to her. "I didn't open it for weeks," she said. "I was afraid it would be filled with hate. A part of me felt I deserved it, too, all the hate you could heap on me. I hated myself. But I was afraid to face it. I had to really work myself up to open that envelope. I held it and held it between my palms, debating if I should have someone else read it or just throw it out. When I finally opened it…"

Roxanne choked, swallowing back tears.

"I was so surprised. I never expected…"

Jenene consoled her one-time nemesis, encouraged her to go on, to purge herself. By that time Jenene had compassion for her. She understood the karma she had brought on herself with regrettable—avoidable—actions.

"I wasn't able to forgive myself," she continued. "Not after I really realized what I had done. Then I had these kind words in my hands. I expected blame and I got forgiveness. And encouragement. I hadn't thought it was possible to come back from what I did. I had gone into a shell. I never wanted to come out. Your letter gave me hope again: enough to come out of my shell, enough to begin forgiving myself, enough to make the commitment to be a better mother. I came here to thank you for that."

"It took me a long time to forgive you," Jenene said. "But I knew Bill wanted me to release that burden from my heart. He was just that kind of man. If anyone should get credit, it's him."

"I used to stop by to see the horses," she confirmed our long suspicion of how she had known Bill. "He would come out of the barn and talk to me. He was my friend."

"He was a lot of peoples' friend," Jenene said. "He would be tickled to see us here. He never held it against you. He knew it wasn't personal. Just a terrible coincidence, two paths meeting at the wrong place at the wrong time."

"I was so messed up then. I've been clean a long time now. I plan to stay that way. The whole thing…it really sobered me up in a lot of ways."

Isn't that what it always comes back to, lessons?

Listening to Roxanne, in my mind she was transformed from the demon that had killed my favorite uncle into a fractured human being for whom I too felt compassion. I was able to respect that she had made it so Bill's death wasn't in vain in her case. It meant so much she was conscious of the impact of her crime and felt huge guilt: that her self-forgiveness was not complete even if Jenene's letter had granted her the ability to seek it and the courage to try.

"I read your letter until the words faded," she said, emotion brimming in her quavering voice. "The paper absorbed so many tears it got soft. It eventually fell apart. But I'll always remember the words."

Forgiveness is powerful. It helped replenish Jenene and rehabilitate Roxanne. Even though she had taken someone very important to us, in forgiving her, we were able to give not only her but also ourselves something more precious than money, almost as precious as Bill: mercy. In feeling merciful toward her, we gained a better understanding of what it means to be human.

Chapter 86
Lessons

In the mid-90's Jenene made a breakthrough in knowledge that has only in recent years come to full fruition. She found books that taught her how illness, injury, and even addiction are connected to "issues" we must address in order to balance our health. Fascinated, the notion we bring on our own problems—meaning we have the power to solve and/or avoid them—got Jenene thinking.

Before long she began to believe in a slightly different view of "issues" because it seemed there was more to it than accepting she had an "issue" and saying some affirmations. It seemed something had to be learned to truly overcome, so she began tweaking what she had gleaned through thorough research and began calling what she had come up with "lessons." No doubt owing a debt to her research material, as well as her healing angel, who I will get to later, she has nevertheless assembled a personal book of lessons separate enough from existing works to be her own.

Through her research Jenene continued to learn more and more about disease, illness, pain, and injuries being linked to emotions, to the mind.

In our humble opinion, disease, illness, injury, and even addiction are attributable to lessons. A lot of people don't want to hear they invite their own physical and mental problems but as Jenene and I have learned, it's true. It's only when you face up to your lessons that you can heal anything. In my case, this knowledge has meant I have not needed to see a doctor in fifteen years. In Jenene's case, this means she was able to heal diseases predicted to kill her.

What's our proof, you may ask. To that I reply:

How is it that bar revelers across the nation can be tossed off mechanical bulls with enough violence to shatter bones but walk away mostly uninjured while actor Christopher Reeves was crippled by a fall from a horse?

Why within six months of diagnosis do some people go into remission while others die from cancer?

Why do the infants of healthy people who do not abuse drugs come into the world with birth defects?

Why can some people smoke for years and give it up without a problem while others try to quit repeatedly only to fail? On that same train of thought, why do non-smokers die of lung cancer while some lifelong smokers live to be over a hundred?

These are only a few examples of the subjectivity of what does and does not cause grave injury or death. There's no scientific explanation as to why in the very same circumstance some people can and will survive and others wilt and die. The concept of lessons explains a lot. We believe lessons are why an apparently minor infection can kill while a serious disease can be healed.

Lessons even explain predisposition to disease, not genetic susceptibility, but susceptibility through learned mechanisms of thought and action imparted inadvertently by parents, meaning because the mother never learned her lesson, she passed the pattern of thought leading to the lesson to her daughter. This explains why some children are exempt while their siblings suffer: some children buy into their parents' mindset, some don't.

In many cases of remission, I believe people unknowingly, and very luckily, learn their lesson. Of course they attribute their convalescence to doctors or religious belief or some other miracle cure and in the process deny themselves the accolade of having taken a turn in their life so enlightening it saved their life.

In some cases it can be incredibly simple, a relatively small though difficult change, giving up a job that compromises your ethics, exiting a bad relationship, or forgiving someone a transgression against you, the sort of move someone could conceivably make without consciously knowing it was exactly what they needed to do to heal.

Of course knowing a lesson is only part of the battle; learning a lesson can involve deep introspection and personal admittances about one's thoughts and feelings that are not necessarily easy to make. It can involve admitting weakness, jealousy, and fear; accepting an unfavorable or unfair situation; and even becoming a different person to reflect a heretofore-unidentified personal ethos.

For some death proves preferable to making whatever concession or compromise was necessary to heal.

For us the belief in lessons has freed us from the fear our health has the power to control us. Lessons may be another element of this story that is not quantifiable, but from our experience they are the difference between life and death.

Jenene's next career move would put her integrity in the crosshairs and cause her new lessons to learn before she had learned all her old ones.

Chapter 87
Lessons in Action

In another sink or swim situation, Jenene was able to tread the waves until a necklace of anchors was forced around her neck.

I call the company Jenene transitioned to Generic Safety Company (GSC) because the owner would certainly sue for what he would call slander and I call the cold hard truth. In the beginning GSC offered abundant opportunities to those able and willing to put in the time and effort. Later it would develop into what can be termed unscrupulous at best and a scam at worst.

Jenene excelled through the training course and earned her own office. As a manager it was up to her to recruit and train new managers, who during training were also salespeople for the company, which sold quality safety products. It was up to Jenene to mold the recruits, to make them informative and able to teach.

Jenene was truly in her element when teaching. Over the course of that summer I watched as she worked with potential managers at all levels of instruction. They dressed slick from the start but it was only by the end of training that they were slick in manner.

Those with fears of standing up before a class had to get over their phobia quickly and learn to be engaging and interesting speakers. I saw a lot of sweating. Literally. Brows awash in sweat beads as they waited for their turn to shine. Jenene coached them, worked on their weaknesses, and helped them gain the necessary confidence to achieve their goals.

I was impressed. I attribute a large part of my indifference toward school to my teachers' apathy. If I had any teachers like her I may have been inspired to be a better student.

The job had perks, sort of, extravagant corporate trips to fun and exotic locales among them. These were little more than an excuse for the managers from around the country to exchange notes for a couple of hours and then cut loose in a mecca-like setting. Jenene felt the trips were little more than indulgence and didn't look forward to these mini-vacations. They seemed like little more than an excuse to waste money. Her previous years of financial deprivation made her acutely aware of the importance of not squandering hard-earned money.

It was before one of these trips that a medical emergency would be the catalyst that would help Jenene find her truth.

Spring, 1997.

Suitcase open on her bed like a clamshell, an array of possible clothing selections laid out on her vanity and rocking chair, Jenene was in the usual pre-trip rush to get everything done before departing for a long weekend. Russ wondered if he should pack a suit or only casual wear. Jenene had bigger concerns.

"My arms and feet are on fire," she declared. The skin was breaking out in huge, bulbous blisters. Her skin has been extra sensitive ever since the severe allergic reaction, reflecting her sensitivity in other regards. "I can't believe how much it hurts."

"What's causing it?" I enquired worrisomely. I had seen similar symptoms when I was a child—the time all the skin on her body nearly sloughed off from the allergic reaction to triple antibiotic ointment. I spent a few days living with a babysitter while she was in the hospital growing back her skin.

A moment of thought and Jenene was able to pinpoint the precipitator. Earlier that afternoon she had a manicure and pedicure. It was a business expense: she had to maintain her facade. She often sported elaborate designs attached to her fingernails.

She made the mistake of allowing the manicurist to use a high-quality lotion to perform a hand and foot rub. Her skin was selectively sensitive to various skin creams. When the product being used was expensive and purported to be a good hypoallergenic, usually it was safe. She just wanted to relax with a touch of pampering before traveling and now she was in agony.

Pain levels spiking as her skin erupted in inflamed red lesions, she knew her decision was a grave gaffe.

The blisters began to break, to weep plasma—less than ten hours from boarding a plane. Though the lotion was purported to be safe for even the most sensitive skin it caused a reaction that made the skin practically fall off her hands and feet, a reaction terrifyingly similar to a flesh-eating disease.

"I can't believe I'm considering this," she said resignedly, "but I think I need to go to the emergency room."

It had been three years since Jenene saw a doctor. Part of her was resistant to put herself back in the hands of the sort of gloom and doom sorts who kept imposing expiration dates, but the pain—stinging, burning, ever-present—was sweeping and made her reconsider her reservations. Besides, she doubted they would let her on a plane if she were openly weeping—from eyes or sores.

In the ER Jenene was presented with a difficult decision. Of all the pharmaceuticals in the world, what medication would help her? Which one would give her fastest relief? Which one would do the job in time for her to go on her trip without the hassle of open sores?

The ER doctor assured her that besides reducing the pain her old frenemy steroids would make fast work of drying up the sores.

With a working vacation upon her, what choice was there? The sad thing was, if it were merely a vacation, canceling or at the very least postponing would've been an option. Her integrity made it impossible to not live up to her career responsibilities. Even when she was firing from both ends, even when she hurt, she never missed work. Take a sick day? Only if she felt like death was imminent. And since she refused to capitulate to the notion that meant no sick days.

Years since her steroid-spurred bout with psychosis, even if relief would be immediate and lasting Jenene still had to weigh her options carefully before jumping headlong.

What became apparent was that much had changed. Even her. She had grown. Back when Russ caught her on the tracks waiting for the next train, her life was so overwhelming steroids pushed her to a saturation point and she just couldn't absorb more. There were worries mounted on worries and only so much she could do.

Now she was mostly in charge of her life. She was happier. More content. Run down by far less responsibility. Her outlook was far more positive and her life all around in a better place.
There had been hard losses tempered with devotion to overcome. There had been a lot of healing. There was a lot of reason to think the circumstances would bring about an entirely different outcome.

No repeat struggle with temporary insanity would happen, why would it?

She decided alleviation was worth what she hoped was a minimized risk.

One dose told her everything. Relief greatly lessened the chances she would lose her mind. The painful stingy, itchy skin lesions might have driven her over the edge on a plane.

Feeling much better, she was on her way to paradise. She put the intense allergic reaction out of her mind and tried to enjoy her trip.

The call Jenene received the Wednesday following the trip was unexpected.

"I have news," the ER doctor said staidly.

Unaware he was running any tests or anything, Jenene was curious but also nervous. The tone of his voice revealed his news was going to be bad. "Let me have it."

"There's a reason you broke out so badly," he reported. "You have systemic lupus erythematosus. It's an autoimmune disease. In collusion with the Crohn's"—she did not bother telling him she believed she had the Crohn's in remission—"all of your organs are under attack. It's like having full-blown cancer throughout your body. I advise you to see a specialist as soon as possible."

Stunned, Jenene hung up. She would go see a rheumatologist but she knew there was little a specialist could do for her. She had to learn her lesson, whatever that may be. That was all there was to it. Simple. But it was in no way effortless. SLE could literally liquefy her organs.

Jenene continued to learn about disease being linked to emotions. She learned that even the medical establishment acknowledges the connection between the mind and disease, which probably explained them pushing her toward therapy. They recognize stress level, outlook, and other mental factors can play a significant role in a patient's ability to recuperate and the simple act of talking about their problems can play a significant role.

Even though SLE was a different monster altogether, a big ugly hairy one with warts and goiters, knowledge was a battleax she could use to chop it into submission and it bolstered her.

Jenene would soon see a rheumatologist to address this new concern and the man made the cardinal mistake of saying to her, "You poor baby." From then on he was a Peanut's comic adult droning in her ear with no more articulation than a buzzing bee and was tenfold as annoying. Dreaded pity. Why was she always deemed pitiful? Because they assumed she was going to die? Who were they to make such assumptions?

No one outranked God and the universe, no matter how schooled they were, how proficient in medicine.

Jenene left the office that day feeling deterred and would not speak about the SLE to a doctor again for seventeen years.

The real problem had to do with a shift at GSC.

The higher-ups recognized the potential profit in convincing unqualified people to put down the deposit knowing full well they would fail and forfeit their investment. This required selling the job in a way that suggested it was easy money—selling it basically like one would a get-rich-quick scheme. That way more would sign up only to discover the true difficulty and requisite diligence and washout. The company was left with their deposit for a minimal investment.

Jenene recognized the unethical nature of such an arrangement and refused to lie and bilk unsuspecting people.

Putting her finger on why her skin flared up contained little challenge after addressing SLE and connecting it to her dissatisfaction with her job. Due to poor performance in his office, one of the managers Jenene trained was uninvited to the corporate retreat by the company's president. She felt it was uncalled for and unfair. It took time to establish consistency, to gain a rhythm; because he missed a few number goals wasn't enough of a reason not to include him on a trip for which she knew he had already paid.

A manager with scruples, she realized being involved in such activity, even being aware of it, was causing the SLE to flare up because even the notion of harming others, especially for profit, literally made her sick.

Here she thought she had a wonderful career only for it to develop into what she recognized as a scam. She still believed in the products and the tenets of safety but if she did not knuckle under to raise her turnover she was as good as gone. This unfairness made her have hard feelings toward life. She worked hard to establish herself. She loved teaching. She loved spreading awareness. Yet the only way to hold onto it was to be someone she could not be…if she wanted to continue to live.

There was only one way to maintain her integrity.

Jenene had to learn to be courageous enough to change the situation so her negative outlook could transform. That was exactly what she did. A year after she was diagnosed with SLE, Jenene felt she had cornered it into remission by making perhaps the biggest decision of her life.

The thing of it was, when she thought about what was the biggest achievement outside her personal healing, only one sprang instantly to mind. Finally convincing Russ to open his mind and become a student of Reiki. With that accomplishment under her belt, she felt bolstered.

After all those years of resistance and suffering, he had been attuned in January of 1998 and our whole lives changed. Within hours The Headache—the bane of our existence—lifted, never to return. He was able to stop taking assistance from disability and go back to work. Seeing so much positive change in another inspired her to want to teach others all she had learned. Even though welcoming clients would be quite a different situation.

Those who would come to her would be open to healing or else they would never bother seeking her out. To heal herself she had to make the decision to heal others, or at least help others heal themselves.

"I had to draw a line in the sand and challenge myself to cross it," she told me. "That was when I had to make the decision to leave the corporate world. I was worried that world was going to cause the Crohn's to return—I had beaten the lesson mostly, but my superiors were trying to change me into someone who would be susceptible to the lesson again. It had already caused the Lupus to flare up."

Teaching was her passion. Healing was what she loved. So it was time to teach what she loved. Not someone else's curriculum. What she had learned. What she had an unbending passion to impart to those facing the sort of challenges she had faced.

So with the GSC chapter of her life closed, with the business savvy and healing acumen she had gained through years of tireless research and ardent self-healing, Jenene decided her path had brought her to where she could begin fulfilling her dream of helping others heal. It would not be easy opening a healing clinic. Debt from investing in GSC notwithstanding, she decided it was now or never, she had to follow her truth.

To add a credential to her roster of achievements, Jenene sought and obtained a degree in natural health consulting. She earned the degree with high honors. Shortly after establishing her business, her work was rewarded by her inclusion in the Lexington's Who's Who as a healer, a distinction she did not seek but accepted gratefully because it established her credibility beyond her own word.

In the meantime Jenene directed her attention to helping those motivated to help themselves.

Chapter 88
Old School Master's Training

The best solutions are found in positive actions....

For a woman told she'd be lucky to see thirty, two years before Jenene had little doubt she would see forty, she undertook maybe the largest step in her healing journey. It was time. From humble beginnings in the porch and the basement office, where she had sharpened herself by giving so many readings, she was again ready for a bigger challenge. She was ready to open her own healing clinic, what we have always affectionately referred to as The Shop.

The location she sought was in St. Paul, right in the heart of the medical district. It seemed appropriate. If she were serious about helping people heal, she needed to go where the ill, maimed, and undiagnosed congregate in the united goal of finding help.

The apartment was on Seventh Street, on the seventh floor, in apartment 707. At the time she was only beginning to understand the numerological significance of the location. In retrospect it's easy to say it guaranteed her time there would be enormously enlightening. Seven is the number of wisdom. The number 707 translates into a five, the number of change. The building's address number was 291, which adds up to 12 and 1 and 2 add up to 3, which is the number of spirituality.

The space quickly proved optimal for spiritual wisdom and positive change.

There was immediately an influx of clients. There were curiosity-seekers, the desperate, and the skeptics who came to make Jenene a fool and oftentimes left feeling themselves a fool. By that time Jenene's spiritual connections had been so prospered that insights big and small would fill her head the entire time she was with her clients. This means she would without exception tell people info that was deeply personal, accurate, and prognostic.

The Shop offered tarot readings, classes on personal spirituality ranging in subjects from stones to meditation, and healing cleanses.

Foremost a Reiki Practitioner, offering Reiki treatments was a no-brainer. They became a favorite among her clients. Many found treatments were a good way to achieve balance. Besides pain relief, recipients are often granted a level of deep calm followed by invigoration. This is all done without Jenene touching the client. Keeping a distance of about an inch, the healing heat, her hot hands, would radiate throughout them.

At the onset Jenene was able to sense differences in the transference of energy. This skill honed over time allowed her to be clued into injuries or illness by detecting imbalances. One client, a diffident and unconvinced doctor, told her of none of his aches and pains. Only to be amazed when she listed them off to him as she read his body, starting at his crown and proceeding to the tips of his toes, down to his smallest gripe.

During this time she also learned that to truly help people she had to be a therapist insomuch as providing an ear and a shoulder for sake of unburdening is a necessity for many people to heal.

This skill prospered over a lifetime came in very handy when an old friend needed a little miracle to bring her little miracle into the world.

Maggie was one of those friends. Someone Jenene rarely saw too regularly even if it was like no time had gone by when they did reunite. They met years before. Just a happenstance that led to a friendship that somehow endured. They shared similarities in regards to past relationships and hardships overcome.

By the time Jenene opened the shop Maggie was at the tail end of an unhealthy relationship. Even though this was her ultimate decision, she had yet to wake up to the epiphany that would improve her life. It can be so hard to admit something once so treasured can corrode to a point it's unsalvageable. She needed strength. Sometimes that can come better from a friend in the position of helpful guru.

Not one to expect even a friend to give for nothing in return, Maggie set up an appointment.

Jenene was leery to take on friends as clients. Her blatant honesty could too easily drive a spike into a friend's heart. When she channels messages, as true now as it was then, she is a conduit without mind. If she stopped to think about the words spilling out of her mouth, the messages would be waylaid, even halted. Adding thought to messages only muddles things. Examination is for after not during. This means harsh truths can cascade out even in the presence of sensitive ears.

But Maggie was insistent. She listened to Jenene's warnings and said she could take whatever might come. In no uncertain terms, she made it clear she felt at a crossroads and was willing to do the work to help herself. She needed to figure out the right way to go and she felt with Jenene's assistance it would be a more attainable goal.

Maggie was hooked.

Reiki treatments were her jam. As calming, healing energy was conducted Jenene would read her body and among other things they would discuss her ailments. She opened up to Jenene about a lot. Troubles seemed always to be heaped at her door. Her faltering relationship was only one aspect at the tip the iceberg of many things she wanted to change, fix, or altogether jettison from her life.

She confessed she felt lost too often.

Even though to any objective observer she was a twig, Maggie was a little heavier than she liked. Highlights more often than not frosted her sandalwood-colored hair. She was a devout believer in the virtues of cosmetics applied without restraint. She had an odd fashion sense that involved layering different shades of the same color. She also possessed an attitude that would lead her to tell you to bugger off if you voiced judgment of these sensibilities.

Marriage had yet to materialize, which meant one of the larger aspirations of her life had failed to come to fruition. The problem was she had poured energy and many prime years into a relationship with a man who had no interest in deeper commitments. He might as well have been the man in his early twenties who won her over with all the enticements that draw along a young woman maybe too naïve for her own good. The problem was Maggie had begun to grow up and not only had he not his goal seemed to be the exact opposite.

Peer pressure from a partner is perhaps the worst kind. Even as they edged toward their forties, Maggie and her partner at his instigation continued to party like rock stars. Together for a decade, there was a divide in priorities but it was Maggie's desires that were always plowed under.

Ready to shoot for the higher aspirations of adulthood, she wanted to have a family before it was too late. Her burdensome man wanted none of that, having long made it clear he had no interest in children.

This meant that two times before pregnancies ended in abortion. Maggie was spiritually and emotionally hollowed but she had felt little choice in the matter. He was persuasive. He made it certain what had to happen. He always lessened the blow with endearments later proven lies due to his prerogatives never changing.

Yet she stayed for a long time. Relationships can be like an addiction, bad but damn near impossible to shake.

Jenene encouraged Maggie to find her inner strength. Through their friendship and her counseling as a healer, the woman found much-needed self-empowerment.

Between the healing energy, a listening ear, and logical but heartfelt advice, she felt balance returning to her life. The problem was she kept limping along a relationship worse than any beater vehicle Jenene and Russ limped along in the early days on the farm. First talking about it helped; later being in a position to listen to advice helped even more.

Late in the spring a final blowup led to the dissolution of Maggie's relationship. She was mournful more for the time wasted than the actual end. By then she was ready to be done with the whole thing, and knew she had only cost herself opportunities by sticking around too long.

A weekly visitor for several months, Jenene was able to track the changes in her body.

In late July of 1998 to her surprise Jenene noted in her file the possibility her friend was pregnant, a feeling that cultivated over several weeks. It was such a shock. She had spoken of no rebound, no new romance. With each treatment Jenene became more adept at reading her client's bodies but had yet to experience the energy of a new life. Still, even though Maggie being pregnant seemed so unlikely, Jenene's certainty would have led her to bet she was right.

So not yet completely sure and not wanting to get Maggie's hopes—or concerns—up, she made the note without voicing what she felt.

There was no denying when her hands were over Maggie's uterus the draw was intense…and her hands read the area much differently than they had before. She wrote in Maggie's file: *Possibly pregnant?*

Early in August a doctor confirmed Maggie was nearly two months pregnant.

Later she would explain that just when she thought she was out she got pulled back in.

Maggie succeeded in instigating the breakup and even found her own apartment. Passion can't be completely doused with logic, though. No, not when other sweet words are coupled with other…enticements. It's funny how a man unwilling to compromise can so quickly become a charmer when rejected. Many women have fallen prey to this sad facet of the game of love; the man spurned who turns to the most manipulative tactics he can devise.

Carried on a tide of sentimentality, promise, and party favors, Maggie let herself be swept away....

By the time she confessed all this to Jenene she had concerns.

The baby was conceived during a cocaine and white wine weekend. The circumstances were by no means ideal. When the conception happened they were really flying high.

This made Maggie scared and for good reason. She didn't want her wanton and self-destructive behavior to translate to the child in her womb. They had used birth control...or had they? That was the thing, during a crazy spiraling sex and drug-fueled weekend with an ex showing his nice side, she couldn't even recall how much emphasis was put on protection.

It was the sort of immaturity she wanted to distance herself from...would distance herself from when she learned the elating news.

Maggie considered a pregnancy a happy accident. It seemed like it was in her best interest for the relationship to remain over. But the baby she always wanted seemed a nice consolation prize. Even if there would be difficulty being a single parent and she would need to change her whole life. Even if the daddy was going to be furious if he couldn't make her bend to his will.

A fling with an ex isn't the best idea. Getting knocked up by him when he never wanted children while under the influence of drugs? Maggie felt she had some major atonement to do. She hoped not only that Jenene would help her. She hoped she wouldn't judge her a bad person for all her mistakes. It seemed to be how she was judging herself.

To begin with not one to judge, even had she been, Maggie's willingness to acknowledge and take on responsibility for her mistakes certainly would've brought Jenene around. But she never felt Maggie was a bad person. Confused, misled, maybe too openhearted, her mistakes were very human. It's in the context of how we frame and deal with our mistakes that determines just how good of a person we are.

"I don't think this is a mistake," Jenene told her. "Reiki brings about the best results even if we don't quite understand how they're the best results. You've wanted a baby for a long time, right?"

"I have, only I don't know if I can do this alone and I know I won't have any help—"

"You won't be alone. We'll get through this. Together."

"You think?"

"I know it."

Jenene encouraged her to be strong not for herself but the precious life she carried in her womb. By virtue of being strong enough for her baby she would be strong enough for herself too. Jenene spoke from experience. She encouraged her to do what she felt was right. To be the person her integrity wanted her to be and outside forces had previously compromised. To be a mom if that was what was most important to her.

"I just can't believe I let myself be so stupid," Maggie bemoaned. "It would be one thing if we had slept together without everything else. But then it never would've happened."

"You can beat yourself up all day but that doesn't help anything," Jenene said. "All that matters is that happened and you've been blessed if you choose to see it that way."

Maggie thought about it. "I'm totally blessed…I think this could be the best thing that ever happened to me."

For the ending of such a longstanding entanglement to include the conception-tryst was understandable. The heart could be dumb when tricked with promises of love. All that mattered was how she moved forward.

Jenene admitted she had felt for some time that Little One, as they called the baby, was there. More importantly, reading her now, she felt the baby was in good health. Since Maggie had come to believe in Jenene's ability to read her body with incredible accuracy, she felt relieved and resolved to move forward with a positive outlook.

Maggie still had her concerns.

In her late thirties, Maggie wasn't old, not at all compared to celebrities giving birth at fifty, but she felt there was reason not to push a pregnancy off any farther. Besides aborted pregnancies, she had lost others to miscarriage too. Every passing year would bring new risks besides. Especially when you've lived a heedless life full of unhealthy choices. If she were going to get her baby this was probably her best chance.

Maggie worried her body would reject this child too and it would be all her fault for being so stupid for so long. She told Jenene she was bound and determined to see her pregnancy through to a baby in her arms.

"I will do everything I can to help you," Jenene said. "I know you. You'll give everything to this."

"You're right about that."

What was the main reason Jenene wanted to help her friend? She believed in redemption. She had seen her friend make huge strides to order and repair many aspects of her life. Watched her get over herself to take even bigger strides to end a harmful relationship. And she wanted to help her keep her baby.

Besides, with what she had read confirmed, Jenene felt a sense of personal recognition: she could trust what she read.

For Jenene Little One would help her grow immensely as a healer and better hone her ability to channel.

"It was really incredible," Jenene told me, "Little One would communicate with me concerning her mother's health directly. If Maggie had a bladder infection, Little One would tell me. When Little One heard my voice, she would begin to move around. Early on, I heard her tell me, 'You touch me I'll touch you back.' I asked Maggie if I could lay my hand on her abdomen and sure enough the baby pushed."

Little One's Guardian began communicating with Jenene when Maggie's obstetrician suggested that due to her age she undergo an amniocentesis. This involves withdrawing a small amount of amniotic fluid from the amniotic sac. This routine test can determine if a baby has abnormalities such as Down's syndrome. Little One's angel felt it was unnecessary. Even if the odds are low, miscarriage is also a possibility.

As his avatar, the angel—I am not allowed to write his true name so I will call him Wisdom Keeper—sent her a vision of a cherub holding Little One like Atlas holds the world. Jenene saw a perfect baby, a perfect baby boy. That was the first revelation of Little One's sex and much like in my case, the message proved true.

Maggie took the advice against her obstetrician's recommendation. Little One, proven by tests and measurements upon birth, was absolutely perfect.

The next challenge Wisdom Keeper came to Jenene with was huge. Little One needed to be attuned in the womb. Maggie had good reason to fear her actions could permanently harm her baby. The attunement was necessary to avoid complications Wisdom Keeper feared would develop later, after birth. Jenene was given a great deal of knowledge to facilitate this feat.

"Wisdom Keeper communicated with me mostly through visions. He made it clear I needed to become a Reiki Master to make it happen." Jenene had always intended to finish her Reiki training with Dee. What stopped her? Dee had gone on a sabbatical from teaching to tackle her own health concerns.

Wisdom Keeper told her that through being a loyal student of Reiki she had convinced him she was worthy of his tutelage. He would make her a Master—without requiring a teacher in the flesh. She had learned the lessons necessary to become a Master by healing herself. Had earned it with consummate obedience and devotion to her belief in and utilization of Reiki. Many Masters are fortunate to never be faced with their mortality. Those who do stare down probable death are blessed with a deeper understanding…those who beat their illness, that is, since not all do.

"Only after achieving a deep meditative state could Wisdom Keeper impart his amazing gifts. Little One's cherub channeled the master symbol along with other symbols I could use not only to heal myself but also help others.

"Once I had delved deep enough there was a series of visions, beginning with him showing me how to perform an attunement"—the sort of information charlatans upload on YouTube as if that was Usui's intent—"as step-by-step instructions. He showed me the method. I didn't have the benefit of being taught by another physical presence, so I had to learn the proper breathing technique on my own. This was crucial for attuning Little One in the womb. I do not know if there is anyone else who knows how to attune an unborn baby."

Shortly thereafter Jenene was taught perhaps the greatest gift of all. She was clued into the fact Reiki could be augmented enormously. She was channeled a symbol formula that multiplies Reiki energy infinitely. Heretofore she was forced to send treatment by treatment, a laborious task often resulting in writer's cramp.

Throughout the years she read every Reiki book she could get her hands on. One mentioned briefly thinking of Reiki in terms of volume, which struck a chord with Jenene, since it seemed very similar to the information she was channeled. "I thought of such amplification as slightly farfetched at first. But the more I thought about it, the more I thought it was possible."

She decided to run with the concept and trust what she was taught. She titled this new method Accelerated Reiki. It could be said her work with Wisdom Keeper was how Jenene earned her doctorate in healing.

"I was also shown how to connect deeply while giving a treatment, how to use symbols to connect more thoroughly. This was when I honed my ability to read bodies." Like metal detectors spot metal, Jenene's hands identify the energy imbalances caused by pain, illness, and disease. Invariably, she can point out the smallest to the largest, paper cuts to cancer. This fine-tuned what before had relied more on intuition.

This skill has often warmed even the most ardent skeptic, from the religious to doctors, who find it amazing that she can pinpoint their ailments. We find it less amazing. It is a very useful skill certainly. But we know through Reiki anyone can develop the ability to read bodies. Few are committed enough to hone what can be natural to all of us.

In the early part of 1999, Maggie's little one was born, a healthy, cherubic little boy.

Wisdom Keeper would appear to Jenene one final time after Little One's birth. Not as the tiny cherub but as a giant, a form truer to his personality. During this vision he granted one final reward to Jenene by channeling what became her Personal Power Ceremony. This empowering invocation is a favorite among her students and was an apt capper to the gifts bestowed for her part in this event.

So much was gained, incalculable in terms of numbers.

Estimating the true value of her rewards would require taking into account the status she had earned both as an individual accomplishment and as an avenue of helping others. While also considering the rareness and uniqueness of becoming a Reiki Master the old-fashioned way: through turmoil, service, and meditation. It meant not only that she was better able to control her own health. But as a facilitator and teacher of Reiki she could propagate healing in a far grander way.

What she received was invaluable, a trade she would say was much more to her benefit than not, priceless even. True wisdom comes with a toll but the value far exceeds the cost when what was gained is put to good use. That was Jenene's intent from the start.

Attuning Little One in the womb was monumental to our understanding of healing. Jenene never really considered it as anything other than another wisdom gained when most needed.

This author was one of the first outside-the-womb recipients of a Jenene attunement. Depending on devotion and utilization, the healing energy conducted by practitioners can be a streamlet or a river. Most begin very narrow. After this attunement I felt like my energy channel had widened, that I was a more vital healer. It was after this I would shuck the final vestiges of the chronic bronchial asthma that vexed my childhood.

There altogether seemed to be something other attunements lacked. Of course that is subjective and I might not be in the most objective position to judge. As before there was no great vision to describe, no journey into the rainbow, not like there would be later. But what I found was a sense of greater openness, a sense of a closer conduit to…infinity or maybe just the energy that makes up everything. Maybe those things are synonymous.

With her efforts to aid Maggie banked, Jenene had all the tools to be a Master. Yet she wouldn't feel like one until after her first major healing success beyond her own. As life is wont to do, such an opportunity would soon be presented.

Chapter 89
A Lesson About Lessons

Jenene's aunt Diana was dying of brain cancer.

Although there had been a long interim between their last visit, Jenene was fond of her aunt and offered to help her heal. By the time she made it up to Minnesota from Illinois, Diana had lost all sensation in her right arm and was completely unable to put it to use. This paralysis was devastating because she was a gifted painter and also enjoyed hair styling as a relaxing hobby.

Diana was Jenene's first face-to-face attunement. Keeping their expectations low so as not to set up disappointment, what happened was truly astounding.

Diana healed literally overnight. Sensation returned to her arm. She was able to move her fingers. Even dexterity came back and before leaving on Monday she was able to style Jenene's hair.

Was the attunement a cure all in this case? Nothing could be further from the truth. The real reason Diana healed so fast was that Jenene helped her pinpoint her lesson.

In this case she needed to learn to not live outside her comfort zone for sake of monetary gain. Although she was a talented portrait artist, the work was not consistent enough for her liking. To earn a more reliable living, she worked as a cosmetologist in a funeral home when she would have preferred painting on canvas rather than the faces of corpses.

The decision was killing her and its reverse, to give up the job, gave her back her life. Diana's doctor called her sudden remission miraculous. Helping Diana in this way was the feather in Jenene's cap she needed to feel confident enough to teach Reiki.

There is another point to Diana's story because in the end her victory was short-lived. Three years after recovering from brain cancer, Diana died of pancreatic cancer. Fast moving, diagnosis to death was a matter of two days. How it was described to us, she felt the symptoms one day and a couple days later she was dead.

Diana made the fatal mistake of allowing the lure of money to make her return to a job she detested. The funeral home enticed her back. Against her better judgment, she took their offer and sealed her death warrant. Due to Reiki Diana is now a healing angel.

Diana's death had a profound impact on Jenene and from it she chose to take a lesson about lessons. "Even if you learn your lesson, if you forget what you learned, your illness will return. Losing Diana was a huge lesson not to forget what I have learned. When you get caught up in the flow of life, it's all too easy to forget."

Not learning a lesson completely and permanently is like improperly removing black mold; the problem appears to be dealt with but will later resurge, worse, and, as in Diana's case, even fatal.

Chapter 90
The Contract Struggle

After escaping an abusive marriage, losing important loved ones, healing trauma from the past, finding forgiveness for one once considered a nemesis, disavowing herself of corporate dastardliness, and surviving enough illness to ruin several lives, it could be said Jenene found her stride. She had put so much distance between herself and the prospect of death one shuffling inch, step, and leap at a time she no longer worried she was dying.

By the dawning of the new millennium she had utilized Reiki, meditation, visualization, affirmations, stone energy, and lesson acknowledgement to put Crohn's and lupus in remission. She had defied all expectations. She outlived Western medicine's expiration date by a decade and on top of that she felt healthy.

No longer did she suffer constant sickness. Long gone were the humiliating and painful symptoms. She had reached the hard sought peak of a mountain purportedly not climbable, beating all the doctors' assurances, and found her true calling, fulfilling a prophecy she once found laughable.

It was freeing.

Whatever toll sickness had taken she took back and then some.

There was a worldwide sense of relief when Y2K fears resolved. We didn't share in the prior anxiety so neither did we share in the collective sigh of relief that swept the nation. We had reason to believe life would go on as usual.

Jenene had prospered several…otherworldly connections.

This equated to the first year of the new millennium being jam-packed with emergent awareness. It also meant prospering her spiritual side in ways she never imagined. Healing is reciprocal and the more she put out into the world the more she in turn received.

What was a sure sign she was succeeding in her chosen business? She was busy. Subsequent to some initial marketing missteps—ads in free papers tended to draw men under the impression they were contacting an escort—she managed to calibrate her advertising to the most beneficial channels. Even then she found word of mouth was probably her best publicity.

Someone expressing how much his or her life had improved was better than any purchased ad space.

So it was a variety of means that steadily built a clientele representing all walks of life who had all manner of reasons to see her. In the spectrum of personalities she found greater unity than she had ever known. No matter how different, how separated by the things humans use to justify disunity, among them they shared the same desire to heal.

All her trials and tribulations made Jenene an avowed humanist, optimist, and high achiever. By traveling the proverbial hard path, she had evolved into a natural therapist too. She was able to apply all she had lived and learned to a variety of situations and problems. This meant she almost invariably had an applicable wisdom for whatever problem was brought to her.

With few pitfalls, guiding people on healing journeys was mostly rewarding. Her devotion was reflected in her own renewed health. There was no doubting healing was her bailiwick.

A lot of gratification came from actively helping an ever-growing assemblage of enthusiastic students. Appreciative and grateful, they tunefully sang her praises. Witnessing their growth confirmed how right she was to devote herself to helping those willing to help themselves.

Positively impacting the lives of others felt fabulous. Even if becoming a healer was never about glorification—grandstanding was never her style—there was glory in what she was doing, the glory of peace of mind, the glory of genuine contentment.

So much changed and opened up for her. She had no idea what she was into until she was in the thick of it.

Reiki her primary tool, she used symbols to better connect with her students. In so doing, awareness began to grow that what she was doing, offering insights and guidance, wasn't entirely up to her alone, that others—angels, spirits, crossed-over family members—contributed to the counsel and advice she dispensed. Connecting with Wisdom Keeper had evidently unlocked a door and now she was more open to channeling than she had ever been before.

Speaking with spiritual beings and witnessing miracles large and small were becoming usual occurrences.

What was unusual was Russ and Jenene's relocation from the farm to Irvine Park Towers. With civilization encroaching, the decision to sell was difficult but necessary. Enough time was spent worrying about the liability, worrying about a trespasser getting injured and taking the farm from us through litigation.

After over a decade in the rural badlands of Grey Cloud it was like going from a breeze into a whirlwind.

The city never sleeps even if it does doze; quietude existed in the wee hours of morning but those streetlights were lit all night (good curtains are a prerequisite to a decent night's sleep). At earliest dawn began the clinks of bottles as the bars emptied their bins. The jangling of glass was caught in the echo chamber of the city and made a counterpoint to the incessant noise of street sweepers scouring the asphalt and the ever-present traffic.

No longer hampered by a long commute, Jenene ran her business with even greater commitment. Often working late into the night, she saw as many students as time allowed.

One student took particular interest in learning everything Jenene was willing to teach. Getting attuned to second degree as soon as he could, Randy was one of her first Reiki students and remains one of her most dedicated. His interest derived from a desire to turn around a string of misfortune. Straight up he wanted a better life and was willing to work toward what improvement he could earn. After other methods purported to help failed he found Reiki was the answer he had been seeking like a treasure hunter willing to hazard any terrain to find his fortune. For Randy his fortune was good health.

Another aspect of spirituality she was learning about was soul-level connections, karmic attachments that transcend life and death. Some people come into our lives because of unions forged throughout the timeline of history. Such revelations were new and fascinating and through giving him Reiki treatments Jenene learned she and Randy shared such a karmic connection.

This maybe explains his immediate adherence to Jenene's teachings; his trust in her preceded this life.

What was also interesting about Randy was his Guardian Angel. Unlike other Guardians, who only came forward in an apparent way when necessary (Jenene's Guardian for instance spoke so little she still had no idea his or her identity), Randy's Guardian greeted Jenene as an old ally, friend, and confidant.

David claimed he and Jenene shared a deep karmic bond. One that went so far back he said they had "walked together in the time of Christ," an endorsement that says it all about the existence of Jesus Christ when some claim the man never existed. Whether Jesus is what Christianity and the heavily edited Bible has made him out to be, the man was real, and a great healer undoubtedly, even a necromancer if we are to believe the story of Lazarus.

An unforeseen spiritual ally who professed unshakeable caring, Jenene felt an immediate kinship with David. With his openness he inspired her to seek the identity of her Guardian. Using Reiki, she forced a meeting of sorts. Adam proved curmudgeonly and terse; he was in no way personable. Yet his influence was unmistakable; what else assured my ultimate first name? Based on his surly disposition, Jenene felt as if her Guardian considered her an inconvenience. In time she would learn why.

Two massive events would transpire the following year. The latter would be the events of 9/11. The former would be Jenene's death.

As it turned out Jenene had an expiration date after all. Not one imposed by doctors but one determined by the powers that be, powers we even now only vaguely understand. June 19, 2001 was determined to be the day Jenene was to cross.

How she came to this knowledge exposed perhaps her most prodigious alliance. The ordeal began quite unexpectedly a few months ahead of the date with a message from a voice she suspected belonged to her Healing Angel.

The structure of the spiritual realm, hidden behind the chimerical veil that has clouded the vision of many for millennia, was slowly gaining patches of transparency. Part of what she was learning besides confirmation that we have Guardian Angels was the possibility that Healing Angels are assigned to those attuned to Reiki. With a sliver of this knowledge she sought to know her Healing Angel, and it would be in service to giving her the most important message of her life that they would formally make acquaintances.

"You're going away," the voice told her vaguely.

Jenene misunderstood. "I thought she meant I was going to move or something along those lines. Stranger things had happened and I *would* eventually move back to Wisconsin. I was still learning that the angels often speak proverbially and in metaphor. Belle was tiptoeing around the real message. She was breaking the rules by giving any forewarning and she was trying to be careful."

"You aren't my Guardian," Jenene observed in her early communication with the angel. "Who are you?"

"My name is Belle."

"Who are you to me, Belle? Angel, guide, karmic ally?"

"It is as you suspected. I have been with you since your first attunement. But I was nearby before. Waiting."

"That would mean…you knew I was going to be attuned?"

"Not all fates come to be, but I felt it was your destiny to outlive your first contract."

"What contract?"

"Each who walks does so under an agreement that determines the time each is allotted. Some are very short. Some are very long."

"When was my first contract up, I don't understand?"

"You were not meant to see the age of thirty-three."

Thirty-two was an easy year to remember. It was a hard year, a crossroads year. She struggled painstakingly that year. As it turned out she fought arduously enough to earn an extremely rare reprieve. How had she lucked into such a monumental achievement? No luck was involved. Jenene soon learned she had earned more time. How? Through being a consummate student of healing, such a dedicated student the universe had taken notice.

"So what's going on now?" she implored Belle. "What do you mean I'm going away? I feel like you're leaving out information I think I might need."

Belle was reticent.

Spiritual laws bind us. And even angels have to follow the rules. There is a secret, though. Intent and motive can mitigate those laws. If there is good enough reason to pass along a message of great import, exceptions can be made. Belle took a chance by offering even obfuscated information, but she continued to, until Jenene was able to theorize her way to the answers without being given one iota explicitly.

Before Jenene had her answers it would take what from Belle's end must have felt like an extended interrogation. Whenever she had a chance, she posed more questions. She turned different angles. Came at it from all directions. Jenene pieced the tidbits together. Piece by piece, sections of the puzzle were revealed until the truth was staring her right in the face.

The image that emerged was the specter of death pointing at a date on the calendar.

Surrounded by beautiful stones and lush houseplants, in her shop Jenene broke the news to me. In its own way consoling, Elton John music played softly on her boom box. A wallpaper mounting Russ had affixed at her behest, the backdrop of her desk was a gorgeous scene of a tropical beach, all sand and palm trees stretching off seemingly forever.

How badly I wished I were on that beach, the waves crashing at my feet, the sun warming my shoulders, the wet sand squishing between my toes, a gentle breeze caressing my face, and the reality I was being presented with about a million miles away.

"I don't want to believe it," I said and in my own ears my voice echoed because it came from a hollow place, as if I had spoken from inside a big bass drum. Healthier and happier than I ever remembered seeing her, I was struck by a tremendous sense of the absurd. I was heartsick. "Is there anything that can be done? Healing we can send?"

"Adam doesn't think so," she said. "Belle isn't so convinced but no matter what there are no promises."

"I just don't understand."

"All I know is I thought you would want to be told," she said. "I would feel terrible if this happens and I didn't warn you."

"If your contract was renewed or rewritten or whatever, why can't it be done again?"

Born with an agnostic bearing, I came by my belief in angels, spirit guides, and all the rest honestly. I was never one to believe anything without what I judge irrefutable evidence. The information Jenene channeled turned out to be amazingly accurate too many times for me to doubt. It also opened me up to listening for the voices of my guides and angels.

"It comes down to my Guardian," she explained. "Adam has no choice but to call in all his wards."

"But why?"

"You know how souls work on their spirituality until they ascend to becoming guides and angels?"

I nodded.

"The way it seems, that can work in reverse too; angels can make mistakes that cost them the level they've achieved. Seems Adam screwed up. He has to come back and live another life."

"So he's being punished?"

"I think it would be looked at more as being given a chance to relearn lessons he's forgotten."

"How crazy the world's getting it sounds like a punishment to me," I said. "And even if it isn't, I don't understand why you have to be punished because of what he's done."

Jenene didn't understand, either. At the time she presented a strong front for my sake but was as confused, frustrated, and angry. She explained the situation in no uncertain terms. She didn't want me banking on another miracle.

Years later she would explain it to me like this: "I felt like I had earned my life. I wanted to live. I wanted to keep helping people. Yet I couldn't be resentful. I had already lived longer than I was supposed to. Adam made that clear. There were no bells and whistles, but I had beaten that first date years before without even knowing how close I came to dying. Six months and nineteen days after my thirty-second birthday I was supposed to be finished."

"It's not a punishment," Jenene said. "Don't look at it that way. I could've died when you were eleven. Please don't take for granted how much extra time we were allowed."

"I get it," I said. "I do. But I really don't like it. I just lost the farm; I don't want to lose you too."

"You won't lose me. You know I'll always be with you."

"It's not the same."

"You're right. But it could be worse."

Even if she kept a brave face, at first Jenene felt like all she had worked for unraveled in an instant.

After so many years of fighting for her life on so many fronts and in so many trenches it seemed diabolic the war to live should be lost due to matters so outside her control. If her journey had taught her anything, it was that if she put in the effort her health was within her control. Suddenly that reassurance was a rug that was pulled out from under her. Sitting back as her day of death approached was so out of character but what else could she do?

Was it wrong to feel her Guardian failed her?

More appropriately, he had failed himself. His terse manner summed it up. After she began hearing Adam it became apparent his glacial voice was all too familiar. When a dream might have helped, it was he who so coldly told her she would lose her son or father. A part of our lessons include learning compassion and empathy. Hardnosed Adam's bearing suggests his failing was in that he had risen to such prominence he forgot his lessons.

Jenene would seek consolation from an unexpected source.

Adam remained aloof, almost indifferent. On the opposite side of the spectrum David took it upon himself to offer solace. Compassionate words and unflagging wisdom erased many doubts and granted a grander perspective. To consider her life as anything other than well lived would diminish all she had accomplished. After all was said and done she had to be upbeat about how much she had learned, changed, and grown on her long healing journey.

She had become the sort of empowered person who pursues her desires and dreams in the face of all hardship, chin held high. To go to the hereafter with any less aplomb than that wouldn't befit the dignity she had earned.

So rather than submit to bitterness Jenene didn't so much resign herself as decide to be grateful for the time she had earned and open to what was to come. She had seen The Seniors through to the end of their lives. She had seen me through to adulthood. She had also lived up to that outrageous prediction and helped others heal after healing herself.

Jenene could accept her time was up. Back when her prospects were most ominous, when she had no choice but to face down her mortality, she prepared herself to leave the mortal plain. There was no choice. She had to come to terms to release all fear of death. That way it held no power over her.

Fear still had no resonance with her.

It was the resounding injustice that put the thorn in her side David so tactfully removed. Even after David's diplomacy she had to keep reminding herself I had grown up and could take care of myself. Russ had been warned long ago she was living on borrowed time and would survive. Most importantly, she had helped those she could. She could pass at peace even though there was still so much she could do because she had done what she could.

Belle wasn't so sure it was as cut and dry as Adam implied.

Summer days can stretch to epic proportions when you're young and carefree; unfortunately for me the days of the summer I was nineteen were a countdown and went so fast time seemed sped up. June came and what had been the final weeks were suddenly the final days.

I was at a loss. Was I ready to live without my mom? I didn't think so. There was absolutely no one else in my life able to fill her role. I had no real friends even if I had a lot of friendships. No one who cared in a genuine way and who would be there beyond all doubt to lean on. A young person can use that; the stability of knowing there is someone in the world who will always be there for him or her.

The relationship wasn't there even though Russ and I developed a friendship. If we lost her, we would suffer alone, maybe too alpha in our thoughts to see the support we could get from each other. Between males there's often a transitory period when roles change and evolve.

I insisted on sleeping over on the night before the dreaded date. I had to be nearby. "Imperative" for its four syllables fails to express how important it was to me to be close at hand. I had no idea why it was better to be there. I had no doubt about the outcome.

Maybe it was important to be there to say goodbye.

Knowing beforehand was truly a gift if my mom dying was how it had to be. The opportunity—one many are deprived—to say a final farewell and I love you was worth more than a mountain of pure gold studded with fine-cut diamonds. These final words I would remember.

"I'll miss you every day," I told my mom. "Thank you so much for all you've been to me, all the times you've been there for me, all you've given me. Thank you for helping me learn so much and believing in me. I don't know what I'll do without you but you've prepared me enough I know I'll survive."

"Send healing and you'll be able to hear me."

I said I would.

As a family we discussed keeping her up all night in the hours leading up to bedtime. Jenene decided if it were her time to go humble acceptance would be more dignified than trying to defy reality. The will of the universe cannot be subverted on a whim. There are no Faustian deals, at least not for ones with souls as pure as Jenene's. Brain aneurysms strike at any time, when people are jogging, when they are cooking, when they are making love. We didn't want to witness her keel over dead.

Russ lay awake with her until the specified time elapsed. They knew that meant nothing. From there all she could do was drift off to sleep and face her destiny.

Obstacles intertwined with miracles, she had survived many trials. Was this where her underdog story ended?

After adjourning to the couch in the other bedroom, sleep eluded me like a stray cat unwilling to be caught. Understandably. My mind was at once whirring and inert.

I tossed and turned on the couch, wide awake. To distract myself I would stare into the white wall until my vision went blurry and my head ached. I had only begun to hear my own angels. I felt fogged because their answers were none of what I wanted, were too free of supplication and hope.

Put simply I was in a state of turmoil. I feared the thing I had always feared was here finally, delayed, no doubt, but here now. In the dark I lay for hours…until I heard a voice. "Go check," the voice advised.

I snapped to, quick to oblige. Left the room I occupied. Strode toward Jenene's bedroom. Glided through the darkened apartment like a wraith headed toward an uncertain reckoning. The shadows seemed to contain sinister shapes, hints of things not seen but there watching.

There is a hierarchy on the other side, regulations, and the territory I was being led to at the very least manipulated rules. There is no certainty as to who captured my attention. Just who solicited me to go to my mom at that moment to this day remains a mystery. All I know is timing can mean everything.

What else did I know? Across town Randy's Guardian roused him from sleep in a way similar to how Jenene was roused the night I had a grand mal seizure. Only now it was Jenene's life on the line. David rolled him out of bed and demanded he send Reiki to Jenene immediately. A connection needed initiation, creating a bridge of sorts. It was up to Randy.

The apartment bedroom was diminutive. To get beside her I had to negotiate the narrow space around the foot of the bed, careful not to bark my shin on a chest of drawers.

Faint city illumination lent to details of every object in the room being clear. Crystal. In all the hours I had lain in the near lightlessness, I had become one with the darkness, become another extension of the shadows that seemed to watch me. My eyes were too well adjusted.

My real trouble was three seconds of denial followed by crushing recognition of the truth.

I could tell immediately. If you've ever examined a dead body you can quickly zero in on the details that betray a being has ceased to live.

For one, she wasn't breathing. I put my finger beneath her nose and felt no warm shush of air. Nor was there a visible pulse, nor a pulse to be felt, either in wrist or throat. No movement of any kind. Her skin was pale and drawn. The penultimate nail in the coffin, she was cool to the touch, the warmth of life draining away since there was no longer a source to sustain it.

The vividness of my perception belied the notion I had unknowingly slipped off into sleep and this was all the intangibles and make-believe of dreams.

This was cold hard reality. This was the real world, where any number of tragedies occurs at every instant, meaning no one should believe their misfortune exclusive. No matter our divides, in love and pain we are a collective species. Such a philosophical notion wouldn't enter my mind for years. No such consolation was available.

So it was true.

Her contract had expired.

She had died.

Part of me was so shattered it took everything I had not to explode and let off a scream that would have shaken the foundations.

Much of my life she had readied me to lose her but now that the eventuality was here before me I wasn't at all prepared. That I could care for myself sufficiently meant nothing. That I was a survivor meant even less. I felt like a little child entombed by my worst nightmares and fears made manifest in one implacable image.

Death is natural, inevitable, but no less of a sucker punch. She warned me. I had no reason other than denial not to believe her. Her psychic intuition too often blew my mind to have true doubt. I had just wanted her to be wrong about this one, this crazy prediction that said her time was up, her contract was being pulled.

This end was obviously gentle but no less unfair. But who ever said life was fair? "Fair" is just a word in the dictionary after all. Just a toothless word because for it to have bite it would need enforcement.

I was compelled to place my hands up by the collarbone. She wore a white silky nightgown and the skin of her shoulders was bare. It felt clammy under my palms. She was so cold. On those points alone I couldn't refute it, not when I could feel that she was too cold to be alive. Skin does not get a chill like that on a warm night unless the blood stops flowing.

The confirmation I wanted to avoid, the final nail, was she had no heartbeat.

The word "no" my internal mantra, I refused, absolutely refused to accept it, refused to believe that this woman I loved so much could be gone from the mortal coil, accessible only through channeling, a means that is nowhere near as reliable as a phone call. I could already feel a crater hole forming in my soul and a piece of my heart dying.

That was when it happened. The only way I can describe what occurred is to say my hands acted as defibrillators, sending a life-restoring jolt through Jenene's vessel.

In the same instant Jenene gasped in a gusty breath so mighty it was like she was drawing air after almost drowning. She sat bolt upright under my hands with such force I was shoved away.

My skeleton about jumped out of my skin. Few startles have challenged that one. None have quite equaled it. I was sure she was dead. When a dead body revivifies under your touch, it's freaky, like nothing else.

Shocked, amazed, and all at once doubting all the assessments I had just made, I croaked hastily, "I had to check on you"—*no freaking way*, I thought, *she was so cold and I swear stiffening*—"sorry to wake you."

Jenene knew different. "I wasn't asleep, I was gone," she said flatly. "I died. Something big happened while I was gone. I feel like I went to some meeting."

Grateful for the gift of life, she embraced me and we held each other as the warmth returned to her body.

What followed was assembling the pieces of another puzzle; only the image that would emerge this time was to our immense relief far rosier.

A trifecta of participants converged in Jenene's time of need to overturn an unfair verdict predicated not on her accomplishments but the failings of one tasked with protecting her. They represented three legs of the stool that propped up her life; the fourth leg was made of a combination of Jenene's spiritual conviction and my unbending love for her.

Next morning Randy called and received quite a shock when Jenene answered. "Jenene, you're alive!" For some reason he was sure she had passed. The way it felt when he sent, the intensity of it, convinced him a crossing was involved.

Jenene explained that he wasn't so far off.

"David tossed me out of bed in the middle of the night and told me to send."

"You're a good student," she commended. "You played a big role in saving my life."

Soon we learned David played maybe the most important role by stepping up and absolving Adam of his responsibility. Using the bargaining chips of Jenene's indomitable will and the positive message she proliferated, Belle oversaw the accord. In so doing a new contract was executed, with David signed on as her Guardian.

Even if all in the end played out to her benefit, the ordeal was a lesson in humility. Powers higher than her would remain in charge of pulling the strings, no matter how much she advanced as a healer. Such a fact in no way demeaned Jenene's resolve to spread healing, though, which was only all the more bolstered, a passion driven to new heights. It's a matter of pride how many she has helped heal and attuned to Reiki.

Beforehand Jenene appreciated every day; now she was grateful for every hour and minute that makes up her days.

There was definitely newfound wonder at the majesty available to us all if only we seek it out. Longevity can be a state of mind, splendor an insight so simple yet so deep; she had decided to live and live she would, a life worthy of yet again writing a new contract.

Chapter 91
Fresh Sights

Carried on the cascading ebb and flow of the universe, Reiki has a way of taking us where we need to go....

Following three years of fulfilling work in the Twin Cities, in March of 2002 Jenene relocated The Shop to the village of Woodville.

A variety of factors contributed to returning to Wisconsin, not the least of which their building going condo and they had to buy or leave when they had no interest in owning. From the boondocks of the farm to the heart of the city, a happy medium was sought. Woodville seemed a good compromise.

Family also factored. An option to reconnect with her mother in a way never before possible, it was a chance to mend old hurts. After years in separate states, she and Lois became neighbors, living less than a block apart. Jenene saw it as a chance to maybe shed light on some of those little mysteries that always vexed her. At the very least it was an opportunity to know her mom better.

Turned out there was a lot to know.

Subsequent to retirement from Hartford in the wake of a flourishing career Lois naturally fell into the role of civic-minded dowager. Not one in need of a man, she never remarried. She was content to live alone in her big house. Content to spread her time among a number of causes, reading, and card club. Committed to community life, in the role of retiree she was busier than ever.

Besides reading the library out of books, the American Legion and Lion's Club alike could always count on her to volunteer. She often worked the counter of the village office. She joined the board of the village nursing home and with her colleagues spearheaded a transformation that led to awards and national prominence. She was even for a time elected to the village board, a thankless job we were too happy to see her leave.

All this meant was Jenene had inroads where someone completely new to the area would be directionless. Between her past acquaintances and Lois' current reputation, she lucked into a lot of much needed networking. Whatever help she could get was welcome. After a dicey couple of months she managed to begin adding to her student base.

In regards to Jenene's method of teaching there was what those who are more concerned with profits than compassion would consider a real problem. Jenene's goal was to teach her students healing self-sufficiency.

No one is ever exploited as a cash cow. Success means students move on.

Though she had a handful of regulars, the majority learned what they needed and only checked in occasionally for advice or to share elements of their healing journey. She never wanted to put anyone in the position of feeling like they would need to rely on her in perpetuity. Gurus who want to be relied on forever maybe share too much in common with cult leaders.

The owner of the local newspaper took notice. Jenene was offered print space for a column based on her teachings and wisdom. I offered editorial advice. *Jenene's Word* gave insight on everything from stones and Reiki to herbs and visualization. Some minds were opened, others changed. She gained quite a readership during the few years she wrote the column.

Jenene's personal spiritual growth was leading to many shrewd observations and keen revelations. For one thing, she was learning how smell could be associated with spirits; case in point, if the rich scent of buttered grits hit her nostrils and it could not be accounted for with actual grits, it meant her dad was nearby. A boy out of the south, he loved a mess of grits.

As for Bill, our beloved uncle had ascended befittingly to the level of a spirit guide. Students would often profess to having witnessed a kindly old man standing over Jenene's shoulder while receiving Reiki treatments.

For these occasions, she hung a small reproduction of Diana's charcoal sketch of Bill in a place not noticeable automatically. When someone said they saw an old man, she pointed out the image. They would be stunned to see the face in the sketch and the one they had seen were one and the same.

Driven by their individual pursuits, mother and daughter still made time to meet for lunch every week. They would often engage in competitive games of Scrabble. Surprises never cease; a rapport proliferated.

Send enough healing and you'll soften towards those for whom you have the hardest feelings. No family disconnection is so great as to be insurmountable. Not if there remains a willingness to put in some effort. Some barricades exist to be broken down. Sometimes the past just needs to be irrelevant if there is to be a present and a future.

Lois often enlisted Jenene to join her when volunteering. Happy to give, Jenene accepted such invites good-naturedly. These opportunities to bond led them to ever greatening understanding. Many years in a row they worked the beer tent for the Lions during Syttende Mai, trading drink tickets for cash.

Jenene always felt like her mother's judgment was in limbo, pending. Before she knew it their strengthening relationship seemed to bring a positive verdict.

Never one to be concerned about the approval of others, pleasing Lois through actions and time spent together was in many ways a fringe benefit to the bonding they were granted. Yet once she had the approval, she appreciated it more than she suspected she might. Maybe in some way we all want our parents' approval. Such judgments are more paramount than we like to admit.

What best demonstrates the importance of their reconnection? Proximity led to their usual lunch dates, which ultimately led to the revelation that brought Jenene to reassessing their entire relationship.

So much comes down to how information is framed. For too long she believed without reason to doubt her harried mother had abandoned her on the farm because she was deemed an inconvenience and only through the tireless actions of her noble dad did they become a family.

The effort led to the defrosted former ice maiden Lois broaching the disputed period on ice all those years. Without coaxing she reminisced openly. Out the story spilled. With it the truth that was according to her dad too taboo to mention, the truth that reshaped Jenene's entire understanding of everything, was conveyed so casually it was a wonder it had never come out before.

The level of healing required to facilitate the sequence of events is unknown but I suspect it was bountiful and unstinted in a way hard for puny human minds to comprehend.

Jenene ended up with so much more than she ever dared hope. For all those years she proved her loyalty; she never betrayed her word. When Lois opened up, she asked questions, no longer bound by her promise. What she learned was a lesson in how false realities are constructed and the wastefulness of their long-lasting consequences.

Why had her not-so-noble dad made the information forbidden? She concluded he was worried she would judge them both harshly, him in particular. On some level he felt guilty for his early inaction. Maybe he feared too many questions from his naturally inquisitive daughter. No matter what his motivation, he allowed a misunderstanding to be a wedge between daughter and mother.

Jenene felt so grateful for the truth. If her life had taught her nothing else, it was to recognize universal gifts when they are bestowed. Her mother opening up and revealing the truth restructured their entire relationship for the better. She saw how useless all her hurt feelings had been. Though they have their differences, there were mutual understandings too.

Reiki dissolved a wedge that was once like a Gordian knot.

An infusion of much-needed truth can do that.

Jenene accredited such an amazing turn-about in her life to blessings from a universe fairer than she was taught. Fair to those who earn their way on the spiritual path anyway.

Even when her healing lessons shrank, no longer requiring her mortality be on the line, she nitpicked the little things, intent on bettering herself and better understanding how to help others. For her vigorous devotion she received many rewards, not the least of which enlightenment, understanding, and closure in matters that long vexed her.

Reiki has a way of ordering or reordering life through the simple action of bringing about the best results. Synchronicity in action, unexplainable like most workings of the universe, but very well attributable to all the Reiki sent, all the healing assisted, and the inexhaustible desire to reconcile the past to better take pleasure in the present.

Reiki could even lead to some of the most significant if unlikely showdowns.

Chapter 92
Out of Nowhere

Days of reckoning often bear every semblance of a normal day right up until...

The phone beside her desk rang. Jenene was busy in her office. If she wasn't putting the finishing touches on a column she was assembling a new class. Attached to her home but in a separate second story apartment, the space was filled with her plants, her many books, and her large amethyst geode among hundreds of other stones. Sage smoke more often than not spiced the air.

Jenene answered and was greeted by an unfamiliar masculine voice. It was so low and raspy his words were nearly muffled to inaudibility. "Jenene?" The caller ID indicated the caller was in Maryland. No surprise. Due to the diversity of her students getting calls from all over the country and even the world was usual.

"Yes."

"This is your brother Bobby," the man said trenchantly. Even with him hundreds of miles away Jenene felt an eclipse steal across her heart and enclose it in a self-protective cowl. "I need to talk to you if you'll let me. I've been trying to reach you for a long time."

Mind-blowing. Just like that Jenene was reconnected with the half-brother she had long thought vanished, incarcerated, or dead. Her own journey one of self-actualization, she never needed her abuser to play any part to offset her healing. So much so she never used Reiki or spiritual connections to learn more about what became of him. She felt it better to leave it all up to karma.

And here he was on the phone.

Jenene made a quick decision to proceed evenhandedly.

What was his purpose?

Hm. She was interested to know if he would own up or evade now that she had a chance to confront him. Not that it mattered for her wellbeing, but it never hurt to satisfy her curiosity. She would only be able to do that if she could avoid making him so squirrelly he dashed. Pounce too fast and he might be startled and hang up, gone forever. She had to ease toward it. For all she knew he was calling for different reasons entirely.

So much time had elapsed since she dealt with the abuse. She had to for sake of healing the degenerative disc disease. Facing such hard truths saved her from a wheelchair. Saved her from her self-destructive nature. Saved her from the self-recrimination that tinctured her whole life beforehand.

One enigma of a fraught life, it could be said that no matter how negative his contribution, out of it she had gotten something too—the sort of damage that forces a person to grow or perish.

Self-contempt aside, she had grown not because of him but because she was a survivor even before she knew she was strong. There's no doubting he adversely compromised her life. Without that influence better decisions might have been made; but all the bad decisions shaped her life and helped her develop into the self-empowered person she was now. Even though the journey was full of diversions and pitfalls, it would be disingenuous to say what she had gained wasn't more valuable than what she lost.

"How are you?" she proceeded cautiously.

Bobby's story was full of woe.

The desperado had lived largely off the grid after the collapse of his last marriage and those pesky accusations. By the time he got in touch with Jenene he was a gargantuan five hundred pounds and confined to a nursing home. His life had been one of little triumph, too many hurt feelings, and bad dealings. He survived male breast cancer but felt his time was drawing short.

He wanted to make right if making right were possible.

Jenene was able to tell him about his mother at the end of her life; they had coincidentally shared a hospital room shortly before the woman's death. Bobby was able to fill in gaps from the early years concerning their dad and her mom. Then the conversation worked around to what might have been a touchier subject had Jenene not forgiven and had Bobby not been willing to own up.

Not so much seeking atonement or even forgiveness as simple understanding, it turned out Bobby was ready to admit to his inappropriateness.

"I did bad things to you," he admitted rather courageously considering the possible ramifications of his confession. "I can't tell you how much I regret hurting you. I'm so sorry."

Jenene was able to express her forgiveness by explaining the path her life had taken, the journey his actions very well in some way instigated, and how in the end she had evolved into the big-hearted, strong, and enduring woman to whom he was speaking.

The gratefulness Bobby in turn expressed showed her their eventual coming to terms likely benefited him more than her. For him the guilt was still a raw wound. Whatever old scars she had were so faded they were invisible.

Chapter 93
Ultimate Praise

The proof Jenene was on the right path manifested in many ways.

The greatest payoff was her students' appreciation. She worked tirelessly and determinedly to help those willing to help themselves. Even as she discouraged it some valued her the way gurus are valued. All she did was listen, offer advice, teach, sometimes mentor, and lead them to the ability to cull insights from their own experience, knowledge, and spiritual connection.

In a world of so many different points of view, there were still detractors. Naysayers who delight in using skepticism as a scalpel to undercut belief, they left niggling doubts in Jenene's mind.

The validity of her work was given maybe the greatest confirmation possible on June 19, 2005.

Channeled through a new Reiki student named Susie, all Jenene's diligent work inspired a message from the Master himself, Dr. Mikao Usui. The day before, after her first attunement, Susie had a lucid vision of Usui and afterward wrote down two shorter messages from the Master: *"You are doing well—you are a true disciple,"* and, *"All that you need you already have."*

These had surprised the lovely woman, as she was not used to channeling messages. She was open to the experience. But she never expected to channel such a profound and beautiful message as:

"It is a truth that all are not given the energy to rise above the rainbow—but all are welcome to enjoy its beauty. The spectrum of color is as the spectrum of each of us...each living thing holds within itself. It is only in sharing this knowledge of love and light and color that we will totally achieve our mission. Our lives are an opportunity. The light and love it brings is a gift. The ability to share this knowledge is more than a responsibility—it is our destiny."

After Susie wrote down this message, she handed it to Jenene and said, "I don't know what this is. It might be a recipe. But it's for you." Her talent running toward the artistic, not the literary, Susie was quite surprised by the words she had transcribed.

Jenene looked at the words as the ultimate praise.

That honor is part of the reason this book was possible. Jenene is too modest to be self-aggrandizing enough to write her own story. She never even would've felt right hiring a ghostwriter to tell it entirely from her point of view. It took a lot of cajoling on my part to get her to be a participant in its writing, and she was oftentimes like a pile of oysters I was prying apart in that my questions not always sprung pearls.

I pointed out to her that her story had to be important if even Master Usui had taken notice. It had to be worth telling.

This would only happen after the proof she healed herself was irrefutable. Of course this knowledge would begin with a scare.

Chapter 94
New Lesson

Even when lacking other symptoms, one symptom can be so egregious it makes it easy to let speculation run wild.

Jenene began noticing traces of blood in her stool again. Maybe not the horror-show of the past, but even a small amount of red in the toilet bowl had her worried. Had her bowel movement been black, meaning the blood from the colon, she would have feared cancer. The lessons that caused the Crohn's disease no longer fit yet blood was no doubt evidence something was amiss.

Jenene expressed her problem to me: she needed to pinpoint the dilemma and the only way she could know for sure was to go to the doctor. It had been so long the very notion filled her with uncertainty.

Trepidation aside, she wondered what I might think since we had resolved to live without the infringement of Western medicine. Unwilling in regards to my own health, she feared I would be disappointed and part of me was because I believe her strong enough to learn her lessons and heal any ailment. I expressed my belief in her and together we came to a hard realization: there needed to be a rapprochement to Western medicine because then she would know for sure.

Able to recall readily the previous saga of her health, she retraced that old path to remind herself of all she hoped to avoid.

In the days when she was dealing with Crohn's every minute of her life, every pound lost was a pound lost forever, and her doctors would never let her forget it. It was practically a mantra. Even though the disease made eating agonizing because it felt as though she was digesting broken glass rather than edible food, she had to force food down to keep up her caloric intake or else, as the physicians warned, she would waste away and die from malnutrition as much as from Crohn's.

As it was, her body was unable to absorb nutrients. This caused a scarcity of hair growth for years. And by the time she was convalescing actively all the teeth had fallen out of her mouth save for the six bottom front teeth. Her dentist told her they were saved by the salivary glands. Good thing too—dentures work better if there are more than gums for bracing.

After coming through such a trying ordeal she was adamant she would not allow herself to get so sick again. Had she somehow done just that?

Fear of Crohn's possible return took me instantly to an aspect of the past I would as soon forget. It's funny and sad and kind of amazing how an adult man can be reduced to a child in an instant. Fear has that power. Even being a little older and wiser had ill prepared me for the loss half-expected all my early life.

In the intervening years since those darkest days I had almost forgotten the constant nagging dread that each time I saw my mom would be the last. That if I let something go unsaid between us I would never get the chance to say it to her face. That sooner than I was willing to accept, my future would be without her.

Fearing Crohn's had reappeared, after years of seeking no medical testing, in the end Jenene knew she had to get a colonoscopy. She needed to know if our fears were founded. Had ulcers returned? Or was it something else?

For those of you who don't know, here's the bad news: once you hit middle age, your doctor is going to want to stick a tube up your works and regularly get a peek. This lovely procedure involves examining the large intestine via a colonoscope, a fiber optic camera, inserted into the rectum. The good news is that nowadays sedation makes the odious procedure less uncomfortable and painful than in years past.

Jenene suffered several colonoscopies when the unpleasantness of the procedure was masked by nothing.

A terrible way to spend a morning even if there would be sedation, Jenene was not exactly anxious to go through with another scope.

If the Crohn's were back, the doctors would press her to get prodded again and again. Crohn's sufferers like clockwork get scoped four or more times a year.

Numbed up or not, that was one routine she would prefer not resume. It was a coordinated nightmare.

After the anal fissure, Jenene had been particularly observant to protect that region of her body. The discomfort of the procedure brought to mind the stories of distress people tell following alien abductions. Even if there is sedation, the feeling wears off. You will feel that there's been some monkey business going on down below.

There was no getting around that she had to know if her worst fears were true. She learned long ago it's better to face your demons. Shying away from them does not make them go away; it only gives them time to grow stronger and become scarier.

No longer faced with suffering through the examination without anesthesia, the worst part this time would prove to be the preparation. Prescribed powerful laxative tablets and syrup-thick polyethylene glycol, the intended result is easy enough to guess: a poop-propelled human rocket.

Jenene was advised to drink a half-gallon of the polyethylene glycol. The pharmacy gave her a pre-mixed gallon-sized jug. I marveled at how the liquid was so clear.

Not one to be wasteful, I offered to join her in the cleansing process, partially out of sympathy, partially because of that myth that at autopsy they found five pounds of impacted waste in John Wayne.

The night before the scope we followed the instructions to a tee. First we swallowed laxative tablets. Then the object was to drink eight ounces of the mineral-flavored purifier every fifteen minutes until the viscous fluid was gone, camped out near to and on the toilet.

"To our health," I said before we doffed our first glasses. I choked a little, not used to the thickness and weird flavor of the drink. All I could do was open my gullet and let it cascade down. I wiped my mouth and smiled. "Not so bad."

"Wait 'til it kicks in," Jenene replied.

We were sitting at the dining room table, having one of those difficult but necessary conversations.

I only had one question. "If the Crohn's is back, do you have any doubts you can heal again?"

"I can tell you one thing, I want to avoid the prescription drug route," Jenene replied. "As much as they've advanced and improved, and they definitely have, the possible side effects are still scary."

It's true that today there are more drugs available to combat Crohn's. But how safe are these drugs, really? By their own admission, there's a list of possible side effects to rival the prophecies of Nostradamus, from malignancies to heart failure.

That Crohn's sufferers would risk death to get relief is a testament to, if nothing else, the huge inconvenience Crohn's represents. But Crohn's is more than a nuisance; it is a constant threat that can cause among other indignities seronegative arthritis, anal fistula, and festering ulcers.

Quality of life is an important thing. Some argue that regardless of quality, life is sacred…but how sacred can your life feel if you are in constant pain, living through the horror of Crohn's? For the fortunate, the drugs reduce their symptoms and allow them to live their life; for others, well, they are not so lucky.

Unaware how she ended up on their mailing list, Jenene was inundated with mailers hocking the Crohn's drug Humira. Out of curiosity she had perused their advertisements to see how far prescription drugs have progressed. The last time she had been to the doctor, steroids were the main option, which if you recall Jenene found caused devastating psychological side effects.

When she was finished scanning the possible side effects, she said, "I hoped it would be better. Scary as ever."

After scanning the list myself, I had to agree. In a perfect world, drugs such as Humira would work for every sufferer who took them. I wish it were that simple. I'm sure doctors wish it were that simple. The makers of Humira would especially wish it were that simple. As the small book of side effects attests, unfortunately it's not, and no drug is absolutely certain to help every Crohn's sufferer.

"I would hope even if it's back you would be better able to control the symptoms," I said. "You know so much more now."

"Oh, I don't doubt I could back it down," she assured me (the pledge I was waiting for); "I would just be really disappointed in myself for letting it return."

The colonoscopy went as smoothly as can be expected and the news was good.

Our beliefs were rewarded: lo and behold there was absolutely no sign of Crohn's disease. None. Not even scar tissue from the previous bout. A decade after Western medicine turned its back on her—as confident as they were she was a lost cause, we believe out of frustration rather than dispassion—Jenene was proven completely Crohn's-free.

"I knew I healed it," she said, "but it's great to get confirmation."

This outstanding news meant Jenene had defied every medical expectation, did what she had been told repeatedly was impossible...and proven that if applied intelligently, the methods by which she brought about her good health could save a life doctors have deemed lost.

The bleeding turned out to be from a small ring of fissures deep in her rectum, a lesson that pertained to her life and therefore could be learned and the issue healed.

After the wonderful news, besides being ecstatic, we began reminiscing about Jenene's battle throughout the years, the ups and downs, the good and the bad. We discussed the day almost two decades before when she was given the diagnosis that changed our lives.

Recalling it all, I said the very thing many doctors had throughout the years: "Your story would make a remarkable book." A self-proclaimed hermit, Jenene acknowledged that her story could be beneficial to others facing a war against disease but felt she was not the sort of person who would be so self-important as to write an autobiography.

"Come on, Mom, this story could help people and do all the things you are trying to do with The Shop," I said. "You're like a living miracle."

Too humble to see it in such terms because she believes it's within all of us to heal ourselves of life-threatening illness, my appeal to her vanity fell on deaf ears. Sure, she had to find the tools and put together her own survivor's toolbox, but the methods she used are available to anyone willing to open their minds and put in the work to save their own lives. Some of these methods have existed literally for millennia.

"I don't know if I would want to get any attention."

"It remains to be seen if anyone would be interested," I pointed out.

"My life written out…I don't know if that's a good idea."

"I think Master Usui would feel whatever it takes to get the message to the largest audience possible. People need to learn about twenty-first century Reiki. They need to learn about how much farther it can be taken than is conventionally known. You're sort of the perfect poster child for how far healing can be taken."

Jenene mulled it over. "Maybe you could write it," she suggested. "You could tell it better than anyone else. You were there through the worst. You saw it all."

I had to mull that over. "I don't know. I'm not sure I could deal with those who would be our detractors."

"What do you mean?"

"There will always be skeptics," I said sepulchrally. "Your story is so incredible there will be those who don't believe it's possible."

"Different strokes for different folks. I don't think I can tell it. I think you can. If you think my story will help isn't that what's important?"

She had me there.

Not even taking into consideration the wide gamut of diseases, illnesses, and other ailments healing can help and even beat, so many people suffer from digestive issues this whole book could exist just to address that aspect alone.

Consider, almost invariably when I turn on the TV, I see advertisements for products to control ulcerative colitis, irritable bowel syndrome, and Crohn's disease. Of these life-altering ailments, Crohn's is the archetype of digestive tract disease. From athletes to regular Joes, many people are afflicted with the painful and sometimes fatal malady.

Filmmaker Dan O'Bannon lost his decades-long battle with Crohn's in December of 2009. The project he is maybe best known for, penning the game-changer script for 1979's *Alien*, was directly inspired from his experience with the disease. Concerning the life cycle of an alien monster that gestates inside a living person only to burst out of the victim's chest in one of history's top five scares, the film probably stands as the best and most visceral visual insight into how Crohn's makes a person feel.

Crohn's, for something that so little was known about when Jenene was first diagnosed, has become frighteningly common. Sufferers endure so much horror and unpleasantness. They bear extreme weight loss and inconvenient bouts of diarrhea, excruciating ulcers, painful and humiliating procedures, and their only chance at remission comes through extensive, expensive, and exact drug treatment.

Unless they are clued in to and put to use the alternatives Jenene utilized to reclaim her health.

With all this in mind, I decided it was worth the effort to tell this story, even if it was a direction I had never before considered. In some way or other, my whole life prepared me. My childhood was unique in that I lived under the dark cloud of fear my beloved mother would die and instead was privy to witnessing what I have no qualm against terming miraculous recovery.

I never considered events in my own life in literary terms. Life seems rather prosaic when the days are being lived. In retrospect, having heard the stories and lived the rest, I saw what an amazing life Jenene has lived. I put together how I could use the love of words she inspired in me to honor her achievements.

So I began writing the story you have read to this point, intending this to be the end, the valedictory scene when Western medicine proved Jenene's methods work.

At the onset of the project I had no idea about the chapters that lay ahead. After so many tests and lessons learned, we never expected those yet to come.

Chapter 95
Fallout of a Spirit Intervention

In the dreamscape all possibilities are laid bare....

Jenene sits in the passenger seat of an old car. She's riding shotgun, her dad behind the wheel. The dash rattles. The seat feels hot. There's just a touch of dustiness. The radio plays a song she can only identify as old. Cheeks florid and red, her dad graces her with his warming smile, and she feels good about this trip, wherever it may take her, because she would always in some way trust her dad.

They are in the old neighborhood. Cottage Grove. In fact, they are coming to a stop in front of her childhood home, the one they lived in before the move to Wilson. It looks just the same....

So many memories came about in this house.

Many were made in the neighborhood too. It's too easy to recall they were the family looked upon as different. Her mom worked. Every other mom in town was a housewife. A two-income home, they were the first family who could afford an air conditioner...and color TV. Neighborhood kids would line up at the screen door. Just to catch a gander at the flickering screen.

There was another downside to her mom working: on her birthday she was the only kid who brought store-bought treats. Every other kid's mom baked cookies or other confections. She felt the distinction singled her out in a bad way. It made her believe her peers thought her mother didn't care enough to provide homemade treats.

How different it was when her son went to the very same elementary school. By then it was store-bought or nothing.

Her dad puts the car in park. He glances at their old house before turning to face her. "It looks about the same," he comments.

She agrees. Right out of her memory, the house is exactly as it was way back when.

Their old house is only one stop.

They drive. Familiar sights, but from long ago—time has gone on while their route exists somewhere between then and now, a slice of amalgamated nuances combined to make the ultimate representation of a road she used to drive all the time…because they are going to the farm, and she knows the way well. The path to the farm, from any direction, she would never forget.

As it was for decades, she sees the old red house with white trim bracketed by trees. Of all the places she had lived in her life, this was the only one she truly identified as home. It saddened her greatly when she heard the old homestead burned down. Yet here it stands. The wheels crackle over the gravel driveway where she has gleaned many agates. The sound is so achingly poignant it makes her want to cry for what was and what can never be again.

Bob parks and ushers her to the front door. She is so happy to go inside. This is the important place in her heart of hearts, where she felt the most secure. The house represented the kind of unshaped but tangible happiness that can sustain a difficult life.

Lal, Bill, and Herb wait for her in the sun-lit living room. Seeing them makes a wellspring of emotion burst. They welcome her with the warm hospitality that epitomizes these wonderful people she loves so much. They look good. Each had a period of old age when they were still hale and hearty and that is how they appear to her.

The familiarity she feels towards them warms her as much as the balmy light pouring through the windows.

There is a realness to them that belies her belief that they are dead.

A large man attired in a dark suit stands with them. He is a stranger. At the sight of him, there is a shift, as if clouds have blotted out the sun suddenly, and the room is cast in dimness and shadows. Dust motes float languidly, visible only barely in the sudden gloom. He doesn't frighten her even though she knows instinctually his presence is a bad omen. He stands back from the others, tall and solemn, like one of those monolithic heads on Easter Island, a guest polite enough to wait to be introduced.

"He's a doctor," her dad says. "He has to tell you something. You have to listen. It's very important. Your life is on the line."

The doctor steps forward, so that The Seniors are at his back. He says eight words she will never forget: "You have breast cancer and need treatment immediately."

Cancer? Cancer!

Looking around at her beloved relatives' faces, they all earnestly nod agreement. Bill's deep, wisdom-filled eyes bore into her and in them she sees all the truth she needs.

"I won't get chemo," she asserts. It had long been her conviction that she would not seek health through poison. "Not ever."

Then the wispy stuff of which dreams are made blows apart and Jenene awakes in her bed in Menomonie, Wisconsin.

It was the morning of June 13, 2010.

Jenene was being greeted by the enthusiastic licks of a little Chihuahua named Pinto. Her constant companion, the cute-as-a-button lap dog was more than a pet; he was a constant source of hope. He had come into her life the Thanksgiving of 2008 and with cuteness and jubilancy endeared himself immediately.

Pinto's person died from an asthma attack. After going through a string of abusive homes, he wound up in the care of my dad. When Guy took a trip, I offered to dog sit.

During his week with us we became very fond of the adorable little pooch, Jenene in particular. I offered to take him off my dad's hands permanently. I had witnessed him offer the little guy to someone for which neither of us much cares. I knew it would be cool.

Quickly it became apparent Pinto was meant for Jenene. We do not seek the animals we care for; they come to us on their own. Pinto came at the right time, too.

Scratching Pinto's little skull as he lay down his ears submissively, she thought: *I can't have breast cancer. I can't.*

There was no reason to panic. Not yet. She hoped. But her gut feeling, pesky instinct, gnawed at her.

At the first opportunity she discussed the dream with Russ. There was a time she may have avoided such communication but her husband had matured and grown. It could be said he was committed to embodying a spiritual renaissance.

New problems emerged for Russ in the years after The Headache lifted. Since a nod's as good as a wink to a blind horse, he could never see the upside. Unfulfilled, he went through jobs like rolls of toilet paper. As he got older and the sort of job he could tolerate never materialized, he became increasingly unhappy which lent naturally to cynicism.

His attitude ran invariably toward the negative. He would argue with Jenene uselessly. He claimed to have troubles controlling his mouth. The same squabbles went on for years. A point came when Jenene was fed up with his antagonism. She gave him an ultimatum. Seek help or free her from the burden of living with a man who couldn't go a day without picking a fight.

Russ professed to not being able to see a future without Jenene and swore he would do whatever it took to save their marriage.

This vow led to difficult admissions. He spoke to a doctor about bipolar-like symptoms and suicidal thoughts. Depressive lows and manic highs marked much of his life. Speaking up led to a pertinent discovery. His lithium level was low. It accounted for his dour mood.

A simple affordable prescription brought about a total metamorphosis. He was a new man—a man intent on making a better life and stronger relationships.

Even after conquering The Headache Russ remained a resistant student. For too long, he only sought Jenene's counsel when he recognized she was teetering toward wit's end. Once he was open to guidance, a lot of disharmony was excised from their relationship like a lanced abscess.

At last he wanted advice. He recognized he had to come to terms with his past to reconcile the present and he needed help. The problem was that he had no idea what exactly needed to be healed. He had wronged and been wronged. There was so much.

There was also his desire to make up to Jenene for all the time he was, his word, a "butt."

What was Jenene's idea? A proposal and challenge: no matter what send Reiki faithfully. Every day. Committed. Unbending. She suggested there be a minimum of two recipients. This way he would receive whatever healing he sent and without knowing exact specifics would heal his bad karma.

After a fair amount of grumbling, it seemed like a lot of work, Russ decided he was being stupid. He conceded he hadn't always been the best or most gracious person. Maybe through healing he could grow roses in the manure he had scattered over his life.

People and situations personal to him could only be part of it. There were many good causes in need of healing energy. She felt that if he continued to send it would be proof of his conviction to their union. It would also heap healing back on him.

Russ established a list and encouraged everyone to contribute.

Henceforth he sent to those he had slighted and hurt; bridges burned; enemies prospered.

To the family he had harmed and those who harmed him.

He sent to missing children, refugees, American soldiers and their allies; to abused and neglected animals, to premature babies, to people harmed in accidents, to the victims of terrorist attacks.

He sent to endangered species. Whales. Wolves. Polar bears. And bees. He sent to natural disasters: hurricanes and earthquakes and tornadoes, the usual troika of apocalyptical events that prove that for all the civilization chiseled out of the world Mother Gaia can reduce us to scurrying ants in an instant.

He sent to all the people, events, and other things Jenene did and maybe more.

Russ's fresh new attitude restored her faith in him and she fell in love with him all over.

What ultimately manifested Russ's change? A lot contributed but I wonder if all the Reiki Jenene sent over the years brought about her best results. She didn't want to breakup. She really didn't want to divorce. Only she needed her husband to be open to life and at least the prospect of contentment if not happiness. It was taxing being married to someone so curmudgeonly. She had enough of her own lessons. She needed a solid mate and wanted him to have a healthier outlook.

Russ undergoing a resurgence of spirit meant he was better able to address her needs. He encouraged her to share and be open. He wanted to be close again. He wanted her trust.

Even with Pinto there Jenene would've felt very alone had Russ not committed to doing his best to be a devoted husband.

Possible estrangement quashed, feeling safe expressing all the anxiety, fear, and other elements the dream dredged up meant so much. Dread predominated but there was a sense of wistful nostalgia too. What was maybe strangest was the wonder also inspired. The bad news aside it was quite a reunion, an aspect of the dream she would savor.

Russ was at a loss except to suggest she follow her best instincts. Before they could discuss it further, he was wracked with chest pains. Jenene rushed him to the ER. Extensive testing—including going through his femoral artery and up through his body to his heart—proved what he experienced was a panic attack.

Russ lost his mother to cancer, cancer that began in her breast and metastasized to her brain. He believed in his wife's uncannily accurate "psychic" dreams. It was understandable the prospect of Jenene harboring cancer freaked him out so much he was convinced he was suffering a heart attack.

Russ's ordeal meant his heart got a clean bill of health and Jenene learned how devastated her husband felt at the prospect of losing her. It also served as a distraction from the dream.

She wanted to believe the phantasm could be attributed to an agitated stomach or unfounded unconscious fears. She did not want to capitulate to the fact her dream was at that time an unheeded warning delivered at precisely the right time…so long as she did not dawdle.

As it turned out, she would have a mammogram before Russ was released from the hospital.

Chapter 96
Impetus

Since returning to Western medicine, Jenene underwent regular checkups as a baseline for monitoring her health. She happened to have an appointment soon after the dream with the intent of scheduling a bone density scan.

Dr. Brown had been her dad's general physician and she trusted him. "When was your last mammogram?" he asked offhandedly near the conclusion of the appointment.

"It's been over twenty years," she said coolly, struck by the coincidence of the timing of his inquiry. "I don't like mammograms." The way the procedure pressed her breasts was extremely unpleasant and left her sore for days. Because she never thought she could have the lessons for breast cancer, she had decided to avoid the discomfort. The decision was coming back to haunt her.

"Wow, that's a long time. I think it's important to check this out."

"I would prefer not to get one."

"I think it's necessary," Dr. Brown concluded. He escorted her to the reception desk, where he had her future appointments scheduled, including a mammogram.

Without the dream there was no way she would have left Dr. Brown's office that day with an appointment for a mammogram.

After delays and postponements, Jenene finally underwent both procedures on June 23. Shortly after, she was called in for a second mammogram. Then she met with surgeon Dr. Greg Ruth on June 29 to discuss the results.

For starters the bone density scan revealed she had osteopenia, an early form of osteoporosis. She had to work on it. That wasn't the diagnosis she sweated over, the one that had her insides coiled up tighter than springs.

Jenene had a bad feeling the rest of the news was going to be even less promising. The problem was that all she could do was look within. In so doing she learned some things. Introspection determined she very well had the lesson for breast cancer. She couldn't deny the possibility. There was no choice other than to move forward ready to face the worst.

Even with the pertinent relationships improving all the time, residual bits of negativity with all the ugliness, clinginess, and pervasiveness of barnacles stuck to her still. In an attempt to purge of the vitriol and scrape those suckers off her hull, she wrote down all her gripes, angers, and hurts. Then she burned the spewed-upon sheet of paper to release the negative energy.

Even as she had undergone the ritual, she felt the cleansing was too late to avoid a diagnosis. Cleansing herself of it all was no less cathartic for the knowledge. She recognized it was long in coming.

So it was no surprise when Dr. Ruth confirmed her suspicions. He showed her a suspicious spiky speck on the computer screen. Miniscule, only about ¼ centimeter, for its smallness, it nonetheless represented a huge potential danger.

Flushed with the immediate panic that comes from feeling intimidated by forbidding prospects, Jenene's mind whirled. Reviewing all she been through, would have to do, and how she would deal with this new beast, she concluded she may be in for it again.

"I'm scheduling you a sentinel node biopsy," Dr. Ruth concluded. "We need to find out exactly what this is."

Jenene nodded. "I need to learn as much about this as I can," she said. "I need to heal this."

August 7 was the day of reckoning—when it all became real. For a biopsy, the experience was less cumbersome than she anticipated but it in no way lightened the burden of the news it would ultimately bring. The radiologist was thorough, and though it was painless, Jenene was anxious to be done.

Two days later, Jenene received a message from Dr. Ruth. It was a Friday. She had never gotten good news when a doctor called her on a Friday. Good news can be put off until Monday, only bad news, such as that time was of the essence so not even a weekend could be spared, warranted a Friday call.

Jenene and Russ were walking Pinto when the call came.

Words were not minced. "We found invasive tubular carcinoma," Dr. Ruth said levelly. "It's a very rare form of cancer. We also found ductal carcinoma in situ or DSIC."

Even if she had mentally prepared herself for this eventuality, it still had all the impact of a battering ram right to her midsection. She harbored two different forms of cancer? She didn't want to believe it but knew she couldn't afford the luxury of denial.

The idea of losing her breasts terrified her. The cosmetic aspect aside, the whole idea of losing a section of her body to cancer repelled her. Actress Christina Applegate, *Married with Children's* Kelly Bundy, lost her breasts; Jenene thought it so brave of a sex symbol to undergo a mastectomy and it seemed even braver now that she was facing the possibility herself.

"You need to come in immediately so we can schedule surgery."

Feeling as if she had fallen into a kaleidoscopic tumble down a very deep pit, it took her a few seconds to regain her faculties. "I need time to think about this," she said shakily, feeling suddenly out of sorts, almost ill.

"There is no time. You are so lucky this was caught now. We have to move fast, while we still can."

In recent years, dreams had come less and less, perhaps because messages transmitted more directly. It was as if Jenene's psychic sixth sense had been calibrating, trying to strike the right chord, the right balance. In some cases she has been able to receive messages and omens at appropriate times to make a difference. Other times not so much. How appropriate that the most vivid and straightforward dream would be the one that was her personal life preserver.

The dream afforded her just enough time…if she heeded her doctor's warning.

The unpredictability of life and lessons blindsided her again.

As a seasoned survivor she refused to wallow in self-pity. Overshadowed by shock, any initial grander feelings were washed away in a tide of baser speculation, such as how the hell could she let this happen? What for some would be unanswerable questioning was for Jenene stone cold acceptance that the enigma of her lessons could only be unfurled and solved through introspection.

She had proven her healing cred. She had achieved a certain status. With that came the maturity to turn her high-powered perception on herself. She could look within the way she read a student seeking solid advice. She could acknowledge she was imbalanced. Acknowledge she had courted the lesson that brought cancer inexcusably into her body.

Still, there was a period of moving leadenly, thinking sluggishly, during which terms had to be reached. There was never a conflict. She would fight for her life but she would not grovel.

If only Belle could have told her sooner….

It is not in our Angels' purview to interfere beyond minimal advisement. Aspects of our paths have to be dealt with in a personal, lone way. When they arise it is up to us to pinpoint and learn our lessons. What Belle had done by warning her of the impending end of her contract was a no-no that was only tolerated because of Jenene's tireless healing efforts. This was another chance for her to demonstrate why her reprieve was justified because her survival would mean she had gained another way to teach and inspire others.

She had learned not to underestimate her opposition; breast cancer was perhaps the fiercest dance partner ever on her fight card, a real killer. The research is too concrete to ignore: many sufferers lose the battle.

She was determined to live; single-minded was she toward that end.

Less than a week after Jenene learned she had cancer, a blazing hot Wednesday in August, Dr. Ruth laid out all the scary possibilities: a full mastectomy, chemotherapy, another sentinel node biopsy to check the lymph nodes, breast conservation surgery, radiation, hormone therapy. One thing he had to say that was interesting: like the outer layer of a geode, the DCIS completely covered and contained the inner lining of tubular carcinoma and likely stopped it from metastasizing into the lymph nodes.

"But it's likely, as early as this was caught, that a mastectomy won't be necessary," he said, much to her relief. Two other doctors floated the possibility of a full mastectomy; she told them no way and she would quit treating if they insisted. "Both cancers are stage one, a very promising prognosis."

"How soon do you want to do this?"

With solemn eyes looking suddenly right into her, he said, "Friday, no later," and the tone of his voice made it sound as if he were ordering military air strikes against a hostile enemy right then marching him and her down.

The gravity of the situation could not be mistaken: Jenene committed to her doctor's orders.

From the dream to setting up surgery, a span of one month, her life had changed irrevocably.

What could she do? She didn't want to be viewed as weak for taking medical help. As a Reiki master, she felt she should be able to heal herself. Some lessons, it turns out, require greater sacrifice. And in reality she was faced with a tremendous opportunity to combine all that she knew with what her doctors could do for her. In melding the separate methods she would be an example of what was possible through integration of both philosophies, what could very well be the future of medicine.

Even the humble need be humbled more.

Oh, did she regret opening this can of worms! The thing of it was, now that it was open, it was open all the way, and the creepy-crawlies would be wiggling until dealt with, whether she liked it or not.

Surgery was scheduled for August 22.

Chapter 97
Breast Cancer

Breast cancer calls to mind some powerful and evocative words. Tumor. Malignancy. Mastectomy. Death.

With that revelation this book took on a new dimension: it morphed into the story of a woman who not only fought and beat two dangerous autoimmune diseases in the past but, like a retired gunslinger forced to participate in another gun battle, had to face yet another, perhaps the worst opponent of her life. Even famous and wealthy people have lost their breasts and even their lives to cancer.

To disease, your account balance, status, and achievements mean nothing. No amount of money could save multimillionaire Elizabeth Edwards. In the unblinking and non-judgmental eye of cancer, wealthy and paupers are no different. That's why the proven information in this book bears such importance. For a minimal investment anyone can gain the tools to save their own life.

Looking down the barrel of any cancer stuns, confounds, and terrifies. It took terrific resolve for Jenene not to unleash a scream out of frustration…and disappointment. Allowing cancer in made her feel like she had let herself down. Maybe she got too complacent.

Just her nature, or the nature she prospered, Jenene had no choice other than to take this catastrophe in stride.

She couldn't let cancer bully, intimidate, or scare her; at least not so much she lost her psychological edge. It was up to her to repel the invasion. Her edge had brought her through before and it would again. What it amounted to was her belief that all disease is conquerable…so long as she was willing to look into herself and learn her lessons.

Maybe the greatest lesson Jenene ever learned along her extended journey was that illness and injury are the body's clues there is something we need to reconcile, repair, or resolve. In some cases the reason can be relatively minor, such as a need to slow down and rest when life gets too overwhelming. Or it can be infinitely more difficult; the need to accept someone close to you will never change; relinquishing control; even cutting someone harmful out of your life.

Sometimes it can involve reconciling old hurts and newer regrets.

"The doctor in the dream was right," Jenene dropped the bomb. "I have breast cancer."

Galvanizing news has the power to shellac, pellet, and bulldoze in one swoop. I was again filled with all those old fears. Knowing her history of hurdles leapt, I was also bolstered. I have seen my mom be the exception to the rule so many times. I knew cancer was just another stumbling block she would hurtle right over.

"So the dream was a warning," I said.

"I had a feeling when my dad took me to the farm and the Seniors were there."

"The moment you told me about it I was worried it wasn't just some fluke. It's almost like your history of prescient dreams culminated in this warning."

I was positive she would heal. The dream was meant to allow her the chance. Why doubt? I had witnessed her overcome. I had watched her conquer Crohn's, degenerative disc disease, and lupus. I had the privilege of being there when she helped others overcome everything from Tourette's syndrome and anxiety disorders to diabetes and cancer.

"I'm grateful they let me know."

"What would've happened if they hadn't?"

I recognized breast cancer was a daunting challenge, one that would likely test her more than any other. But she would walk away with her life.

"I maybe wouldn't have known to read that part of my body until it was too late," she acknowledged. "This form of cancer is fast acting. I might not have survived."

"Seems like there was a reason they warned you. Like you aren't supposed to die…only learn a new lesson."

Despite all the healing I've witnessed, I walked away from this conversation acknowledging the peril.

Statistics don't lie.

One out of seven women will also suffer breast cancer. This makes the odds of knowing someone who will face breast cancer—your mom, your aunt, your sister, your daughter—far higher than the likelihood you will know someone who dies in a plane crash or a terrorist attack, two major modern fears that are astronomically unlikely to personally affect most people.

How many of these women will die? Another hard stat to swallow is that potentially one fifth of breast cancer sufferers will succumb to this devastating disease. As many drunk driving fatalities as there are and as many murders, statistically far more women will die from breast cancer.

Especially lacking early detection….

All I can be is deeply grateful the spirits of our beloved family orchestrated the dream and ensured she got the message she so desperately needed. Ignoring messages only reaps more harm. There was a reason our family beseeched her to get her breasts checked. There was a reason for the spirit intervention.

It saved her life.

Chapter 98
The Prospect

Carried from dream to surgery on a cyclone of anxiety, in the interim Jenene worked overtime to pinpoint her lessons…and accept her choices.

This was to be a test of her durability, perseverance, and open-mindedness.

The decision to take aid from Western medicine was difficult. She was certain she could heal on her own. Once the adversary has been identified the beast can be slain. Again she was at a crossroads. She could do it but why bargain against a structure of support she never before was offered?

The situation was all different. Doctors turned their backs on her before because they had run out of options. Her new doctors were better prepared. They wouldn't try to chisel away her hope to lessen the blow of their failure. They wouldn't abandon her.

Making the rational decision to ignore the illogic of pride was bigger than testing her health against her ego.

This was the perfect opportunity, actually. To show how Western and alternative medicine could and should be integrated.

Reiki and other forms of natural healing have the potential to help every patient in the world have a smoother medical experience—if not eliminate the need altogether—and I knew Jenene had all the tools to prove the point.

Even if recovery was maybe more attainable by integrating Western medicine with her methods, there was no illusion it would be easy. The prognosis was beleaguering from the standpoint of her doctors. She was warned to anticipate pain. She was warned when it got to the radiation to anticipate burns. She was warned to anticipate slow and trying recuperation. But healing was her wheelhouse and she was intent on making a point.

As always, my mom would use healing to prove the exception to the rule.

Chapter 99
Healing Crisis

With the help from some of her students, the angels, and her friends, Jenene devised a healing plan, creating a routine she as before followed every day. Intent on pushing the cancer out of her body, she used Reiki symbols, stones, affirmations, visualization, garlic tea, and apple cider vinegar, Herb's old cure-all. She researched foods that fed cancer and in changing her diet learned more about letting go.

Even what amounts to a small sacrifice can make for a glum disposition.

The worst dietary change was renouncing soymilk. Under the impression it was good for her health, she had gotten in the habit of drinking a glass every morning. A treat, she enjoyed the smooth cold silkiness. Never much for breakfast, soymilk was a good way to kick-start her metabolism and get on with her day. But her research revealed soymilk feeds cancer. It had to go. For her it was worse than when she renounced smoking.

To boost her strength and because Pinto loved it, soon after relocating to Menomonie after scaling back The Shop when the economy spiraled, Jenene began to go for walks every day. She worked her way up to as many as three or four a day. Her doctors praised her ambition; they were amazed someone missing a kneecap, an infirmity once predicted would require her to use a brace and cane, could so far exceed limitations.

Exercise is conducive to healing and she wanted to heal; every mile walked felt like a mile turned back on her odometer. There was also the fact that a body in motion stays in motion. Forward momentum reminded her that all things pass.

Menomonie is a college town and UW-Stout has provided many sidewalks throughout the sprawling campus. Adding to the workout are many hills; a veritable wealth of verticality, some are brief, others long, some gradual, and a few steep. Russ and/or I often joined her because walks boost heart health, we liked the company, and there could be hooligans about.

Most of the college kids are friendly but some appear a little rough around the edges. There was also the matter of the Thirsty Thursday party tradition. We would often encounter large migrating groups of pre-drunken or post-drunken students. When alcohol is involved, people can get aggressive when there's a cute little dog they want to pet.

The school supports many athletics and our walks often involved circling their Nona William's Stadium, Johnson Fieldhouse, and through the park in front of the art building. We tallied many miles. Considering her missing kneecap was supposed to require her to always need a brace and a cane and the degenerative disc disease was supposed to put her in a wheelchair long ago, her ability to journey so far is something I consider remarkable.

Anyone seeking to improve his or her mental outlook should go for a walk. Getting the blood circulating and the muscles working has an amazing effect on the spirit. Even fifteen minutes a day can improve your health drastically. Once in the habit Jenene tried to walk as often as possible.

"With a missing kneecap there's always a chance my knee will give out and it does happen once in a while," she said on one of our walks. "But it's worth the risk when I consider where I *could* be. To think there was a time I was told I would be saddled with a cumbersome leg brace the rest of my life. Now decades later all I need to worry about is the occasional give out. It's worth the risk. I trust I won't fall and get hurt…unless I have the lesson."

To think she walked for leisure now. I thought back to all the paper routes she delivered on foot and was struck by how far she has come. She logged so many miles just in the course of her life then. The notion of taking a walk for pleasure was absurd.

It was fortuitous before going into the battle with cancer Jenene built up her stamina and endurance. Improved physical prowess combined with Reiki had so far lent enhanced physicality. And the time to think or converse revealed better perspective on many things. She hoped the trend would carry over into cancer treatment.

To a degree it worked.

She never thought walking could factor in her health and mental outlook so much during a time of crisis but as part of her routine it helped immensely. "When dealing with breast cancer every walk helped me find a little peace of mind," she explained. "I'm so thankful Pinto came into my life and I discovered what walks could do for me. Without them I would've had a lot less enjoyment in my life during those dicey months."

We also used walks to discuss much of what has been written in this book. Out under a blue or star-studded sky, it was easier to delve into the past.

The walks helped but even when she went with no companion other than Pinto and had time to really think, the quandary of cancer continued to stymie her.

Looking ahead to surgery, she felt overwhelmed and outmatched. Cancer was this whole other beast. She had sent huge amounts of Reiki and was faithful to her healing plan, yet she felt no different. For the first time in a long time, her body was too much of an enigma to her.

Nothing had happened that made her feel bolstered.

She needed a clearer sign.

One of her students who had progressed far led a Reiki I class around that time. Jenene was invited to receive an attunement and treatment. The opportunity couldn't have come at a more opportune time.

Like a flash grenade going off, following the class her sign began with the sort of intense perspiration that envelopes your entire body. The extreme sweating lent to an overall feeling of exhaustion. Staying hydrated was like running a marathon.

Jenene knew what she was experiencing. For all the discomfort—agony—welcomed the onslaught. It meant she was healing.

Not to be mistaken with ordinary sickness, a healing crisis occurs when the body is undergoing purification. The burst of discomfort and discharge of sweat is the body working double time to flush illness or disease. Nothing about it is pleasant. It can feel akin to dying. But the cleansing process can make a world of difference, all the difference that might be needed to repel death.

She knew something big was happening as she continued to perspire like a jug of cold milk on a hot day, something life changing, probably life saving. All she could do was drink glass after glass of water to stave off dehydration cramps and ride out the miserable part.

Before bed an aluminum flavor all at once suffused Jenene's mouth. It tasted like she had dipped her tongue in aluminum shavings. She was unsuccessful brushing the ick out with any amount of toothpaste. Even swishing with mouthwash did nothing to reduce the permeating flavor.

In the night, she rose, skimming consciousness, and urinated, neglecting to flush before returning to bed. A couple hours later, she awoke feeling surprisingly refreshed, even reinvigorated. She went into the bathroom.

There was a foul odor.

She looked in the toilet…and there was her sign.

Whatever she expelled had left a dank green ring in the toilet bowl. She flushed. The ring remained. She squirted some toilet bowl cleaner and tried to scrub the ring away. Like the awful aluminum taste of the night before, it wouldn't fade. She soon learned even straight bleach lacked the power to clean the toilet bowl or even whiten out the discoloration.

Whatever it was she expelled lacquered the porcelain.

Jenene was sure it was the caner. I tend to believe her. I wonder if some sort of testing could prove what caused the damage. It was clear as day for ages.

Next day she was going into surgery and she had never felt more positive about it: she was certain she had peed out a significant amount—if not all—of the cancer. Dr. Ruth would remove any that was left, if there was any—he did say the first sentinel node biopsy could have gotten the entire tumor.

Then she would jump through their hoops and get radiation, even if she was all but certain the cancer was already gone.

Chapter 100
Surgery

Friday, July 23.

Why are operations always scheduled so early? At the hospital early in the morning, Jenene knew the protocol. Surgery was old hat. She had been through so many operations there was nothing new except the procedure and that it was under Dr. Ruth's knife she would be going.

There was still anxiety. If she had peed the cancer out, was she being true to herself by going through with the surgery? There was no question she had to learn to reconcile her feelings. She had to remind herself of the point she was attempting to prove.

A quick walk with Pinto calmed her before the trip to the hospital. She kept up her walks throughout the ordeal. She even planned to walk later that day when she got home. She concentrated on that plan as she was prepped.

Before she was transferred to surgery, six wires were inserted around her nipple and pushed all the way back to the lymph nodes in her armpit. Had this been described to her as a medieval form of torture she would not have been surprised. If this is what she had to look forward to in regards to radiation, she knew the worst was likely still ahead. Anesthesia was welcome.

Lois was waiting when Jenene awoke after surgery. "Dr. Ruth said he got everything," her mother informed her reassuringly.

Dr. Ruth informed Jenene he had removed two lymph nodes and about 20% of her left breast. Then it was a matter of waiting for the test results. That call could not come fast enough. In the meantime, Jenene had two small incisions with which to contend. She tried to believe the cancer was behind her. She would not be sure until she had gotten confirmation. It would come less than a week later.

Chapter 101
Transcendence

It's only after facing real darkness that all the light that exists in the world seems brightest. After a lifetime of doozies, Jenene again faced such a patch, during which she had doubts about everything, her husband, her son, her beliefs, and even her continued existence.

Not Pinto, but everything else. She would never have doubts about that little dog.

Life is all about lessons.

Knowing didn't change that she was finding it increasingly difficult to learn hers.

Then illustrating the importance of her efforts, she received a call from a college professor interested in learning Reiki. The woman was adamant in her resolve to learn. Jenene realized obstacles may have beset her path, but it was her mission to teach and spread healing. Why else had she survived so many diseases that could have ended her mission? So long as she could teach, her life had meaning.

If there is any chance her message can reach a larger audience is there really a choice if we can help even a handful?

The world is a frightening place. What if we as a species sent healing collectively to all the situations tearing the world asunder? Could we change the world for the better with universal life force energy?

Jenene sums it up like this: "I realized there is still so much to be done. Even if every day is a struggle in some way, even if I have to face new lessons, I have to do it because it's my mission to teach the knowledge I'm blessed enough to gather. I have to believe all that I have gone through was for a reason…if for nothing else it would serve as inspiration to help others."

Chapter 102
Cancer Free and Beyond

July 28.

Really important days dawn like all others, with the sun rising over the horizon and casting the world in its life-giving radiance. In that way all days begin with equal hope. It's the light at the end of the darkness that has always given man solace through the longest and darkest nights. The sun will always come up and banish the gloom and shadows for another day. In that we can trust.

Jenene had no idea when she woke that hot summer morning and took Pinto out to do his business it would be a day she would always remember.

Like any other day, she took Pinto for a walk around the campus. For a college town there is a great deal of nature and wildlife. Deer. Rabbits. Squirrels. Opossums. Skunks.

Dragonflies. Even giant water bugs would scamper across her path. She took to carrying her camera phone because she came upon many photo ops.

Each time she confronted death she found new ways to value life and this amateur photography had given her a lot of pleasure and distraction. You may not be able to squeeze blood out of a turnip but Jenene had learned joy could be extrapolated from even the worst times in life. The effort could be large and the return small. Yet it was the little glimpses of happiness that bridge the gaps between the larger returns.

Seeing Dr. Ruth's office come up on the caller ID made her heart flutter. Ignoring the call would only put off the inevitable. Doubt was a bane on her back. The doubt made her afraid. Yet she was never one not to confront her fear.

"From what the tests are telling me, you're cancer free." Dr. Ruth's candor was far welcomer now that he was saying things Jenene wanted to hear. "There was only one small tumor," he said over the phone. "It was only about ½ centimeter. Besides that, your lymph nodes were clean."

"I don't have cancer." The words felt good in her mouth, sweet and chewy like salt-water taffy.

The sense of victory that overcame her was so prominent and pure she felt that all the weight she had accumulated on her shoulders was lifted...if only for a little while.

"You may be cancer free but you still need to continue your treatment with an oncologist. Otherwise, our time together is over. You did really well."

For some reason the sound of that was the one discordant note in the exchange. The one dark cloud in an otherwise blue sky, she wanted to know how bad the storm was going to be. "Can you give me an idea of what I'm in for yet?"

"Probably radiation. Possibly chemo."

Even if on some level she had reconciled herself to jumping through every hoop she needed to, she still had reservations about subjecting her body to more poison. She thought she had made the decision to follow through on treatment and yet she found herself reconsidering. If she was cancer free, was it really necessary?

"Even after getting the good news, I felt fed up with the whole cancer situation. I wanted to be done. I had to make a decision I had already thought was made. Now the idea of chemo or radiation was so repellent I just couldn't set up the appointment. My procrastination probably helped nothing, but it gave me time to come to terms with my feelings and what I needed to do."

Luther Midelfort, Mayo Health System, Eau Claire, Wisconsin.

It would not be until the sixteenth of September that Jenene would see an oncologist to learn what would come next in her treatment.

Knowing all along it would be unreasonable to believe the oncologist would suggest no further action, she had to decide if she would go along with the program or forfeit any help if she experienced a relapse. The impetus behind her decision finally to go was a message Belle had broken to her shortly before: the breast cancer would return unless she underwent more treatment. Overcoming one facet of the lesson in no way meant she had overcome other facets, her guilt concerning my childhood most prominently.

The oncologist, Dr. Daniel Burns would deliver good news: the cancer had been caught early enough that chemo was unnecessary. "Thirty radiation treatments will give you a 97% chance of living as long as you would have if you never had cancer," he said. "I'm sending you to a radiation specialist."

Jenene would recall later: "At that point I was still stunned cancer had invaded my body so forcibly it could be found by Western medicine. Because of the lessons, I suspect cancer has come and gone a few times throughout my life...but I had hoped doctors would never find it. I was really bothered by how the whole mess affected my family.

"When the oncology radiologist told me on the fifteenth of October my only choices were a mastectomy or radiation, it was almost worth it to me to sacrifice my breasts just to be finished. From the research I had done, I knew radiation treatments went on for weeks—four to seven—and that once it began it would be inescapable, I would have to go five or six days a week until it was finished. It would be a lot of driving....

"And there were the side effects to consider. I was a high risk for serious skin problems, fatigue, and severe pain besides a whole list of other side effects. Since I've had allergic reactions so bad a great deal of the skin fell off my body anything to do with the skin is a real concern. What would radiation do?"

Really it was not even the individual side effects that had Jenene worried but the cumulative effect on her body. So far, despite the breast cancer, she had kept the Crohn's and lupus from returning, a remarkable accomplishment. Would radiation compromise her ability to maintain that aspect of her health? Radiation wears down the body.

"What made me decide to do it was the idea of showing how Reiki and other methods could ease, even alleviate, the side effects. I was determined to get through radiation with a minimum of fuss. Reiki brings about the best results. I have to trust in that. My faith would be rewarded."

One day short of the twenty-two-year anniversary of Bill's death, October 20, 2010, was the first radiation treatment.

Russ escorted her to every appointment; his presence was bolstering.

The radiation was targeted. All went to one small square area. Three small tattoos were placed to mark the area. To her surprise, she did not even feel whatever it was the machine did to her. "The treatment seemed like nothing. I was perfectly positioned and then the machine moved over me, making noise and stopping twice." It was quick, in and out, but she was warned the painful part came in the wake of treatment.

Jenene had decided to use apple cider vinegar on the affected area. She had always used it to treat sunburn. Since it has the same pH balance as the epidermis, apple cider vinegar neutralizes the burn and restores the skin and in the case of sunburn, often prevents peeling. When she told the doctor and nurses this, she was met with open skepticism and encouraged not to go through with her plan.

A doctor was sent for from Mayo in Rochester to come and convince her to use lidocaine on her skin. "Apple cider vinegar will dry your skin out," he claimed ignorantly.

Day after day she was in and out consistently. She usually exited around the time her appointment was scheduled. She was prompt, even the day her alarm was set wrong. If only the weather were as reliable. Thirty minutes away, she had to take I-94 to Eau Claire. Some days the wind was blowing so ferociously her knuckles would be white gripping the steering wheel.

There were also the side effects:

"There were times it felt like my nipple was being yanked by a vise grip, then twisted! There were nights I got no sleep. In some ways, my worst fears were realized because I was getting more and more fatigued. You can't heal if you never get quality rest."

And more of what had made her turn her back on Western medicine:

"You would think this would afford me some compassion but I found my radiologist was intolerant toward me. He felt the vinegar was causing the pain and wanted me to use 'aquaphor.' He needled me. Even implied I was weak and should maybe stop the radiation and get a full mastectomy if the pain was too bad. I had to work hard not to be angry. I couldn't believe he would undermine me that way."

The skin never burned as terribly as she was warned. Every time she saw pinkness she would spray on more apple cider vinegar. Toward the end, she began using aloe as well as the apple cider vinegar. Both worked well.

"The pain was humbling. On some level I obviously believed for whatever reason I deserved the pain."

As often as she could, Jenene would go to Luther Midelfort's healing garden to meditate after therapy. The size of a small gymnasium and outfitted with a fireplace, a grand piano, a wide selection of seating, potted trees, and a variety of other plants made to look as if they were growing from the floor, it was a place designed to be favorable for healing and she found it was a peaceful spot to calm her mind.

There was also a magnificent fountain. Some days sunlight poured through the glass ceiling and made the spouting and cascading water a dozen shades of orange, among them aurora, saffron, apricot, corral, and peach. She would toss coins in the water. Made wishes she saw come true or not come true day by day.

It was a calm place, humid and warm and rich with the smell of greenery. She would sit on one of the stone benches and soak in the tranquil ambience, listening to the trickling water and enjoying the simple warmth.

She was able to meditate until the pain was all but gone. On those days, schedule permitting, she would take her sweet time. In a life plagued by adversity, she had learned to savor the small joys. It was an energizing place, a reward after the thing she did not want to do, the prize.

A reward of affection waited at home.

In her absence a truly tortured soul, whether she was gone ten minutes or five hours Pinto's enthusiasm was no less fervent, ecstatic, or zealous. While she was gone he howled the blues; upon her return his tail whipped with the ferocity of an airplane propeller.

At her return his cheerful barks rang through the house. Angry she left but overjoyed she was back, Pinto would nibble and lick her fingers, dozens of little I-love-you's.

The first of December marked the last of the scheduled thirty radiation treatments.

A rough couple of days on the heel of one of the roughest months of Jenene's life, the day before the car broke down right after therapy. After all these years and car problems could still be prevalent. But she still felt better for the simple elation spurred by knowing cancer was going to be in her past.

Turning back not an option, she had gone into a dark cave without knowing with absolute assuredness if she would ever emerge again into the light. Never had she come so close to defeat. She had felt like she dropped the ball. She had allowed herself to become weak. But in facing the cancer she once again learned not only that she could *be* strong but also that she *was* strong.

Almost anticlimactic, the last treatment went off without a hitch. Some monsters can be vanquished without a grand battle. The machine did its little dance, made its whirs, did its flashing, and it was over.

"Ring the bell," the nurses encouraged afterward. The bell was to signify that she had completed radiation therapy.

Ding! Triumph. Ding! Victory. Ding! Success. Ding! The most important one of all: freedom from cancer.

The dings signified that she had bested another scourge. A cheer went up. The whole staff congratulated her. Other patients took consolation in her achievement. When asked for advice, she said, "Keep your heads up and remember all things pass. And that it's up to you to be strong enough to get through this challenge in your lives."

Chapter 103
Illimitable

In the days after radiation therapy ended, Jenene was extra fatigued and needed a lot of rest. There was some pain in her breast but it was negligible compared to what she was told she could face. The vinegar completely prevented burning. In fact, there was a perfect square tan. Herb would have been proud.

Never one to be held back, she still got in as many walks as she could, even more than Pinto was willing to take. This resulted in her acquiring a dog carrying harness so he could watch the world from chest-level. He was very agreeable to the situation. And even though her breast should have been very sensitive to touch, she could handle his weight pressed against her.

There was a real sense of victory in being cancer free and you could see it in her bounding step. There was more bounce to Russ's step too; relief changed the complexion of his life.

In many ways, Jenene was lucky. Early diagnosis, spurred by a psychic dream, saved her many indignities.

The lessons, going back to her childhood and my childhood, may have been too much for her to deal with sans the tools of Western medicine combating the cancer on one front while to deal with it on another she worked on learning and accepting her lesson.

The entire medical establishment long ago became her bugaboo. She felt like they turned their backs on her at a time she needed the reassurance of support if nothing else. Such a betrayal is hard to come back from and yet she had learned to trust again.

Throughout this work I've alluded to the scientific box that closes many doctors' minds to greater possibilities. Much of that was originally written before the breast cancer diagnosis. This ordeal demonstrated to Jenene and me that all that could be true but maybe our minds had been closed too. We saw ourselves as irreproachable, above the need for medical help. Now we recognize that for our health, as well as the health of everyone else, the future of medicine needs to be integration of all methods that work.

Awareness of lessons has saved me many injuries…yet under some circumstances I concede that I would need a doctor. I still refuse to ever undergo a colonoscopy.

At times Jenene feared she would lose my respect, that I would view her as weak or pathetic for using Western medicine. To some extent maybe she was right. But to not learn and understand would have made me the sort of closed-minded person I never want to be. The treatment helped her. I am so grateful it did and I will always be thankful to the doctors who facilitated her healing.

After the breast cancer was weeks behind her, she thanked Dr. Brown for saving her life.
"How did I do that?" he responded uncertainly.
"You made me get the mammogram."
"I did?" He was puzzled. "I don't remember doing that."
"You insisted I needed one. You even escorted me out to the nurse to make the appointment."
"That's probably the only mammogram I've ever ordered. Still, I don't recall that at all." Spirit possession? Who knows? The educated doctor did not remember what for even him was a somewhat significant event. I wonder. "Well, I'm glad it all worked out."

Chapter 104
Contemplation

During and after the ordeal, we contemplated why this had to happen to Jenene and I have outlined the overall theme. No reason ever seemed completely satisfactory. It only came to me when I began to think of the grander scheme of things, the whole picture. I had a moment of eureka. There was real significance to Jenene surviving breast cancer and the way she did it, and the reason was that it made her story all the more amazing.

"If for no other reason I think this happened for the book," I told her. "People don't automatically relate to Crohn's disease or lupus. But everyone knows about breast cancer. Because you went through this, the message of the book will be stronger and more relevant. What was that National Cancer Foundation statistic? 200,000 new breast cancer cases will be diagnosed in the next year, one in seven women, and it's assumed 40,000 of them will die? Not to mention the 1,700 men a year diagnosed with breast cancer."

"I hope it was for a reason so noble," she said. "I could live with that. This whole experience was very humbling. It showed me I could still be weakened; even after all I've dealt with and learned. That one's hard to face after working so hard to be strong."

"I don't agree. I think you're stronger now than you've ever been. Stronger even than when you were totally healthy before the cancer."

"You think so?"

"If you weren't, you would have given up," I said. "People give up all the time. Getting up and facing every day, with all the frustration and pain, you proved you're stronger."

"Maybe you're right."

"Not only that. You kept the Crohn's and lupus from returning. Wasn't that viewed as sort of an upset win by your doctors on par with Buster Douglas knocking out Mike Tyson?"

"I don't know if the odds were *that* long."

Either way, she came through breast cancer remarkably well for someone who had already dealt with Crohn's and a bunch of other health obstacles. Anyone facing disease should feel bolstered. Miracles can be earned. Between what doctors have to offer and the benefits of Reiki, miracles can be won by anyone willing to step up and take control of their health.

Jenene proves it.

Chapter 105
Final Thoughts

After all that has come and gone, what would Jenene consider to be her paramount lesson?

Simple: she will always have more to learn, prove, and teach.

Learning lessons goes hand in hand with her life. It's her destiny to inspire others by demonstrating what can be accomplished with the many charms in her healer's toolbox. No matter how many diseases she conquers, her past has taught her she needs to maintain her guard. Knowledge is illimitable but only attainable through new challenges. Counterbalances will always have to be struck. Mountains climbed. Battles fought.

Along the way Jenene had to not only discover self-worth; she had to nurture her worthiness in direct defiance of a self-defeating nature. She learned you have to believe you are worthy to have a life, worthy to chase and capture your dreams, worthy to succeed, worthy to be happy.

She has gratitude for every misadventure that has redirected her path. Every time she was waylaid, misdirected, or forced to outwit an obstacle she was gifted with a little more knowledge, a splash of wisdom…and another facet of what makes up who she is as a person.

The past seems like the golden oldies now. A lot of hard times, sure, but a lot of good times too. I guess you can only measure the good against the bad; I pity the person who faces no adversity and therefore never knows true appreciation for all that is great and wonderful. I have read showing gratitude elicits immense happiness, not for the receiver but the giver.

If you treat life like a mad dash of physical acquisition to the finish line you miss all the quirkiness and uniqueness—the humanity—that makes the journey meaningful.

In simple lives of so much complexity, chance of confusion, and inevitable tragedy Jenene has learned and taught me we have to be the sculptors of our own contentment and happiness; chiseling our way to masterpieces. We have to be the artists who use frequent brushstrokes to add the vibrancy and energy of color to the drab gray world in which we too often find ourselves; do our best to infuse rainbows in the lives of others to add the full spectrum of color to our own lives.

We have to be the comedians who find humor in the absurd and unbelievable, the sad and scary.

We have to be the architects of great towers of hope. Even if sometimes we feel it is up to us alone to erect every beam and install every window.

We have to mine for the decency, integrity, and justice in the world.

In all these pursuits we have to stay mobile and never give up.

For many of us at some point it becomes mandatory to become skilled life cartographers because we are responsible for mapping our lives and some effort needs to be made if you want a good one.

That's what Jenene does and it makes for a full existence. That and working to avoid falling in the trap of underestimating herself; not so difficult as it once was, she knows she's on track so long as she aspires to inspire, is reliable, dispenses earned praise, stays tolerant, accepts the randomness of life, and helps those willing to help themselves.

All she can do is be content with who she is, being just Jenene.

Today her credo remains the same. No one label sums her up. She's a survivor, a healer, a Reiki Master, a dispenser of wisdom, a pursuer of justice, a mother, a wife, a friend, a channeler, a bit of a guru, and so much more. She teaches Reiki and offers all sorts of counseling.

She assembles Uniquely You life readings based on her years of numerology study for which she receives many accolades for accuracy. In her pursuit of this knowledge she learned why she was in many ways so unlike herself during her first marriage. Her married name gave her a number that made her weaker than she resolved to be. Perhaps a clue as to why so many marriages fail: unforeseen number changes. Russ's name, as her life has shown, gave her a strong name number.

She helps animal shelters, attends the yearly Cancer Survivors dinner, and attained a Reiki license plate to advertise the top implement in her healer's toolbox.

She has had a lot of success exorcising malefic, lost, or confused entities by utilizing Reiki and spiritual connections. She has even dealt with dangerous poltergeists. She has also honed her skills channeling spirits for sake of information and closure.

She opened The Rock Shop on Main Street in Baldwin, Wisconsin to fulfill a long-held desire to sell stones while practicing healing.

None of this sets her apart, or so she would say. Everyone can learn what she knows and follow their truth.

Through versatility and being open-minded to alternatives, she saved her life and figured out "fair" may only be a word in the dictionary but fairness does exist and can be found. Death can be outrun. Contracts can be exceeded. Miracles can absolutely be earned.

Broadcasting kindness and humility makes us all stronger.
Dispensing hugs will only help matters.
It's good to allow love in. And mirth. And joy.
Seek resolution.

With every breath, with every heartbeat there is hope. That may be the mainspring of life—maybe only a guidepost.

As for me, the record keeper and bard, the spreader of legends not to be mistaken with myths because my tales are truth laid bare in words, the greatest consolation I find is that art is long even though life is short.

Epilogue

At about a quarter after eleven on January 29, 2014, Russ arrived home from work. Jenene was in bed, down with a bladder infection (hers always being a life of lessons), and he ultimately told her goodnight without ruining her night with bad news. On the way to work the roads were slick; he'd had a collision with a curb and the car's alignment was wrecked.

When Jenene asked from bed how his day had gone, Russ expressed that it had not been good but they could talk about it tomorrow. She pressed him to talk more but he averred; he knew telling would only light a fire he at the moment didn't have enough water to douse.

They said their goodnights, exchanged declarations of love. Russ had devised a little poem he said to her every night for years and that he said right before they parted: "If you dream make them sweet, even if you don't dream have a sweet night because I sure do love you with all my might."

Then Russ was off to go through his nightly routine before bed while Jenene slept, Pinto by her side. A hour or so later, after eating a snack of brats and filling the refrigerated water jug, Russ climbed the stairs to his room; he went inside and shut the door so the sound of his television wouldn't carry.

With divergent schedules and desired conditions—Russ liked it hot, Jenene liked it cool—they had decided separate rooms better suited their needs; there was also the fact that as a sufferer of sleep apnea, Russ slept with a CPAP machine. So alone in his room, Russ watched a little TV before turning in.

As a man of routine always one to stay on schedule, at the predetermined time Russ switched off his TV, stood to shut off his light, took a step…and everything changed in an instant. During that step Russ's body fell, no longer a living vessel, and his soul stood in place; he was surprised the ending of a contract could be so painless because he never lost consciousness even though his body had fallen down dead.

There was a familiar figure before him, posed in that contemplative way he stood; Russ had to be consoled, looking up into the face of wisdom, of forgiveness, of god in the eyes of a small child.

"It's over, son," Bill said…and guided him to where they watched Jenene and Pinto sleep peacefully for the last time for months…and later took him into the light after the discovery of his vessel.

At 5AM on January 30 Jenene found the love of her life dead on the floor.

Russ Lehman ascended to the spiritual plain in the early morning hours.

As day broke the skies opened and wept ice. Snow fell all morning. It snowed eight inches in four hours. The flakes mounted like the sadness in our hearts until the world was buried as we were buried.

On February 1, Rus was reborn as a Healing Angel—all that sent Reiki paid dividends; a righted karmic scale tipped far into the good—and a voice Jenene Lehman will hear for the remainder of her time on earth, a connection that will transcend the flesh and time and all we understand as eternity. For a wife shattered before the return, the validation of knowing her beloved husband is here, and that his death was unpreventable no matter how much she had learned, was what she needed to heal from the worst event of her life.

For all of us losing Russ was difficult beyond words. Yet…

Knowing he is here is an amazing story…one to be told another time.

We live to transform our soul. We exist to transcend to the highest levels of spirituality.

About the Author

Adam James lives in Wisconsin with his wife and cats.

Made in the USA
Middletown, DE
24 February 2017